THE ONE MINUTE MEMORY MANAGER

UPGRADING AND USING YOUR PC'S MEMORY FOR FASTER, MORE EFFICIENT COMPUTING

THE ONE MINUTE MEMORY MANAGER

UPGRADING AND USING YOUR PC'S MEMORY FOR FASTER, MORE EFFICIENT COMPUTING

PHILLIP ROBINSON

M&T Books
A Division of M&T Publishing, Inc.
501 Galveston Drive
Redwood City, CA 94063

Limits of Liability and Disclaimer of Warranty

The Author and Publisher of this book have used their best efforts in preparing the book and the programs contained in it. These efforts include the development, research, and testing of the theories and programs to determine their effectiveness.

The Author and Publisher make no warranty of any kind, expressed or implied, with regard to these programs or the documentation contained in this book. The Author and Publisher shall not be liable in any event for incidental or consequential damages in connection with, or arising out of, the furnishing, performance, or use of these programs.

Library of Congress Cataloging-in-Publication Data

Robinson, Phillip R.
The One Minute Memory Manager
p.   cm.
Includes index.
ISBN 1-55851-102-4
1. Memory management (Computer science) 2. Microcomputers--Programming. I. Title.
QA76.9.M45R63 1990b
004.5--dc20
90-21529
CIP

Trademarks:

All products, names, and services are trademarks or registered trademarks of their respective companies.

Cover Design: Lauren Smith Design

94 93 92 91   4 3 2 1

Acknowledgments

Thanks To:

For the input—thanks to the writers, editors, and production professionals of such computer magazines as *BYTE*, *PC Magazine*, *PC Computing*, *InfoWorld*, and *PC World*. I've learned about memory management by reading these magazines, listening to computer users, and experimenting with my own systems.

For the output—thanks to Brenda McLaughlin, Christine de Chutkowski, and the other editors at M&T Books. They were patient, helpful, and diplomatic. I thought this was a good book idea, so did Brenda, and now I hope you'll think the same.

For the images—thanks to the many companies that provided screen images or pictures of their wares. You'll see the particular credits with the pictures.

Contents

STEP 2: TAKE INVENTORY

STEP 3: USE LESS MEMORY

STEP 4: FIND MORE MEMORY

STEP 5: ADD MEMORY

STEP 6: CHANGE YOUR ENVIRONMENT

STEP 7: DO MORE WITH MEMORY

STEP 8: MANAGE YOUR PERIPHERAL MEMORY

STEP 9: DEFECT FROM DOS

STEP 10: THE QUICK SOLUTION GUIDE

APPENDIX A: GETTING CHEAP AND FREE SOFTWARE

APPENDIX B: PRODUCT LIST—ALPHABETICAL

APPENDIX C: COMPANY ADDRESSES

GLOSSARY

BIBLIOGRAPHY

INDEX

Preface

What It's About

This book explains PC memory management, a critical skill for fast and easy computing with a PC, PS/2, or compatible. It is for those who run programs, not for those who write them.

I call it the *One Minute Memory Manager* for three reasons.

1. Because it is loaded with ideas, tools, and techniques that will take you little more than a minute to master. (Naturally there are some others that can take considerably more than a minute.)

2. Because I believe that if you devote just a minute regularly to organizing and streamlining your use of memory, you'll multiply your computer's performance and your effectiveness. (Much the same can be said of your hard disk, incidentally.)

3. Because it sounds good.

In my own use of PCs I discovered that sloppy and ignorant memory management was holding me back. To play the PC game well today I needed to know more about memory; to play at all tomorrow I had to arm myself with memory understanding and tools. I found a number of programmer's guides to memory, full of technical details and algorithms, but I couldn't find any users guide, anything written for the person who wants to run programs, not write them—so I made my own.

It is based on more than a decade of experience reviewing PC hardware and software, and on research into the latest software and hardware memory tools.

The first few chapters explain how memory works. The rest of the book is devoted to listing and describing the tools and techniques to:

Discover how much memory is in your PC

Find more memory in your PC

Squeeze memory to do more

Add memory to your PC

Use found, squeezed, and added memory to compute faster and easier

How It's Organized

Memory management is a tangled and interdependent subject. Many of the relevant tools and techniques apply to more than one aspect. To force some order, this book is organized into ten "steps":

Step 1. Learn About Memory: How It Works

Step 2. Take Inventory: What You've Got

Step 3. Use Less Memory: Put Your Programs on a Diet

Step 4. Find More Memory: Relocate TSRs* and DDs*

Step 5. Add Memory: Expand, Extend, and Go Virtual

Step 6. Change Your Environment: TSR Managers, Task-switchers, DesqView, and Windows

Step 7. Do More With Memory: RAM-Disks, Caches, and Spoolers

Step 8. Manage Peripheral Memory: Printers, Video-adapters, and Networks

Step 9. Defect From DOS: a New OS* If You Must

Step 10. The Quick Solution Guide: My Advice

* *TSRs (terminate & stay resident programs) DDs (device drivers) OS (operating system)*

How to Read It

As I see it, there are three ways to read this book: Straight through—you'll learn the most and understand all of the connections. Dip in here and there—you'll gradually become memory smart.

Read Step 10 to get a general idea of what you might do, then read only the relevant sections of the book—this takes the least time and can still lead you to superb memory management.

Managing PC memory once demanded great technical experience and skill, plus plenty of tedious tinkering. That approach still works, but there are now programs that can handle all that work for you, as long as you understand a few terms and know where you want to go.

PCs, PS/2s, PS/1s, and Compatibles

Most of this book will use "PC" to mean all computers compatible with the IBM PC, including IBM's own PC, XT, AT, PS/2, and PS/1 systems as well as many similar systems from other manufacturers that are built on the same hardware foundation and can run the same software as the IBM systems. (You can see why I prefer the short term.) Where there are differences between the generic "PC" and other PC-compatibles, I'll let you know. And some of these differences are crucial in memory management. But for the most part the techniques of memory management explained in this book remain the same across the entire world's complement of approximately 60 million PCs.

A Request for Your Help

Part of managing your PC's memory well is knowing methods and tricks for particular programs, computers, and peripherals. You may find a way to shave a few K off the memory demands of a popular program. Someone else will know how to make a memory-management program grab more unused memory. Together our common knowledge will far outweigh what any one person can learn and explain. So please send me tips, hints, and advice about memory management that can improve the next edition of this book. And let me know if you want more details or fewer. I'll credit any tips I do use. Send them to:

Phillip Robinson

c/o M&T Books
Memory Manager Tips
M&T Publishing
501 Galveston Drive
Redwood City, CA 94063

Why this Book is for You

Anyone with a PC, PC-compatible, or PS/2 personal computer, running the DOS operating system can use this book. It doesn't matter if you have a simple PC with 256K RAM and a single floppy disk drive or the latest 486-based powerhouse PC with megabytes of RAM and several hard disks.

Anyone with such a computer can compute more easily and productively by understanding the terms and using the tips contained in this book.

How much do you need to know to read the book? Only how to turn your PC on.

However, novices should have some other materials on hand, such as your PC's manual, your DOS manual, and any manuals for your applications programs. You should also have the phone numbers to call for technical help with your PC and programs. (Those numbers are probably in the front or back of the manuals.) One book cannot explicitly explain every step of starting every program or type of PC. However, with those other materials on hand for occasional cross-checking and particular explanations, even complete beginners should be able to use this book. Some of the explanations may seem too detailed initially, but you can still skim them for the sense of the matter. Pay attention to the Key Ideas in each chapter, and use the chapter descriptions to choose hardware and software to manage your PC's memory.

Intermediate users may get the most from the book, from understanding just what their memory has been doing all this time to how they can inexpensively improve any PC.

Will experts be bored? I hope not, and I think not. I've been reviewing computer hardware and software for more than a decade and there are some things in this book that I hadn't bumped into in all that time. What's more, although computer gurus may find the technical explanations overly simple, the collection of memory management hardware and software in this single volume should make the book useful as a catalog of solutions.

Learn About Memory: How It Works

Key Ideas:

- PCs use memory for almost everything they do.

- More memory means faster and easier computing.

- PC memory is limited by hardware and software—the limit depends on your PC model.

- The main limit is to 640K of conventional memory for most programs.

- Not all of the 640K is available to programs because parts of it are occupied by utilities and drivers.

- Expanded, extended, high, and virtual memory are different schemes you can use to get around the 640K limit.

- You can also get to use more of the 640K of memory by relocating utilities and drivers to high, extended, or expanded memory.

Introduction

There are two ways to manage your PC's memory: do it yourself or let memory management programs do it for you.

To do it yourself, you'll need to thoroughly understand how memory works. And you'll probably end up using some memory management programs anyway, customizing them to your particular system.

If you let memory management programs automatically handle your memory, you can get by without much knowledge—but not without any. To choose the best memory management program and employ it most efficiently you'll need to be familiar with the language of memory.

That's what this Step is about. It's a long step, by the way. Please don't feel that you must read it all at one sitting. You can just treat it as an extended glossary, with explanations and definitions of terms you'll be bumping into.

And if you're already knowledgeable, please be patient with the easy stuff, or skip it altogether. Remember that it was once unknown territory for you too.

Why Memory Matters!

Perhaps you're wondering why memory management is so critical. Here's the case for its importance.

The Memory Shortage

Your PC needs memory to hold programs while they run, to catch data results as they're processed, and to hold images—both text and graphics—that are shown on the screen. In short, it needs memory for everything it does. Memory holds the program instructions that tell your computer what to do, and the files of information you do it to (text, graphic, spreadsheet, sound, or whatever).

But PCs rarely seem to have as much memory as we want. And they never have all the memory we could use, as you'll see in this book. As memory gets cheaper and so more plentiful, computers find more ways to use it. The demand always keeps ahead of the supply.

Many of us know about the memory shortage in PCs because we've smacked into it. A spreadsheet might have been too large to load, a word processing document might have saved slowly, a database might have crept through a search operation, or a new program might have just remained caged on disk, unable to fit into the computer's memory. If your PC doesn't have enough memory, some programs will run slowly, others will only work on small documents, and some programs just won't run at all.

The PC is particularly famous for the "640K limit," as you'll read later, that prevents you from running more than one program at a time, and limits the power of any one program.

The Memory Wastage

For every person hurting from too little PC memory, there's another who's not using all of their PC's memory. Memory can make computing faster and easier in lots of ways, but is often left fallow and indolent because the PC's owner doesn't know it's there, or doesn't know how to make it get up and work.

In fact, often the memory shortage and the memory wastage turn up in the same PC, run by the same person. At the same time that the computer owner is bemoaning too little memory to load a spreadsheet, he or she may also be ignoring hundreds or even thousands of K (kilobits) of memory that could load that spreadsheet and manage it's printing, save it faster to disk, and make room for useful utility programs. (I know, I've been guilty of precisely this computer crime.)

Memory Management Isn't Obvious

Why not just solve the problems of wasteage and shortage by adding memory to your computer? Because it's not that simple. You need to know how much memory your PC has and where it is, how much the PC can hold, how much more you need, what kind to look for, where to insert it, and how to configure it. Then you need to know how to set the memory up so your programs can find it and use it. This book is a list of answers to those questions.

Memory Management Helps Any PC

Skillful memory management means faster and easier computing. In fact, clever management can increase your PC's memory before you buy a single extra chip, board, or utility program. And when you outgrow your PC's current memory, apt selection of more memory and of management software can multiply your computer's performance for quite a small price.

Fast (quick operations and display changes)

Easy (to learn and to use)

Pretty (sharp and attractive working displays and printed results) are the holy grails of computing.

Memory management is a key to all three, and is one of the least expensive improvements you can make to your computer and your computing. In fact, if you were only concerned with speed, after the speed of the main processor chip itself (which mainly means your choice of a PC, XT, AT, 386, or even faster computer), memory can be the most important factor in PC speed.

More memory wisely used lets you compute with:

Stronger programs

Larger files

Better graphics

More programs at once and

Higher speed

Stronger programs need more memory because they have more instructions. They can process larger and more complicated documents.

Larger files are important because people are no longer using computers just to write letters and calculate departmental budgets. Today they're writing and publishing books, and calculating entire company accounts

Better graphics depend on memory, because graphics files are huge. Yesterday's page of text is only 1/100 the size of today's desktop-publishing document with fancy fonts. Yesterday's simple black and white picture is only 1/1000 the size of today's color video image. And that memory is vital in both the computer that creates the pictures and the printer that puts them on paper.

More programs at once means easier computing. Simple *task switching* that lets only one program actually run, with the others in suspended animation, eliminates the time needed to move between programs. Sophisticated *multitasking* that actually lets multiple programs continue their work at the same time lets you immediately get to work on a new document while another one is printing, or allows you to look something up in a database while a spreadsheet is calculating a result.

Higher speed is always nice in computing. Studies prove that even a half-second wait for your program to respond means lower productivity—our attention drifts

6

away. Programs run fastest when they and the information files they work on are entirely in memory, instead of being partly in memory and partly on disk.

Memory Building Blocks

To manage your memory, you need to speak the language. If you're not already conversant with bits, addresses, extended vs expanded, cache hit rates, and so on, read on. The easy stuff comes first, the more difficult a little later. So if you're a pro, fly over these first pages until you come to something you're not familiar with. If you're a beginner, don't sweat it. You don't need to memorize this stuff. Just slide through it, and come back later for particular sections when you know better just what you need to know.

Bits

Computers retrieve, process, and store information. The information can be anything: words, pictures, numbers, sounds, you name it. All of it is broken down into the smallest possible units for storage and manipulation in the computer. Text becomes letters, numerals, and punctuation. Pictures become dots of dark and light. Sound becomes "noise here, no noise there," like dots of sound and silence. Put enough letters or dots or noise instants together in one big group and you've got a document, or an image, or a voice.

Every kind of information, therefore, can be stored as groups of "bits," the most elemental information piece possible. A single bit can have one of two values: "1" and "0". A "1" could mean a dark dot or a noisy instant; a "0" could mean a white dot or a silent instant.

Bytes

One bit can hold one of two values, 1 or 0, as noted above. Two bits as a team can hold any one of 4 values: 00, 01, 10, or 11. Three bits can hold 8 values, four bits 16 values, and so on to eight bits holding any one of 256 values.

To store letters, you need to be able to store at least 26 different values, one for each possibility in the alphabet. If you want to store both lowercase and uppercase (capital) letters, the numerals 1 through 10, foreign characters, and a dozen or more

7

punctuation marks, you'll soon have more than one hundred and fifty different values to contend with. For that, you need at least eight bits for each letter or mark you want to store. You would just assign one pattern of eight bits to each letter, and then have the machine translate them for you into their assigned letters. For example, you could use these assignments

a   00000000

b   00000001

c   00000010

and so on.

A set of eight bits is called a *byte*. Each byte can store a single character, or a number in the range from 0 to 255. You could also assign these bytes to graphics, to sound, or to any other information.

Data and Programs

Computers don't only store data of text, numbers, sound, and pictures in memory, they also store their own programs in memory. *Programs* are lists of instructions for the computer's processor chip to follow or execute. These programs can be thought of as recipes for handling data. The instructions are such things as:

Add two numbers

Compare two letters

Retrieve whatever is stored at a particular memory address

Each instruction can be represented by bits and bytes, just as data is. A simple system might use this assignment:

0001   Add

0010   Compare

0100   Retrieve

The computer would have to be told in advance whether to recognize the bits as text, sound, program instruction, or whatever.

Files

For both programs and data, bits and bytes are collected into larger units called files. A file can be data—such as a word processor document or a worksheet. A file can be a program or a part of a program—such as the word processor itself or the spelling checker for that word processor. Files are the smallest chunks of computer information that earn a name—each file in a PC has a name that can be up to eight letters and numbers long, with three more letters or numbers as an extension. (The extension typically is an abbreviation telling what kind of file it is, such as TXT for text or WKS for a worksheet file. Files with COM and EXE extensions are programs that the PC can run.)

Kilobytes and Megabytes

Storing a single character isn't much work, but storing a full page of text, about 2000 characters and punctuation marks, is something substantial. That takes about 2000 bytes, one for each character, or 16000 bits total. Storing a usable graphic image can take even more memory, often as much as 1,000,000 bytes.

To make those values easier to talk about, computer memory uses metric lingo, putting K and M before large quantities. There are bytes, kilobytes (KB), and megabytes (MB).

But there is a confusing factor here. Because computers work with bits that can have only two values, 1 and 0 as mentioned above, everything they do naturally falls into mathematical powers of 2. That is, although you count in powers of 10 (1, 10, 100, 1000 the natural size jumps) computers count in powers of 2 (2, 4, 8, 16, 32, 64, and so on). When it comes to K and M, computers mean 1024 not 1000, and 1048576, not 1000000. Although at the moment this may seem confusing, the values aren't that different.

In these terms, storing that page of text takes about 2K. A full 1MB could store a 500-page book.

Addresses

But just as a page of text is meaningless if the characters are all jumbled together without the proper order, so is a set of 2000 bytes meaningless if they don't have any order. Computer memories use an order called *addressing*. Each byte of storage has a numeric address starting at 0. The next byte has address 1, the next 2, and so on. If the addresses are read in order, by moving up the scale from one to the next, the information in them can be neatly ordered.

Remember that there are two linked ideas—the address of a byte and the information stored in that byte. Think of it in terms of mailboxes in a post office. If you want to know what someone has written to you in a letter (the information), you first need to find the particular box the letter is in (the address), and then to read the letter (learn the value stored at that address).

Memory Maps

When you're talking about megabytes, it isn't enough to simply have addresses. You need a memory map that can give you the general layout of what's in memory. Memory maps crop up a lot in memory management. The maps rarely show the values at each and every address. You don't need to know what's in every house on a street to drive down that street or to figure out the fastest way through town. Figure 1-1 is a simple memory map. It follows the tradition of showing the address as boxes, with values inside those boxes if they're relevant.

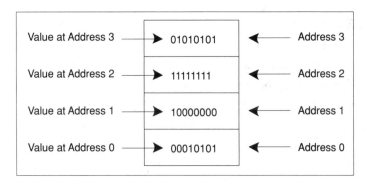

Figure 1-1. Simple Memory Map

Binary

As I mentioned above, computers operate in powers of 2 because of the two and only two values a bit can have: 0 or 1. So where we count: 0,1,2,3,4,5,6,7,8,9,10,11, and so on; computers count: 0,1,10,11,100,101,111, and so on. The computer's 10 is the same as our 2; its 1111 the same as our 15. The computer is counting in base two or *binary* arithmetic; we count in base-ten or decimal.

It helps to know this, but you don't have to be adept at translating binary into decimal. There are programs that will do that for you.

Hexadecimal

As if memory weren't confusing enough with bits, bytes, addressing, and so on, you'll also sometimes run into hexadecimal values in memory maps. These look like **A000** or **FFFF**. This is base-sixteen or *hexadecimal* arithmetic. For programmers it translates easily into binary—there is one hex value for each four binary values—and it saves them from writing painfully long binary values and addresses. Instead of

Value 0100101001101110 at Address 101000000001

hex gives the shortcut of

Value 4A6E at Address A001

Decimal counting can only get as high as 9 before needing two numerals at a time to represent a value. Hexadecimal goes up to the value of 15 before needing a pair of numerals. Because hexadecimal needs more symbols than our traditional decimal system can supply, it borrows a few letters. After the first ten 0,1,2,3,4,5,6,7,8,9 hexadecimal uses:

A in hex = 10 in decimal

B in hex = 11 in decimal

C in hex = 12 in decimal

D in hex = 13 in decimal

E in hex = 14 in decimal

F in hex = 15 in decimal

You'll often see hex values on memory maps. Don't let them throw you. Just remember that they have decimal equivalents. Figure 1-2 is an example memory map of a PC with hex addresses in place of the decimal addresses (shown in parentheses). It's really no different than moving from a country (such as the US) that has postal Zip codes made entirely of numbers to a country (such as Canada) that has Zip codes with letters and numbers. You get used to it pretty quickly.

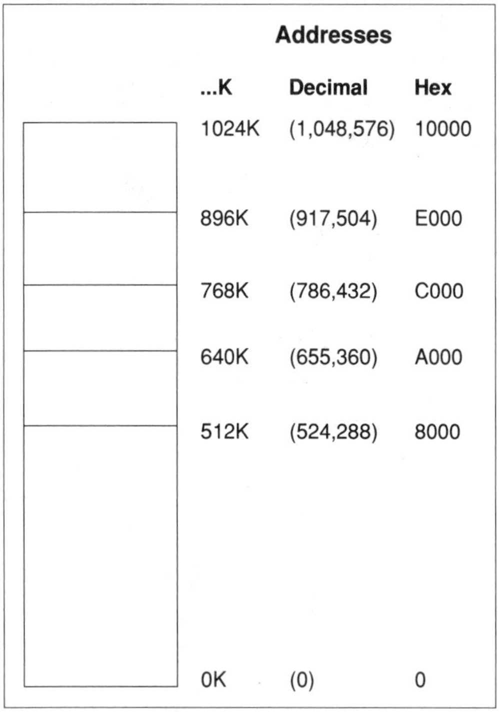

	Addresses	
...K	Decimal	Hex
1024K	(1,048,576)	10000
896K	(917,504)	E000
768K	(786,432)	C000
640K	(655,360)	A000
512K	(524,288)	8000
0K	(0)	0

Figure 1-2. Example PC Memory Map with Hexadecimal Addresses

Banks and Segments

Don't worry about understanding Figure 1-2 right now. Just see how hexadecimal addresses line up with decimal addresses. Notice too how the standard 1MB of a PC's memory is organized into *banks* or *segments* of 64K addresses each. Those banks are labeled 0,1,2,3,4,5,6,7,8,9,A,B,C,D,E,F, from the hexadecimal addresses.

The latest PCs—the 386 and 486 generation—aren't founded on 64K segments as their predecessors were. But because so much PC software was created with those segments in mind, even the memory maps of the latest PCs show the bank and segment divisions.

Reading and Writing

Reading from memory is looking up an address and learning the value stored there. It doesn't destroy the information in the memory, it just makes a copy of it for the computer's processor and program to use.

Writing is sending information to an address. Since any location in a computer can only keep a single value stored at a time, the writing process will destroy whatever information might have already been at that address, substituting the new information.

Memory and Hardware

Your PC doesn't just have a single, homogeneous kind of memory. It has a variety of hardwares used to store information, each with different advantages and disadvantages. You need to know something about these to manage your memory well, just as you would need to know about the employees of an organization to manage them well—their strengths and weaknesses, experience and education.

Chips and Disks

There are a number of physical ways to store a bit, to save it as memory for use or inspection later. You could use electricity and refer to an electric charge as a "1" and no charge as a "0". Or you could use magnetism and refer to a magnetized area as a "1" and an unmagnetized area as a "0". Computers happen to use both of those schemes, storing electric charges in tiny circuits on chips and magnetic fields on iron-coated disks and tapes. The information is the same, only the medium changes.

Disks are considered *non-volatile memory*, that is, they keep their stored information even when the computer's power is turned off. Many memory chips, on the other hand, are *volatile*—they forget their information the second they lose power. That's a factor to balance in memory management.

The term, memory, in this book refers to chip memory. That's the traditional use of the term in computerese anyway. Disks and tapes are important too, but they aren't the primary memory storage in a computer. It's the chip memory that determines if you can load a program or file, run more programs at a time, and so on. There are plenty of books on managing disk memory; this one focuses on chip memory.

RAM and ROM

There many kinds of memory chips, but they basically fall into two categories: *RAMs* and *ROMs*. RAM stands for Random Access Memory. Any bit on a RAM can be read from and written to at any time. ROMs (Read-Only Memory) can only be read from. You can't write new information to a ROM. They are unchangeable to protect the important information, typically programs, stored inside them.

All PCs use a mixture of RAMs and ROMs for their chip memory. The ROMs hold some fundamental programs that animate the computer; the larger amount of RAM is the working area to hold computer programs and data files.

EPROMs, EEPROMs, and Flash EPROMs

There are certain types of ROM that can be written to in special circumstances. EPROMs can be removed from your computer, then erased and written to by a special machine with an ultraviolet light. But to your computer they're still just ROMs, typically used to hold configuration information (such as what type of disk drives are in the system and what sort of video adapter)—basic facts that can change, but don't change often. Flash memory combines EPROM and EEPROM ideas to make a simple and relatively inexpensive (though not as inexpensive as DRAM) memory chip that is both non-volatile and fast—with DRAM-like speed. EEPROMs and Flash EPROMs can be erased electrically, while still in your computer. Writing new information to an EEPROM or Flash EPROM is much slower than writing it to a RAM chip. Flash memory is therefore better used as a replacement for a disk drive than as a replacement for DRAM memory because it uses less power and is more reliable than a disk drive.

CMOS RAM

Standard RAMs are volatile—losing their information as soon as you turn off the computer's power. But some PCs use special CMOS (it stands for Complementary Metal Oxide Silicon—which doesn't matter here) RAM chips that don't use much power when they run. These chips are so frugal with power than they can hold their information even when powered only by a battery. Because CMOS RAM is more expensive than regular RAM, it is only used for the following:

- Small configuration memories in desktop PCs—where you want the information to last even when power is off.

- Portable computer memories—where the whole system may need to run on batteries.

The only time you need worry about managing or testing your CMOS RAM is when your computer has lost its configuration or you've changed the configuration and need to update the computer.

DRAM, SRAM, and VRAM

There are several types of RAM chips. The most common is the *DRAM* or Dynamic RAM. This kind of RAM can hold the most bits on a single chip, and is the least expensive, however, it is the slowest. DRAMs need anywhere from 80 to 150ns (nanoseconds) for each "access" (reading or writing) by the computer. (A nanosecond is a billionth of a second.) DRAMs make up the bulk of any PC's memory chips. The most common chips today are the 1Mbit (that's megabits, not megabytes) size. The PC uses 8 of these to make up 1MB of memory. (Actually it uses 9, the extra is for "parity" checking, to see if the other 8 show any errors. Parity is explained just after this section.) Some PCs still use the older 64K and 256Kbit chips. Some are already using the newer 4Mbit chips. Chips with a memory capacity of 16 to 64 Mbits are on the way. Each new generation of chip carries more bits, meaning more memory in less space and using less electrical power than before.

SRAMs (Static RAMs) are faster than DRAMs, but can't hold as many bits of information. They're also more expensive than DRAMs. SRAMs can read or write information in 30 ns or so. Today's typical SRAMs hold 256Kbits. SRAMs tend to be one generation behind DRAMs in memory capacity.

VRAMs (Video RAMs) are faster than DRAMs for video operations, because they can be written to and read from at the same time.

Parity and Memory Errors

Memory chips can make mistakes, just as other parts of a computer can make mistakes, just as any machine can break or misfire. It's not common, but it does happen.

One simple way to monitor memory mistakes is called *parity*. The bits in each byte are automatically added up to a sum. For example, 11100001 has four 1s, and 10101011 has five 1s. Then a parity bit is added on the end, a ninth-bit. In an even parity design, the parity bit's value is set to make the entire 9 bits give an even number of 1s. For 1110001 the ninth bit would be 0, to leave it at four 1s. For 10101011 the parity bit would be 1, to change the five 1s into six.

Then whenever the computer reads the byte, it checks to see if the parity is even—if all the bits add up to an even number of 1s. If they don't, the system knows that some bit in that byte has failed, changing mistakenly from a 1 to a 0 or a 0 to a 1. On the PC, you'll see an error message telling you there has been a parity error.

Then you can choose to replace the chip with the bad byte, or to hope that it was a "soft" error—a temporary condition that won't happen again. (This can happen when a chip is hit by a stray radiation burst from the sun or some other source.) If you want to distinguish a hard error from a soft error, use one of the diagnostic and testing programs mentioned in Step 2 to thoroughly test the chip.

Unfortunately, if there are two errors in the same byte at the same time, they could cancel each other out in the parity test. There would be a mistake and parity wouldn't show it. There are some other EDC (Error Detection and Correction) circuits that can be added to memory to find and fix any such mistakes, but few PCs use them. Unfortunately these EDC systems add a fair amount to the cost of a memory system to fix a problem that rarely occurs.

Speed Versus Expense

Changes in memory medium can be important—determining how quickly the computer can read or write information, for example. Chips are far faster than disks, and SRAMs are more expensive than DRAMs. Disks need 20 to 100 milliseconds (thousandths of a second) for their work. Chips need 20 to 100 nanoseconds (billionths of a second) for theirs. So chips are a million times faster than disks, and speed is vital to computing. Most programs spend much of their time reading and writing data to memory.

But chips are more expensive than disks, and SRAM chips more expensive than DRAM chips. Part of memory management, as you'll see, is balancing the expense of various memory forms against their speed.

Computer Speed

The speed at which you compute depends on many factors, from your own typing speed and knowledge of your programs to the speed of the memory chips in your computer, the efficiency of the algorithms in your programs, the speed of the processor, the speed of the disk drives, the speed of the printer, and the speed of the video display. But the central factors for typical computing are: the disk speed and the processor/memory speed.

Disk speed is always important, but is most important for programs that are *disk intensive*, that is, they spend lots of time reading and writing information on the disk. Database management programs are prime examples. But disk speed is not a subject for this book except in one sense: memory caching which can be used to speed up the disk speed, as mentioned later on in this Step and in Step 7.

Processor/memory speed is always important, but particularly so for programs that have many complex calculations and data manipulations to perform. Spreadsheets, graphics programs, and desktop publishing stand out as *compute intensive* applications.

Processor/memory speed is written that way because the two are intimately linked in the latest computers. There's not much point to improving one without improving the other at the same time.

Processors

The central processing chip in the computer sets the pace of processor/memory interaction. There are two aspects to this: the clock speed and the number of bits handled by each instruction.

Processors work through program instructions to the ticking of an electronic clock inside the computer. This clock beats millions of times a second, in MHz. The original PC with its 8088 chip had a 4.77 MHz clock. The original AT with its 80286 chip had a 6MHz clock. But then ATs moved into 8, 10, and 12 MHz speeds. Processor performance leapt forward. The most powerful PCs now have either 80386 or 80486 processor chips running at 16, 20, 25, 33, and some even 40 MHz clocks. A PC with a 40MHz clock will get calculating compute-intensive work done ten times as fast as a PC with a 4 MHz clock.

Processors have also grown to handle more bits with each clock tick. The original PC's 8088 worked on 8 bits at a time. The 286 chip in the AT took 16 bits at a time. And the 386 and 486 chips grab and manage 32 bits with each instruction. Roughly speaking, a PC that handles 32 bits with each instruction is four times faster than one that handles only 8 bits.

Combine that increase in processor speed (from about 4 to nearly 40MHz) with the increase in bits-per-instruction (from 8 to 32) and the latest PCs can process at 40 times the speed of the original PC.

Fighting Wait States

But there's a hangup in this tale of processor power: memory speed. When processors cranked at 4 or 6 MHz, the average memory chip with a 150ns access time had no trouble with reading or writing. But when a processor runs at 10, 20, or even 40MHz, a 120ns or 100ns memory chip can't give or take information fast enough. It makes the processor chip sit in a wait state, idling while the memory chip finds or stores information. These wait states cut the real speed of the computer. That's why you'll see computers advertised sometimes as having "0 Wait States."

What can a computer designer do about wait states? There are about a half-dozen choices:

1. Nothing

That's not great, but it's cheap. You just put a faster processor in your PC and hope that most of the time the wait states aren't too bad for performance. You certainly won't have the fastest PC in town.

2. Use faster DRAM chips

If you spend more per chip, you can buy DRAMs that are 100ns instead of 120ns, or 80ns. Then they'll be able to respond to faster processors without a wait state. Unfortunately, DRAM chip speed hasn't improved as quickly as processor speed has. Even if you don't mind spending more for your memory chips, you quickly run into a wall: a 16MHz processor needs a 60ns memory chip to run without wait states, and there just aren't DRAMs that are that fast.

DRAMs have an Achilles' Heel: they must be refreshed regularly. The information in them must be checked and recharged. Because of that, they cannot perform at their rated access time for even two or three reads or writes in a row. Their cycle time is in fact a more accurate description of the rate at which they can give and take information. And that cycle can be two to three times the access time of the chip. SRAMs, however, don't need refreshing. Their access time is good over and over—it's the same as their cycle time. So even when an 80ns DRAM isn't fast enough for a 16MHz 386-based PC, an 80ns SRAM is.

3. Use SRAMs

This would give you the speed for most systems, because SRAMs can easily be found in 60ns speeds. In fact, you can find SRAMs with 35, 25, and even 20ns access times, though these can be expensive. All SRAMs cost a lot more than DRAMs and take up a lot more space. Do you want a big, expensive computer just to get the speed? Maybe that's not the best solution. (Dell was one of the few computer makers to actually create a fully SRAM PC, but they quickly abandoned the technique for some of the less expensive ones that follow.)

4. Change the Memory's Architecture

There are some clever ways to structure DRAM chips both internally and as groups of chips to make them act faster, without actually using faster chips. The three most popular are *interleaved*, *static-column*, and *page-mode* memory. All three work from two facts: that programs tend to read from consecutive memory addresses and that DRAM chips use part of their access time to refresh themselves (to charge back up the electric bits).

Interleaving divides the DRAM memory into banks, and alternates the reads between them. While bank 1 is being read, bank 2 is getting refreshed. When bank 2 is read, bank 1 is getting refreshed. Then back to reading bank 1 again. By overlapping their refreshment times, Interleaving can make the DRAMs seem nearly twice as fast. A few machines even divide memory into four banks, overlapping these for yet a bit more efficiency. This architectural change speeds up memory access using standard DRAM chips. All it needs is a bit more design care and the right controller chips built into the PC's foundation.

Static-column and *page-mode* memory actually use modified DRAM chips. Static-column DRAMs have some SRAM features. They're more expensive than DRAMs but less expensive than SRAMs. Such chips divide the memory on each chip into small pages of 2K or so bits. Reading consecutive bits from a single page doesn't cause any wait states. Jumping to read a bit from another page does cause a wait state. If your program reads mainly from areas of 2K or less for long stretches of computer time, Static-column DRAMs will be nearly as fast as SRAMs. Page-mode DRAMs work in the same way, only differing in the technique they use to break memory into small "pages". Consecutive reads from a single page don't cause any wait states. (A computer designer could even use interleaving with page-mode chips, to cut wait states even more.)

5. Use an SRAM Cache

But to explain SRAM caching, I should first explain caching in general.

Buffers and Caches

Most computing programs tend to intensively read from or write to a small area of memory for quite a while, before moving to another small area of memory and reading from or writing to that area. Memory architectures such as interleaving and static-column DRAMs use this fact to avoid some wait states. ("Quite a while" in computer time, by the way, is measured in thousandths and millionths of a second.)

Some bright person noticed that pattern and came up with the idea of a buffer or cache—teaming a small area of fast, expensive memory with a large block of slower, cheaper memory. (The term *buffer* is often used to mean a small or simple cache.) The large block would store all of the information. When a program asked to read some information from that block, the item asked for, and all other items in the small area around it would be copied into the small, fast memory cache. Then on the next read request from the program, the request would be sent first to the cache. If the information was there (which is likely because most requests are for information close to the most recently requested info), it could be sent at the fast cache speed. If the desired information wasn't in the cache, it would be found in the slower, main memory—and that new piece of information and its neighbors would then be copied to the cache.

If most requests for information stick to an area the size of the cache, this can give the computer the apparent speed of the fast, expensive cache memory, without spending the money to actually fill the entire computer memory with the faster stuff. The percent of read requests that can be satisfied by the cache is called the *hit rate*. Most PC manufacturers that use a cache claim 90 to 95% hit rates, but this depends quite a bit on their testing method. When the hit rate is high, the entire memory will appear to operate at nearly the speed of the cache. But it won't cost as much as building the entire memory with the high-speed kind of memory used in the cache. That's the trick.

Disk Cache

One popular cache scheme is to use chip memory as a cache for disk memory. The most frequently used disk information is kept in part of the chip memory. This can speed up the disk work tremendously. See Step 7 for details. See Figure 1-3 for a diagram of disk caching.

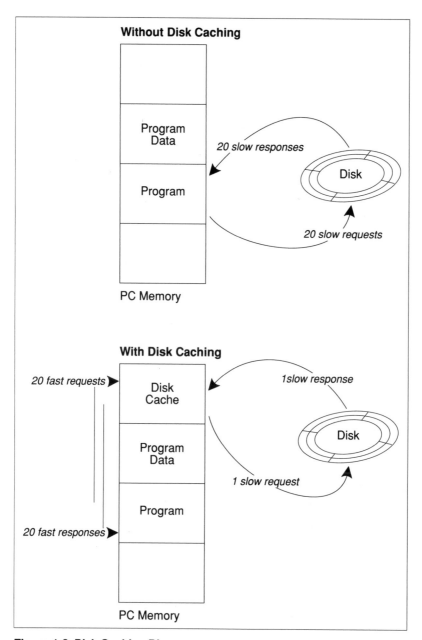

Figure 1-3. Disk Caching Diagram

22

RAM Cache

SRAM chips are faster than DRAM chips, but they're more expensive. Many of the latest PCs with the fastest 386 and 486 processors use small amounts of especially fast SRAM (in the range of 4K to 128K, but typically 32K or 64K) to cache for their main DRAM (1MB to 4MB or more). These SRAM caches can make megabytes of inexpensive DRAM rated at 100ns or so seem to run as fast as megabytes of expensive SRAM would, rated at 25ns to 35ns or so.

In fact, the latest processor chip in PC compatibles, the 80486 chip, has 8K of SRAM cache built right onto it. Some PCs with the 486 chip don't use any other cache. Some add a second cache of SRAM. Which works better? That depends on how well the caches are designed and whose performance measurements you believe. There is no clear answer.

But the question of second caches for 486 machines does lead to a more general question: How much SRAM cache is enough? It depends on what kind of work you're doing, how fast your processor runs, how efficient the cache controller algorithm is at keeping the most recently used information in the cache, and other such factors. For small programs that get small chunks of program and data frequently, 8K is probably enough. But for large applications working on large files, or for multitasking, 8K is probably not enough. Then 32K or more might be more appropriate. The 82385 Cache Controller chip supposedly has a 95% hit rate with a 32K cache in a 386-based PC, if you want a technical estimate.

But there will definitely be a point of diminishing returns as you increase the amount of SRAM in a cache. To use some hypothetical but not extreme numbers, if an 8K cache gives you a 90% hit rate, a 32K cache might only improve that rate to 95%. You've increased memory speed by about 5% by spending four times as much for SRAM. Increase that 32K to 128K and maybe you boost memory speed another 1% by spending 16 times the original amount on SRAM.

Watch out for systems that are sold as superior because of larger caches—you may be paying more for advertising sizzle than for real performance. Figure 1-4 is a simple diagram of SRAM caching.

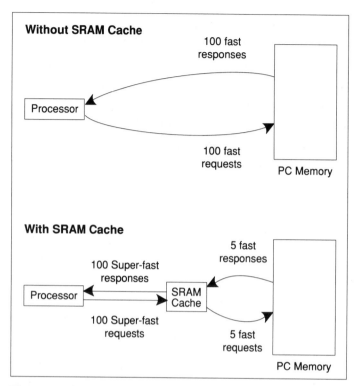

Figure 1-4. SRAM Caching Diagram

Read-ahead

Caches are found to improve memory reading speeds. How well they do this depends on how often the information your program needs to read is in the cache: this is called the hit rate. Simple caches just keep the most recently used information in the cache. But more advanced read-ahead caches guess what information will be wanted next by monitoring program activity over time. These grab not only the information the program needs from slow memory now, but the information that is close to it or related to it—the information your program might need next. If the cache does a good job of guessing, the hit rate will improve.

Write-back and Write-through

Caches must also tackle the question of writing. When there's a new value to write to memory, does the computer just write it to the cache? Does it also write it to the slower memory at the same time? If it doesn't write to the slower memory, than the cache and the slower memory will have different values for the same address. That won't do, so at some point the new value must be written to that slower memory. A write-through cache does this immediately, caching only read requests, then letting writes take the extra time to write to both cache and slower memory at once. Some cache schemes, however, don't like the slowdown in computer processing this can cause. These impatient cache schemes hold on to the newly written values in the cache until there's a lull in the computing action, then they write them to the slower memory. To prevent any mistaken use of the older value in the slower memory before the final writing operation, these high-performance caches must keep track of which addresses have changed values. If any of those addresses are called for by the computer before the final writing operation, some sort of cache controller (either hardware circuits or a software program) must interrupt the request and finish the writing. That makes these write-delay or posted-write caches more complex, but lets them run faster than write-through caches.

You don't need to worry about these details of caching much; the computer and software designers take care of it automatically. But having heard about it will help you understand computer ads that refer to details of caching designs.

The 486 processor's "burst mode" allows tremendously fast movement of information in memory, but it requires a burst cache that has read-ahead and write-back abilities.

DMA and Caches

Most movement of information to and from memory is directed by the main processor chip. But many PCs have a special feature called *DMA* or Direct Memory Access that lets other components direct such information movements without bothering the processor. For example, a PC with DMA could move a big block of information from a scanner or disk drive into memory without the processor having to monitor each step. The processor just says "go ahead and get that much" then turns its attention to other things. When the peripheral is done moving the information, it tells the processor, which resumes work where it left off.

DMA is built into programs, and so is something you don't have to worry about. It can be a great help in computer processing. But the people who create caching hardware and software have to think about it, because a DMA operation could write information to the slower memory and would have no responsibility to write it to the cache. That would leave cache and slower memory with different values: always a danger to memory integrity.

To avoid running into that problem, cache controllers such as the 82385 chip mentioned above often have bus snooping that watches for DMA. When some DMA writes to the main, slower memory, the 82385 marks any copy in the cache as invalid. When the processor wants that information, it will get it from main memory where the latest copy is.

Bus Width and Speed

Speaking of DMA, there's another important element in computer processing speed: the bus. This is the collective set of wires, and the signals on those wires, that moves information around the computer. The bus connects to the processor, the memory, the disk drives, the video, and the slots for adding memory and peripherals. The bus has a clock rate of its own. The bus also has a data-width and an address-width. The data width tells how many bits the bus moves at a time: 8, 16, or 32. The address-width tells how many addresses the bus can specify: 20-bit (the original PC's 1MB of addresses), 24-bit (the AT's bus for 16MB), or 32-bit (the 386 bus for 4GB). The clock rate and bus data width dictate the maximum speed at which the bus can move information.

In the PC the bus ran at processor speed. But as processors got faster, many peripherals that connected to the bus did not. So most PCs now have a slower bus than the processor. Most boards now work at 8MHz, so that is a typical bus speed. Some fast PCs have two buses: one for slower peripherals running at 8MHz or so, and another for fast memory-processor interactions running at the processor's speed. This is important when you want to add memory to your system. It's better to plug memory into the high-speed bus.

Bus and Slot Types

There are at least five types of buses, that differ in the physical shape and placement of signals in the slots where additional circuit boards can be plugged into the computer.

The original type is an 8-data-bit PC bus. You'll still find some expansion slots for this on many PCs for adding slow peripherals.

The original 16-data-bit AT bus or ISA (Industry Standard Architecture). You'll find many of these expansion slots in today's PCs. There are probably more plug-in circuit boards with memory, modems, disk controllers, and other appurtenances for this bus than for any other.

The new 32-data-bit EISA (Extended Industry Standard Architecture) bus. This bus was specifically made so that cards for the ISA bus could plug into it, alongside new cards with 32-bit data abilities.

IBM's 32-bit-data MCA (Micro-Channel Architecture) bus. This appears only on IBM's high-end PS/2 systems, though it has also been promised for a few PC compatible systems.

Proprietary 32-bit-data buses for memory cards on 386 and 486-based PCs. Each company that makes these PCs has its own design for this bus, because it provides the fastest memory path. But all of those different designs make it impossible to buy 32-bit-memory add-in cards on the open market.

MCA competes with the EISA bus to be the next PC standard. Because IBM is behind it, it has a good chance. However, because IBM is charging license fees to copy it (which IBM did not with the AT's ISA bus), MCA isn't a shoo-in. Both EISA and MCA have special capabilities for bus mastering that will be useful in future systems that have more than one operating processor chip. This doesn't concern today's PC user much. The MCA and EISA buses, and slots to plug in to them, are particularly useful for networking and hard disk controllers that need to move lots of information at high speed. Buses are wonderful for memory add-ons, though there is not a clear standard as mentioned above.

The most flexible PCs have a couple of 8-bit slots, some 16-bit slots, and some 32-bit slots.

Processor Modes

Processor chips have different modes of operation that determine how much memory they can handle: real mode, protected mode, and virtual-8086 mode. These modes are part of the hardware, but dictate the kind of software that runs on the chip, so they are an appropriate final hardware topic before the software section.

The 8088 and 8086 chips (of the PC and XT) operate in real mode, and so can address 1024K, 1MB. This is the mode that the DOS operating system uses.

The 286 has real mode, and adds protected mode. In real mode the 286 acts just like an 8088 or 8086, only faster. The 286's protected mode can address 16MB. (A processor running in protected mode also understands and will perform a few commands that real mode doesn't provide.) It was called protected because it has some features to help protect multiple programs from stepping into each others area of memory. DOS doesn't understand protected mode, so it can't use that extra 15MB (called extended memory as you'll see later). The 286 can switch easily from real mode to protected mode, but has a very hard time switching back to real mode, so the PC can't easily jump to the protected mode to get at extra memory.

The 386 and 486 chips have real mode, protected mode, and a new Virtual-8086 or "V86" mode. In real mode the 386 acts just like an 8088 or 8086, only faster (even faster than an 80286). In protected mode the 386 acts like a 286 in protected mode, only faster. The 386 has an easy time switching from real to protected and from protected to real, solving that problem of the 286. In V86 mode the 386 can run many real mode programs at the same time, each in its own 1MB of memory. Each of those megabytes can have DOS and a program running within it, not knowing about any of the other real mode operations that are running at the same time.

Memory and Software

Software refers to programs; lists of instructions that the computer hardware "obeys." It plays as big a role in memory as does hardware. There are many kinds of software, and you need to know the differences before you can manage your memory.

Operating Systems

The *Operating System* or "OS" software is the most basic stuff, the first instructions the PC runs when it starts and the instructions that keep the various PC parts—such as disk drives, screen, and processor chips—talking to each other.

Applications

Applications are the programs that do your regular work, such as word processors, database managers, drawing packages, and spreadsheets. These applications are written to work with a particular operating system.

Utilities

Utilities are applications too, but are typically smaller pieces of software and are dedicated to functions such as tuning up a disk drive, keeping a calendar, counting words, and so on.

Spoolers

A *spooler* is a utility that controls information headed for a printer. It captures and stores that information temporarily, then feeds it to the printer at the optimum rate. This lets the processor and application program get back to working on other things.

Device Drivers

Device drivers, or just "drivers" are programs that help the operating system and applications, most often by showing them how to communicate with peripherals such as printers, display screens, and modems. To connect an application to a particular printer, for instance, you need the printer driver for that printer. To send high-quality graphics from an application to the screen, you need the right graphics driver.

Utilities and drivers play a big role in memory management. Some utilities help you analyze your system's memory and memory limits. Special drivers can sometimes bypass the memory limits set by the DOS operating system.

BIOS

The PC has some *BIOS* (Basic Input Output System) software that it always needs. Some of these programs are the first things to run when you start the computer, testing memory and setting the PC up for use. Other BIOS programs set up and communicate with various parts of the computer's hardware, such as the disk drives, printer, and display screen (and in early PC's, even with cassette drives—before the days of disk drives). Because these programs are constantly needed, and don't change, they can be put in the permanent and fast (faster that disk drives) memory of ROM chips. (Most computers keep additional BIOS and OS—operating system—software on disk, and load it into the computer's RAM after the ROM routines have run. Some laptop computers keep all of their operating system on ROM chips.)

DOS

DOS—an abbreviation for Disk Operating System—is the operating system for most PCs. There are others, but DOS is what you'll find on more than 90% of the 50 million PCs, PS/1s, PS/2s, and compatible computers in the world. (The D for disk is added because most of the operating system is on a disk, and is loaded into chip memory only after you turn on the computer.)

DOS has the very unfortunate and deserved reputation for severely and painfully restricting the PC's use of memory. (The restrictions didn't seem so bad when DOS was invented back around 1980, but have become a serious liability by the 1990s.) Those restrictions and DOS's popularity led to this book, which deals primarily with understanding and making the most of DOS memory.

OS/2 and Unix

There are other operating systems, such as OS/2, UNIX, and the Macintosh OS. Each has its own problems, but most allow you to use more memory more easily than does DOS. (Step 9 has some details on these other OSs.) Many also offer other advantages such as improved graphics and better networking. Unfortunately, they won't easily run the thousands of applications, utilities, and drivers created for DOS, so most people for now at least prefer to stick to DOS.

Extended DOS

But there's an unofficial new operating system strategy called *extended DOS* that's winning converts. Extended DOS is DOS transformed by some of the memory tricks and schemes I'll explain in this book. It has some of the advantages of other operating systems and eludes some of DOS's restrictions, but can still run DOS software because, after all, it is DOS.

PC-DOS and MS-DOS

By the way, IBM calls its version of DOS "PC-DOS." Microsoft, which developed DOS originally and works on it in close conjunction with IBM, calls it's version "MS-DOS" Most firms that make computers compatible with IBM's license MS-DOS from Microsoft and sometimes re-label it Z-DOS or A-DOS or some other variation. All of these varieties will run nearly all the same applications, utilities, and drivers. They'll mostly—with some small exceptions—all obey the same rules described in this book. That is, they are largely compatible.

DOS Versions

Microsoft and IBM (and therefore all the other companies that license it too) have improved DOS over the years. Each version has a number. Large changes warrant large number changes, such as from version 1.0 to version 2.0. Smaller changes come with smaller number changes, such as from version 3.1 to version 3.2. The improvements typically include new commands, new options for older commands, and compatibility with newer hardware (including newer processor chips and peripherals).

Each version has been designed to be compatible with previous versions. That means that programs written for version 2.0 of DOS will run on a computer that has version 2.1, 3.0, 3.3, or 4.0 of DOS.

However, programs won't necessarily run on previous versions, because they may use commands and features that appeared only in a later or higher version of DOS. For example, a program that is said to run on a PC with DOS 3.3 may not operate on a PC that is equipped only with the older DOS 2.0.

The latest version of DOS as I wrote this book in late 1990 was 4.01. DOS 5.0 was scheduled to appear soon, offering some new memory management abilities. Many computer users were still using version 3.3, having chosen not to pay for the upgrade to version 4.01 because they wanted to avoid its bugs (it was famous when new for having some troubles), didn't want to lose the extra memory it used (4.0 eats up more RAM than 3.3), or just because they couldn't be bothered. There are even some PCs still running older versions such as 2.0, though very few 1.0 models are around. DOS 5.0 may appear by early 1991, and may have some of its own memory management tools. See Step 3 for more information on DOS.

Environments

There are now several environment programs you can choose from that will automatically handle such things as expanded, extended, high, and even virtual memory. They also give you file management, a graphic interface display with windows, and even utility programs. These environments can eat up part of the power of your PC's processor, but they can certainly simplify computing life (and memory management) by automating a large part of it. DesqView and Windows are the best known. Step 6 describes environments.

Memory Types and Limits

PC hardware and software communicate with memory in several different ways, treating them as different types of memory. This is similar to the various ways you might communicate with friends—through telephone calls, letters, or visits. Just as your friends are friends no matter how you communicate with them, so the very same memory chips can be used for each of the different memory types.

But the PC's hardware and software set limits on its communication with memory. Consider what you'd do if you had such limits, if you were limited to calling only two friends, for example. If you wanted to communicate with any other friends, you'd have to do it via letters. And if there were also a limit on the number you could write to or read letters from? Then you'd have to visit the rest, or depend on news carried by friends. Any given communication path could carry information, but not all would carry the same amount (letters can't let you hear a voice, for instance) or work at the same speed (calls are clearly faster than visits).

The PC works just that way. There is some memory that it can call directly, and more that it cannot. In fact, memory can be divided into at least five major types: conventional, high, expanded, extended, and virtual. And there are some smaller divisions even within those types. The hardware and software in your PC set limits on how much of each type of memory you can have and use. Each type has its own advantages and disadvantages. The following pages explain those limits, pros, and cons, and the terminology surrounding them.

Conventional Memory: the 640K Limit

The regular RAM memory in your PC is called *conventional* or "base" memory. This was as little as 16K in some early-model PCs. Most now come with at least 512K. The hardware in a PC or XT allows a maximum of 1MB. PC hardware that is 486-based can handle as much as 4096 MB—4GB (4 Gigabytes). But the software in both standard PCs and high-powered 486-based PCs typically allows a maximum of 640K. If you have 640K or less, then your PC is limited solely by how many memory chips are in the system. But if you plug in more than 640K of chips, there are other limits.

Hardware Limits for Conventional Memory. There are two hardware limits to PC memory: room and addresses. By "room" I mean the physical place to plug in memory chips and boards and the electrical juice and connections to power them. Some PCs—such as the smallest laptops—don't have any slots where you can plug in memory boards. At best they might offer a special socket for adding a few memory chips, perhaps as much as a megabyte. Big desktop PCs with lots of slots will have plenty of room for memory chips, but will have a limited amount of electrical power for them.

By "addresses" I mean the processor's ability to find the chips for reading and writing information. With six or more slots, for instance, you could theoretically plug in boards with as much as a 100MB of RAM chips. But the typical PC's processor can't address that much RAM. Plugging in boards that the processor can't address would be like building homes without any streets. Sure, you've got the building, but no one can get there. (Later in this step I will mention some "off-road" tricks for getting past these limits.)

Different generations of PCs use different processor chips. Each kind of processor chip can address a certain amount of memory, which depends on how many address bits at a time it works with. The direct address space is the memory address range that a processor can reach directly, quickly, and efficiently. You could compare it to all the homes that could be built on a street of a certain length. Just as a longer street means more possible building sites, a processor with a wider address bus means a larger addressing space.

Just remember that the memory address space and the memory in the system are different. Just because the processor chip could reach a certain address, doesn't mean there's a memory chip waiting there for it to talk to. And just because there's a memory chip there, doesn't mean the processor can address it. To be useful, memory needs both.

Figure 1-5 lists some of the processor chips inside various PCs and compatibles. The 8088 chip in the original PC, and in the XT, worked with 20 address bits at a time and could address 1MB (1024K). (The previous generation of computers worked with 16 address bits and could handle only 64K or 65536 bytes of memory.) The IBM AT—and all the AT compatibles including those built around the 286 chip can address 16MB. The 386 and 486 chips can address as much as 4GB. Various PS/2 models use 286, 386, and 486 chips.

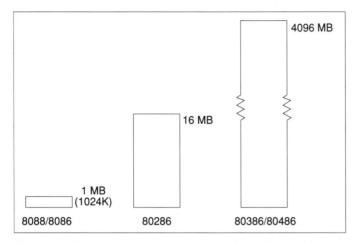

Figure 1-5. Processors set a hardware addressing limit on memory.

Software Limit for Conventional Memory. But none of these systems, the PCs, XTs, ATs, or even the PS/2s, can use more than 640K of memory as conventional memory for their programs, no matter how many megabytes of chips or of memory addresses they have. The software limits stop them cold from touching anything more. It's as if the street construction company had the vans, tools, and time to lay down pavement to more homes, but was prevented from doing so by union or management rules. Software limits may not feel as tangible as hardware limits, but they're just as effective in restricting a PC's use of memory.

DOS, the operating system software that nearly every PC uses, only recognizes 640K of conventional memory for your regular programs and data. That limit is the single largest factor in memory management for PCs. Running into it was traumatic for computer owners who expected memory to keep growing. The open frontier suddenly had a limit, the expansion of a country ran right up against an ocean. And the limit is so fundamental to DOS, built right into the very core of the operating system, that it cannot just be eliminated. But, happily, there are plenty of schemes for slipping around the limit, for avoiding enforcement of the 640K law.

35

Not Even a Full 640K of Conventional Memory. In fact, you can't even get 640K of conventional memory. DOS uses part of the 640K—from 40K to 100K or more—for itself. (The amount depends on the version of DOS you use. The new version 5.0 will use less. [See Step 3 for details.]) If you have less than 640K in your computer, the DOS bite can be painful. The "TPA" or Transient Program Area that's left for your applications can be far smaller than you'd like. Ways to diminish this DOS use are strewn throughout this book.

High Memory: 384K Above Conventional Memory. The 384K of memory addresses above the DOS limit of 640K are called high memory or reserved memory, as you can see in the memory map of Figure 1-6. Your regular programs and data can't use high memory the way they use conventional memory. In fact, under regular circumstances, they are barred from using it at all. And any RAM chips that would have been at those addresses in high memory are pre-empted by the reserved uses. That is, the messages to high memory are automatically detoured to the reserved uses. That 384K was reserved by the programmers who created DOS for:

BIOS and other ROMs

Video memory

Future uses

BIOS and Other ROMs. Just as RAM memory chips have addresses, ROM chips too must have addresses. The PC sets some high memory addresses aside for its BIOS and other ROMs. Some memory must also be set aside for system functions such as keeping track of the PC's configuration (as you might dedicate part of a file drawer in your home office to keeping insurance, bank account, medical, and other such records). Often parts of this configuration information are kept in CMOS RAM chips, connected to a battery. (DOS also reserves the first few K of conventional 640K memory for housekeeping functions. These include such things as remembering the most recently touched keys (a 16 byte keyboard buffer) and the interrupt vectors, special address values that programs need and change while at work.

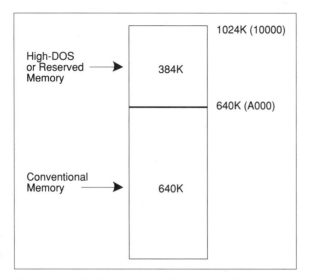

Figure 1-6. PC Memory Map Showing 640K Conventional and 384K High Memory

Video Memory. Besides keeping video-control software in ROMs, video also eats up memory for a frame buffer. This holds the bits that determine the image on the display screen. (This is explained in detail in Step 8.) The actual chips they may use for graphics are often on the video adapter boards—not the chips on the main computer board. But the addresses are given to the video boards, so those chips on the main computer board that would be at those in the upper 384K are just ignored.

Reserves for the Future. Most good computer designs leave room for future changes and improvements. Most computer activities need memory, and newer abilities typically ask for more memory than older abilities. So smart designers leave some memory addresses empty for future assignments. (If there wasn't this slack, for example, PC's wouldn't have so easily accommodated new, higher-resolution displays, as mentioned in the previous paragraph.) The PC left some fallow memory addresses for just this reason, and many have already been used by successive generations of PCs since the original.

Borrowing From High Memory. DOS reserves but rarely uses all of the 384K of high memory. Which addresses actually are used depends on the graphics adapter in the PC and the other peripherals that are plugged in. For instance, the 128K part of high memory just above conventional (the A and B banks) is dedicated to the graphics adapters. Adapters such as the original Monochrome Display Adapter (MDA) and Color Graphics Adapter (CGA) don't use much of this 128K, and the right utility program can liberate it from those adapters and add it to your conventional DOS. It doesn't work for all programs, and it limits your graphics, but it could give you 704K, 736K, or even more, of conventional memory, memory your programs and data can play with just as if it were below the 640K line. Figure 1-7 shows how it works. Step 5 covers this in detail.

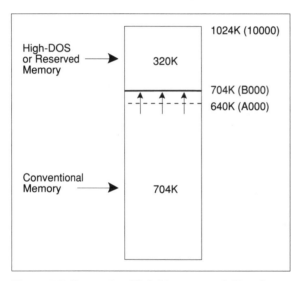

Figure 1-7. Borrowing High Memory to Add to Conventional RAM

Relocating TSRs and DDs to High Memory. In most any PC, there are probably tens and perhaps hundreds of K of addresses left free in high memory, reserved but unused. If your system actually has memory chips behind those addresses—that is, if your system has a full 1MB of RAM—then the right memory management software can relocate some utilities and driver programs to the unused high memory. (The 386 and 486 chips are especially adept at this relocation, because they can remap memory. It can also be done on an 8088 or 286 system with the right software or hardware additions.) Figure 1-8 shows an example of this; Step 5 covers this in more detail.

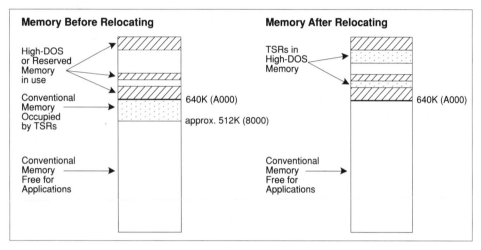

Figure 1-8. Relocating Memory-Resident Programs to High Memory

Shadow RAM. *Shadow RAM* is another element in high memory handiwork. ROMs are sometimes much slower than RAM chips, so some PCs copy the contents of their ROMs, such as graphics adapter ROMs, into RAM chips at the same addresses. Then they redirect the addressing so that whenever the system needs some graphics adapter program instructions, the requests are sent to the shadow RAM chips that hold the programs, instead of to the original ROMs. That speeds up the computer's work, but doesn't work with all software or hardware. Figure 1-9 shows how this works. Step 8 digs into its advantages and problems.

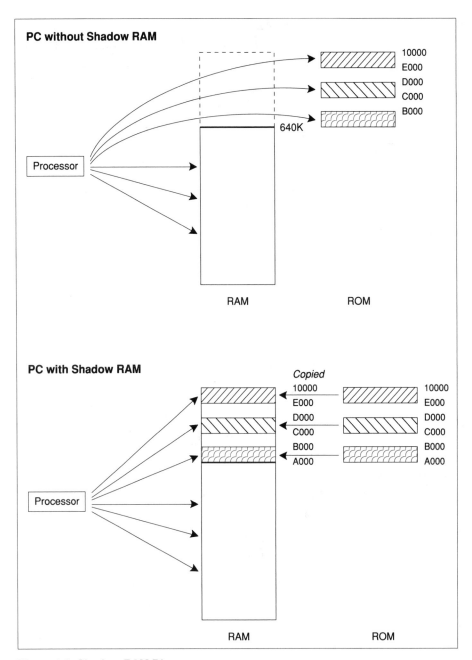

Figure 1-9. Shadow RAM Diagram

Expanded Memory

The first major scheme for slipping around the DOS 640K limit on memory was *expanded memory*; it's still one of the most important. Expanded memory still forces programs to deal only with conventional memory, or with borrowed parts of high memory, but it swaps information from other memory in and out of these conventional addresses. Figure 1-10 shows how this works in brief.

With the right software and hardware to handle this swapping of memory information, a PC can have as much as 32MB more memory. Only programs that are written to understand expanded memory can use these megabytes, but there are quite a few of those these days.

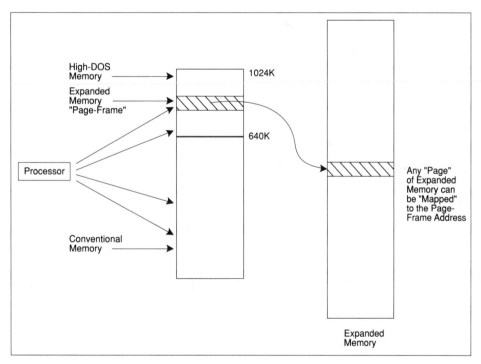

Figure 1-10. Expanded Memory Map

Expanded memory can be slower than conventional memory, but that's a minor price to pay for getting so many megabytes. And in fact, under certain circumstances such as multitasking, swapping even more of conventional memory in and out in expanded memory fashion—a practice known as backfilling—can be faster than traditional conventional memory.

Extended Memory

Extended memory is memory at the addresses directly above 1MB. That is, it's the memory above conventional and high memory.

It is not the same thing as expanded memory. (It's too bad the names are so similar.) Expanded memory swaps information in and out of conventional; extended memory holds its own information. expanded memory works on any PC with the right added hardware and software; extended works only on PCs, PS/2s, and compatibles built around the 286, 386, or 486 chips. These days many of these systems ship with enough memory chips to fill 2MB, 4MB, or more.

Unfortunately, DOS limits what you can do with this memory—that pesky 640K wall appears. But any PC can use it for caching or spooling. And some new software called DOS Extenders, special programs that push a 286, 386, or 486 processor into protected mode, can use as much as 16MB of extended memory directly, almost as if it was conventional memory. Other operating systems such as OS/2 and Unix can also use extended memory. Extended memory can also be used as expanded memory through the magic of emulation . An emulator program can set up software registers and the other necessities of the expanded memory specification, and then tell your PC to treat extended memory as expanded. It won't be as fast as expanded memory that has real, hardware registers, but it will do the same jobs. Figure 1-11 shows where extended memory is on the map; Step 4 explains it.

High Memory

The first 64K of extended memory, the addresses from 1024K to 1088K, are sometimes called Hi or High memory, in a confusing similarity to the 384K of high memory between 640K and 1024K. Microsoft discovered a trick with the 8088 chip's addressing (that also works with the later processor chips) that lets it actually reach more than 1MB in real mode. With the right high memory driver software DOS applications can use this 64K just as if it were an addition to the lower 640K. Figure 1-12 shows Hi memory; Step 4 explains it.

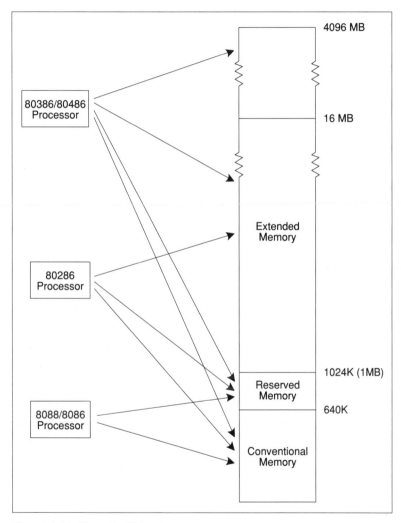

Figure 1-11. Extended Memory

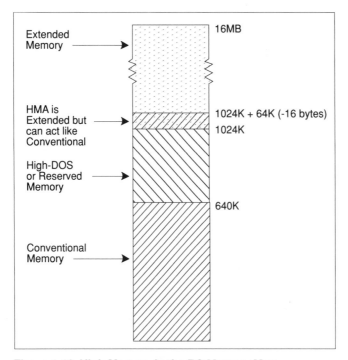

Figure 1-12. High Memory in the PC Memory Map

Virtual Memory

There's almost always lots more disk memory in a computer than there is chip memory. After all, disks are cheaper. But programs that want a certain number of KB or MB of memory don't want disk, they want RAM chips. Virtual memory software exploits the presence of large, cheap disk memory by tricking those programs into thinking that part of the disk is RAM memory.

It does this by telling the program that there is more RAM memory than there really is, and then keeping track of how much memory each program and information file wants, and where they are. Each time some software requests a program or information from memory, the virtual memory software intercepts the request. Then the virtual memory software checks for the needed stuff in real RAM. If it's there, fine, it is used. If the requested stuff isn't in real RAM, the virtual memory software looks for it on disk. When it finds the needed program or file, it copies it into the real RAM that is available, making room by moving something else to the disk. Then it doles out the requested information from RAM. There's virtually more RAM than is really in the computer. Figure 1-13 illustrates this process.

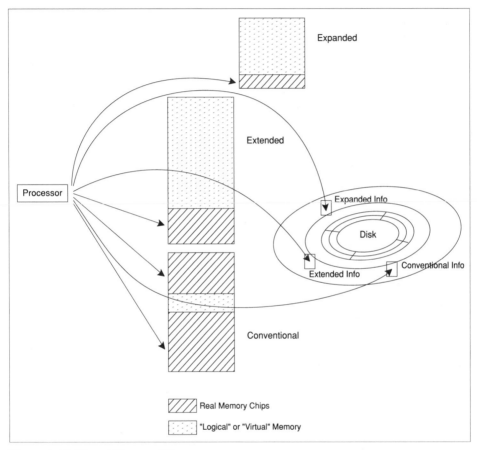

Figure 1-13. Virtual Memory Diagram

Virtual memory may seem similar to disk caching, but is actually quite different. In virtual memory the disk space holds information that is supposed to be in RAM, calling it in as needed. To the program the virtual memory on disk looks like RAM. In disk caching, the most used disk information is kept in RAM, and is used only when the computer is looking to disk . (Unfortunately, IBM chose to call it's RAM disk program VDISK for "virtual disk," confusing things a bit more than they need to be.)

386- and 486-based PCs have hardware that's designed to efficiently provide virtual memory; but they don't have virtual memory for all programs because DOS does not provide virtual memory. (Some other operating systems, such as OS/2, do.) However, some programs have their own virtual memory routines built in. These are called overlays where a program is broken into parts that are pulled into and pushed out of chip memory as they are needed. There are also utility programs you can add to DOS that will create virtual memory for many programs.

A Final Step 1 Note

I hope you're now comfortable with such technobabble as: "Can I run these two programs under DOS 4.0 using LIM 4.0 EMS expanded memory and some extended memory, without a virtual memory scheme, on a 386-based PC with 1MB installed, 16MHz, 0-wait state, page-mode RAM, expandable to 8MB through internal, proprietary, high-speed 32-bit slot, with 64K write-through 30ns SRAM cache, expandable to 256K, with 1MB of VRAM on 16-bit VGA EISA graphics board, shadow RAM as an option."

This Step tried to explain all that. But don't worry if it didn't all catch. You don't have to know it all immediately to get on with memory management. And you'll be surprised at how quickly you learn it when you start using the management software and hardware in this book.

STEP 2

Take Inventory

Key Ideas:

•   You need to know how much memory is in your system, what type of memory it is, whether it is working properly, how well it works, and how it is being used.

•   You can get basic answers from a technical support person, user group colleague, or a computer sales person.

•   You can get more detailed answers if you're experienced with PCs and are willing to open the PC case to count memory chips, and to use DOS to ferret out memory use.

•   You get the most information by running an analysis and diagnostic program.

Why an Inventory is Important

Before you manage your PC's memory, you should know how much it has. You should also know how that memory is being used—which programs take up how much. That's the focus of this Step.

This may seem an overly simple question. If you're an experienced PC user dealing with a single PC that you know intimately from countless hours of tinkering, it is painfully obvious how much memory you have. You'll already know, probably from all the times you wished you had more, and ran into some limit in loading utilities or running a large program. But you may not know just how that memory is being used. The tools in this Step can still help even such a grizzled pro.

Even if you're a beginner with a brand-new PC, you may well have some clue to the memory stockpile in your system. You were probably clutching a discount-store ad at some point or were told by the salesperson in a computer retail outlet how much memory was in your box, in phrases such as "this PC has a full 640K" or "comes with 512K standard." So what's to count? How much more do you need to know? Plenty, though knowing at least that much gives you a headstart.

And think of the poor folks who are supposed to help others with their PCs, from the neighborhood computer whiz to the corporate MIS (Management Information Systems, or "computer support people") adviser. (Perhaps you're one yourself.) These people don't have first-hand knowledge of each and every PC, but are supposed to quickly suggest how to maintain, operate, and upgrade a wide variety of them, often with little-help from a frustrated and anxious user or owner. How does an expert find out what memory is in a PC?

And what about more sophisticated and tricky questions, the kind you don't need to answer for basic memory smarts, but that are vital to the advanced and most efficient use of memory? Even experienced users can sometimes be stumped by such questions as "does your system have shadow RAM?" or "how much memory does your mouse driver eat up?" You don't need to know the answer to every such question to make smarter use of memory, but to get the absolute most out of your system, you should know where to find the answers. (And experienced tinkerers will undoubtedly want to know just to have a more complete and so more comfortable grasp of their hardware and software.)

Finally, the facts about your computer's memory changes. Not only do they change in a big way when you buy and install more memory (or get a new computer), they change whenever you add a new program or driver to your computer's diet, when you adjust the size of a cache or RAM disk, or when you plug in a new card to connect to some peripheral. You certainly don't need to know every minute what's happening in your computer's memory, but it helps to be able to find out what is there and how it is used when you have any trouble.

What to Inventory

There's more to counting memory than coming up with a single number total. Years ago it was enough to say "I have 128K" or "comes with 512K." You can get by with those numbers today, sort of, but for memory efficiency you sooner or later want to know this much about your computer:

1. How much conventional RAM is in my PC? (This is the sort of number mentioned above).

2. How much extended RAM is in my PC?

3. How much expanded RAM is in my PC?

Those are the basics. Then there are other questions just slightly less crucial:

4. What speed chips does my PC use?

5. Would faster memory chips add to my PC's speed?

6. How much cache memory does my system have?

7. What kind of cache memory is it?

8. How much expansion memory can I add on the motherboard?

9. How much memory can be configured as extended? As expanded?

10. Is my PC's memory 8-bit, 16-bit, or 32-bit? Is there a special memory-card slot for 32-bit memory?

11. How much video memory does my system have? Is it DRAM or VRAM? How much more video memory can I add? Is the video memory 8-bit or 16-bit?

12. Does my system use shadow RAM ? Can I disable the "shadow RAM"?

And those dozen questions just cover the hardware. Then there are software memory questions, such as:

13. How much memory does my DOS use?

14. How much memory is taken up by RAM disks or caches?

15. How much memory do my drivers use?

16. How much memory do my TSR utilities use?

17. How much conventional memory is left for applications to run in after loading DOS, drivers, and TSRs?

18. How much extended memory is left?

19. How much expanded memory is left?

20. How much memory does my application (spreadsheet or word processor or database manager) want?

21. How large a file can I load into my application?

22. Do I have a CMOS-memory storage spot for system configuration?

23. What addresses in memory are my drivers and utilities using?

24. What memory areas between 640K and 1MB are unused?

If you're worried after that interrogation, relax. Remember, you only need to answer the first three to get started with memory management. But the more you do know, the more clever you can be with your system, and the more time and money you can save. Incidentally, if any of those terms were foreign to you, either don't worry about them for now, read about them in Step 1, or turn to the glossary for a quick definition.

How to Inventory

There are several ways to take a census of the memory in your computer. Some are quicker and easier; some somewhat more involved but more complete. They are:

1. Ask someone who knows more about computers to do it for you.

2. Do it yourself, manually (by opening the box and by using DOS and whatever utilities you have).

3. Do it yourself, with software (by running a program dedicated to counting and analyzing your system).

Ask Someone To Do It For You

This is the easiest way to go, and it could be the cheapest. I say "could be" because if you have to pay a consultant, for instance, the cost could be significant. If you have to wait a while for an answer from a friend or corporate support person, the time could add up. However, it is also the least flexible way because it leaves you stranded if and when (when is more likely) anything about your hardware or software changes. Then you have to go ask again. But if you want to go this way, you can ask:

• Computer sales people (they are sometimes knowledgeable)

• A computer-wise friend (they are also sometimes knowledgeable)

• A user-group acquaintance (probably knowledgeable)

• Corporate or technical support person (at your company or at the company you bought hardware or software from—these folks are the most knowledgeable).

Do It Yourself—Counting Chips

Another option is to just open up the computer and see what you've got. This one is tough unless you're unafraid of fiddling with the hardware and conversant with chips and circuit boards and DOS.

Do It Yourself—With Software

This is the best way to go. There are many programs, some free, that will quickly and accurately assess your PC's memory.

Counting Chips

To make your own hardware memory count, you need to open the computer case and find the memory chips. There will be some on the main circuit board, and possibly more on plug-in circuit cards. To do this:

Unplug your system

Ground yourself (this eliminates static charges that could destroy chips)

Open the case

Then look inside

Step 4 describes the look of memory chips and boards, if you're not already familiar with them. For instance, you might see a row of nine identical chips that could be 256K of memory, or a full megabyte, or even more—depending on what the individual chips are. Figure 2-1 shows an example. You'd also have to check for any added memory boards, note any empty sockets (to see what the expansion possibilities are for the system), and squint at the tiny print on the chips to see their speed. If you are or want to be a hardware hacker, you'll soon be able to run through this process in just a few seconds on friends' PCs. If you don't have the time or interest in such details, rest assured that you don't have to. Not only can you turn to one of the other counting and analysis methods (and learn much more than anyone can from inspecting the naked chips), but you can even get a bit more done manually, and cheaply, by looking to DOS. I won't go into any more detail on chip identification here because you can find more information in Step 4, and because it's more practical for almost anyone to use DOS and utility programs to more thoroughly count and analyze your memory.

Figure 2-1. Example of Memory Chips Inside a PC (courtesy Hauppage)

Inventory

There is quite a range of abilities and prices in assessment software.

Power-On Self Test

Most PCs have a power-on self-test (*POST*) that tests and counts memory (among other tasks) when you first turn the system on. Often you'll see a display on screen showing either the progress of the results of this test, giving you the total conventional and extended memory in your system. Most systems with expanded memory have an expanded memory driver that makes a similar test, and shows the results on screen. Unfortunately, the displays are transient—you'll have to watch closely to see results this way. What you'll see for a few seconds is a result such as this:

BASE RAM Test	640KB
Extended RAM Test	0K
Total Memory	640KB

The BASE RAM line refers to conventional memory. This is not a test of how much conventional memory will be free to use; just how much is actually plugged into the system. Before you use that 640K, some will be taken by DOS, TSR programs, and device drivers.

Inventory with DOS

DOS provides two ways to count memory: *CHKDSK* and *MEM*. *CHKDSK* is available with all versions of DOS. MEM is more powerful than CHKDSK for learning about memory, but is only available in DOS 4.0 and 4.01, not in previous versions. DOS 5.0 may have some new memory counting commands when it arrives.

If you don't know which version of DOS you have, you can watch the POST displays—they'll mention it—or you can just type **VER**. This DOS command reports immediately on the DOS version you're using.

CHKDSK. The DOS program *CHKDSK* comes with every PC as part of DOS. It is designed to examine disks (check disk) for damaged files and repair those files, but when it works it will tell you how much overall conventional memory you have.

CHKDSK isn't an internal DOS command like DIR or COPY that's always available no matter which directory you're in. You must first find it on your disk—probably in the DOS directory. To use CHKDSK to count memory, just type **CHKDSK**. You'll soon see a listing of the total memory, free memory, and disk memory available in your PC. The difference between total memory and free memory is the amount of memory used by DOS, TSR programs, and device drivers. Free memory is what's left for running applications.

MEM—CHKDSK only gives you bare conventional memory totals, but MEM can lay out lots of details on conventional, expanded, and extended memory. You can use it in three ways:

MEM   for simple results

MEM /program   for a list of programs in memory

MEM /debug   for a list of drivers in memory

If you merely type *MEM* you'll see a report on:

bytes total memory

bytes available

largest executable program size

C>mem

    655360 bytes total memory
    655360 bytes available
    462288 largest executable program size

    393216 bytes total extended memory
    393216 bytes available extended memory

C>

Figure 2-2. Simple MEM Report in DOS 4.01

But if you type **MEM /PROGRAM** you'll see the report of Figure 2-3—a list of all the programs in memory. This list displays the name of each program in memory, the type of program, the starting location or address for each, and the size of each in bytes. Those memory areas listed as IBMDOS are free.

C>mem /program

Address	Name	Size	Type
000000		000400	Interrupt Vector
000400		000100	ROM Communication Area
000500		000200	DOS Communication Area
000700	IO	002510	System Program
002C10	MSDOS	008E20	System Program
00BA30	IO	002FE0	System Data
		0000C0	FILES=
		000100	FCBS=
		001F40	BUFFERS=
		0001C0	LASTDRIVE=
		000CD0	TACKS=
00EA20	COMMAND	001640	Program
010070	GRAB	000030	Environment
0100B0	COMMAND	0000A0	Environment
010160	GRAB	005AB0	Program
015C20	SKN	000030	Environment
015C60	SKN	019570	Program
02F1E0	MEM	000030	Environment
02F220	MEM	012F00	Program
042130	MSDOS	05DEC0	— Free —

655360 bytes total memory
655360 bytes available
462288 largest executable program size
393216 bytes total extended memory
393216 bytes available extended memory

Figure 2-3. MEM /program report in DOS 4.01—The Programs in Memory

If you type **MEM /DEBUG** you'll get a report of the device drivers in memory, along with the programs. See Figure 2-4.

C>mem /debug

Address	Name	Size	Type
000000		000400	Interrupt Vector
000400		000100	ROM Communication Area
000500		000200	DOS Communication Area
000700	IO	002510	System Program
	CON		System Device Driver
	AUX		System Device Driver
	PRN		System Device Driver
	CLOCK$		System Device Driver
	A: - C:		System Device Driver
	COM1		System Device Driver
	LPT1		System Device Driver
	LPT2		System Device Driver
	LPT3		System Device Driver
	COM2		System Device Driver
	COM3		System Device Driver
	COM4		System Device Driver
002C10	MSDOS	008E20	System Program
00BA30	IO	002FE0	System Data
		0000C0	FILES=
		000100	FCBS=
		001F40	BUFFERS=
		0001C0	LASTDRIVE=
		000CD0	STACKS=
00EA20	COMMAND	001640	Program
010070	GRAB	000030	Environment
0100B0	COMMAND	0000A0	Environment
010160	GRAB	005AB0	Program
015C20	SKN	000030	Environment
015C60	SKN	019570	Program
02F1E0	MEM	000030	Environment

| 02F220 | MEM | 012F00 | Program |
| 042130 | MSDOS | 05DEC0 | — Free — |

655360 bytes total memory
655360 bytes available
462288 largest executable program size

393216 bytes total extended memory
393216 bytes available extended memory

Figure 2-4. MEM /DEBUG Report on Drivers in Memory

Note that this is the debug option for MEM, not the DEBUG utility that comes with DOS. The *DEBUG utility* is meant for programmers and experts who want to inspect or change what's in memory or in programs. DEBUG isn't simple to use— you must be able to deal with hexadecimal addresses and values, and remember the cryptic DEBUG commands, such as shown in Figure 2-5. But if you do know how to use DEBUG, you'll be able to see each and every bit in memory. This can be useful, but is not a practical way to get an overall sense of how much memory you have and how it is being used.

```
C>debug
-d
3461:0100  01 8E 33 E8 00 00 5B 50-8C C0 05 10 00 8B 0E 1E   ..3...[P........
3461:0110  01 03 C8 89 4F FB 8B 0E-26 01 03 C8 89 4F F7 8B   ....O...&....O..
3461:0120  0E 20 01 89 4F F9 8B 0E-24 01 89 4F F5 8B 3E 28   . ..O...$..O..>(
3461:0130  01 8B 16 18 01 B1 04 D3-E2 8B 0E 16 01 E3 1A 26   ...............&
3461:0140  C5 B5 10 01 83 C7 04 8C-DD 26 03 2E 18 01 83 C5   .........&......
3461:0150  01 03 E8 8E DD 01 04 E2-E6 0E 1F BF 00 01 8B F2   ................
3461:0160  81 C6 10 01 8B CB 2B CE-F3 A4 58 FA 8E 57 FB 8B   ......+...X..W..
3461:0170  67 F9 FB FF 6F F5 00 00-00 00 00 00 00 00 00 00   g...o..........
-d
```

```
3461:0180  00 00 00 00 00 00 00 00-00 00 00 00 00 00 00 00   ................
3461:0190  00 00 00 00 00 00 00 00-00 00 00 00 00 00 00 00   ................
3461:01A0  00 00 00 00 00 00 00 00-00 00 00 00 00 00 00 00   ................
3461:01B0  00 00 00 00 00 00 00 00-00 00 00 00 00 00 00 00   ................
3461:01C0  00 00 00 00 00 00 00 00-00 00 00 00 00 00 00 00   ................
3461:01D0  00 00 00 00 00 00 00 00-00 00 00 00 00 00 00 00   ................
3461:01E0  00 00 00 00 00 00 00 00-00 00 00 00 00 00 00 00   ................
3461:01F0  00 00 00 00 00 00 00 00-00 00 00 00 00 00 00 00   ................
-
```

Figure 2-5. DEBUG Utility—A Different DOS Command than DEBUG option of MEM

Inventory with General Software

There are applications and utilities that clue you in to the memory facts of your system, either as one of their important features or as a byproduct.

In the first category are utility packages such as The Norton Utilities, which include a routine called SI (for System Information). Give the SI command (from the Norton Integrator menu or by typing SI at the DOS prompt) and a disk drive letter, such as C: (the common hard drive symbol) **SI C:** and you'll see a list of lots of system facts, including how much memory the utility could find. (Although this book doesn't spend any time on factors such as coprocessors and disk drive speeds, those too are important to computer performance—and it's nice to learn about them while you're also learning about memory.)

Many programs tell you something about your memory in passing. For example, Borland's SideKick is one of the most popular PC utilities. Because SideKick loads into your memory chips and stays there, ready to use, even when you return to DOS to manage your files or when you use another application program, it needs to know how much memory you have. When you first load SideKick, you'll see a message that tells you the total amount of memory you started with, the occupied memory (what SideKick and DOS and already loaded drivers and TSR programs used), and the free memory (what you have left for use by applications and other TSR utilities after loading SideKick). By subtracting free from occupied, you can learn how much memory SideKick itself has taken.

Inventory With Analysis Software

With memory so important, and counting memory a vital first step to understanding and using it, it's natural that many programs have been developed to help you with this. These range from quick-and-dirty programs that do little more than DOS 4.0's own MEM command to comprehensive packages that can measure, test, organize, explain and optimize memory use.

Some of the programs are free (that is, public domain, meaning that anyone can use them without charge). Some are distributed for free to customers of a specific software or hardware company, to entice people to buy or use other programs from that company. Some are shareware (meaning anyone can try them for free, and is then expected to pay a registration fee if he or she uses the program). And some are just commercial packages that you pay $50 to $200 for to get more out of your PC.

Public Domain and Shareware Analysis Software. There are no inexpensive analysis programs as complete as the best commercial analysis programs. But there are many that can do something for you. To find them, ask friends, a local users' group, or look to the sources mentioned in the "Cheap and Free Software" appendix in this book. Here's a list of some programs you'll find through such sources, in order of preference.

MEMMAP.EXE.—This public domain program is like DOS 4.0's MEM, but does more and does it for DOS versions 2.1 and 3.3 as well as 4.0. It displays all of the blocks of memory that have been allocated. This includes TSR programs. If you use its "/v" option (type MEMMAP /V) you'll see a display of the variables in each environment block. It even works for OS/2 Extended Edition 1.1 in the DOS Compatibility box. It is easier to read than MEM and brings MEM-like abilities to DOS 2 and 3. MEMMAP is available from PC MagNet.

SYSID.EXE—This public domain program produces a dozen display screens of information on your PC. It will tell you the PC type, the BIOS information (who made it and when), the current operating mode of the PC, details on conventional, extended, and expanded memory, TSRs, device drivers, and interrupt lists, video adapter modes, keyboard information, DOS environment settings, and more. Available from PC-SIG.

PMAP—This free program from The Cove Software Group is available on CompuServe as PMAP.ARC in Library 1 of the IBMSYS forum. It shows where device drivers and memory resident (TSR) programs are. It also shows how expanded and extended memory are being used, except for any memory controlled by the HIMEM.SYS driver.

Scout—This shareware program is a TSR utility file manager. It lets you copy, move, alter, delete, or rename files while you're using another application program. It can display directory listings, has a built-in calendar and an ASCII table. Scout can display the amount of memory used by each TSR. It is available from PC-SIG.

P-CEM—This public domain program handles more than just memory counting. It simplifies use of DOS commands such as copy, delete, rename, execute, view, or print. It can encrypt or decrypt a file, change file attributes, switch directories, change CGA colors, and change the cursor size. Where memory's concerned, it will list either the total memory or currently available memory in the PC, as well as display system configuration details. It is available through PC-SIG.

MEM.EXE—This public domain program is for the OS/2 operating system. It can show the largest block of RAM available for use. It is sometimes listed as OS2MEM.ARC on bulletin boards.

Commercial Analysis Software. There are some excellent independent analysis programs. Typically they'll cost you $100 to $200. If you look around carefully, you may find them bundled for free with other programs or with memory boards. For example, Quarterdeck's Manifest comes with the QEMM 386 memory manager program. System Sleuth was at one time bundled with Teletek's X-Bandit board.

Most of the commercial analysis programs do far more than test memory. Most also test and report on all the other features of a PC. Some also pack utilities such as disk caching programs. The best come with "adviser" commands that can suggest to you what parts of your system are the weakest links—and how to improve them.

Here are some leading analysis programs:

Control Room—Ashton-Tate's Control Room program is a complete PC inventory and analysis package. It operates as a small TSR program (taking only 5 to 20K) that's always available. Control Room combines many features of PC utility packages, including system analysis, performance testing, and system customization. It includes screen blanking, virus scanning, macro saving, disk caching, disk optimizing, print-to-disk (great for laptops that aren't always hooked up to a printer), and DOS Shell features. Control Room packs an editor for changing CONFIG.SYS and AUTOEXEC.BAT files. And it lets you customize your keyboard (for everything from the click it makes to the repeat rate when you hold a key down).

As shown in Figure 2-6, Control Room can tell how much memory your PC has and how it's being used. This search finds conventional, expanded, extended, cache, and any other memory in the system. It lists applications, caches, device drivers, TSRs, DOS pieces, and anything else in memory. It also tests CPU, disk, and video performance, keeps an inventory file on disk of your PC's equipment, and tracks the use of memory. Control Room makes it easy to view and change the settings and configurations of all your hardware too. It comes with on-screen help to explain all the various parameters and settings.

Control Room wraps all this investigating up in a 15 to 20-page "Expert Opinion" report that tells you how your system measures up to other PCs, and where you might change it, including what memory would improve it. Figure 2-7 shows a page of an example report.

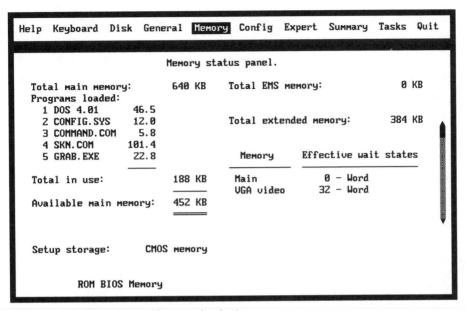

Figure 2-6. Control Room Memory Analysis

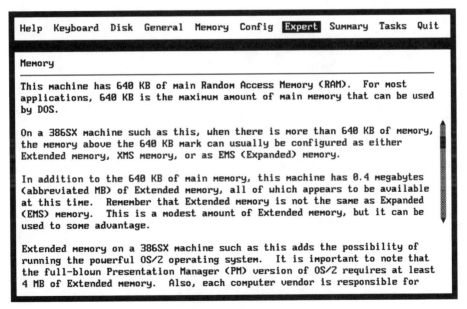

Figure 2-7. Control Room Expert Opinion Report

Manifest—Quarterdeck's Manifest is a hardware analysis and testing program. It can run as a standard application or as a TSR utility to analyze the type and amount of RAM your system has, tell you how it is used, and suggest which parts are unused or under-used. It even details the speed of various parts of RAM in the PC. This is vital information for knowing how to relocate network, buffer, and mouse drivers, and TSRs. Manifest can tell you what is in your AUTOEXEC.BAT and CONFIG.SYS files and what sort of processor chip your PC is built on. It has on-line help. And, using all of that information, Manifest will generate a report for you on what to change or improve about your use of memory. You can buy Manifest on its own, or with Quarterdeck's QRAM memory optimizer or QEMM memory manager. Figure 2-8 shows a Manifest improvement suggestion.

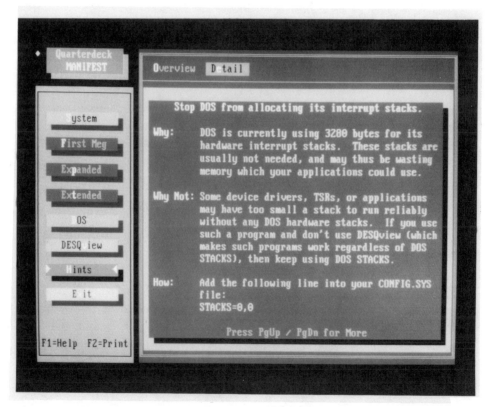

Figure 2-8. Manifest Memory Improvement Suggestion (courtesy Quarterdeck)

ASQ—The 386Max memory management program from Qualitas comes with a memory analyzer called ASQ. This program both analyzes what memory is doing and explains memory management terms. You can download a copy of ASQ for free from the Qualitas bulletin board.

Discover—The Headroom and Netroom utilities (see Steps 5 and 6) from Helix Software come with a memory analysis program called Discover. It is really three utilities, to analyze and report on memory, and a text editor to change your batch files that control memory. Discover can find device drivers and report on expanded, extended, and high-DOS memory use, as well as on other system factors (such as disk drives).

InfoSpotter—Merrill & Bryan make memory management programs such as Turbo EMS (see Steps 4 and 5). They also make InfoSpotter, a full diagnostic and analysis program for memory. It works on any PC from the original design to today's 486 machines, detecting bus and mouse type, analyzing all kinds of memory (including HMA) and even lets you edit batch files and CMOS memory values.

System Sleuth—Dariana Technology's *System Sleuth* is a computer analysis and inventory program. It is available for PCs running DOS, for PCs running Windows and DOS, and for Apple Macintoshes.

System Sleuth reports on every aspect of your PC's hardware. It runs as a standard application—not as a TSR utility. It reports on the memory content and use, disk and video features, and other features of the hardware. It lists the amounts and uses of each type of memory. Sleuth gets down into such details as configuration switch settings and interrupt request trapping, important details for finding and solving conflicts between various peripherals that want to use the same parts of memory. Figure 2-9 shows a System Sleuth map and listing of memory use.

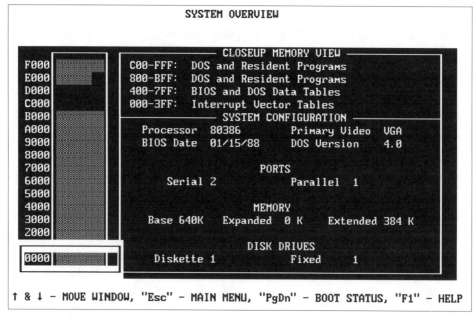

```
                        SYSTEM OVERVIEW


                    ┌──── CLOSEUP MEMORY VIEW ────┐
  F000│▓▓▓▓▓│     C00-FFF:  DOS and Resident Programs
  E000│▓▓▓▓▓│     800-BFF:  DOS and Resident Programs
  D000│▓▓▓▓▓│     400-7FF:  BIOS and DOS Data Tables
  C000│▓▓▓▓▓│     000-3FF:  Interrupt Vector Tables
  B000│▓▓▓▓▓│     ┌──── SYSTEM CONFIGURATION ────┐
  A000│▓▓▓▓▓│       Processor  80386      Primary Video  VGA
  9000│▓▓▓▓▓│       BIOS Date  01/15/88   DOS Version    4.0
  8000│▓▓▓▓▓│
  7000│▓▓▓▓▓│                   PORTS
  6000│▓▓▓▓▓│            Serial 2        Parallel  1
  5000│▓▓▓▓▓│
  4000│▓▓▓▓▓│                   MEMORY
  3000│▓▓▓▓▓│       Base 640K  Expanded  0 K    Extended 384 K
  2000│▓▓▓▓▓│
                               DISK DRIVES
 │0000│▓▓▓▓▓│       Diskette 1            Fixed     1


 ↑ & ↓ - MOVE WINDOW, "Esc" - MAIN MENU, "PgDn" - BOOT STATUS, "F1" - HELP
```

Figure 2-9. System Sleuth List of Memory Use

Sleuth also includes a powerful application for finding and deleting files across any number of disk drives, a disk cache, a driver to convert extended memory into expanded, and a driver to allow use of the high memory area (64K above 1MB), the interrupt table is in the first 1024 bytes of system memory.

WinSleuth, the Windows version of Sleuth, runs under Windows 3.0. It gives the same basic information as the DOS System Sleuth, but adds information about the windows environment in the different modes. Information covered includes, how much various applications are using, and the differences between free unblanked, uncompacted, RAM (before any reorganization by the Windows memory manager) versus free global, uncompacted RAM, (available before Windows rearranges programs to maximize space).

hDC First Apps—This set of nine Windows 3.0 utilities includes: autosave, character set (for special symbols), font viewer (to see which system and printer fonts are installed), art gallery (a scrapbook for graphic and clip art), alarm clock, desk calendar, and others. The memory viewer utility reports on what memory is usable in real, standard, and enhanced modes. It reports on how much memory there is, how much an application is taking, and how much is left.

Performance Testing

You need to know what's in your system; it's also good to know how well it works. Traditional performance testing was fairly academic, just seeing how fast the processor, memory, disk, and video could zip along. Most of the commercial inventory and analysis programs include some performance testing along this line.

But there are also programs devoted to more thorough and realistic testing. These performance testing programs can run benchmark tests that are more realistic, working on word processor documents or spreadsheet numbers instead of on hypothetical laboratory algorithms. They'll tell you which parts of your PC hardware are holding back performance, and can compare your PC's speed against results from other PCs.

Personal Measure from Spirit of Performance and Power Meter from The Database Group are well-known performance-testing programs. Personal Measure, for example, can run in the background as you use your regular programs. It will then give you a report that's precisely on target for your own computer demands—what you need to consider upgrading in your system and what is working just fine. Figures 2-10a and 2-10b show what such a benchmark display looks like.

You can also find performance tests in most popular computing magazines, such as *BYTE* and *PC*. These magazines have laboratories that cook up testing programs. You can often get the programs for just the cost of a phone call or letter.

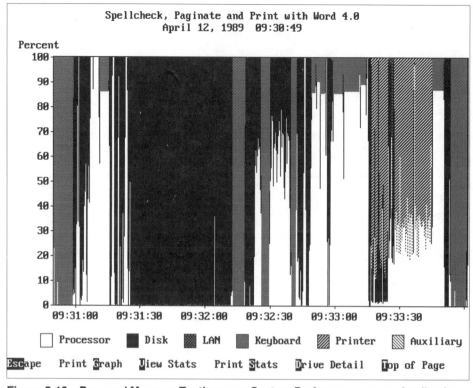

Figure 2-10a. Personal Measure Testing your System Performance on an Application.

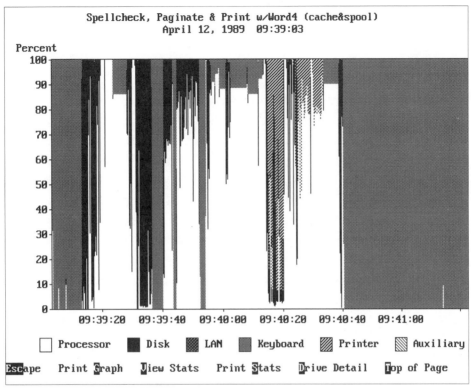

Figure 2-10b.

Finding Memory Failures

Chips can fail or break, just as any device can. RAM failures aren't as common as software conflicts or human mistakes, but they do happen. Of all the chips in your PC, the RAM chips are the most likely to fail.

You can repair memory problems in one of three ways:

1. You can give the machine to someone else to repair.

The repair person will then, in turn, probably do one of the following:

2. You can replace each RAM chip or bank of chips in your PC until the problem disappears. (See Step 4 for details on replacing chips.)

3. You can use a diagnostics program to identify the bad chip and replace only that one.

Types of RAM Failure

There are three types of RAM hardware problems.

The first is the catastrophic failure. When this happens, the chip just isn't working at all. You'll see a **MEM ERR** message on the PC's screen and that's where the POST (Power On Self Test) will end. If your PC has a catastrophic memory chip error, you won't be able to use any diagnostic program to find the problem chip. Your only choices will be the second option (replacing each chip or bank in turn and then trying to turn the system on), or sending the PC to a professional repair shop.

The second problem is the device-fault-related error. In this case the POST will not freeze in its tracks. It will inform you of a memory error, but the RAM chips will start and boot the computer. A diagnostic program can detect such a memory error, and pinpoint the chip that has it. Then you only need to replace one chip.

The third problem type doesn't even rate as a MEM ERR to the POST. But at some point after the computer has been running, it will freeze or reboot, without warning or explanation. In fact, this error can occur at random intervals, because of a circuit inside a RAM chip that sometimes works and sometimes doesn't. Some diagnostic programs won't detect this kind of error. Others are able to run tests over and over until such an error reveals itself. This same process can be used to identify and pinpoint chips that are weak, and that may fail soon.

Diagnostics

Some system analysis and inventory programs have diagnostic abilities. Control Room, Manifest, and System Sleuth do. But they don't match the depth and completeness of the programs listed that follow.

Unfortunately, RAM diagnostics are not very advanced. For instance, none of the programs diagnoses trouble in a processor RAM cache. And most can only pinpoint the faulty chip in PC, XT, and AT RAM arrangements of DIP chips. Expanded and extended memory sometimes elude them. And they are often confused by 386-based PCs RAM arrangements with 1MB SIMMs or with mixed

DIPs and SIMMs. These faults may ease in the next year as the popularity of 386 and 486 systems pressure the developers into meeting those needs. But even now these programs can save you time and trouble, especially if you use one that points you to an imminent failure in a weak chip.

POST—Of course the cheapest diagnostic is the built-in one: the Power On Self Test in every PC. Not only can this testing find any serious chip failures, it helps you find the chip that failed. Unfortunately, you must be able to read the diagnostic messages and code numbers to use this information. They tell you which bank of chips and which chip within that bank is making trouble—but the code is in hexadecimal and varies from PC to XT to AT, and from company to company. See your system documentation if you really want to cipher this out.

RAMTEST—This shareware utility tests RAM to tell you which chips are faulty and should be replaced. You control it through menus, telling it how many times to test, what sort of report to make, and so on. It tests expanded memory if there's an expanded memory manager program mentioned in your CONFIG.SYS file. It will also test extended memory on an AT. RAMTEST. You can get a copy from PC-SIG.

Burn In

Most chips fail at the beginning or near the end of their expected life. This is called the "bathtub curve" for reliability. To winnow out those flawed chips that are going to fail early, most PC manufacturers use a "burn-in" process of intensive use and testing. You can carry out such tests yourself with this Shareware program. It will run your memory chips for 24 to 72 hours, putting ASCII characters on the screen, running graphics for CGA, EGA, and VGA displays, and generating random numbers to store on disk and display, then erasing those numbers and starting over again. It is available from PC-SIG.

DR-Chips—This commercial program from the Alpha Group costs little more than shareware would. It tests only memory, not the disk or any other parts of the PC.

CheckIt—TouchStone Software's CheckIt is a compete diagnostic program for PCs. It also provides the sort of inventory information you would get from one of the programs mentioned earlier in this Step, such as Control Room or System Sleuth.

CheckIt has tests for the main system board's processor (in real and protected modes), the numeric coprocessor, the interrupt and DMA controller chips, the disks, the video adapter (in character and graphics modes, and including tests of the video board memory), the communication ports, the printer, the input devices (mouse, keyboard, joystick), and the memory. The memory tests can handle up to 16 MB of base and extended memory. You can limit the memory tests to a particular address range.

There's a quick Test Everything selection, or individual tests for the various hardware. The tests include benchmarks to show comparative performance. And the memory test includes a RAM locator to show the chip to replace. CheckIt 2.1 can be confused by 386-based systems.

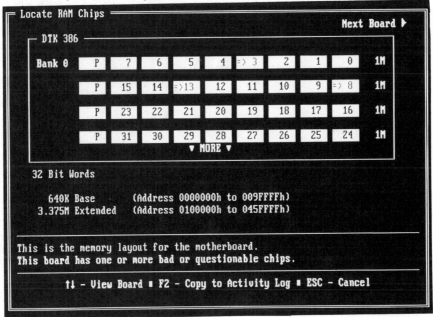

Figure 2-11. CheckIt Display Showing Chip Failures (courtesy TouchStone Software)

TouchStone also makes a less expensive program called PC Test that runs a series of Pass/Fail tests on a PC then generates a report.

AMIDIAG—Named for its developer, American Megatrends Inc., this program tests the RAM, system board, hard and floppy drives, video, keyboard, and I/O ports of a PC. It stores the results of those tests on disk for each machine tested—a handy database for a technical support professional in charge of many PCs.

There are six memory tests in AMIDIAG 3.14, to detect and graphically pinpoint RAM errors. Different tests, naturally, are preferred in different circumstances. For example, when there's a permanent problem, you don't need to run pattern tests. Instead a walking 1s and 0s test will give the quickest result. But when there's a random error, you'll need a pattern test that can run for a while.

Service Diagnostics: The Kit—This sophisticated diagnostic package from SuperSoft can test a PC that won't even start. It's the sort of program a full-time service expert might use for testing disk drive alignment on other niceties of a smoothly performing PC. For memory testing it has both quick and intensive RAM tests, that can find a permanent error in minutes or run all night to burn-in chips.

Use Less Memory: Put your Programs on a Diet

Key Ideas:

- You can choose your programs for minimum memory use.

- You can configure DOS to use the least possible memory.

- You can configure many programs to use less memory than they would by default.

One great way to manage your memory more prudently is to use less to get the same work done. There are general rules of thumb to follow—such as types of programs that use less memory—and there are specific rules—such as how to tell your particular program to conserve. There are also DOS tricks for conserving memory—and because everyone (or nearly everyone who might read this book, at least) uses DOS, everyone should pay attention to these tricks. This step describes both general and specific rules for your programs, and DOS memory conservation rules.

General Rules

Here are some general rules of thumb for using less memory. Some are obvious; some not so obvious.

- Configure DOS to the smallest size

- Use the smallest version and configuration of your application

- Use small applications

- Use TSRs

- Use Integrated Applications

Configure DOS to the Smallest Size

This book is about managing memory for PCs running the DOS operating system. DOS uses memory itself, and you have some control over how much. You can select a version of DOS that uses less memory, or you can use commands within DOS to limit the memory it grabs.

For example, DOS 4.0 uses lots more memory than DOS 3.0, leaving less for your application programs. DOS 4.0 also comes with some new features, but if you don't want those features, you can get along quite well, and use less memory, but sticking to the older DOS 3.3. Or if you want DOS 4.0, you can cut down on its memory use by restricting such options as BUFFERS. DOS memory conservation is discussed in this Step.

Use the Smallest Version and Configuration of Your Application

There are several ways to go about this. One is to use the options that come with many programs to limit their memory use. This Step mentions such options for particular versions of many programs. You can always look to the manual of your particular program to discover its memory switches and options. If you don't find information there, you can call the technical support staff and ask them.

Another approach is to choose your program version for its memory needs. Most programs grow through a series of versions, such as Word 2.0, Word 3.0, Word 4.0, and so on. (DOS has evolved this way, too, as mentioned above.) The newer versions are compatible with the latest PCs, fix bugs discovered in the older versions, and also add more features and commands. Often they are also faster—though a few unfortunate programs get slower, perhaps because of all those new features. As programs evolve through versions, they often change in the amount of memory they use. For several years most programs used more memory with each version. If that's true of your word processor, spreadsheet, or database manager, you might want to opt for an older version to save on memory. You need to be careful that you don't choose a version that's buggy or that won't be compatible with your hardware.

76

In the last couple of years, because of the common problem of "RAM-cram," or too little memory, many new program versions use less memory than their predecessors. Many of them too offer an option of loading into expanded memory. Because of this trend, you should always keep up to date on the latest versions of whatever programs you use. Know what they offer and what they demand. Even a small version change, such as from Version 3.0 to Version 3.01, could mean elimination of some nasty bugs and a significant cut in memory demands. In that case, you'll need to decide if the improvements are worth the upgrade cost—which can range from free to $100 or more, depending on the program and the company selling the program.

For example, Lotus Development wanted to put the latest features into its spreadsheet 1-2-3, but knew that these features would require more than 640K of memory. So they developed two new versions—2.2 with some new features, able to run in 640K, and 3.0 with many new features, requiring 1MB of memory. Some people will want to move to version 2.2 or version 3.0, but some will want to stay with their older version 2.1. In another example, the latest version of Freelance, a graphics program from Lotus Development, uses less memory than older versions. It also has more commands—so every Freelance user interested in memory conservation will want to get the latest version.

Use Small Applications

Not all programs take up the same memory, obviously. But you may not realize how much memory you could save by using a smaller application program. Some such programs save memory just through clever, tight programming. Others save by eliminating some features. That may sound too much like the worst part of dieting—going without the food you really want. In fact, it may just mean discarding features you never use. Don't see it as eliminating all bread from your diet. More likely it means not having any cans of octopus in the cupboard. Because it's typically the advanced features such as automatic indexing and thesaurus in word processors or back-solvers in spreadsheets that push memory use to new heights. Although those features are boons to some (some people live for canned octopus, I suppose), they are unused menu items to most. And you can find applications without them that are smaller, and often quicker, than the one's you're used to. Don't become obsessed with getting the most features in a program. Look instead for the best price, speed, and memory efficiency in a program with the features you'll actually use.

For example, the Quattro Pro spreadsheet competes quite favorably with Lotus 1-2-3 Release 3.0, but uses less memory: 512K instead of 1MB. For another example, instead of using PageMaker or Ventura Publisher for desktop publishing—each needing several MB of memory for good performance—you could turn to DTP, for instance, can use Avagio, Express Publisher, PFS: First Publisher, or Publish-It, and pay only a third as much for a program that needs 640K to handle most desktop publishing work.

If there's a smooth and easy upgrade path from that slim program to one with the more powerful and memory-hogging features, you'll be able to move up if and when you do need those features. Sometimes you'll be able to move fairly smoothly because one company has labored to make its program compatible with other companies: Quattro Pro, mentioned above, can work with the same command-keys and files as Lotus 1-2-3. But there's an even stronger kind of compatibility—when the two programs come from the same company, as part of the same line. (Sometimes such programs are advertised as the laptop versions, because they were designed for laptop computers which once had less memory and disk space than most desktop computers. This title is obsolete, now that the latest laptops have as much memory and disk as the average deskbound PC.) For example, WordPerfect Corporation makes the most popular word processor, WordPerfect. The company now also makes a smaller, simpler program called Letter Perfect, that's essentially a slimmed-down version of WordPerfect. Buttonsoft now makes PC Write Lite, a slender version of its word processor, PC Write.

Use TSRs

The previous section discussed the advantages of using small applications to save memory. These slim programs may lack a few features, but they'll often run in 384K or 512K, instead of 640K or more memory.

If, in fact, you don't even need all the features of a small application, if you only use the basic half-dozen or dozen features of your application program, you could save even more memory by using a TSR replacement. That is, there are miniature versions of most applications—word processor, spreadsheet, database, or whatever—that run as *Terminate and Stay Resident* utilities. These may use as little as 50K to 100K of memory, less than any standard application. And though many are rudimentary, some pack almost as many features as the big applications.

For example, New England Software's Graph-in-the-Box is a TSR chart-making program that uses as little as 10K when it's not active. When you do want turn it on, it uses less memory than standard graphics programs such as Freelance or Harvard Graphics, but has many of their features. For another example, Lucid 3D is a powerful, inexpensive, and memory-thrifty spreadsheet stuffed into a TSR form.

Some TSRs boost programs that you're already using. The TSR called @Base connects to Lotus 1-2-3 and turns it into a database manager. That saves you the memory that a separate, independent database management program would have eaten.

Use Integrated Applications

Once upon a time, many experts thought integrated applications would become the standard in software. These programs combine word processor, spreadsheet, database management, and other applications (such as communications, graphics, and desktop publishing) into a single program. These applications are often called modules. They are popular, particularly among beginners and small businesses, but they didn't conquer standalone applications.

Integrated applications typically ask for at least 512K or 640K of memory. So why mention them when talking about rules for memory conservation? Because they manage to handle all or most of your computing tasks in that memory. They don't start small, but they don't ask for yet more memory or provide a slow and cumbersome process when you want to switch from one application to another. If you pick an integrated application with all the features you need, and you have enough memory to run that one program, you won't have to worry much about memory management. (It's still nice to manage your memory to make more room for utilities, to spool and speed your printing work, to cache your disk accesses to boost performance, and so on.)

Integrated applications also offer other benefits, such as easy movement of data from one task to another (such as copying spreadsheet charts into word processor documents) and easy learning; because once you learn one module you've learned many of the commands for any other module. They also take up less disk space than a suite of dedicated applications would. And because they are popular with beginners, they are often inexpensive. One disadvantage is that no integrated application is likely to have all the features in any one field that a dedicated application would have. If you use all of the most sophisticated features, you may want to shy away from integrated applications, or to supplement one with a single, dedicated application in your special field of interest.

Some of the most popular inexpensive integrated applications are:

Microsoft's Works
Lotus Development's LotusWorks (which used to be called Alpha Works)
Software Publishing's PFS:First Choice
Spinnaker Software's BetterWorking Eight-in-One

Some of the more powerful integrated applications are:

Lotus Development's Symphony
Ashton-Tate's Framework

GeoWorks Ensemble is both an environment and a suite of applications—and together they don't need much memory. See Step 6 for an explanation.

Specific Rules

Most programs can be fine-tuned to use less memory, or to work faster by using more memory. The rules for each program and for particular versions of each program are different. You can learn these rules by:

Reading the manual

Reading any "readme" file on the program disk

Calling the technical support experts at the software company

Asking friends and colleagues who use the same program

Foraging through magazines for tips and ideas

To use less memory, you'll generally be:

- Selecting a particular version of the program

- Using configuration, setup, or setting options for minimum memory. These are often switches, optional letters you type after a slash mark and the program's normal starting command, like this: program /x.

- Break large document files into smaller pieces, then linking those pieces

- Stripping certain optional features—such as spell checkers, background printing, and mouse support

- Use text mode instead of graphics mode

To use more memory for more performance, you'll generally be:

- Selecting a particular version of the program

- Using configuration, setup, or setting options for maximum performance (such as using expanded or extended memory)

- Adding certain optional features—such as spell checkers, background printing, and mouse support

- Adding background printing through a built-in or utility spooler

- Copying important program elements to a RAM disk, and running the program from there (see Step 7 for details on RAM disks).

When listing files to copy to the RAM disk, I'll use the DOS wildcard symbols, where the asterisk * stands for *any letters* and the question mark ? stands for *any single letter*. For instance, telling you to copy **.ovl** means to copy all files that end in .ovl, no matter what letters begin their names.

This part of Step 3 runs through some of the versions, settings, and RAM-disk relevant files for popular programs and DOS. Environments such as DesqView and Windows are handled in Step 6.

Special Note About Windows Programs. Programs that run under Windows get their memory management from Windows. See Step 6 for some of the rules on Windows memory management.

DOS

DOS is the fundamental Disk Operating System program your computer runs. DOS offers you a number of ways to manage and conserve memory. This Step won't describe them all, not by a long shot. After all, there are entire libraries devoted to understanding and tweaking DOS. This step, however, will cover some of the most important considerations.

Don't worry about knowing just how DOS works. You don't need to know details such as what the TPA or Transient Program Area is and how COMMAND.COM loads—those are the sort of things any DOS manual can explain. All you really need to know is that DOS takes up part of conventional memory, but that different DOS versions use different amounts. Knowing a bit more about DOS lets you set DOS options such as buffers to use the least or optimum amount of memory. Don't waste too much time trying to save a K here or there, however, by scrimping on everything DOS does. That was more important when memory was more expensive than it is now. Instead, look to get good performance without wasting memory on DOS features you don't care about.

Several DOS commands and options are described in other Steps, where they are relevant to particular aspects of memory management Those are merely mentioned here, with a reference to the other sections for more details.

Versions. The most important memory decision you make about DOS is which version to use. Different versions of DOS use different amounts of memory. Later versions of DOS—with higher version numbers—offer more commands and compatibility with the latest hardware. But up to version 5.0, they also used more memory. This is explained in some more detail in Step 9.

This is how DOS evolved:

1.0	1981	The original DOS.
1.25	1982	Added support for double-sided floppy disks.
2.0	1983	Added support for subdirectories.
2.01	1983	Added support for international symbols.
2.11	1983	Fixed some bugs in 2.01.
2.25	1983	Added support for extended character set.
3.0	1984	Added support for 1.2 MB floppy disks.
3.1	1984	Added support for networks.
3.2	1986	Added support for 3.5 floppy disks.
3.3	1987	Added support for PS/2s.
4.0	1988	Added a shell and support for large hard disks.
4.01	1988	Fixed bugs in 4.0.
5.0	1991	Improved memory management.

You can use the VER command (just type VER and then the Enter or Return key) to discover which version you're using.

There's also a difference, by the way, between PC-DOS and MS-DOS, because the first comes from IBM and the later from Microsoft. MS-DOS runs on both compatibles and IBM PCs and PS/2s, but PC-DOS will only run all of its functions and features on IBM machines. They are quite similar, but not identical. What you learn about one is almost sure to work with the other, though a few options differ and many of the actual file names may differ. See your own DOS manual for details on what you're using. Just remember that you can't go entirely smoothly from MS-DOS 3.2 to PC-DOS 3.3 because of the change in file names—including hidden files that you won't see when you run a DIR directory of your disk.

DOS 2—DOS 2 didn't use a whole lot of memory, but is growing rapidly obsolete, and doesn't have many of the support and command features of later versions. I suggest you give it the slip, and move on to DOS 3, 4, or 5.

DOS 3—The various DOS 3 versions generally use the same amount of conventional memory—about 70K—and are perfectly fine for most people's PC use. The precise amount of memory they use depends on their configuration, as explained in the rest of this section. DOS 3.00 added the RAM disk programs VDISK.SYS and RAMDRIVE.SYS. DOS 3.3 added the FASTOPEN command.

In many ways DOS 3.2 or 3.3 are the best choices until DOS 5 appears and is proven bug-free, because DOS 3.3 is well tested and stable, and doesn't have some of the TSR conflicts that DOS 4.0 suffers from. Also, when you move from 3.3 to 4.0 you sacrifice 18K more of conventional memory.

DOS 4—DOS 4.0 added new utilities and some minor improvements to old utilities in DOS. It can handle hard disks larger than 32MB and has a DOS shell with simple pull-down menus for most DOS commands. It also added the XMAEM.SYS and XMA2EMS.SYS expanded memory device drivers (in PC-DOS), the EMM386.SYS expanded memory driver (in MS-DOS), and the HIMEM.SYS extended memory driver.

Version 4 can be installed in three ways: a minimum, medium, and maximum size and function configuration. It generally uses more memory than Version 3, especially if you use the Shell—which eats at least 10K of conventional RAM. It also uses more disk space than Version 3.

Version 4.01 cleaned up some bugs in 4.0; you won't see many systems actually running 4.0 anymore. These troubles were mainly with TSR programs, disk optimizers, and network drivers. DOS 4 also added direct support for EMS 4.0 expanded memory, but you probably don't need this unless you have an IBM PS/2 with the IBM expanded memory card. IBM's cards have some compatibility problems with other drivers.

Few programs demand DOS 4; most will run with DOS 3. Because of that, and DOS 4's buggy reputation, many people choose not to move to DOS 4 just to gain the new commands and the larger disk support.

DOS 5—DOS 5.0, which was not released as this book went to press, will use less memory than 4.0, both because it is written more compactly and because on 286, 386, and 486-based PCs it will allow you to relocate some portions of DOS to high memory (memory between 640K and 1MB). This could leave up to 630K or so of conventional memory free for your applications. DOS 5 will also be the first version supported directly by Microsoft, with a telephone number to Microsoft you can call if you have any questions. Previous versions were only supported through the company that sold you the computer containing the DOS.

DOS 5 will replace the old "GW Basic" that came free with DOS with Quick Basic. DOS 5 will have a file-search utility, an improved editor, and will support the DPMI (DOS Protected Mode Interface—see Chapter 4) extended memory standard. It will still have the shell with menus, but this will take up less memory than in DOS 4.

ROM DOS—You may also bump into a new Microsoft ROM-executable version of DOS, especially if you have a laptop computer. This version runs from ROM chips instead of RAM and so saves about 40K of RAM.

DOS Memory Use. The versions of DOS used this much conventional memory (these are ranges of the typical amount used—the absolute amount depends on the computer and the configuration.)

PC-DOS #	MS-DOS #	# of bytes
1.0		10,240-13312
1.1	1.25	12,400
2.0-2.11	2.0-2.11	24,688-40,960
3.0	3.05	38.928-60,416
3.1	3.1	38.960
3.2	3.2	46,000
3.3	3.3	54.992
4.0		65,424-108,270
4.01	4.01	68,608

Tips for Selecting a DOS Version. My advice is to choose with these rules in mind:

• Choose a DOS version that will handle the programs you want to run.

• Use DOS 5.0 when it's available, and has been proven bug-free and compatible with your programs. (DOS 5.0 should have the ability to free some conventional memory by relocating drivers and TSRs to high memory.)

• Use DOS 3.1, 3.2, or 3.3, whichever is most easily available, until DOS 5.0

is available and bug-free. DOS 4.01 is fine in some ways—for instance it has the MEM command for telling you about what's in your memory—but it uses more memory than DOS 3 or DOS 5 will.

- Whatever you do, avoid DOS 4.0—it's buggy. Use DOS 4.01 instead.

Batch Files and RAM disks. Batch files are those files with names that end in .BAT. These files are a sequence of text lines. DOS tries to run batch files like little programs. It opens the file, reads one line, closes the file, tries to execute the line (as a DOS command or a command to start some program), then opens the batch file again to find the next line, and so on. Because it keeps opening and closing the file, it reads and writes disk information quite a bit. That's why putting your batch files on a RAM disk can speed their action.

AUTOEXEC.BAT and CONFIG.SYS. AUTOEXEC.BAT is a special batch file. It is the file that DOS looks for in the root (main) directory and then automatically runs when first starting.

CONFIG.SYS is another text file that DOS also reads when starting. The lines of CONFIG.SYS tell how to "configure the system." Many of its lines consist of device driver assignments for peripherals and memory management utilities. These use the form

```
device=drivername.sys
```

Many memory management utilities and options can be found and dictated within the AUTOEXEC.BAT and CONFIG.SYS files. To see what's in these files, you can read them by entering the following commands: **type config.sys** or **type autoexec.bat.** The files don't necessarily exist on every PC's disk. DOS can get by without them—using default (assumed standard values) for the various configuration and setup details.

Editing AUTOEXEC.BAT and CONFIG.SYS. Some programs automatically change your CONFIG.SYS and AUTOEXEC.BAT files when you run their installation routines. Many times, though, you're the one in charge of making

86

changes, for the optimum setup for a particular program or for the best memory management.

You change the AUTOEXEC.BAT or CONFIG.SYS files (or make new ones from scratch) by editing them with any text editor or word processor that saves ASCII or plain text files. If you change AUTOEXEC.BAT or CONFIG.SYS, you must restart your computer—either turn it off and then on again, or press **Ctrl-Alt-Del** (those three keys at once)—to see the changes affect the PC.

DOS has the built-in EDLIN text editor for this, but it's not that easy to use. Most word processors can handle ASCII files. Also, DOS 5.0 and some DOS compatible operating systems such as DR DOS provide text editors. Just use any of these to load the .BAT or .SYS file, make the changes, and save the changed file to the same directory. If you want to save alternate versions, you can give them other extension names, such as AUTOEXEC.BAK or AUTOEXEC.1.

You can also change CONFIG.SYS and AUTOEXEC.BAT in DOS 4.0 by putting the letters **rem** before any line. This command will then turn that line into a remark that remains in the file but is ignored by the PC. This makes it easy to retrieve the older file version, just by removing the "rems" later. DOS 3 can do basically the same thing if you put a colon (:) before any line. You'll have to put up with "unrecognized command in config.sys" error messages when you start your PC, but you can just ignore these. DOS 4 won't even send these errors if you use the colon approach.

Don't just delete things from CONFIG.SYS unless you know what the effect will be. You might stop your mouse or video board from working if you delete a necessary device driver. There are also some .SYS files that DOS needs in certain circumstances. DOS 3 contains the following .SYS files:

ANSI.SYS

COUNTRY.SYS

DISPLAY.SYS

DRIVER.SYS

that aren't always used, but are necessary for some configurations. ANSI.SYS, for example, uses more memory but enhances keyboard and display processing. DOS 4.0 adds several more .SYS files:

PRINTER.SYS

RAMDRIVE.SYS

VDISK.SYS

XMAEM.SYS

XMA2EMS.SYS

If you use memory management programs, you'll also be adding .SYS file lines such as **device = qemm.sys** to **CONFIG.SYS**.

In DOS 3 and later you may use the **attribute** command to make CONFIG.SYS and AUTOEXEC.BAT read-only, so others can't change or delete settings. Use the command like this: **attrib +r \config.sys** to make CONFIG.SYS read-only. The same line with **-r** will change CONFIG.SYS back to read and write.

Here are some text-file editors (some with their commands):

DOS—You can make a new text file, for AUTOEXEC.BAT or CONFIG.SYS, without any text editor. Just type **copy con config.sys** and then press Enter. Then anything you type on the keyboard, such as **device = qemm.sys** will be copied to the CONFIG.SYS file. Type each line you want, and press Enter at the end of each. When you're done with all of the lines, press **Ctrl-Z** (the Ctrl and Z keys at once). This procedure will erase any older CONFIG.SYS file, though, so be careful. (You might want to rename that older file before using this scheme.) You can use the same procedure to make an AUTOEXEC.BAT file.

EDLIN—This is a crude text editor, but it does work and is free with DOS. (You can get more EDLIN details from a DOS manual.) To start it, type **edlin filename** while in the DOS directory. (The filename we're talking about here will be CONFIG.SYS or AUTOEXEC.BAT.) You'll see the prompt: *. Then you can use any of these EDLIN commands (type the command letter and then press the Enter key):

L   means list file, displays the lines of the file on-screen, along with the line numbers. If you then press Enter again, a new line number will appear. (The line numbers don't appear in the file itself, and won't appear if you use some other text editor. They're only here because EDLIN works on a single line at a time; most editors work on all of the lines at once and so don't need the identification numbers.)

I   means be ready to Insert text.

D   means Delete a line.

Ctrl-Break or Ctrl-C   means stop editing

E   means End or Exit, to save what you've done and return to DOS. It will also make a backup copy of the pre-changes file.

Q   means Quit, and returns you to DOS. This will not prompt you to save your file first, so make sure you do before hitting Q.

QEdit—This is a small, inexpensive (shareware), fast text editor with lots of commands. You can find it on many bulletin board systems.

The Norton Editor—The Norton Editor 2.0 is small and has pull-down menus for easy use. Because it is aimed at programmers, it deals well with ASCII files. It even comes with a "Norton Classic Editor" version that runs as a TSR and uses only 50K of RAM. It is compatible with Windows 3.0, DOS 2.0 or later, and DR DOS.

WordPerfect—Many people are familiar with this text editor. To use it with ASCII files such as AUTOEXEC.BAT and CONFIG.SYS, load the file you want to change, then enter the contents on individual lines. Press Enter at the end of each line (that's important). Then, when you're done, press **Ctrl-F5** the Text In/Out command. Next press **T** for DOS Text, and then **S** for Save. Finally, type the filename you want to save stuff under (such as **CONFIG.SYS**) and you're done.

Handling Multiple AUTOEXEC.BAT and CONFIG.SYS files. If you have many AUTOEXEC and CONFIG files you might want to keep them in a separate subdirectory, to protect them from being overwritten when you make a new configuration. One approach to multiple files is to create one that has all the possible features, and one with the best memory conservation, and then make batch files that automatically copy and rename the one you want to use. Your prompt could then show which one was in effect. This kind of tweaking is definitely for those quite comfortable with DOS, however.

There's an easier way for people who aren't DOS gurus. There are a number of programs that make it easy to create and choose from various AUTOEXEC.BAT and CONFIG.SYS setups. You can do this on your own by creating multiple files, and then renaming them when it comes time to restart your computer. But that can be a lot of typing work. Use one of these utilities and you won't have to rename files.

RECONFIG—This utility can store multiple AUTOEXECs and CONFIGs and then automatically switch between them. It then restarts or "reboots" your computer. It has a built-in editor for changing the files, and has pull-down menus for ease of use. It is shareware, and can be picked up from PC-SIG (see Appendix on "Cheap and Free Software").

Bootcon—This utility from Modular Software Systems modifies your CONFIG.SYS file so that it branches to any number of CONFIG.SYS and AUTOEXEC.BAT variations. You can choose the configuration you want as your PC boots. A menu will appear on the screen listing your choices, and you select the ones you want. If you don't make a selection for something, the default is used. Bootcon then makes a CONFIG.SYS and AUTOEXEC.BAT file to fit those choices, and uses them. Bootcon uses only 200 bytes of memory. Bootcon isn't very easy for beginners to use, but it does save a lot of time for PC users with lots of AUTOEXEC.BAT and CONFIG.SYS files. You can get it through the Programmers Shop or the Programmer's Connection (see the Address List at the end of this book).

CONFIG.CTL and BOOT.SYS—These are shareware programs that do pretty much the same thing that BOOTCON does. CONFIG.CTL is from PC Magazine, and you can find it on their bulletin board, PC MagNET (see Appendix on "Cheap and Free Software"). BOOT.SYS is available from Hans Salvisberg (see the Address List at the end of the book) and from bulletin boards or from the Public Software Library company (again, see the Address List).

PATH. The PATH command in DOS is important when you're setting up configurations and RAM disks. It tells DOS where to look for a program or batch file, if that file can't be found in the current directory and subdirectory. You may put PATH commands into CONFIG.SYS, or you can use them any time the PC is on. See your DOS manual for details.

Buffers. DOS has a built-in disk caching feature called BUFFERS. These keep the most-used information from disk in memory. Using more buffers, to a point, can increase disk performance. But using more buffers also eats up memory. You dictate the number of buffers with a **BUFFERS=XX** line in CONFIG.SYS. Some programs need a certain number of buffers.

DOS Environment. DOS uses memory for its environment variables. These include the PATH statements, COMSPEC statement (such as that above for the RAM disk holding COMMAND.COM). The minimum size is 160 bytes, but long PATH statements and other variables might exceed this amount. That's not a problem in some cases because DOS lets the environment memory grow automatically as needed. However, if a BATCH file is running, or if there's any TSR in memory—including a DOS TSR such as PRINT or FASTOPEN—the environment is trapped and cannot grow. You would see the error message: "Out of environment space" To see what's in the environment, you can use the SET command at any time. Just type **SET** and you'll see a list something like this:

COMSPEC   C:\COMMAND.COM

PATH   C:\DOS; C:\123

PROMPT pg

You may also use the SET command to change what's in the environment.

You can set aside more memory or space in advance—in DOS 3.2 and later you may have up to 32768 bytes—with SHELL line in CONFIG.SYS. Use the shell command, like this: **shell = command.com/p/e:size** The **/p** option instructs DOS that this is a permanent change (until you use the shell command again).

The /e:size option tells it the environment size. This can be a little confusing because in DOS 3.1 the size is measured in multiples of 16 bytes. For example, /e:**10** would mean 160 bytes. But in DOS 3.2 or later the size is just in plain bytes, so /e:**512** means 512 bytes.

STACKS. DOS has a STACKS setting to determine the amount of memory dedicated to handling interrupts—such as when a disk drive "tells" the PC that it is ready to send or receive information or is done with such an operation. If the STACKS setting is small, and there are interrupts of interrupts, you might see the error message: "Fatal: Internal Stack Failure, System Halted" You can set aside more memory for STACKS with the line **STACKS=stacknumber, stacksize** The number of stacks can range from 8 to 64. The size of each stack can be from 32 to 512 bytes. If you use too few stacks, you may have these errors. If you use too many, you're eating up memory. A typical setting that works well is **STACKS=8,512**.

RAM Disks: VDISK and RAMDISK. Most DOS owners don't realize they have free RAM disk programs on hand: VDISK.SYS or RAMDISK.SYS. By putting either of these as a device driver line in CONFIG.SYS, you can set up a RAM disk in your PC's memory, to improve performance. (See Step 7 for details.)

Initial DOS 4.0 Setup. DOS 4 generally uses more memory than DOS 3, but you do have some immediate control over the difference, and in some cases you can even pare DOS 4 back to less memory occupation than DOS 3. When you originally install DOS 4 you are presented with this choice:

- Minimum DOS function; maximum program workspace

- Balance DOS function with program workspace

- Maximum DOS function; minimum program workspace

No matter what DOS features and commands you like, you shouldn't choose a DOS setup that's beyond your PC's conventional memory. In a PC with 256K, always stick to the first option. A PC with 512K can use the second option, and a PC with more than 512K can use the third option.

If you're willing to voluntarily live without certain DOS features, though, you can choose the first option or the second option to have a smaller DOS and so more conventional memory for other uses.

TSR installation. DOS 4 can install some TSR programs when it starts, by making them part of the CONFIG.SYS file. To do this you use the **INSTALL** command. TSRs can work more efficiently this way. You can use INSTALL with DOS's own TSRs, such as

FASTOPEN.EXE
SHARE.EXE
KEYB.COM
NLSFUNC.EXE

or with your own TSR utilities. The line looks like this: **INSTALL=tsrname** There are other options for INSTALL. See your DOS manual for more details.

FASTOPEN. FASTOPEN is not a disk cache, but like a disk cache it helps disk speed. This command of DOS 4 lets your PC quickly dig several levels into a subdirectory on a disk. It helps DOS remember where files are that are in a subdirectory within a directory. It is particularly useful on disks with many levels of directories. You can speed your disk reading times by including FASTOPEN in the AUTOEXEC.BAT file. It looks like this **FASTOPEN driveletter=number** where the *number* is anything from 10 to 999. The default is 34. Few people need a value above 100. A larger value uses more memory (though this can be expanded memory), but improves performance more.

DOS Shell. DOS 4 comes with a Presentation Manager or Shell. This is an extra utility that presents DOS directories of files and DOS commands in menus on screen. It is supposed to make DOS easier to use for beginners. Unfortunately, it uses at least 10K (9800 bytes or so) of Conventional memory in the process, more with the options mentioned below. Even if you remove it from memory at some point, it still takes up 5K if it was ever in memory since the PC was turned on.

The Shell loads when **DOSSHELL.BAT** is the last line of your AUTOEXEC.BAT file. You can remove this line if you don't want to use the shell.

The command **SHELLC** lets you configure the shell. There are plenty of options, that you put after the shellc to dictate its behavior and use of memory. The options are:

/DOS	includes the file system in shell
/mul	permits multiple directories in the file system
/date	displays the time and date
/exit	turns on the exit shell option
/menu	turns on the Start Programs display
/maint	lets you change programs and groups in the Start Programs display of the shell
/color	permits you to change the display colors
/mos:driver	specifies the name of the mouse driver—for a mouse to control the shell

The more of these options you leave out, the less memory the shell will take.

The following are a couple of options that also don't eat up more memory:

/tran	lets the shell swap part of itself to a disk when a application runs, giving that application more conventional memory. The part then returns from disk when the application is finished.
/B:size	sets the size of memory given for the file system. Set a smaller value here to save memory.

Expanded Memory: XMAEM.SYS, XMA2EMS.SYS, and EMM386.SYS. PC-DOS 4.01 comes with several drivers for turning extended memory into expanded memory in 386-based systems: **XMAEM.SYS** and **XMA2EMS.SYS**. These are necessary because some DOS 4 command—including FASTOPEN and VDISK—can use expanded memory.

You may get these drivers working in your PC by including them as: **DEVICE=XMAEM.SYS** and **DEVICE=XMA2EMS.SYS** in the CONFIG.SYS file. XMAEM.SYS transforms extended memory on 386 systems into expanded memory. It emulates the PS/2 80286 Expanded Memory Adapter/A. It would look like this **DEVICE=XMAEM.SYS somenumber** where the word *somenumber* is actually a value for the number of 16K pages you want to create. The minimum is 64K pages, for one MB of expanded memory.

XMA2EMA.SYS is a LIM 4.0-compatible expanded memory manager for the memory transformed by XMAEM.SYS. Its line would look like this:

```
DEVICE=XMA2EMS.SYS [FRAME=location] [P0=location] [P1=location] [P2=location]
[P3=location] [P254:location] [P255:location] [/X:pages]
```

where the square brackets indicate optional parameters tacked on to the one line. The **FRAME:location** parameter specifies the address of the default frame, somewhere between C000 and E000 in high memory. The location parameters specify the addresses of the pages used by DOS. If they aren't specified, DOS commands cannot use expanded memory.

The **/X:pages** parameter tells the amount of expanded memory to make, in 16K pages. The minimum is 4 pages. For more details on these drivers, see your DOS manual.

MS-DOS systems have the **EMM386.SYS** driver instead of XMAEM or XMA2EMS. It does the same work as the two: transforming extended memory on 386 systems into expanded memory, and then managing that memory.

These drivers don't offer all the features and options of other extended-to-expanded memory converters or LIMulators, such as those mentioned in Steps 4 and 5 (QEMM and 386-to-the-Max are the best known). For example, they don't support 386 remapping for use of high memory.

Extended Memory: HIMEM.SYS. DOS 4.0 includes the HIMEM.SYS driver, which you can also find bundled with some programs such as Windows. This driver lets some programs—those written to understand it—use the first 64K of memory above 1MB. This is called high memory. It is up in the zone of extended memory, but because of a special accident in the construction of the 286, 386, and 486 processors, it can be used as additional conventional memory for some programs. (See Steps 1, 4, and 5 for more details.)

COMMAND.COM. DOS always loads the COMMAND.COM part of itself—which is about 25K to 30K of program—into memory automatically. This is the part with the internal DOS commands, such as DIR and COPY. Then, when you start a large application, such as WordPerfect or Lotus 1-2-3, that needs some of the memory COMMAND.COM is in, DOS unloads part of COMMAND.COM to make room. When you finish with that application, DOS must load COMMAND.COM in again. If you switch tasks a lot, that means repeated reading of COMMAND.COM from disk.

To speed that process, you can put COMMAND.COM onto a RAM disk. If your RAM disk is **d:** you can use these commands to move COMMAND.COM: **copy command.com d:** and **set comspec=d:command.com** The second line tells DOS where to find COMMAND.COM. You can do the same thing with other DOS utilities that you use frequently, such as FORMAT or DISKCOPY.

PRINT. This DOS command is really a simple print spooler. It can use anywhere from 512 to 4096 bytes of memory. Look to Step 7 for details. Most people find that the default of 512 bytes is just fine for PRINT, and in fact rarely use the command at all. It is a TSR that occupies memory, and you're better off with a more sophisticated spooler if you print much at all. PRINT does not have to be in the CONFIG.SYS or AUTOEXEC.BAT files.

MEM. DOS can tell you how much memory your system is using, and how much is available. The commands for this—such as MEM—are explained in Step 2.

Word Processors

The simplest word processors don't ask for much memory, but advanced features such as spell checking, on-line thesaurus, and on-screen font selections do. Word processor memory demands range from 256K to 2MB (IBM's Interleaf Publisher uses a DOS extender to get to multiple megabytes of extended memory).

Two general rules for word processors:

If there's a text mode, use it to conserve memory

See if you can improve performance with a RAM disk

WordPerfect

This leading word processor runs in 384K of memory (that's version 5.1). It automatically handles expanded memory. If you want a smaller version, WordPerfect Corporation offers Letter Perfect, which is entirely compatible but lacks a few of the most advanced features, such as table editing. There's also an older small version called WordPerfect Executive, made for laptop computers.

If you see the WordPerfect error message "Not enough memory" the manual suggests 15 ways you can get more memory. The most important are:

1. Remove TSR programs

2. De-select the soft keyboard (**Ctrl-6**)

3. Turn off hyphenation or choose internal rules as the hyphenation type

4. Don't print in background (WordPerfect has its own spooler)

5. Don't use the mouse

RAM Disk Use—It a document won't fit in conventional memory, WordPerfect moves as much of it as possible into temporary files in expanded memory, and puts the rest in overflow files on your hard disk. You can redirect those files instead to a RAM disk, by starting WordPerfect with this command line switch: **wp /d-x:** X is the RAM disk letter.

You can also copy some of WordPerfect's overlay files to the RAM disk, and throw in a few WordPerfect option switches, to make the program run faster. Put this into config.sys:

```
device =c:\vdisk.sys 1024 512 64 /e
```

Then these lines into AUTOEXEC.BAT

```
mkdir d:wp51
```

then these lines for a batch file to start WordPerfect 5.1:

```
cd c:\wp51
copy wp{wp}us.* d:
copy wp{wp}.spw d:
copy *.wpm d:
copy *.prs d:
wp /w=*.*/r/d-d:
copy d:\*.sup c:\wp51
copy d:\*.wpm c:\wp51
```

You'll need a RAM disk of about 1MB. The first five lines copy important files to the RAM drive D. The sixth line is the optional switch telling WordPerfect to use expanded memory for temporary files and a RAM drive for overflow files. The last lines copy files that can change—such as the supplemental spelling dictionary and the macros—back to the hard disk to save any changes. Copying the main dictionary to the RAM disk is especially useful for spell-checking long documents with few errors, such as documents that have been checked before. Copying the supplemental dictionary is not as important, because it changes frequently and will have to be copied back and forth between hard disk and RAM disk to stay current on both.

To change the setup permanently, start WordPerfect from the directory on your C: hard disk. If you start from the RAM disk any changes you make will disappear later because you'll have saved them to the RAM disk.

Expanded Memory and Overlays—Using the Expanded memory switch /**r** with less than 1M of expanded memory and with large documents can actually slow editing. Previous versions (to 5.0) used the /r switch to load all of the overlays into conventional memory. Now it loads them into expanded memory. This requires about 328K of expanded memory—if any less is available, you'll get an error message.

Graphics Tip—When using large .TIF graphics files in documents, keep those files on disk so they won't load into memory.

Ami Professional. Ami runs under Windows, so its memory management comes from Windows (See Step 6). It doesn't have any command-line switches, but it can run faster if you put the ***.exe** files on a RAM disk. (This takes about 2MB of RAM disk.) Then place the RAM disk's letter at the beginning of the PATH statement, and run Ami from the RAM disk.

98

Set the TEMP variable to the RAM disk's letter as, **SET TEMP=d:.** Use the Windows disk cache if you have enough memory for it, with the line **DEVICE=SMARTDRV.SYS 1024** in the CONFIG.SYS file. Finally, load the HIMEM.SYS driver to get that 64K more RAM of high memory, so Ami can get files without going to the hard disk.

MultiMate. MultiMate 4.0 requires 384K of conventional memory and can use expanded but not extended memory. Its built-in memory manager swaps program pieces in and out of expanded memory automatically, and uses disk space for this swapping when there isn't enough expanded memory. The grammar checker, E-mail, indexing, and red-lining functions automatically use expanded memory.

You can improve MultiMate's performance by putting the following graphics and dictionary files on a RAM disk.

```
usa.*
custom.lex
*.key
*.pix
*.fsl
*.fst
```

Then from the Systems and Document Defaults options under the Main Menu, specify RAM disk for the temporary files. Also change the PATH statement to direct the program first to the RAM disk.

Word. You can also improve Word's performance by putting the spelling, thesaurus, printer, and fonts files on a RAM disk.

```
spell-am.lex
updat_am.cmp
wfbg.syn
*.prd
*.dat
```

Then use the Options menu to identify the files on the RAM disk. Put the RAM disk's letter in the PATH statement so Word can find the files it needs.

There are several options and switches to tell Word to use less memory or to run faster. One is the /c switch, which instructs Word to operate in the faster Text mode instead of Graphics mode. Another is the **/Bnn** switch that tells Word the number of 512-byte buffers to use. The default is 60. If you can fit the entire document into these buffers, then operations such as search and replace will be much faster. Word won't let you set this /B so that no memory is left.

If expanded memory is installed, Word automatically uses it for search and replace operations, and for pagination, macros, and sorting.

PC-Write. PC-Write is an inexpensive word processor, but it can be replaced by an even smaller and less expensive version from the same company—PC-Write Lite from Quicksoft. A key difference in function between the two is that Lite has fewer formatting features. PC-Write Lite needs only 256K of memory, or 384K with the spelling checker.

There are no command-line switches for PC-Write, but if you put all of its files on a RAM disk, you'll improve performance.

PFS: Professional Write. Professional Write offers neither RAM disk performance improvements nor command-line switches for memory conservation. It does use expanded memory to speed spell checking and address functions, however.

Word for Windows. As a Windows program, Word for Windows gets most of its memory management from the Windows environment . However, you can speed it by putting these files into a RAM disk:

lex-am.*
syn-am.*
conv*.dll

(That's the spelling dictionary, the thesaurus, and the dynamic link library.) Then in the WIN.INI file, under the Word entry, add the line **UTIL-PATH-=d:** (assuming d: is the RAM disk). You should also use the SMARTDRV.SYS Windows cache, with a setting of 384K.

WordStar. WordStar depends heavily on overlays, and will run much faster if you put the main file **ws.exe** on a RAM disk. Then, at the installation menu set the following to *On*.

WS RAM resident

Main DCT in RAM

XyWrite. The most recent versions of XyQuest's XyWrite can use expanded or extended memory. Putting the spell-checking dictionary and thesaurus into expanded memory takes about 112K. This frees conventional memory for other uses. The spell-checking utility in XyWrite III Plus needs a disk cache, or it can be very slow.

In moving from XyWrite III Plus to XyWrite IV, static overlays were changed to dynamic. That means that instead of just telling you that there's not enough room in memory for some part of the program, XyWrite now looks to see what isn't being used and swaps that out to make space for any additional commands you request.

Desktop Publishing

Desktop Publishing, or DTP, combines fancy text with graphics in large documents, and so asks for lots of disk and RAM memory. Disk Caching and RAM disks can help with overflow files in DTP, especially with very large documents, However, there's quite a range of memory needs in DTP, from 256K for the least powerful programs, to 640K (plus 256K to 512K of expanded memory) for Ventura Publisher, to as great as 4MB or more for IBM Interleaf Publisher.

Ventura Publisher. The president of Ventura Software once said that the most important advice for a Ventura user was to be as efficient and wise with memory as possible. That's still true now that Ventura Publisher has evolved through several versions, and has been acquired by Xerox. Memory management is particularly important with Ventura not only because the program is so large, but because it has not traditionally run under Windows therefore it has needed its own memory management. (A new Windows version takes its memory management cues from Windows—see Step 6 for details on Windows.) In fact, having too little memory for complex tasks can even crash Ventura Publisher.

Ventura 1.1 Standard Edition needed less RAM than version 2.0. The Professional Extension needs yet more memory than the Standard Edition. Each demands a full 640K of conventional RAM, and can use expanded or extended memory (as long as the extended is configured as expanded). Try not to run your Ventura at the minimums though—it will run slower with less memory. A memory shortage can show up in the middle of work, in errors such as "Frame Too Complex." Then you'll be forced to leave the program to fix the memory troubles, before continuing with your work.

You may use all the standard tactics to increase free conventional memory, such as configuring DOS to a minimum, discarding unnecessary TSRs and drivers, relocating TSRs and drivers to high memory, adding HIMEM.SYS to CONFIG.SYS to get 64K more conventional memory, and using a task switcher or environment—such as DesqView—to swap utilities in and out of memory. (Task switching can be very handy with Ventura, because you may need a word processor or graphics program as you lay out pages.) DesqView with EMS 4.0 expanded memory, for instance, can load Ventura program code into expanded memory.

Command-line Switches—Ventura offers quite a selection of switches for memory management. These are typically put into a batch file called VP.BAT. You start Ventura by running that file. The switches are:

/o= use with the standard edition to say where to send overflow files. (Ventura loads as much as it can into conventional memory, and then spills the rest to a disk.) If you have the Professional Extension and EMS memory, you don't need /o because Ventura automatically spills the extra to that EMS. For example, to send files to a RAM disk **d**, use /**o=d:** at end of the vp.bat line that begins with **drvrmrgr vp %1/f=** to increase the size of the screen font buffer for faster screen redraws—if you have expanded memory in the PC. The default is 68K.

You can specify from 32K to 170K. Less than 68K will give more room for other things, to force Ventura to use less conventional memory while loading. Specify more than 68K to reduce the redraw time—the time to put fonts on screen. Don't use both /f= and /a=, as they cancel each other out.

/a= takes 1K to 32K of memory, normally reserved for screen graphics and fonts buffers, and adds it to the text area. Use this switch only with PostScript printers. Don't use this with a JLaser card. If it's not working with a particular graphics converter, try /a=0. However, then if you use many screen fonts, some of screen then might not load. Don't use both /f= and /a=, as they cancel each other out.

/h= set the command /h to zero when himem.sys is installed on the system for other applications, and you don't want Ventura to use high memory.

/e= the command /e lets you see what the maximum amount of expanded memory is that Ventura will use. Only the Professional Extension and the network versions use this, because the basic Ventura Publisher doesn't use any more than 128K of expanded memory. If you have a JLaser card, include /e=0 in the DRVRMRGR line. You can also use /e when multitasking, where Ventura might be competing with other programs for expanded memory. Even with /e=0, however, Ventura uses at least 90K of EMS. You can only stop Ventura from using EMS by renaming or deleting the file GEM.EMS in the Ventura directory.

RAM Disk and Disk Cache—You can improve Ventura performance by copying all of its files to a RAM disk. You must copy all files—a total of about 3MB—to the RAM disk to get real use from it. A cache is probably better, because you don't have to copy everything to it. Also, it would be dangerous to put document files into a RAM disk because they could be lost if power was lost (that's true of any program). You'll want a cache that supports both extended and expanded memory. Use at least 600K of disk cache if you can. More will add even more speed.

Fonts—Ventura will use up to 128K of expanded memory for part of its overlays, but it will keep screen fonts in a certain directory on the drive from which it was loaded. Remove any fonts you don't use regularly so they won't load each time your run Ventura.

Printing—If your HP LaserJet-compatible laser printer contains at least 1MB of memory, you may copy all of the font files to the printer before loading Ventura. To do this, start by creating an ASCII file and naming it HPLJPLUS.CNF in the Ventura directory. On the first line of the file, put the PATH of the files (the drive and directory they occupy on disk). Then add a line with the font ID number and filename for each font to download—one line per font.

If, however, your printer has only 512K, you can avoid some memory limits by installing both 150 dpi and 300 dpi Laserjet drivers in Ventura. You can then switch from 300 dpi to 150dpi when necessary—there really isn't that much difference between the two unless you're turning out a professional quality final product. If 300dpi is required in some instances, you can locate the pages that have very large fonts or graphics, and print them one by one. Then print the rest of the document. Remember, if you stick to 6 and 24-point fonts, the fonts that are automatically installed for a Laserjet, you shouldn't have memory problems.

High, Extended, and Expanded (EMS) memory—Use the HIMEM.SYS driver. This adds 64K to conventional memory, above the 1M mark. Not all programs can use this extra memory, but Ventura can—(For more details on this, see Step 6). To do this, just make sure the HIMEM.SYS file is in your root directory, and then put the line **device=c:\himem.sys** in the CONFIG.SYS file.

Configure Extended Memory as Expanded —Only the Professional Extensions and Network version fully support expanded memory. Version 2.0 of Ventura can put a small amount of its program into EMS. (You can get the EMS through an expanded memory board or through simulation of extended memory as expanded— see Steps 4 and 5 for details). Standard Ventura can load 60K of the program into expanded memory; Professional can use several megabytes. Some sophisticated functions, such as tables and equations, are very slow without expanded memory.

Video Display—You can help dictate the amount of conventional memory Ventura needs by your selection of video display mode, and the memory that supports that mode.

Using these modes and these memory options, Ventura needs this many bytes:

HIMEM.SYS	EMS	HIMEM.SYS and EMS	
EGA 2-color 556,232	506,728	498,360	475,944
VGA 2-color 557,752	508,248	499,880	476,504
VGA 16-color 582,696	533,192	524,824	478,408

The amounts increase for the Professional Extensions and network version. Then, on a system with 640K of conventional memory, this many bytes are used:

HIMEM.SYS	EMS	HIMEM.SYS and EMS	
EGA 2-color 570,024	508,232	464,792	403,000
VGA 2-color 571,544	509,752	465,352	403,560
VGA 16-color 596,488	534,696	467,256	405,464

Checking Memory Needs—Some versions of Ventura have a hidden diagnostic menu that can help you analyze your memory status and needs. It displays the size and allocation of all memory in your system. Use this menu before you modify the VP.BAT file with memory management switches.

To find it, from the Desk select the Publisher's Info menu. A dialog box will tell you the Ventura version number, the date, and the serial number of your program copy. There are two rectangular outlines just above the copyright line. The left rectangle has the Ventura Software company name. Click your mouse on the word Ventura and the diagnostic box will appear.

First Publisher. First Publisher is a simple desktop publishing program that can have increased performance from a RAM disk. Put all of the files on the RAM disk—this requires about 2MB—and then in the setup file, indictate that the program should run from the RAM disk.

Interleaf Publisher. The original version 1.0 of Interleaf Publisher needed 6MB just to run. Now version 1.0.1 needs only 2MB, though more MB will help it run better and faster. (It also demands at least a 386 processor in your PC.) Interleaf Publisher has its own built-in DOS Extender to use extended memory, and has its own virtual memory scheme to stretch large files out on to the hard disk.

PageMaker. PageMaker runs under Windows, and so gets its memory management from Windows (see Step 6). It doesn't have any command-line switches for memory management. But you can improve PageMaker performance by putting its **pm*.*** and ***.fon** (program and font) files on a RAM disk.

Also, as you work in PageMaker, control your file size. Check the size periodically, and break it into smaller parts when it grows large. Remember that file size doesn't decrease after you delete elements from a document. Use the Save As command and a new filename to shrink it back to the smallest dimensions.

Spreadsheets

Spreadsheets were the first programs that cried out for more memory. Large Lotus 1-2-3 spreadsheets, in fact, were the motivating force behind the invention of expanded memory. So it is important to know how to:

Keep as much conventional memory open as possible for the spreadsheet

Minimize your spreadsheet's use of memory

Establish its access to expanded or extended memory

Not all spreadsheets take advantage of RAM disks for performance. Some cannot because they don't make as much use of overlays. They tend to keep the entire program and working data file in memory, so they don't have to read and write disk information as often. However, some spreadsheets do have overlays—Excel and Quattro Pro can run faster from a RAM disk.

One general tip on spreadsheets: small worksheets run much faster than large ones, so think of breaking your large sheets into smaller sheets that are either independent or are linked. (Remember that officially a *spreadsheet* is the program while a *worksheet* is a document handled by a spreadsheet program.)

Lotus 1-2-3 and Symphony. These two programs from Lotus Development are in a single section because they are similar in many ways. Lotus 1-2-3 is a spreadsheet; Symphony is an integrated application that includes a spreadsheet. But the two use many of the same tips, technologies, and utilities.

Memory is so important to 1-2-3 that it was the claustrophobia of large 1-2-3 files in 640K of memory that originally led to expanded memory. Many companies offer utility programs that improve 1-2-3's use of memory. Most of these also work with Symphony. Lotus Development understands the importance of memory: 1-2-3 comes with a MEM warning light to show when a worksheet is growing so large as to fill memory. Lotus offers a free Check 1-2-3 utility that can examine your systems memory to see how much conventional, extended, and expanded memory you have.

The key to understanding 1-2-3 and Symphony is *releases*: instead of versions, Lotus deals in releases and the memory abilities and management of each release differs from those previous.

For 1-2-3, few people still use Release 1. Many are still using Release 2.01, which supports expanded memory. When looking to improve 2.01, Lotus realized that all the features it wanted wouldn't fit into 640K of conventional memory, even with expanded memory. So it created two upgrades: 2.2 and 3.0. Release 2.2 has some more features, and still works on systems with 640K of RAM, and can use expanded memory. Releases 3.0 (and its successor 3.1) have yet more new features but require a 286 or 386-based PC with at least 384K of extended memory. Then there's 1-2-3/G which runs only under the OS/2 operating system. A version of 1-2-3 for Windows should be available in 1991.

As you move up in releases you gain more functions, and sometimes more speed (such as upgrading from 2.01 to 2.2). Sometimes, though, you simply need more memory.

Symphony Release 2.2 manages memory better than Release 2.1. It handles up to 4MB of LIM 3.2 expanded memory. Before this version, Symphony users often ran out of conventional memory before they were out of expanded memory. Symphony will run on a 512K system, but needs 640K if utilities such as Allways or @Base are used.

Version 2.01 and 2.2: Expanded Memory—Version 2.01 uses 256K for its program code; 2.2 uses 340K. Both use the rest of conventional memory to hold their worksheets and any add-in utility programs. (Lotus has a special add-in technology that lets utilities appear within the 1-2-3 menus, as if they had become part of the main program.) Version 2.2 adds such features as a 2D file linking (linking values in one spreadsheet to values in another) and recalculation, improved graphics (by including the Allways utility) and PostScript printing.

Both can theoretically reach 4MB of expanded memory. In fact, these releases of 1-2-3 need expanded memory to hold large worksheets. But a portion of any worksheet—addressing pointers that tell 1-2-3 where to find stored information for cells—must remain in conventional RAM. (Each pointer uses 4 bytes.) Even with unused expanded memory, you can get a "Memory Full" error if you run out of conventional memory for these pointers. Practically speaking, then 2.01 or 2.2 reach at most 2.5MB of expanded memory. You can elude this problem with a special utility—see "Beyond 640K" in the Utilities section that follows.

If you do have a PC with extended memory, you should convert it into expanded memory with a LIMulator (see Steps 4 and 5).

Version 2.01 has a bug for people who use the @DSUM function or data query commands with expanded memory. These functions won't always access all of the data they should. You can avoid this problem by saving the file to disk and then retrieving it—to make sure that data is loading sequentially into memory with all of its pointers. Another fix is to upgrade to Release 2.2, which doesn't have the bug.

There's another bug to look out for when you use the Allways add-in utility. Allways lets you print fancier and more complicated pages than Lotus 1-2-3 or Symphony alone would allow. (Though it is integrated into 1-2-3 as part of Release 2.2.) However, it does not work well with some Expanded Memory Emulators (programs that convert extended memory into expanded). You can avoid the trouble by relocating the portion of Allways from expanded memory to conventional memory: run the AWEMM program on the Allways disks. This does not disable 1-2-3's use of expanded memory. (Incidentally, this problem doesn't appear with expanded memory boards, just with emulated expanded memory.)

Release 3.0 and 3.1: Extended Memory—Releases 3.0 and 3.1 use a DOS Extender (see Steps 1 and 4 for an explanation) to reach up to 16MB of memory, 640K of conventional and the rest extended. (These releases also come with disks with an OS/2 version, but that demands at least 3MB of memory.) In fact, because they can address 32MB of expanded memory, their memory grand total is 48MB—even more than OS/2 programs can reach. Release 3 added new macro, 3D worksheet, better graphics, relational database, and network support features to the 1-2-3 foundation. Release 3.1 loads itself into extended memory so more conventional memory is free for network drivers, TSRs, and the like. Version 3.1 also has its own virtual memory management to let large worksheets spill out to a hard disk. The 123swapsize variable lets you control the size of the swap files on disk while the 123virtsize variable lets you specify the minimum amount of virtual space 1-2-3 will use.

Release 3.1 is compatible with Windows 3.0 in the 386-Enhanced mode. When used this way, Release 3.1 depends on Windows virtual memory manager.

These releases need at least 384K of extended memory to run. Most 286 and 386-based PCs have this much extended memory. Unfortunately for 1-2-3, many of them use part of it for such performance enhancements as shadowing ROM BIOS and video RAM, as well as some disk caching. This is the memory between 640K and 1MB. You need to stop or disable such uses to run Release 3.0. To see if they are a problem in your PC, use a memory analysis program such as the one mentioned in Step 2. Release 3.0 supports VCPI (an extended memory specification mentioned in Step 4), and won't work with expanded memory emulators that don't support VCPI, such as the one that comes with IBM's PC-DOS 4.0.

Lotus 1-2-3/G—Lotus 1-2-3/G (the G stands for Graphics) runs only under OS/2. It can therefore use OS/2's direct reach to 16MB of memory. 1-2-3/G has such advanced features as the Backsolver and Solver, which can search for optimum answers to calculation questions. 1-2-3/G is slower than 1-2-3 Release 3.0, and it needs 5MB of RAM and a 386 processor to run reasonably well.

RAM disk—1-2-3 Release 2.0 and Release 2.2 won't be faster with a RAM disk—as the program and worksheet are entirely in memory. Release 3 can benefit from a RAM disk because it uses overlays. But it will expect all of these overlay files to be in the same directory that the program started from. Copy all but the *.wk3 files to the RAM disk, then estimate the size of the worksheet's memory demands, and add 1MB more for the program, the dedicate that much to the RAM disk. Set the Worksheet Global Default Temp directory (use the command \WGDT) to RAM drive.

Utilities—There are three kinds of utilities that help you manage 1-2-3 memory. The first kind are the utilities you would use with any program: the memory management stuff described in the rest of this book. The second kind are utilities that are dedicated to 1-2-3 or Symphony memory improvements, but that remain outside of 1-2-3 or Symphony. The third kind are the so-called add-ins, utilities that actually become part of 1-2-3 or Symphony menus. Add-ins don't work with Release 3.0 or Release 3.1.

Here are some of the most important utilities:

Allways. This utility lets 1-2-3 print fancier results than it could by itself (and is built into Release 2.2). When used with 1-2-3 you'll need at least 512K of conventional memory. Allways automatically switches to text mode if there isn't enough memory to load a large worksheet in graphics mode. If you want to use graphics with it, you'll need more memory. Allways may be too slow when using expanded memory—if so disable the use of expanded memory with the AWEMM and D option.

Also, Allways may run out of memory when printing because it uses memory to format the output. If you see an error message such as "Out of Memory", when you try to print soft fonts to a laser printer, you need to free some of the main memory so that Allways can download soft fonts to the printer. Do that by creating a new file with just the data for printing. Use the Range Value command to convert all formulae within the Print range to values. Then delete all of the rows and columns outside of the Print Range. Next save the worksheet with a new name. Then Retrieve the worksheet by its new name and print it. Some 1-2-3/Allways users do this so often they create a macro to handle it automatically, and to automatically update this partial file from the main worksheet.

Beyond 640K. As mentioned above in the description of Releases 2.01 and 2.2, 1-2-3 can theoretically use 4MB of expanded memory (EMS 3.2 or 4.0) to hold large worksheets. In practice it can only use about 2.5MB because a 4-byte pointer must remain in conventional memory for every cell, and when these pointers fill conventional memory, 1-2-3 cannot take advantage of any more expanded memory. The Beyond 640K add-in from Intex Solutions breaks that limit. It uses 4K of RAM itself to put the entire worksheet into expanded memory when conventional memory is full.

P.D. Queue. This spooler is a 1-2-3 or Symphony add-in. It works with other utilities, including the printing and publishing utilities such as Allways and Impress, and can run in the background. Once it is added to 1-2-3 or Symphony, you just use the standard printing commands, and P.D.Queue intercepts print jobs and sends them to disk. It uses 36K of RAM.

AboveMem. This is two utilities: Above 640 and AboveMEM. They come as part of the Above DISC package from BLOC Publishing. Above 640 is a TSR that grabs up to 96K of memory from high memory of EGA and VGA systems that isn't being used for video work. AboveMEM can convert extended memory into expanded memory compatible with EMS 3.2. That is, it is a LIMulator. It requires 21K of its own.

3-for-3. This utility from Iris Associates converts Release 3.0 or 3.1 of 1-2-3 into a Windows 3.0-compatible 1-2-3. Without it, 1-2-3 will run under Windows, but without most of Windows appealing features. With a 3-for-3 translation, 1-2-3 will have Windows resizable windows, pull-down menus, full mouse support, printer support, clipboard support, virtual memory, and even DDE (Dynamic Data Exchange) abilities. It will not, however, have the fonts and graphics of Windows.

@Base. Personics' @Base turns 1-2-3 or Symphony into a proficient database management program, it's an add-in utility that can work with disk-based database files, including dBASE III files. Lotus 1-2-3's own database commands are limited to working on the data within the worksheet, which will be entirely in memory. The two add-in parts of @Base, main and utilities, use 86K and 18K of RAM respectively.

Compilers. Spreadsheet compilers can cut your spreadsheet down to size in memory by squeezing out all the unnecessary functions. Some even provide virtual memory. You apply a compiler to a spreadsheet that you use frequently, and what results is a dedicated application, where you can enter values and see the calculated results, but where you cannot then change the formula and labels of the worksheet. Several 1-2-3 and Symphony compilers are available:

@Liberty 2.01 from SoftLogic Solutions
Baler 5.0 from Baler Software
King Jaguar 1.0 from Sheng Labs

Extra K for Symphony. This utility attaches to Symphony like any other add-in utility, and reclaims unused memory for Symphony's use by unloading unused Symphony environments (such as DOC, COMM, FORM, and GRAPH). On systems without expanded memory, Extra K can add about 90K—enough for 3000 cells. On systems with expanded memory, it can use the memory more efficiently. This is particularly useful when working with other add-in utilities.

Here are some examples of the amounts of memory saved, and the number of additional cells that memory will convert to:

Unloaded Environment:

	doc	form	comm	graph	total
W/O EMS	38K	17K	10-17K	26K	93K
cells	1225	575	425	825	3000
With EMS	36K	15K	7-14K	24K	80K
cells	8500	3000	2400	5500	18900cells

General Tips for 1-2-3 and Symphony—

• Link several small files together rather than work with a few large ones. Use the cell-linking in 2.2 or 3.0, or 2.01's File Combine /FC command, or Symphony's file-linking. Don't use macros to consolidate data—they can use up a lot of memory.

• When you do have large worksheets, use the /s system command to remove overlays from memory.

• Convert formulae to values whenever possible.

• Remove unnecessary data, range names, and cell formats from the worksheet, then save it again.

• Take out any TSRs you can live without.

• Disable the Undo feature. (Use the "/worksheet global default other undo disable" series of commands.) Once you do disable it, save your work more often. Once Undo is off and you load a worksheet, you cannot turn Undo back on until you save the file, then use "/worksheet erase yes" and then "/worksheet global default other undo enable quit".

- Save your changes to the 123.CNF configuration file so that they'll automatically be in force next time you use 1-2-3.

- Don't leave unused worksheets in memory.

- If you use the same worksheet layout over and over, compile it (see the Utilities section in this Step).

- If you use expanded memory, attach add-in utilities before retrieving files.

Look to Lotus Magazine for more tips. (And call for their free "Good Ideas" book: 800-635-6887.)

Excel. Excel is a Windows program, so it gets its memory management from Windows (see Step 6). The Excel files to put on a RAM disk are: **excel*.*** and ***.fon** (the program and fonts files). Here are some tips:

Close unwanted worksheets

Design your worksheets so they are longer than they are wide

Eliminate blank cells between full ones

Look for more tips in any discussion of Windows memory management, or in the booklet offered with the Excel documents: "Getting the Most from Your Hardware with Microsoft Excel."

Quattro Pro. Quattro Pro needs only 512K of memory to run, less than any competing powerful spreadsheet. It does this through Borland's VROOM (Virtual Real-Time Object-Oriented Memory manager) technology. VROOM is a software idea that breaks the program into lots of tiny overlays or objects, instead of several large ones. There are about 300 objects, of 2K to 4K each. These are moved in and out of conventional memory as their functions are needed. In fact, the total memory they occupy can even shrink as the worksheet in memory grows. The most frequently-used code segments are assigned priority as you work, so Quattro can guess which is most likely to be used soon and so needs to be kept in memory. Unfortunately this knowledge is lost when you quit the program, so Quattro has to learn your working style again next time you run it. Quattro, incidentally, also shaves its use of memory by *formula and label sharing*, keeping only a single actual copy of each formula or label, and then making references to that copy anywhere else the formula or label is needed. Because VROOM reads and writes those objects of the program frequently, a RAM disk can help Quattro Pro performance, but only if you put all of the files on the RAM disk.

Quattro Pro uses expanded memory automatically to store objects. For faster performance, but more use of conventional memory, when you set up Quattro Pro, use conventional RAM before using expanded RAM. At the Options Other Expanded Memory menu site, choose None or Format to store less in expanded memory. And finally, as with most spreadsheets, break large worksheets into smaller ones, and link them. Then load them one at a time to minimize use of memory.

Database Managers

Database managers work on large files—their most apparent activity is lots of reading and writing of data. This kind of disk intensive computing will get the most performance boost from fast disk access. You can buy a fast disk drive, or you can use memory for disk caching and RAM disks. However, because sophisticated database managers are also complex programs, able to perform intricate calculations on their data, having plenty of memory available for the program itself is also important. This is even more important for database managers that are communicating with larger databases on network or mainframe systems—the interface or connection software needs room in memory too. When a PC database manager is working as a DOS front-end for a SQL database, you know memory will be tight. The connection software might take 150 to 210K. Add what DOS needs, and there won't be much of even 640K of conventional memory left for the database management program. You can ease this trouble for any database management program by using small network or mainframe connection drivers, or by pushing those drivers into high memory (see Step 5).

To make the most of RAM disks with database managers, create indexes and perform file merge operations on the RAM disk. Move the database file itself and any index files to the RAM disk. Be sure to copy them back to the hard disk regularly, or safeguard your data by making sure that you have an uninterruptible power supply (UPS), or you could lose any changes you make.

dBASE. dBASE III needed 450K of its own RAM (that's after DOS and any utilities load) to run, plus some more RAM for any data file. The initial dBASE IV, Version 1.0, needed more than this—520K. But Version 1.1 of dBASE backs down to 450K again. Version 1.1 is also the first version to use expanded or extended memory, but only for it's own disk cache program dBCACHE. (Some competing programs, such as FoxPro, use all of expanded memory automatically.) The Server Edition of 1.1 (the one for network servers) needs yet more memory.

dBASE IV can be much slower than dBASE III. One way to help its performance is to use a RAM disk, but that can take as much as 2MB to fit all the files. Some of the files to put on a RAM disk for dBASE III are:

dbase*.ovl
*.hlp
dbase.exe
dbase*.res
*.pr2
protect.ovl
*.gen
config.db

After you copy these files to the RAM disk, set the PATH for the RAM drive. At the DOS prompt, you can just type **Set TMP=D** (assuming your RAM disk has the letter D:).

dBASE doesn't have any command-line switches, but it does have some variables you can set for memory control. For example, the dBHEAP environment variable specifies the percent of available memory that dBASE IV uses for application space—applications here meaning the programs written in the dBASE language. The rest is used for overlay swapping. When this variable is set higher, there's more memory for complex applications; when it's lower, there's more memory for swapping. The overlays handle such work as defining menus, pop-up information, and windows. These move faster with more swapping space. The TMP and DBTMP environment variables tell dBASE where to create and store temporary files. You could aim these at a RAM disk.

dBCACHE is Ashton-Tate's version of the Hyperware Hyperdisk utility. This cache handles the overlay files, and has fine-tuning options to balance memory use against speed. It uses staged writes as the caching default, rather that using Hyperdisk's standard write-through caching default.

Finally, you can squeeze more dBASE application into memory if you use a compiler to automate and compress that application. Nantucket Corporation's Clipper is a dBASE compiler. It automatically stores memory variables and database buffers in a dynamically sized memory space consisting of main memory, expanded memory (LIM 3.2 or 4.0) and hard disk swap space. That means it has its own segmented virtual memory subsystem that can address up to 64MB of memory.

FoxPro. FoxPro is a dBASE competitor, a sophisticated relational database manager from Fox Software. Although it supports both expanded and extended memory, it will run in as little as 512K on an XT. FoxPro is compatible with dBASE—it can use dBASE files and run many dBASE applications—and in many cases is faster.

FoxPro does not have command-line switches, but it does offer a variety of its own commands for memory analysis and control. For example, the FoxPro command **Memory**() tells you how many K of conventional memory are available for executing the FoxPro RUN command (for running applications written in the FoxPro language). The command **SYS(12)** is similar, but returns the amount of memory in a precise number of bytes. The **SYS(23) and SYS(24)** commands check to see how much expanded memory is available.

The command **SYS(1001)** tells how much total memory is available within FoxPro, while **SYS(1016)** tells how much of that pool is being used. SYS(1016) to find out how much of the pools is used up. Details on all of these commands can be found in the FoxPro reference manual.

Paradox. Paradox 3.5, from Borland, uses an overlay technique called VROOM (Borland's own term) to fit into whatever memory you have. Borland claims VROOM frees an average of 50K of memory. VROOM uses many small objects like overlays, moving them into memory from disk and back out to disk as necessary for the current operation. Older versions of Paradox needed only 512K RAM, and supported both expanded and extended memory. Paradox 3.5 requires a 286 or 386 PC with at least 1MB of RAM. It uses expanded memory for its VROOM manager, disk cache (it has its own), and for temporary storage. In fact, however, it frees 50K of conventional memory, doubling the memory available for PAL (Paradox Application Language) programs that you might use to customize your Paradox.

Paradox 3.5 can use up to 16MB of extended memory because it has a DOS extender built-in, one that supports the VCPI standard but not the DPMI standard. To connect to the Oracle database you'll need at least 1.5MB. There's also an OS/2 version of Paradox.

To improve Paradox performance, you can put all of its files **paradox3.*** on a RAM disk.

PFS: Professional File. This simple database manager from Software Publishing uses all of expanded memory to improve its performance. You may also put all of its files onto a RAM disk to speed things up even more. To do this, copy all the files to the RAM disk, then start the program from the RAM disk. Select Setup from the main menu in the program, and set the work directory to the RAM disk's driver letter.

Q&A. Q&A, from Symantec, is an easy to use database manager that includes some artificial intelligence. It doesn't have any switches to cut memory use, but you can improve its performance by using a RAM disk. There are two levels to this improvement: just the overlay files on the RAM disk (which requires about 235K) or all of the files on the RAM disk (requiring 2MB). Copy the files to the RAM disk, then include the RAM disk in the PATH command of your AUTOEXEC.BAT or Q&A batch file.

R:Base. R:Base, from MicroRim, is a sophisticated database manager that can handle dBASE III and III Plus files. Version 3.1 is faster than Version 3.0, and needs less memory: 470K instead of 520K. This makes it possible to load and use R:Base with a network. If it is still too big for you, you can try Personal R:Base, a smaller version that omits some of the most advanced features.

Though there are no command-line switches for R:Base to decrease your use of memory, you can improve its performance with a RAM disk. Copy these files ***.ovl**

117

and ***.rbf** to the RAM disk (the overlay and database files). Then put the RAM disk's letter at the beginning of the PATH command.

Reflex. Reflex can run faster if you put the temporary, swap, and configuration files onto a RAM disk.

Reflex also has several command-line switches for memory control.

-x+	to use expanded memory
-y+	to use extended memory
-t d:\	to use RAM disk d: to store temporary files
-s d:\	to use RAM disk d: to store swap files
-g d:\	to use RAM disk d: to store configuration files
-i	to make command-line switch settings permanent

Communications

CrossTalk Mk.4. CrossTalk will run its scripts (its own programs or sequences of saved instructions) faster if they are on a RAM disk. Put this file: ***.xtc** on the RAM disk, then put the RAM disk's letter into the Crosstalk's PATH statement, so it will look for scripts there.

ProComm Plus. ProComm Plus, the DataStorm Technologies communications program, needs 192K RAM. You can load it faster if you put these files on a RAM disk:

    pcplus.xlp
    pcplus.prm
    pcplus.dir
    pcplus.kbd
    pcplus.key
    pcplus.fon

and then in AUTOEXEC.BAT or the batch file you use to start ProComm Plus, put the path statement **pcplus=d:** so DOS will know which copies of the ProComm files to use.

However, once ProComm has loaded, it is all in memory, and keeping its files on a RAM disk won't improve performance. The only exception is that if you save downloaded information to files on a RAM disk, then downloading and saving of files will be faster.

Networking

Novell NetWare. Novell's NetWare is the most popular network operating system software. Until recently NetWare used nearly 80K of conventional memory for its low-level protocols (called IPX) and the NetWare shell software.

Use the New Shell—The IPX protocol still cannot use anything but conventional memory. However, the shell has changed. The old shell alone used 40K of conventional memory. The newest version of the shell, version 3.01, uses only 7K of conventional memory because the rest (about 64K) can be installed in expanded or extended memory.

There are three shells—one that runs entirely in conventional memory, one that mainly loads into expanded, and one that loads mainly into extended memory. You can get the new shells for free from the CompuServe on-line information service. See the Appendix on "Cheap and Free" software to learn more about CompuServe. The files are called DSWIN1.ZIP, DSWIN2.ZIP, DSWIN3.ZIP, and DSWIN4.ZIP. Downloading all four will take you about an hour. These files include the complete shell as well as a text file that tells how to install it.

Relocate the IPX—The IPX can use from 20K to 50K, depending on your computer and network adapter. Use a utility such as LanSystem's LANSpace to move the IPX into HMA memory. (Such utilities can also move the shell out of conventional memory, but that is less useful now that the latest shell from NetWare can do the same.)

Manage TSRs—One way to run NetWare more efficiently is to manage your TSRs intelligently. (That's also true of most programs, but becomes critical with a memory-hungry program such as NetWare.) Use one of the utilities mentioned in Step 5 for this work, such as PopDrop Plus or Marknet and Release Net (available as MRKREL in the public-domain and demos library of the Novell A Forum of CompuServe's NetWire forum), to load and unload TSRs on demand. Get rid of the ones you don't need when running NetWare. Or, instead of just eliminating the TSRs, you could run them from high-DOS memory, from expanded or extended memory. Use any of the memory management programs in Steps 4 or 5 for this work, such as QEMM-386 on 386-based PCs or the ChargeCard on 286-based PCs.

Configure DOS for NetWare—A previous section of this Step explained how you should configure DOS to use the minimum amount of memory that's practical. When working with NetWare that configuration should include pruning the CONFIG.SYS demands to get rid of DOS buffers. Set this to 0, even the default of 2 or 3 uses a couple K of memory that there's no reason to give up. The Lastdrive command isn't necessary when you use network drives. Prune that and you can get 2K or more back. Eliminate the ANSI.SYS console device driver—you probably don't need its special screen colors and prompts—and you save 2K to 10K more.

Graphics

Freelance Plus 3.0 from Lotus Development and Draw Applause from Ashton-Tate once needed 640K each. Both were slimmed in more recent versions to run on 512K PCs. In fact, Applause II, the successor to Draw Applause, uses about 450K while Freelance Plus 3.01 uses only 415K (that's the memory they need free after DOS and any TSRs use their bite of memory). Applause II can also use EMS 4.0 expanded memory, but if you have 3MB or more beyond conventional memory you're often better off putting the entire program on a RAM disk. The first version of Applause occasionally would abort entirely if you made a chart so big that it filled memory. Now a virtual memory scheme in Applause II automatically moves a too-large chart to EMS memory or to the hard disk.

Harvard Graphics. Version 2.3 of Harvard Graphics needs 420K of RAM, and so will fit in most systems that have 640K of conventional memory. However, many Harvard Graphics users run into a lack of printer memory. Many laser printers, especially those at least a year or two old, came with only 512K of their own RAM. With that much memory, the laser printer can only print a half page of 300 dpi (dot per inch) resolution graphics. To print a full page of graphics at this high resolution, you need at least 1MB of printer memory. If you have a page that mixes text and graphics, you will need to add extra memory for the fonts, possibly as much as 2MB or more. (See Step 8 for details.)

Freelance Plus. Freelance Plus 3.01 is the latest version of this graphics program from Lotus Development. It has the same functions as Version 3.0, but uses less memory—needing 438K after DOS is loaded instead of 508K. In fact, it can be cut to as little as 415K by a command-line switch that decreases the memory allocated for charts and drawings. This smaller version of Freelance is better for PCs attached to networks or mainframes or those using TSRs, because more conventional memory is free.

For increased performance, put these Freelance Plus document files on a RAM disk: *.drw and *.cht and *.wk? along with any clip art or symbol files. Then use the File, Options, Form command (working through the Freelance Plus menus in that order) to tell the program to find the data files on the RAM disk and that the RAM disk, is the default drive. To reach data files on a RAM drive use the File, Options, Form commands to set the RAM disk up as the default drive.

Freelance Plus can keep two image working areas or "draw pages" active at once. If you have a VGA graphics card, you can install the Freelance Plus EGA screen driver that uses memory on the video card itself to store the entire second draw page—to increase performance by avoiding redrawing the whole screen when switching pages.

If you have more than the minimum amount of memory Freelance Plus needs and you import large spreadsheet files, you can increase the number of rows and columns allocated to the view page under the Chart Options menu.

Designer. Designer, from Micrografx, is one of the most popular graphics programs that runs under Windows. As such, it gets all of its memory management from Windows itself. Look to the Windows notes in Step 6 for details on using Windows memory.

CAD

AutoSketch. AutoSketch is an inexpensive CAD program for basic sketching. It needs at least 512K of conventional memory, but can use up to 2MB of Expanded memory to hold large drawings. (You may use an EMM program to convert

Extended memory into Expanded for AutoSketch's use—see Steps 4 and 5.) Previous versions of AutoSketch could only work on as large a drawing as would fit into conventional memory. Now 64K of any drawing is kept in conventional memory and the rest can be kept in expanded memory or on hard disk—essentially a virtual memory scheme.

While AutoSketch works it creates two kinds of temporary files: an undo file and a vector file (for plotting drawings to a printer). If you put these files on a RAM disk you can speed AutoSketch's performance. The locations of these files are set by the ASUNDO and ASVECT environment variables in AutoSketch. Use these two commands: set asundo=d:\ and **set asvect=d:** in your AUTOEXEC.BAT file

The ASMEMPATH variable in AutoSketch tells the program where to put drawing, fonts, patterns, and other stuff that doesn't fit into conventional memory. The command **set asmempath=d:\ sets it:**

This paging path is set by default to your hard disk, but you could set it to a RAM disk for more speed. Allow about twice as much space in the RAM disk as the largest drawing you expect to work on. Use this command:

```
set asundo=d:\undofile.$$$
```

The ASLIMEM variable controls whether AutoSketch uses expanded memory or not. If it is not present in the environment space of DOS, AutoSketch automatically uses any expanded memory it finds. If it is present and set off (with the command **set aslimem=off** in the AUTOEXEC.BAT file) then AutoSketch won't use expanded memory. Normally you'll want to let AutoSketch use expanded memory, but there will be some occasions when you want to keep that memory for another program or for an Autodesk Device Interface (ADI) display or printer driver or for a TSR utility.

AutoCAD. AutoCAD, like most CAD programs, often works on huge, complicated files. That means memory is critical. As with Ventura Publisher, one of the best things you can do to improve AutoCAD performance is to manage your memory carefully. AutoCAD automatically uses expanded and extended memory, if you have it. If you're running short on conventional memory, try using fewer TSRs.

Instead of versions, AutoCAD has evolved through Releases. Release 10 was giving way to Release 11 as this book went to print. Each release comes with a

"Performance Chapter" in the installation manual, as well as disk files (with names like INCFG.DOC and SYSCFG.DOC) that tell you how to set up for the best memory conservation or the most performance.

Two general tips: 1) Most releases of AutoCAD work better with a good disk caching program. 2) Have at least three times as much extended memory as the size of your typical drawing file, four to five times is even better.

RAM Disk—In Release 10, the AutoCAD files to put on a RAM disk for faster performance are the overlay files (**acad*.ov*** and ***.ovl**) and your drawing files. Don't, however, include the configuration **overlay acadcfg.ovl.** Be sure to copy them back to the hard disk regularly, so you won't lose any changes.

Remember to include the RAM disk statement at the beginning of the DOS PATH statement so AutoCAD can find the overlays. You might also rename the overlay file copies that remain on the hard drive, or move them to a directory that is not in the PATH, so AutoCAD won't find and use them. (A batch file is the best way to do this, and then to undo it when you're done with AutoCAD.)

Putting all these files on a RAM disk may mean you need several MB of RAM disk space. Be sure to have plenty extra, because AutoCAD makes temporary drawing files as you work, and these too will be crowding the RAM disk.

Switches and Configuration—AutoCAD does not have any switches that you type at the DOS prompt for memory conservation. But AutoCAD does have some system configuration variables that affect memory. For example, you set the environmental variable **ACADFREERAM=xx** The lower you set ACADFREERAM, the faster the performance. But complex drawing tasks may need a higher setting. The default is 24.

AutoLISP—AutoLISP is a programming language inside of AutoCAD that lets you customize the program for your own uses. In Release 10, if you use extended AutoLISP (AutoLISP for extended memory), you'll save about 50K of conventional memory.

If you work with very large AutoLISP programs, assign at least a half-megabyte or, better still, a megabyte of extended memory to extended AutoLISP. A good benchmark is to have about 256K of extended memory I/O Space is good for drawings in the size range of 200K to 400K. If, however, you're drawing very large entities, such as large polylines, large meshes, or very large text strings, it's better to use more I/O page space than to use your RAM for RAM disk. If you're not working with such large entities, lean toward using your RAM as a RAM disk for overlays.

To use extended AutoLISP with a memory manager such as QEMM or 386-Max, set up all of extended memory as expanded, then set:

ACADXMEM   to NONE
LISPXMEM   to Null

and allow the memory manager to do its thing. You can use the **ACADLIMEM** configuration statement to control the amount of memory that AutoCAD gets from the memory manager for extended I/O paging. The rest is left for extended AutoLISP to use as node space and for any other expanded memory applications that you may have.

Errors and Memory—If you see the "Fatal Error" and then **EREAD/SMIO/ LTINIT/SCANDR** the drawing file has bad data in it, possibly from a RAM or RAM disk fault. Turn to your .BAK file for a good copy of the drawing, and use diagnostics to check the RAM. Also check the settings you've used for ACADXMEM, ACADLIMEM, LISPXMEM, and the RAM disk. There might also be a problem with any disk caching software you're using.

If you get the message: **DOS/16M: Cannot run program in virtual 8086 mode** you may need to get an updated version of extended AutoLISP, one that supports the VCPI standard for memory managers. (Versions of Release 10 with an EXTLISP.EXE file dated before 02/03/89 may not work with VCPI-compatible memory managers.) Release 10 owners can get an upgrade through the CompuServe ADESK Forum.

AutoCAD 386 Version and Release 11—With Release 10, Autodesk created a special AutoCAD 386 version of the program. AutoCAD 386 eliminates the need for fine-tuning memory use that the general Release 10 depends on for good performance. It looks the same as Release 10 on screen, but runs only on 386- and 486-based PCs with at least 2MB of memory. It loads faster, saves faster, and can draw up to five times faster, and can reach up to 16MB of RAM because it has a built-in Phar Lap DOS extender. It doesn't need a RAM disk for the overlay files because it puts all of the program into memory at once. Using AutoCAD 386 gives more room for larger AutoLISP program files, and for other utilities, network interfaces, and so on. It avoids the slowdown of swapping overlay files in and out of memory. One tip about using AutoCAD 386: have as much 32-bit memory as possible. Many 386 systems can hold at least 2MB of 32-bit memory, but they often fill the rest of memory with 16-bit. That's about 4 times slower than 32-bit. You might use 16-bit memory in a PC as a RAM disk, or to store display lists: those uses won't hurt performance. AutoCAD 386 uses virtual memory to create drawing files as large as 4GB (or as large as your own disk memory).

Release 11 of AutoCAD only runs on 386 systems. This is the first generation that leaves the older PCs behind.

OS/2 and Unix Versions—The multitasking and other sophisticated abilities such as DDE and the graphic user interface of the OS/2 operating system are a boon to CAD work. Most important, perhaps, is the access to much more memory. Users can port AutoCAD files from the OS/2 version to any other platform running AutoCAD Release 10, without file conversion (a standard feature of all versions of Release 10.) AutoCAD for OS/2 requires at least 4 megabytes of memory, a 286 or 386 processor, a math coprocessor, and the Standard or Extended Edition of OS/2.

AutoCAD is also available for Unix, such as SCO Xenix and SCO Unix System V/386 and Unix on workstations. Unix is another operating system that offers much more memory than DOS. And as with OS/2, your AutoCAD drawings can easily move between DOS systems and Unix systems.

Display List Drivers—With AutoCAD, and some other CAD programs, the time it takes to draw any changes in a drawing on to the display screen is a bottleneck. AutoCAD makes a display list of instructions for the way the image should look, and then the PC has to process this display list and put the results on to the screen. Word processor and spreadsheet jockeys won't be used to this, but CAD users know that just zooming in for a better view can mean a 30 second to several minute wait to see a complete display image. One way to speed up this process is to use an expensive special graphics display adapter that will process AutoCAD's display list with its own processor chip and memory. However, you can also buy software display list drivers that will do this in your PC's own memory, and save you the expense of the special graphics board. These drivers claim to gain 90% of the speed of graphics cards.

For example, the Lightning Zoom display list driver (once known as HiRez9 for Release 9 and then HiRes10 for AutoCAD Release 10) works with EGA, extended EGA, VGA, extended VGA, and 8514/A graphics cards. It takes up only 13K of conventional memory, and makes redrawing 2.4 times faster. Various versions of it offer single or multiple viewports and other special features.

Programming

Programmers have a million tricks to conserve memory. Here are just a few examples for non-professionals.

BASICA. This ancient version of BASIC for PCs can only reach 64K of memory. Don't bother looking for tricks to get beyond that: just use another BASIC.

QuickBASIC. QuickBASIC will compile programs faster if you put all of its files on a RAM disk, especially its program and library files. The most important file to put on the RAM disk, though, is the 221K **bcom45.lib** file. To tell QuickBASIC where the files are, put this line **set lib=d:** in the AUTOEXEC.BAT or in the batch file you use to start QuickBASIC.

If all of the files fit on the RAM disk, put the source code files on your hard drive and use a batch file to compile the program on the RAM disk, then link to it, and finally copy the results to the hard drive (to protect them).

Turbo Pascal. Turbo Pascal 5.0 will run faster if the following library files are on a RAM disk: **turbo.tpl** and ***.tpu**. You need to change the Unit Directories in the Options/Directories menu to tell Turbo Pascal to find these library files on the RAM disk.

Microsoft C. The latest version of Microsoft's C, version 6.0, has a debugger that requires very little of the 640K of conventional memory available in a PC. The debugger pages itself in and out of memory or to disk.

Periscope. This debugger from The Periscope Company has its own board to plug into Micro-Channel Architecture bus PS/2 systems. The board's own memory holds such debugging information as symbol tables, and leaves the full 640K of the

PS/2's conventional memory free for the program that's being analyzed and debugged.

Turbo Debugger and Assembler 2.0. Turbo Debugger & Tools 2.0 from Borland has an Undo feature that lets a programmer back up through 300 to 400 instructions on a system with 640K of RAM, or through 3000 instructions on a system with 640K and expanded memory.

Utilities

SideKick and SideKick Plus. SideKick was the first popular TSR program. It comes in several versions, with various combinations of the basic tools: notepad, calendar, calculator, and so on. If you don't need a particular tool or tools, you can choose one of these alternate versions and so use less memory. For example, the full SideKick starts with this command: **SK.** But if you use **SKN** instead you'll only have the Notepad tool, and will have saved all the tens of K of memory taken up by the other tools.

SideKick can be removed from memory if it was the last TSR loaded. To do this, put the SideKick main menu on screen, then press **Ctrl-Home** and **Ctrl-End**.

SideKick Plus is larger than SideKick, but it too can be configured to use less memory. It runs fastest if all 256K of it is in conventional memory. But you can configure SideKick Plus to use only 75K. The rest swaps in and out of either extended memory or a disk drive. This works fastest with a RAM disk. To set SideKick Plus up that way, run the Install program without SideKick Plus in memory, then choose **Design New SKPLUS** and tell the system to use extended memory and the RAM disk. Then choose **Continue SKPLUS Design** and indictate which tools you want to use and which should swap in and out of conventional memory. Then press F2 and save your minimum memory SKPLUS under a new name.

Magellan. Magellan, a utility for organizing your hard disk, has a single memory management switch in Version 1.0. The command /**noex** tells Magellan not to use expanded memory.

Norton Commander. If you have a RAM disk, put these files of Version 1.0 on it: **nc*.*** and **view*.*** and **mci*.***. Then put the RAM disk letter at the beginning of your DOS PATH statement, and include the command **set nc-d:** in your

AUTOEXEC.BAT file, or in any batch file you use to start the Norton Commander.

Norton Utilities. For better performance with Version 4.0, put all the Norton Utility files on a RAM disk. Also, the disk optimizer utility will run faster, the more memory you have.

PC Tools Deluxe. For PC Tools Deluxe, put all files on a RAM disk. Use the **/od** switch to automatically copy all necessary overlay files for desktop and shell to the RAM disk.

DOS Shells

In general, you should avoid DOS shells if you're trying to save on memory. Most don't do anything more than DOS can do—they just make it easier for beginning computer users to do things. If you simply learn the DOS functions then you can easily skip the shells.

Most DOS shells run much faster from a RAM disk, because they remove all but a fragment of themselves from memory when you run an application, then reload into memory once you quit that application. Using a RAM disk can save several seconds for each load. A RAM disk will also help speed some shell operations because shells sometimes use overlays for their features. Even DOS's own COMMAND.COM shell does better from a RAM drive.

Personal Organizers

Agenda. To improve performance of Version 1.0, put these files on a RAM disk: ***.aga** and ***.agb**. Then press F10 while in Agenda to bring up the main menu, choose File Open, and assign the letter of your RAM disk that has the files—that's typically d:. That way Agenda knows where to find the files.

To limit the amount of memory that your Agenda data files occupy do the following:

- Export items marked "Done" to a separate .STF file. Do this by choosing Utility, Preferences, Process Done items, and finally Export to Done file from the menus.

- When you have many Item notes, use the File Notes option to keep notes in external files instead of in the main data file.

Grandview. You can improve the performance of Version 1 of this personal organizer and outlining program by putting the help and spelling files (**GV.HLP GVmain.dct**) on a RAM disk:

Then tell GrandView to find the files there by setting the environment variables in your CONFIG.SYS file like this: **set GVhelp=d:** and **set GVmain=d:**

Financial Software

Dac Easy Accounting. This inexpensive accounting program has a whole slew of files you can put on a RAM disk for better performance. Here's a list of those files, along with parenthetical comments on what the files do (in case you have a newer version of the program with slightly different file names):

```
*.exe              (program)
dea4file.dat
dea4stn.dat
dea4cid.dat        (Btrieve file-creation)
dea4dbcl.db
dea4dbix.db
dea4dbtb.db        (dictionaries)
dea4scr.*
dea4dtl.dat
dea4ndx.dat        (screen and help)
dea4grx.db
dea4prnt.db
dea4repd.db
dea4reph.db        (graphics, printer and report generator)
dea4stb.db
dea4cid.d8         (station and company identification)
all files in the FILES subdirectory
```

The EXE files take up 3MB. If you don't have room on your RAM disk for the EXE and data files, put only the data files on the RAM disk.

You need to tell Dac Easy where to find the data files that you put on the RAM disk. Use the switch mentioned below for this. To run EXE programs from the RAM disk, include the RAM disk at the beginning of your DOS PATH statement.

Dac Easy has these switches:

/db:d:\directory	to tell the program where to find data files
/m:xx	allocates memory xx K of memory for cache buffers. A larger value gives faster performance, but uses more memory. The default is 48; the maximum is 64.

Managing Your Money. For this finance program, improve performance by putting the main program file, **mem.exe** on a RAM disk, and then run the program from that disk.

Quicken. For version 2.0 of this personal finance program, you can improve performance by putting the program and configuration files onto a RAM disk: **q.exe** and **q.cng**

For version 3.0, the files are called: **q.exe** and **q.cgf.**

Version 3.0 also has a memory management switch—/n—that tells the program to increase the proportion of memory allocated to data. This helps improve performance on files larger than 1MB. Start Quicken this way: **q /n**

STEP 4

Find More Memory: Borrow High-DOS Memory and Relocate TSR and DDs

This Step is short because it is relatively simple, but it is one of the most important steps in the book.

Key Ideas:

• Many PCs have unused memory in the high-DOS memory region, between 640K and 1024K.

• Some memory management utilities can borrow a hundred K or more from the bottom end of this memory, and add it to conventional memory—giving you more than 640K of conventional memory.

• Some memory management utilities can relocate TSR, device driver, and network interface programs from conventional memory to high-DOS memory, freeing more of the 640K for use by applications.

• Borrowing from and relocating to high-DOS or reserved memory are the only ways to actually break the 640K barrier, and are important to every PC, even if it uses expanded, extended, virtual, or other memory management schemes.

131

Background

Many PC users run short on conventional memory because that memory must hold a motley crew of DOS parts, TSRs, device drivers, network drivers, and other little programs, alongside their main applications. You've seen some of the fixes for this in previous chapters: using smaller applications, using a smaller version of DOS, configuring applications to use less memory. But there's another clever way to beat RAM cram in the lower 640: use memory from the 384K of high-DOS or reserved RAM.

Remember from Step 1 that much of high-DOS memory—the 384K above 640 and below the 1MB mark—isn't used in the average PC? Remember that the video and BIOS often take up only half of that 384K? Well, there are special memory management programs that can take your TSRs and DDs out of conventional memory and stick them in high-DOS memory, slipping them into the unused areas of that 384K. These professional relocators can bring your PC back to as much as 639K of free conventional memory. You get more memory to use without having to buy any more actual memory.

These memory managers need a PC with one of the following:

- A 386 processor

- A 486 processor

- An expanded memory board

- A memory management chip (such as the All ChargeCard)

- A set of support chips for the processor that include memory management abilities (such as the NEAT chip set from the Chips & Technologies company).

It's called remapping because those systems have the electronic logic to simply reassign the effective addresses of blocks of memory. There are some limits to this forced emigration. Not all drivers will work from high-DOS memory. Also, using high-DOS memory for drivers restricts that memory from other uses, such as for shadow RAM.

There are also some dangers to relocation, for instance, TSRs and drivers sometimes use more memory when they start, or under certain circumstances, than when they are moved to high-DOS memory. If they do, they could conflict with some other program or driver that's in high-DOS memory, causing errors or even a crash in your PC system.

But even with these limits and dangers, relocation of TSRs and DDs to high-DOS memory is a trick every memory manager should use. To do it, get a memory management program with the power, and then either let the program automatically deduce what to put in high-DOS memory and where to put it, or become a guru of the top 384K yourself, using the memory management program's tools to discover and fill each chunk of 128K, 32K, 16K, or even a mere 4K of high-DOS memory.

The 386 and 486 processors are especially gifted at memory mapping and management, able to map any 4K chunk of memory above or below the 1MB mark to any other 4K address in logical memory. The 8088, 8086, and 80286 processors don't have that ability.

Borrowing from High-DOS or Reserved Memory

As explained in Step 1, to use a place in memory, your PC must have three things:

- A memory address that the hardware can reach

- A memory address that the software can reach

- Memory chips at that address

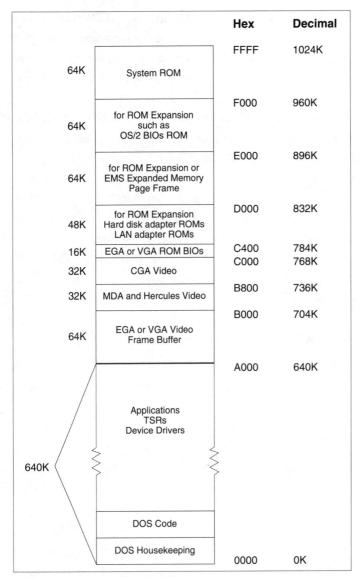

Figure 4-1. Memory Maps of High-DOS or Reserved Memory Use

DOS reserves the 384K of memory addresses from 640K to 1024K (1MB) for system functions. Your programs normally can't get at this memory. It is the home for many PC functions such as the following:

• The ROM memory chips for the system's BIOS (Basic Input Output System) programs

• The video graphics adapter ROMs, (the video graphics adapter frame buffers where the bits that determine the screen image are kept)

• The expanded memory page frame, and other peripheral memory chips

For instance, if you plug in a network interface board, that board's basic program routines will be on a ROM chip that will be assigned an address within this 384K of memory.

But all of these uses don't soak up all of the reserved memory addresses. In fact, in many PCs, all of these uses put together don't add up to more than 150K or so of memory addresses. That leaves 200K or so of addresses unused, addresses which any PC's microprocessor can get at because they are addresses below 1MB. In other words, the hardware can get at them.

Now DOS can't automatically get at those addresses, because it only expects 640K of memory addresses. It won't load a program beginning above 640K no matter what. But some programs don't check for the 640K limit when loading, and so can start below it and continue on through and above it. When you look at reserved memory uses you can see that just above the 640K line is an area of 128K for use by EGA and VGA systems running in graphics modes. If those systems stay out of graphics modes, that memory is fallow—ripe for the taking. With the right utility software, many programs can use some of this memory, as long as it is contiguous—continues without interruption—from the memory below 640K. Therefore, DOS can get at it.

Finally, in many PCs that come with 640K of RAM today, there are actually 1MB of RAM chips installed. It's easier to put the even amount of 512K or 1MB than the somewhat odd amount of 640K, so most PC manufacturers who want at least

640K just go ahead and stick in 1MB. Some 286 PCs, and all 386 PCs, have the ability to remap memory, moving memory addresses as they want. If those PCs have memory chips above 1MB, they can remap some of it to appear as if it is in the reserved memory addresses. So there are memory chips available for use there.

In summary, on PCs that:

• Aren't using all of high-DOS or reserved memory have 1MB or more of memory

• Aren't using memory contiguous to the 640K (typically EGA and VGA systems that aren't running in graphics modes)

• Have the right memory management utility software you can have more than 640K of conventional memory. In some cases, you can have 700K, 800K, or even 900K of conventional memory, as shown in Figure 4-2.

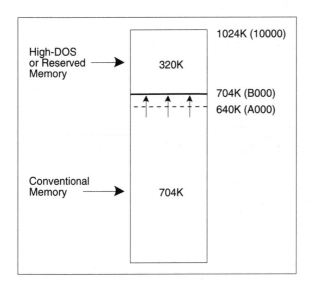

Figure 4-2. Borrowing from High-DOS Memory

Relocating TSRs, DDs, and Network Drivers to High-DOS or Reserved Memory

Many PCs don't actually use a good part of the high-DOS or reserved memory addresses. The unused memory in the reserved area that are immediately above the 640K line can, with the right utility software, be slapped onto the 640K of conventional memory.

But there's another use for reserved and unused memory: relocation or loading high memory. The right memory management software and hardware can relocate some TSR programs, device drivers, network shells, and even DOS utilities such as Files and Buffers, from conventional memory to high-DOS or reserved memory. Mapping hardware is necessary for this work.

This isn't the same as getting more conventional memory, but if part of your own RAM-cram comes from having too many TSRs and device drivers in the 640K, it'll be almost as good—freeing conventional memory for your programs and data. When those drivers and TSRs have been occupying 200K or more of your 640K, it can seem like a miracle. Figure 4-3 shows how this works.

Some utilities can also relocate TSRs and device drivers to HMA memory, extended memory, or expanded memory.

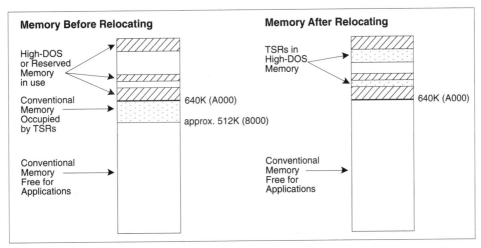

Memory Before Relocating

High-DOS or Reserved Memory in use

Conventional Memory Occupied by TSRs

640K (A000)

approx. 512K (8000)

Conventional Memory Free for Applications

Memory After Relocating

TSRs in High-DOS Memory

640K (A000)

Conventional Memory Free for Applications

Figure 4-3. Relocating TSRs and Device Drivers from Conventional to High-DOS memory

Memory Manager Software and Hardware

To borrow or relocate you need both the right utility and mapping hardware or memory management unit (MMU) that can move programs by changing their addresses, without actually copying them from one place to another. Such a utility is a memory manager or memory management program. Unfortunately, the utilities that organize and handle expanded memory are also called memory managers or EMMs (Expanded Memory Managers). There's a lot of this naming confusion in memory management and in computing in general.

386 and 486-based PCs have mapping built into the microprocessor—a good reason to move to the 386 generation.

8088 and 286-based PCs get mapping through:

- Having an EMS 4.0 expanded memory board

- Having a plugged-in MMU

- Having a Chips & Technologies NEAT chipset (or a similar chipset from a company such as Trident).

286's built with the Chips & Technologies companies "NEAT" chipset (New Enhanced AT)—the group of chips that surround and aid the microprocessor have built-in hardware circuits for memory mapping. You can discover if your machine has the NEAT chip set if you see a notice in the startup screen, when you turn the AT on, or if there's a page of NEAT options when you look at any setup or configuration screen in your system. (Refer to your manual to learn how to find the configuration screen.)

Add-on Memory Management Unit Hardware for PCs, XTs, ATs, and Compatibles

If you have a 386 or 486 system, refer to the following section on software. If you have a 286 or even 8088 system with expanded memory hardware, or NEAT chips, look to the section of 8088 and 80286 memory management software. But if you don't have that hardware yet, aren't ready to move to a 386 system, and want to borrow or relocate, get an MMU such as one of those listed here.

All ChargeCard. The ALL ChargeCard from ALL Computers is a special, small circuit board that you can add to an XT, AT or compatible. You remove the 286 processor from its socket in the computer, plug it into the ChargeCard, then plug the ChargeCard with the processor into the now empty 286 socket. The ChargeCard is an MMU that will allow that 286 system, even without EMS or NEAT hardware, to relocate FILES, BUFFERS, device drivers, LASTDRIVE, TSRs, and some network shells into reserved memory. It also provides memory mapping for smooth multitasking for Windows or DESQview. It does this without disabling any conventional memory, as back-filling of expanded memory sometimes requires. The ChargeCard doesn't come with any memory of its own—it provides the hardware for remapping the addresses of the memory that's in the PC.

HiCard. The HiCard from RYBS Electronics is MMU hardware that adds memory mapping to a PC without 386, EMS, or NEAT hardware. This will let the PC load device drivers, BUFFERS, FILES, STACKS, LASTDRIVE, network drivers, and other software into reserved memory. It works with any PC. HiCard comes with up to 512K of its own memory that can fill reserved memory (from 640K to 1024K), it can backfill conventional memory, or it can act as standard extended memory. HiCard is not compatible with EMS 4.0 expanded memory.

X-Bandit. The X-Bandit from Teletek Enterprises is a memory board for PCs that lets them load device drivers, buffers, and some other DOS software into reserved memory. It comes with up to 2MB of its own memory.

Maximizer. From Softnet Communications, this memory board fits in PCs or ATs. It is a memory-management unit that lets the system load device drivers, BUFFERS, and other software into reserved memory. The Maximizer comes with up to 256K of its own memory that may only fill reserved memory addresses—it cannot be used as extended or backfilled conventional memory. It does not support EMS 4.0 expanded memory.

Invisible EMS. Invisible Software makes a memory manager program that requires EMS or NEAT mapping hardware to work. To help those who don't have such hardware in their PCs, the company also makes Invisible EMS, a small EMS memory board that supports LIM 4.0 and has all the hardware necessary for mapping, as well as the memory management software for relocating drivers and TSRs to reserved memory.

Figure 4-4. Sota MMU (courtesy SOTA)

Memory Manager Software

These are things to look for in a memory manager:

•   Compatibility with your programs and peripherals.

•   Compatibility with your software environment (such as with the mode of Windows you might use—see Step 6 for details).

•   Combined ability to relocate, borrow, emulate expanded memory, provide virtual memory, and other useful tasks.

•   Easy installation and use.

•   Maximum amount of memory from borrowing and relocating. Ability to relocate network and PC-to-host software.

Memory Managers for 386 and 486 Systems. The best known 386 memory managers are QEMM and 386Max (previously known as 386-to-the-Max). Memory Commander is a powerful new contender.

QEMM-386—QEMM-386 (Quarterdeck Expanded Memory Manager) is pronounced "quemm," and comes from the same company that makes the popular DESQview environment and the manifest memory analyzer. It can:

Borrow

Relocate

LIMulate

QEMM-386 is for AT and compatible systems based on 386 or 486 processors. QEMM 50/60 is for PS/2 30 and PS/2 50/60 computers. Either can load TSRs, device drivers, and network software into reserved memory. It can remap and compress the ROM space at the same time and it can convert extended memory into expanded memory, acting as a LIMulator.

Version 5.1, the latest, works with Windows 3.0, opening more memory for each application that runs under Windows. A copy of QEMM comes as part of the DESQview 386 package. In fact, you can use both QEMM 5.1 and DESQView with Windows 3.0, running Windows inside a DESQview window. It supports both XMS and EMS 4.0, and is more efficient than the HIMEM.SYS and EMM386.SYS team of drivers (the first for XMS support, the second to LIMulate) that come with Windows. QEMM automatically puts memory into a single pool and then detects the need for XMS or EMS without any special configuration, providing whichever type is needed.

Because QEMM supports the DPMI standard, it allows protected-mode programs to run under Windows 3.0 Standard mode. If there's a driver that doesn't work well with QEMM, you can put it in CONFIG.SYS before the QEMM.SYS driver.

QEMM is equipped with several utilities, such as:

- TIMEMEM to check the speed of your PC's memory.

- Manifest to analyze your system's memory.

- Optimize to automatically determine the most efficient way to relocate, and to insert the necessary commands into your AUTOEXEC.BAT and CONFIG.SYS files. Figure 4-5 shows Optimize at work.

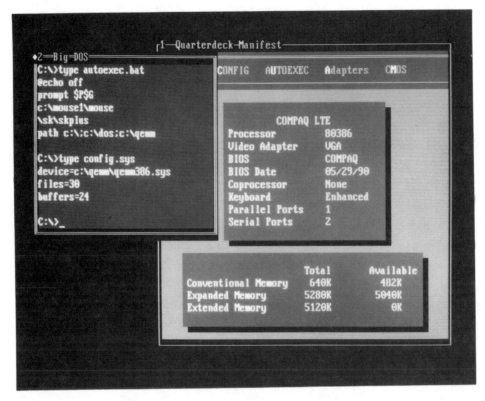

Figure 4-5a. Manifest showing PC's memory before using QEMM
(courtesy Quarterdeck)

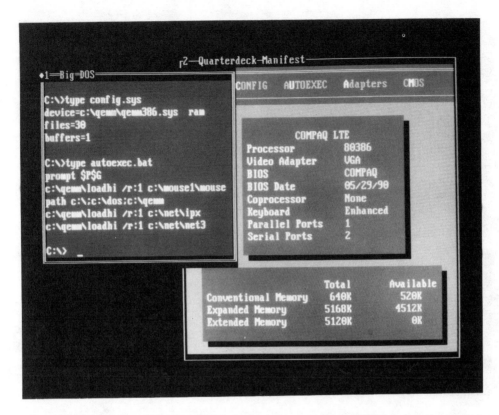

Figure 4-5b. Manifest showing PC's memory after installing QEMM (using the Optimize utility)

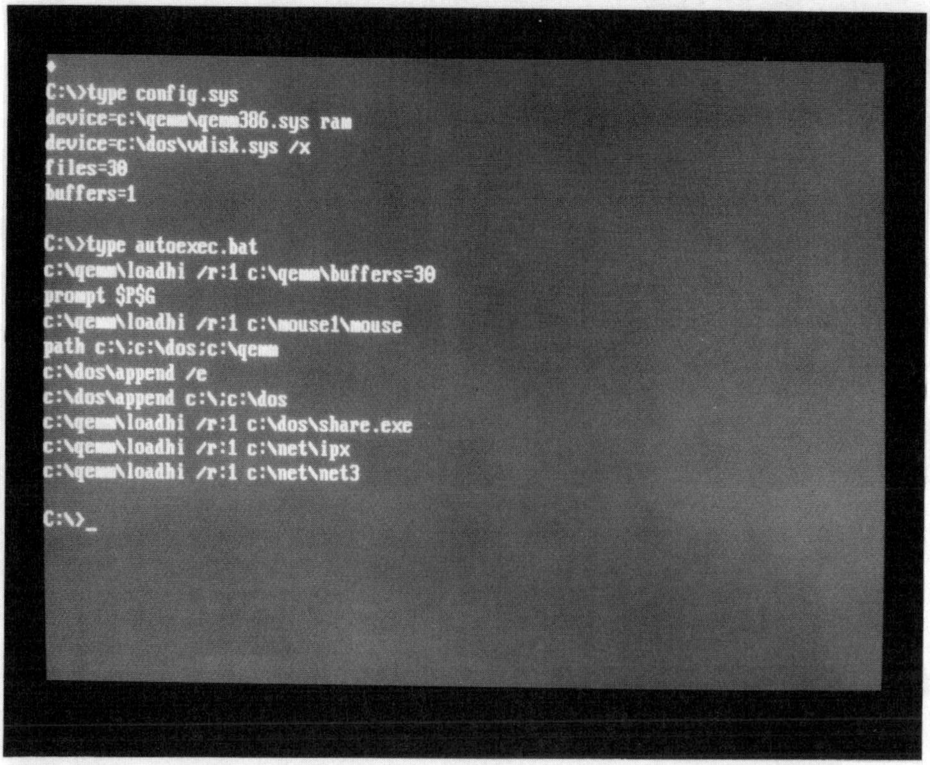

```
C:\>type config.sys
device=c:\qemm\qemm386.sys ram
device=c:\dos\vdisk.sys /x
files=30
buffers=1

C:\>type autoexec.bat
c:\qemm\loadhi /r:1 c:\qemm\buffers=30
prompt $P$G
c:\qemm\loadhi /r:1 c:\mouse1\mouse
path c:\;c:\dos;c:\qemm
c:\dos\append /e
c:\dos\append c:\;c:\dos
c:\qemm\loadhi /r:1 c:\dos\share.exe
c:\qemm\loadhi /r:1 c:\net\ipx
c:\qemm\loadhi /r:1 c:\net\net3

C:\>_
```

Figure 4-5c.

386Max and BlueMax—Qualitas' makes 386Max and BlueMax for 386- and 486-based PCs. Both:

Borrow

Relocate

LIMulate

and map the fastest system RAM into the first megabyte, where it will get the most use.

They load network shells, device drivers, and TSRs into high-DOS memory (above 640K). They borrow unused memory from the bottom of reserved memory, and add it to conventional. And they both perform as EMM programs, transforming extended memory into expanded.

BlueMax is the model for IBM PS/2 systems; 386Max is for ATs and compatibles. The programs come with the ASQ utility for analyzing your hardware and software. This is also free from the Qualitas bulletin board. For Windows users, there's the memory Viewer utility from hDC Computer to handle the same work: mapping memory.

The 386Max programs come with the Maximize utility which automatically analyzes current memory allocation and moves TSRs, device drivers, and network drivers into reserved memory with the best possible fit. Maximize automatically changes your AUTOEXEC.BAT and CONFIG.SYS files so when you start your PC it will use this best fit.

386Max and BlueMax can actually compress the ROM of a PC or PS/2 as it copies it to RAM, by leaving out little used parts such as the ROM BASIC and the POST (Power On Self Test). This can turn 128K of ROM into 44K.

386Max and BlueMax don't move DOS buffers and files into reserved memory—about 20K of memory on a typical PC—on the theory that these are closely tied to the DOS version you're using and that in most PCs configured for memory efficiency, there will be a disk cache instead of buffers anyway.

Two unique features of 386Max and BlueMax are the FlexFrame and the Instancing of TSRs. FlexFrame keeps the 64K page frame of expanded memory out of the way while loading TSRs that take more memory to load than they do while they're in reserved memory. That lets you use more memory. Instancing lets a TSR appear in more than one window of Windows without crashing the system.

Memory Commander—This manager from V Communications works on 386 and 486-based systems. It can:

Borrow

Relocate

LIMulate

Memory Commander can load TSRs, most network drivers, and device drivers into high-DOS memory, can emulate expanded memory hardware, and can copy ROM BIOS routines to shadow RAM to improve performance. By relocating items that were already in high-DOS memory to higher locations, and grabbing memory that would have been used for graphics, it can provide up to 900K of conventional memory for your applications, more than other memory managers. But it demands at least 512K of extended memory to run, more than the competitors. It supports EMS 4.0 and XMS 2.0, and is compatible with the VCPI. It shows memory maps of just what it's doing, and gives you options for the amount of expanded and extended memory you want. It also provides a RAM disk, shadow RAM, and backfilling of conventional memory. Figure 4-6 shows the memory map that Memory Commander presents you.

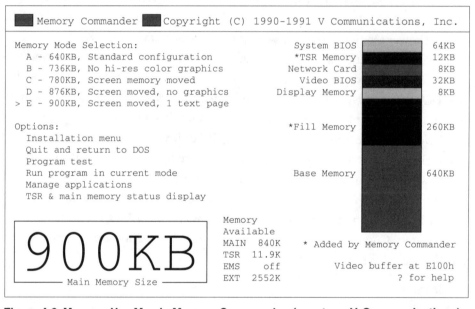

Figure 4-6. Memory-Use Map in Memory Commander (courtesy V Communications)

This utility can optimize memory use without rebooting after each trial, and can map memory uses dynamically—it doesn't depend on changes to CONFIG.SYS and AUTOEXEC.BAT.

ALL Charge 386. This memory manager from ALL Computers is for 386, 386SX and 486 systems. (ALL also makes a MMU hardware device for mapping and relocation on 286 systems.) It relocates FILES, BUFFERS, network shells and emulator programs, device drivers, and TSRs into reserved memory, and it uses only 1K of conventional memory to do the job. ALL Charge 386 uses only 1K of conventional memory itself. ALL Charge 386 supports XMS, LIM EMS 3.2 and 4.0.

Memory Managers for 8088, 286, and 386 Systems with MMU hardware.

QRAM—QRAM (pronounced "cram") from Quarterdeck does pretty much what QEMM does, but for systems that aren't graced with a 386 or 486 chip. It needs LIM 4.0 or EEMS hardware, or a Chips & Technologies chipset to run. It too can relocate and borrow, and has the optimize utility to automatically figure out the best way to do that.

Move'em—This utility from Qualitas brings the 386Max abilities to PCs without a 386. It needs EMS or Chips & Technologies hardware to run. So far, Move'em doesn't have completely automatic installation, but it will tell you the best way to relocate and borrow. You're just left putting the proper lines into your CONFIG.SYS and AUTOEXEC.BAT files.

Headroom—Headroom, from Helix Software, can both manage and relocate TSRs. It comes with the Discover analysis utility to pinpoint what is in memory.

In fact, Headroom can move not only TSRs but network programs (such as Novell NetWare's IPX and Net3/Net4) into reserved, extended, expanded, or disk memory. Headroom can also run mainframe terminal emulators as TSRs, and relocate them. It maintains the communication between the terminal emulator and the mainframe or gateway connected to the network, even when the emulator is out of memory.

Helix's Netroom and Connecting/Room utilities are slightly different from Headroom, and are more tailored to putting Network and PC-to-Host software out of conventional memory. See the description in the LAN section below.

Version 1.1 comes with the RAM-MAN/386 memory manager for converting extended memory into expanded, and so is not useful only for networks, but can be used as a general-purpose memory manager. This requires LIM 4.0 or 386 mapping hardware. Helix Software can tell you whether Headroom, Netroom, or Connecting/Room best fits your situation.

Invisible RAM—This inexpensive memory manager from Invisible Software is made specifically for systems built on the NEAT chipset with 1MB of RAM. It can convert the RAM at reserved memory addresses to EMS expanded memory or to useful RAM for relocating TSRs and device drivers.

Turbo EMS Shuttle—Turbo EMS is a virtual memory utility and EMS emulator or LIMulator. But it also comes with a utility called Shuttle that can load TSRs and device drivers into reserved memory addresses. The shuttle requires 386, EMS, or Chips & Technologies NEAT. It does not provide automatic configuration or optimization. Shuttle requires 34K of memory on an 8088-based systems, 2K of conventional RAM on a 286 or 386-based system.

EEMRAM—This shareware utility from The Cove Software Group can borrow memory on systems that have an EMS 4.0 or EEMS board and EGA or VGA graphics, but stay in text mode. You can find it on PC MagNet, CompuServe, and many other bulletin boards. Instructions and a compatibility testing program come with EEMRAM.

Memory Managers for Network Drivers. There are a few memory management programs tailored specifically for LANs and PC-to-Host software, to push network drivers and shells and terminal emulators into high-DOS or even HMA memory. Many memory managers have a tough time loading network shells high because while the shell can be small—40K to 60K—it is installed by a program of several hundred K. LAN Manager, for example, takes only 34K bytes, but has a 200K installation program. Also, LAN and terminal programs must often remain active: they can't be turned off or put into limbo the way many TSRs can. NetRoom, for instance, swaps a resident portion of the network shell into EMS expanded memory, but maps that shell back into conventional memory when network activity occurs. The latest 3.01 version of NetWare comes with the ability to relocate some of the NET3 or NET4 shells out of conventional memory. This ability sometimes surpasses, and sometimes falls short, of what independent memory managers can provide.

AboveLAN—This Above Software program loads 37K worth of NetWare shell—NET3/NET4—into extended memory (not into high-DOS memory). It doesn't need MMU hardware to do this.

AboveLAN can also borrow memory on EGA and VGA systems, with its included Above 640 program. AboveLAN works with Novell NetWare Versions 2.0 or later. It comes with a utility called ASI (Above System Information) to show system and memory details. Another utility in the package, EMS-CHECK, checks the amount of expanded or extended memory available.

LANSpace—LANSystem's LANSpace utility puts Net3/Net4 up into HMA memory. This may not seem important to NetWare 3.01 users who have this ability as part of NetWare, but LANSpace uses less memory to do it than NetWare does. LANSpace leaves only 672 bytes in conventional memory; NetWare leaves 6K. LANSpace also has a special program to let you load a NetBIOS emulator without rebooting the PC. This saves 20K more of conventional memory. LANSpace does not move any other TSRs or drivers.

Netroom and Connecting/Room—These utilities from Helix Software are similar to the general-purpose Headroom memory manager, but are aimed at network and PC-to-Host operations. They relocate network software (Novell IPX, NET3 and NET4 for instance), TSRs, and device drivers into reserved memory, and, in systems with extended memory, Netroom loads the LAN modules into HMA— the first 64K of extended memory. Netroom can also swap network software to expanded memory, moving the modules in and out of up to 576K of expanded memory on demand.

Netroom works with Novell Advanced NetWare, NetWare ELS, NetWare 386, DCA 10Net, Artisoft LANtastic, the IBM PC-LAN program and Banyan VINES. The Netroom DOS support is generic, and so can handle memory relocation for 3Com 3+, DEC PCSA and AT&T StarLan hardware. With multiple user license fees, Netroom can cost as little as $6 per person for 100 users.

Connecting/Room from Helix is aimed at those who use networks as well as 3270 emulation and other PC-to-host programs. It relocates the software to expanded, extended, or disk memory. The disk it swaps to can be local or on a file server. Connecting/Room lets the connection stay active and functional—the session isn't lost or suspended. When host activity is noticed, such as incoming mail, the user is notified. It can relocate IBM, Attachmate, DCA, and Novell connectivity software, on 8088 through 486 and Micro Channel PCs.

Netroom and Connecting/Room come with the Discover memory mapping utility, shown in Figure 4-7.

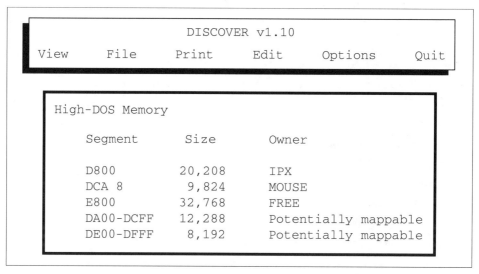

Figure 4-7. The Discover Memory Mapping Utility of Netroom and Connecting/Room (courtesy Helix Software)

Tips on Borrowing and Relocating

Every PC is different in the ways it uses reserved memory. Each has a different memory map. So if you decide to borrow from or relocate to high-DOS memory addresses—and I certainly suggest you do—you'll be blazing your own trail to determine which parts and how much of that memory are yours to use.

Some of the memory managers have utilities to automatically inspect, experiment with, and configure your borrowing and relocating. These generally do a good job. But they can make mistakes, and they don't do the best possible job. Hand "tweaking" can sometimes bring the best results—putting the most into memory—and is sometimes necessary to avoid conflicts that the automatic utilities fall into. Any of the commercial memory managers come with technical support experts who can help you determine if you have the best setup possible.

At the very least you should be able to grab 64K or more of memory, in blocks of 16K or more. If you take the time and trouble, you may be able to slip many more utilities and drivers from conventional memory into reserved, working with chunks of reserved but unused memory as small as 4K. To do that, you'll need one of the memory managers that comes with a good memory analyzing utility, or you'll have to pick up such a utility separately.

Borrowing Basics

This is more straightforward than relocating. Nearly all PCs put their graphics adapters into the bottom of reserved memory, into the so-called A and B banks just above 640K. These are the banks most often borrowed.

In most cases, any PC equipped with a EGA or VGA graphics adapter can capture the A bank of memory by staying in text mode. That's 64K more conventional memory—for a total of 704K, minus whatever DOS and utilities take up. (Incidentally, EGA and VGA systems allow 256K of their own memory—64K each for Color Intensity, Red, Green, and Blue values—into this 64K space through bank-switching, much like expanded memory.)

Systems equipped with CGA graphics, and willing to stay in text mode, can grab 96K. That's a total of 738K conventional memory—minus whatever DOS and utilities take up.

The C bank typically holds the hard disk controller on many PC systems, but this does differ from one to another. Some systems can reach above the A and B banks for borrowing, by relocating whatever is in the A, B, and C banks to other areas of reserved memory. That could give you as much as 192K more conventional memory—for a total of 832K, or even more.

Hardware and Software Idiosyncrasies

There are some memory-design differences between various PCs. If you want to check the automatic memory management utilities, or create your own memory management arrangements, it helps to know and look for more of these.

Designs that use the NEAT (and similar) chipsets and those built around the original IBM AT design and its set of chips. The original IBM AT design had a socket for a future 64K ROM. This ROM was never added, but the socket is there, using 64K of memory addresses. With the right memory manager, you can use these ROM addresses. NEAT systems don't have this socket, so they have 64K more of usable high-DOS memory immediately.

151

Also, memory must be remapped 16K at a time in many non-NEAT designs, where NEAT-design ATs can map memory a single byte at a time. The greater granularity (the ability to work with smaller pieces of memory at a time) on NEAT systems gives you greater chances to put more into high-DOS memory.

Sometimes the automatic installers don't know unused memory from unusable addresses. For example, most PS/2s can't use the E bank for relocation, but the Manifest memory mapper thinks this memory is free—ready for use.

There are some programs that will give you trouble with relocation. For example, Aristocad makes SoftKicker and ExcelMore, utilities that set up a large virtual page for Ventura Publisher, Windows, and Excel users. This page puts the EGA or VGA adapter into a special mode that uses the full A000 to C000 space, including the B000 to B800 area that would be free on most EGA and VGA systems. Your relocation program may not realize this as it arranges the placement of TSRs and drivers at reserved memory addresses.

EMS Page-frame and Expanded Memory Variations

Most PCs that use expanded memory put the expanded memory page frame— the window through which the PC can reach 32MB of more memory—in the reserved memory addresses. If you don't use expanded memory, you get 64K more memory for relocation.

There are EMS 3.2, EMS 4.0, EEMS, and a variety of expanded memory boards that claim to subscribe to those specifications. If your PC is using expanded memory hardware to get its mapping and relocating abilities, you'll discover that the various boards don't all support the same remapping abilities. Some can only work with 16K blocks at a time, others can work with 4K blocks. Some provide both expanded memory and remapping, some provide remapping only if you disable expanded memory.

For an example of a hard-to-diagnose problem, Ventura Publisher 2.0 Professional Edition had a bug that would send error messages if the EMS page frame started above E000. Many memory managers put the page frame up there, because they set it as high as possible.

The 64K page frame could get in the way of TSRs that are larger during installation than after installation. BlueMax and 386Max deal with this by temporarily turning the page frame off during installation. The following section explains this in some more detail.

Initializing Memory Versus Installed Memory

TSRs have three memory sizes: the initial loading size, the maximum size during installation, and the final size. This may be the same, but often they differ. Your memory management must provide enough memory for the largest of these.

Because of these different sizes in each TSR, the order of loading TSRs into high-DOS memory is important. TSRs that are always small should be put into high-DOS first. Others that start large and then get smaller come later. A disk cache might need 60K to start, but only 45K when running. DOS's own FASTOPEN, for instance, needs 68K to start, but only 3K once it's set. If that 68K were set aside immediately, it would use up 65K of memory that would soon be open and left unused.

Shadow RAM Complications

As explained in Step 1, the ROM routines for input and output, and for video display, are kept in high-DOS memory, at reserved addresses. These routines are held in 16-bit EPROM chips, which are relatively slow. To speed these frequently-used program routines, many 386-based systems, and 286 systems with memory management hardware copy them to 32-bit RAM chips given the same addresses. The PCs then use the routines from the RAM. This is called shadow RAM. This can speed video performance by 40% or more. You need to keep an eye peeled for this use of RAM, which may want the same memory used by many LAN network adapter cards, and at the least may use some memory you want for other relocation purposes. Also, some memory managers can actually create shadow RAM, copying ROM routines to the fastest possible RAM in the PC.

8-bit and 16-bit Conflicts

High-DOS memory consists of 6 segments or banks of memory, each holding 64K. These banks are labeled A, B, C, D, E, and F. DOS demands that everything within 128 blocks of memory—A and B, C and D, or E and F—run either in 8-bit mode or in the faster 16-bit mode. You cannot have part of a 128K block operating in one mode and part in another. This can cause conflicts, if for example an 8-bit peripheral is located inside a particular bank, and your memory management scheme then tries to relocate a 16-bit peripheral adapter to this same bank. At best the 16-bit adapter—such as a 16-bit VGA video adapter—will be slowed to 8-bit performance. At worst—with peripheral cards that initialize their own RAM after the PC boots— the clash between the two will cause trouble in accessing or using the peripherals or your entire PC, even if the drivers or ROMs from these devices are using only a few K from the 128K block. This is one problem to keep in mind when you play with the addresses of peripherals, ROMs, and other elements of high-DOS memory.

The Final Word

Keep in mind that your memory manager program uses memory itself, and could possibly take more memory than it gives you back. Also remember that many utilities that are relocated leave part of themselves behind in conventional memory. Finally, remember that if you're scrimping to find each 4K block of high-DOS memory, you may be sweating a lot for a little return. The system you create could be fragile— failing when you add some new utility or driver—and you might be better off getting new applications that use expanded and extended memory.

Add Memory: Expand, Extend, and Go Virtual

You can go a long way using the memory in your PC more efficiently, but in many cases it is a good idea to move beyond conservation and efficiency, to actually add more memory to your PC. In the past few years additional memory has dropped from a price of $250 per megabyte to about $50 a megabyte. It will almost certainly be lower than that by the time you read this book. Memory is nearly always cheaper than it was last year (there have only been one or two exceptions, when market conditions pushed it up again for six months or a year).

This step explains the various ways to add memory to your PC.

Key Ideas:

To get more memory, you can:

• Plug more memory chips into open sockets on the motherboard (the main circuit board inside the computer).

• Plug more chips into open sockets on an additional memory board.

• Swap the motherboard for a newer one with room for more memory—and probably a faster processor chip.

• Plug a new memory board (also known as a "card") into an expansion slot.

• Use a "virtual memory" utility to make part of your disk memory act like chip memory.

• When adding memory, use generic SIMMs because they are the less expensive.

• When adding memory, always match the capacity, packaging, and speed of the chips or modules already in it.

• Added memory chips or boards can be configured as conventional memory (up to 640K), expanded memory or extended memory. Your PC setup limits the configuration choices; your applications' compatibility and needs suggest a configuration.

• All programs can use conventional memory—so you should definitely have at least 640K of that.

• Not all programs can use expanded or extended memory. Many programs use expanded memory. Fewer use extended memory, but the number is growing. EMM (Expanded Memory Manager) programs can turn extended memory into expanded memory.

• Disk memory acting as chip memory is called "virtual," and is inexpensive but slow.

• A PC based on the 386 or 486 processor gives the most flexibility in adding and configuring memory.

Buying and Installing Memory

RAM chips are the fundamental currency of memory expansion. Fortunately, you don't need to worry about the many varieties of RAM chip, or the technologies behind them. For example, although some PCs have SRAM (Static RAM) chips for high-speed caching schemes, you will rarely be faced with buying more SRAMs. (The few caches that can be added to should be explained thoroughly in the computer manual.) And although PCs use EEPROMs and other specialized chips to hold configuration memory, you won't be buying or plugging those goodies in either. What you'll be looking for is good old DRAMs, just called RAM for short.

That said, though, there are some complications. You need to know such things as:

- How much do you need?

- Where will you add it?

- Chips, modules, or boards?

- What size or capacity?

- What speed?

- How do you install without damage

How Much Do You Need?

That's a tough question. Perhaps you should read the rest of this book, and then come back to this question. No? Well, how about this quick procedure to figure out what you need:

1. Use the tools of Step 2 to find out what you have.

2. Know that you'll want a total of (these are my estimates):

640K	for any computing
2MB	for basic business computing
3MB	for business computing with graphics
4MB	for fast business computing with graphics

3. Subtract what you've got from what you might need.

4. Now you know how much you need to add (in a very rough sense). Add even more for more speed and efficiency in your computing.

Where Will You Add It?

The answer to this question also depends on your particular PC and software habits. However, rules of thumb can be quite useful here too.

Rules for All PCs. Fill the Motherboard First—If your *motherboard*, the main electronic circuit board in your computer, has open sockets waiting for memory, that's the place to start. If the PC has less than 640K, it'll certainly have sockets waiting on the motherboard. But some motherboards can hold 4MB of memory, so even PCs with plenty of memory may have empty sockets on the motherboard. (A few PCs will require some other added chips, "PAL" logic, that help additional memory "cope" in the system. Check your manual to see if this is true of your PC.)

Replace memory with denser chips or modules if you can. You should check to see if the sockets that are already occupied on your PC's motherboard (or on any other memory board) can be filled with denser memory. Some PCs let you pull out a 256K memory chip and replace it with a 1M memory chip, or pull a 1MB memory module to replace it with a 4M memory module of the same physical size. Check your PC's manual or ask technical support to see if you can do this. It's as good as having more sockets on the motherboard.

Rules for 386 and 486 PCs. After the motherboard, fill any high-speed memory slot, then add an extended memory board. If you have a 386, or 486-based system, PC, PS/2 or compatible, the next place to look to add memory is in a special high-speed memory slot. Figure 5-1 shows a board that fits such a slot.

This takes advantage of the high-speed 32-bit, processor-speed memory performance that such a PC often offers. (It can move 32 bits of information at a time—2 to 4 times as much as the 8 and 16 bits of other memory boards. And it moves those bits at the speed of the processor, instead of at the much slower electrical speed, 1/2 to 1/5 as fast as the speed of the electrical system bus.) There may already be a board in the slot, with sockets waiting for more memory. Or you may need to buy such a board and plug it in yourself, after adding the memory to it. Unfortunately, these slots are not the same from computer to computer, so you'll end up paying more than you would for a standard memory board. If you're on a very tight budget, skip ahead. Otherwise bite the memory bullet and pay for this board—it'll give you much better performance in every program you run than any other added memory could.

After filling the high-speed board, you should add extended memory boards.

158

Figure 5-1. High-speed Memory Board for a 386 Computer (courtesy Newer Technology)

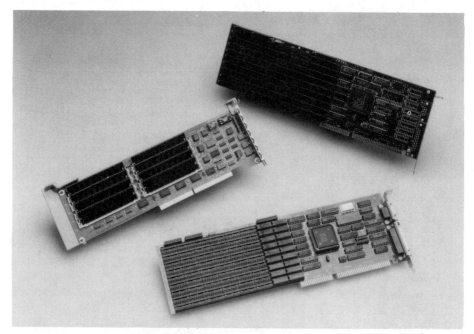

Figure 5-2. Expanded Memory Boards (courtesy Intel)

Rules for PCs and XTs. Fill the motherboard, then add an expanded memory board. Your system can't use 32-bit memory or extended memory. (Although it could if you added a 386 accelerator board--explained later in this Step.) Get an expanded memory board--such as those in Figure 5-2--that supports the LIM EMS 4.0 standard. Add to it as much memory as you need, then plug it into your computer.

Rules for 286 or 386SX Systems. Fill the motherboard first, then add an expanded or extended memory board, as your software suggests. Better yet: add a 386 accelerator board and then add memory to it.

If you have a 286 or 386SX-based AT, PS/2, or compatible you should still start by filling the motherboard. However, if that doesn't give enough memory, the next step isn't as straightforward as it was in the PCs mentioned above. In some cases you'll want to add an expanded memory board, as just mentioned above. In others you'll want to add an extended memory board. This board is similar to an expanded memory board, but is simpler. It doesn't have the extra expanded memory management hardware of the EMS board (read the rest of this step for details on that).

Your choice of expanded or extended depends on your software—you'll need to look to your programs to see what type of memory they ask for. Keep in mind that you can use software to configure either type as the other, though this can be slower and more awkward that just having the appropriate memory in the first place.

When you choose such a board, try to find one that fits into a 16-bit slot before you settle for one that fits in an 8-bit slot. PCs come with various buses and the expansion slots are where add-on boards plug in to those buses. An 8-bit bus moves information at half the speed of a 16-bit bus, which is again half the speed of a 32-bit bus. The original PC had an 8-bit bus. The AT has a 16-bit bus, as do many 286 and 386 computers that follow its general design. This bus is called the ISA or Industry Standard Architecture. The latest AT compatibles have the 32-bit EISA bus, the Enhanced Industry Standard Architecture. EISA is compatible with ISA which is compatible with the PC bus. IBM's PS/2s mostly come with the MCA bus, the Micro Channel Architecture, a bus that comes in 16 and 32-bit editions. MCA is not compatible with PC, ISA, or EISA. There are also proprietary slots, of special designs, for some high-speed memories, as mentioned above. In other words:

- You can plug an 8-bit board PC board into a PC bus slot, an ISA, or an EISA slot.

- You can plug a 16-bit ISA board into an ISA slot or an EISA slot.

- You can only plug a 32-bit EISA board into an EISA slot.

- You can plug a 16-bit MCA board into a 16-bit MCA slot or a 32-bit MCA slot.

- You can only plug a 32-bit MCA board into a 32-bit MCA slot.

- You cannot plug any MCA board into any non-MCA slot.

- You cannot plug a PC, ISA, or EISA board into any MCA slot.

- You can only plug a proprietary high-speed memory board only into the slot designed for it on a particular PC, not into any other PC, ISA, EISA, or MCA slot. (Incidentally, boards don't only differ in their connection to the slot. They also differ in physical size. MCA boards aren't the same size as EISA boards, for example. More important, ISA boards (for ATs) are often too tall to fit into PCs. Even if the slots are compatible, a board for one system may not fit in the other.

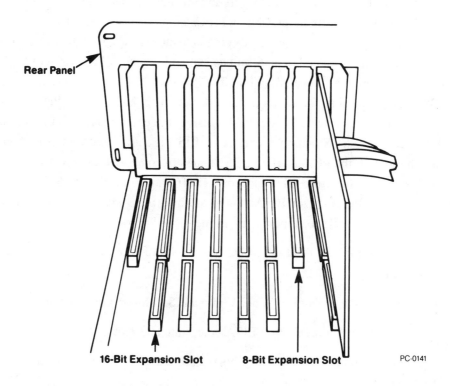

Rear Panel

16-Bit Expansion Slot   8-Bit Expansion Slot   PC-0141

Figure 5-3. Sketch of a typical PC motherboard with 8- and 16-bit slots for adding PC and ISA board (courtesy Intel)

Always try to put a board into a slot that handles at least as many bits as the board. For instance, most older boards were 8-bit, for peripherals such as serial ports. These did well in 8-bit slots, but could also work in 16-bit slots. However, if you fill a 16-bit slot with an 8-bit board, that slot won't be open for any new 16-bit board. Many, but not all 16-bit boards will work in 8-bit slots, but they won't perform as well as if they are in 16-bit slots. Many PCs these days come with a mixture of slots.

162

One more rule: make sure your PC has the power to handle the additional memory. Each memory chip, module, or board eats a certain number of watts, and your PC power supply must be able to supply that much and more—while running all the other parts of the PC too. If your power supply isn't up to the task, you can replace it with a beefier model. Don't cut close to the edge here; barely enough power can lead to lots of memory errors.

Rules for Laptops and Portables. Laptop and portable computers follow the same general rules as other PCs, but they often have fewer or no slots or sockets. You'll have to make do with what you can, following the rules when possible, and probably paying more for any memory that fits the small space and power limits of such systems. (In a few cases there are special memory packages for these machines, such as memory cards shaped like credit cards. There is no standard for these yet, so you'll have to look to the manual or call the technical support experts.)

Expansion Chassis—If you're fresh out of slots, on many desktop PCs and on some portable and laptop PCs, you can sometimes add an external expansion chassis—basically a house for expansion cards. This chassis will provide the slots for plugging in the boards and the power to run them, as well as the connections to the computer's signals. Sources for such chassis include Burr-Brown and Perx. (See address list in the back of the book.)

IBM sells additional memory for the PS/1, but most other memory companies don't. CMS Enhancements does, a 512K and a 2MB module. These plug into the memory socket on the PS/1 system board. IBM sells a 512K module. To add more through IBM you need to buy the expansion chassis and a memory card to go in it.

Chips, Modules, or Boards?

Once you know where you're going to add the memory, you can answer the question: what shape should it come in? Memory chips all look pretty much the same when they're first manufactured, but the last stage in production encases these chips in a variety of different packages, different sizes, materials, and connections to the outside world.

Look at the sockets on the motherboard, high-speed memory board, expanded memory board, or extended memory board, and get memory that will fit into it.

(Or, if you're adding a board that already has memory on it, you don't need to worry about shape and packaging.)

The fundamental package types are:

DIP   Dual Inline Package, as shown in Figure 5-4. DIPs plug into a socket like that of Figure 5-5.

SIP   Single Inline Package, as shown also in Figure 5-4. SIPs plug into a socket with only a single row of holes.

SIMM Single-Inline Memory Module, as in Figure 5-6, which snaps into a special holder such as those on the boards shown in Figure 5-10.

Figure 5-4. DIP and SIP Memory Chips (courtesy Micron Technology)

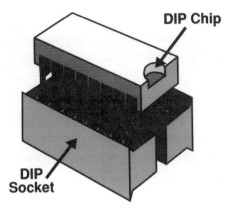

Figure 5-5. DIP Socket

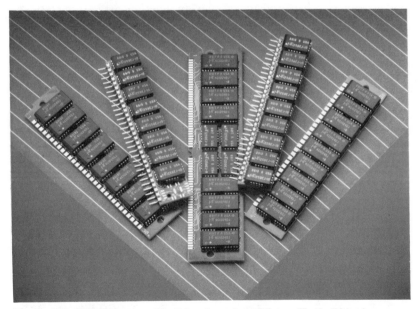

Figure 5-6. SIMM Memory Modules (courtesy Micron Technology)

165

Some DIPs are soldered to the circuit board, so you cannot remove them. Others are pressed into sockets. Most SIMMs, however, are in sockets.

SIMM modules are a newer packaging for the same basic electronics, putting the chips as sets of 8 or 9 onto tiny circuit boards that have electrical connections only on one side. SIMMs are easier to insert and remove without damaging the chips or the computer, and they allow your computer to hold more memory chips in a smaller space—because they stand up vertically. SIMMs are also more reliable because they don't have pins that can bend or break and they tend to stay cooler, (chips can sometimes get quite warm while working).

Not all SIMMs are the same size and construction. If you can, choose a board that uses generic SIMMs, a style that fits into many motherboards and expansion boards. Because these SIMMs are sold in high volume and fit into many different computers, they are the least expensive.

ZIPs (Zig-Zag Inline Package), SIPPs (Single In-line Pin Packages), and others aren't too common, but do appear in some PCs. Understand how to handle DIPs and SIMMs and you'll know how to handle these others by analogy. SIPPs, for example, are a lot like SIMMs. But instead of flat edge connectors they have pins coming out of one long edge of the tiny circuit board.

What Size or Capacity?

Once you know the packaging you need, you need to know the capacity. Do you need 256Kbit or 1Mbit chips? Do you need 1MByte SIMMs? You can try and read the capacity of the chips or modules already in your computer, and put in more of the same, or you can read the manual or ask technical support for the answer.

Many PCs don't let you mix different capacity chips or modules in the same area. Some don't mind. In general you'll avoid trouble if you use the same capacity chips or modules. You might even want to stick to the same manufacturer within a single board or bank, because there are small differences between chips from different companies, even though they're rated the same.

As to numbers? Because DIPS come as individual chips, they are typically measured as a certain number of megabits each. You need 8 or 9 1Mbit DIP chips, 9 if your PC has parity, to make up a megabyte; 8 or 9 4Mbit chips to make up 4 megabytes of memory. You'll know from the arrangement of the sockets, and from looking to your manual. Don't put in only some of the chips of a bank, fill an entire group of sockets at once. A partially-filled bank won't work at all.

Because SIMMs come as a set of chips on the tiny board, they are typically measured in megabytes. You need only a single 1M SIMM strip to make up one megabyte of memory; one 4M SIMM to make up four megabytes of memory. You can probably get SIMMs one at a time.

What Speed?

Once you know if you need DIP or SIMM, 256K, 1M or 4M, you need to know what speed of chips to buy. Just as different cars have different top speeds, RAM chips come in different speeds—measured as the time it takes them to give information to a requesting computer processor. These measurements are in nano-seconds, billionths of a second.

If you buy chips that are too fast for your PC, you'll be wasting money, because the chips will cost more but will only work as fast as the rest of the PC system lets them. If you buy chips that are too slow for your PC, you'll run into memory errors and all sorts of problems. You want memory chips that are just the right speed, or a touch faster than necessary, if you're the conservative type who is willing to spend a few extra dollars to avoid trouble.

The simplest ways to determine the speed you need are to:

• Read the manual to find the specifications for the PC

• Call and ask the technical support people for your PC

• Note the speed of the other chips already in the system (The last part of the number on the chip or module represents the speed. Typically the chip makers only use 2 digits for this work, though. For instance, an 80 ns chip will have an 80, while a 150ns chip will have a 15.

Don't mix chips of different speeds or from different manufacturers in the same bank of memory. The various companies don't make their chips to exactly the same electrical standards, and so the differences could confuse your system.

167

How Do You Install Without Damage?

Electronic parts can be delicate. You can easily break a pin or crack the case of a DIP or SIMM. But those are troubles you can see. The more insidious problem is damage from static electricity. Chips can be ruined or weakened by static, and you may never know this until you run into a problem trying to boot your machine. Even a charge so small you didn't know it was in your fingers can immediately stop a chip from working or cause it to fail soon.

The single most important thing you should do when handling memory, from the time you buy it to the time you plug it in, is to avoid static.

To avoid building static:

- Don't wear materials such as polyester

- Don't wear rubber-soled shoes on wool carpets

- Don't shuffle across the floor

- Don't work on your PC's hardware when the air is too dry

- Ideally, wear a specially designed "grounding strap"

To discharge static that you've already built up, touch something grounded such as an unpainted metal part of the PC's chassis. As a precautionary measure, always do this whether you think you're charged or not .

Touch it again now and then as you work on the memory. An unpainted metal part of the PC's chassis, will do, while the PC is still plugged in, and the case is still closed. (It's best if the power cord's ground line, the third prong, is plugged in—which it should be). The fan grill on the PC case will do. You may also touch a grounded part of your household, such as the plumbing. If you're really worried about it, you can buy a "grounding strap" for a few bucks from an electronics store, to keep yourself static free. You put one end on your wrist and connect the other to some grounded part of the house or work area.

Getting Started

- Unplug the PC

- Open the case

Touch the boards and cards only on their edges—don't touch the connectors that plug into the slots. Any oil from your hands can affect the electrical purity of the connection. You can clean any tarnish off the connectors by gently rubbing them with a pencil eraser.

Write down the settings of any jumpers and DIP switches on the board. If you change these, you may then discover later that you need to return them to the original settings.

Removing Boards and Chips

- Make sure all the present boards and chips are firmly in their sockets.

- If you need to remove a chip, to replace it with a working chip or a denser chip, use a chip removal tool or puller or a flat edge of a screwdriver to carefully pry it out.

- To remove a SIMM, pry away the latches that hold it at each end of the socket, then lean it forward a bit (toward the side with the chips on it) and pull it out.

- To remove any board, grasp it by the top edge and by the retaining bracket—the metal holder that faces the open back end of the PC.

Set any switches or jumpers so the PC will "recognize" and use the memory you've added. Your manual or instructions that come with the memory board will explain this further. The latest PCs, whether with AT buses or the newer Micro Channel or Extended Industry Standard Architecture buses, don't have the DIP switches and jumpers, but instead have software to handle configuration.

Plugging In Boards

• Ground yourself to get rid of static electricity.

• Plug any DIPS or SIMMs into the board while it is flat on a table.

• Next find a bus slot that it will fit in.

• Remove any covering bracket for the slot.

• Check to see that the board won't physically interfere with any other boards—sometimes boards are too thick to stay within their own space, and lap over into a neighboring slot's space.

• Hold the board by the top edge and by the retaining bracket.

• Place the board's connector over the socket, make sure it fits any guide holders on the ends (found in some PCs), and gently press the board into the slot, rocking it to make sure it is firmly down all the way; then screw in the retaining bracket.

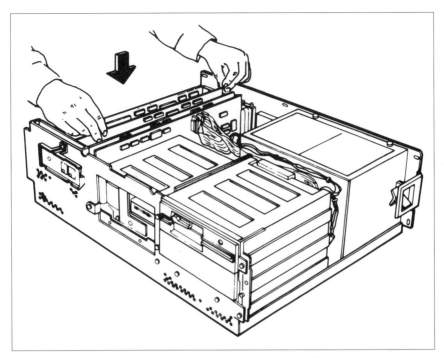

Figure 5-7a. Plugging a Board into a Slot (courtesy Intel)

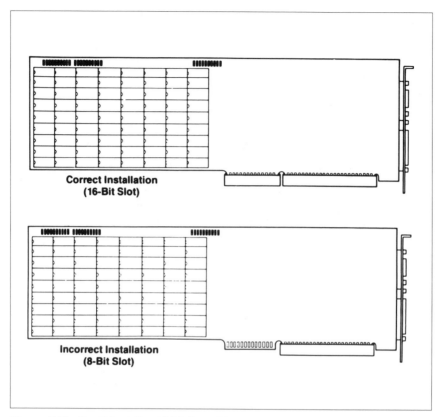

Figure 5-7b. Don't install a 16-bit board into an 8-bit slot (courtesy Intel)

Plugging in DIPs

• Ground yourself to get rid of static electricity.

• Locate the socket you're going to put the chip in.

• Pick the chip up by thumb and forefinger at its ends, or with a chip insertion tool (you can find these for a few bucks at electronics stores—or one may come free with your memory chips or board).

Check the pins. If they aren't straight and evenly spaced, they won't fit well into the socket. If one bends up underneath when you insert the chip, the memory won't work. You may need to place the chip sideways on a flat surface and carefully bend all of the pins on each side inward a bit, all at once, so they'll fit smoothly into the socket. A bit of a pigeon-toed look—with the pins leaning toward the center a bit—can help. You can use a needle-nose pliers or pin straightening tool to carefully fix bent pins. If you break a pin off, though, the chip will be useless.

Find the pin 1 end of the chip—which has a notch or dot, and align it with the pin-1 end of the socket—which also has a notch or dot (they don't need to have the same mark).

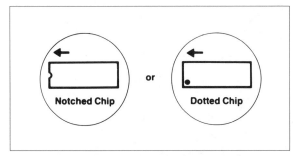

Figure 5-8. Pin-1 Mark Example (courtesy Intel)

- Press the chip down part of the way.

- Check the pins for bending or breaking. Each pin should fit neatly into its hole.

- When you're inserting the chip, make sure you press it all the way down.

Plugging in SIMMs

- Ground yourself, to get rid of static electricity.

- Locate the socket.

- Hold the SIMM by the short ends, without touching the connector edge.

- Orient the notched end of the SIMM toward the notched end of the socket.

(It will only fit in one way, as long as you have the metallic edge "fingers" pointed down toward the board.)

• Point the connector edge of the SIMM into the socket (some SIMMs fit in at 45 degrees, some at 90 degrees—pointing straight out from the main board).

• Gently push the SIMM down into the socket.

Then push the SIMM backward in the socket, away from the side with the memory chips, until it snaps into place. The tabs on the ends of the socket will appear in their holes.

Finishing Up

• Ground yourself to get rid of static electricity

• Check your work

• Close the case

• Plug the PC in

• Turn it on and see what happens

• Run any necessary configuration software

Possible Troubles and Fixes

If your PC won't start at all, open it up again and look for any bent pins or incompletely inserted chips or loose boards.

If there are serious problems, such as a bent pin on a DIP chip, you may not need such a program, because the PC's own diagnostics will give you an error message such as: **201 error 0402** which informs you which chip is bad. (Each type of PC, XT, AT, or compatible is different in this error message, so you need to look in your manual or call technical support to decipher this code.) Chips can also be hurt by cosmic radiation or low power. Some systems, such as micro Channel PS/2s, lock out the bad memory area and run without it.

Sometimes boards that you've plugged in won't work immediately. First try these steps—if you are unsuccessful, then call technical support for help:

Remove TSRs from memory, pulling their installations from your batch, AUTOEXEC.BAT, and CONFIG.SYS files. A particular TSR may be interfering with some part of memory that the board's own device drivers need. If removing them all works, you can add them one at a time to see which one was the cause of the problem.

Check the interrupt, I/O address, and ROM address of the board you're plugging in. These are the addresses that a board needs in memory, and should appear in the manual. If not, you can get them by using one of the analysis programs mentioned in Step 2 or by calling technical support. Then compare these addresses to those your other boards and your TSRs are using. Two of them may want the same address or interrupt—and that's why the new board won't work properly. Most boards then offer you a switch, jumper, or software setting to change from the default interrupt and addresses to some others that won't conflict. If not, you'll have to decide if this board is really worth the trouble, and if it is to search out the interrupt and address changes for one of your other boards or TSRs. Be sure to write all interrupts, addresses, and other configuration settings down before you change anything. as you may want to change these settings back to their original settings. Sometimes you just can't resolve all the conflicts between boards, in which case, look for a different board.

Sources of Chips, Modules, and Boards

New DIPs, SIMMs, expanded memory boards, extended memory boards, and 32-bit memory boards appear all the time. Their prices, options and features change frequently.

Here are some of the most popular boards, and some sources for boards, chips, and modules. Although different PC models and compatibles use different chips, modules, and boards there is some standardization—

• Generic SIMMs fit many expanded and extended boards

• Standard DIPs fit many expanded and extended boards

• ISA and EISA expanded and extended memory boards fit most AT compatibles

• ISA expanded memory boards will fit most any PC compatible

However there are also plenty of exceptions. Compaq computers, for example, call for different memories than most other computers do. So you need to make sure you get a board, module, or chip that is right for your system.

A great source of chips and boards can be found in the advertisements in the back section of computer magazines. The lowest prices come from mail-order, but if you need help installing memory, you might want to pay the somewhat higher prices at local computer shops.

Chips and Modules

Compuadd
Intel
JDR Microdevices
Micron Technology Inc.
SCI Semiconductor Express International

What To Ask for In Chips

• Make sure you get the right speed, capacity, and package.

• Match the chips in your system. If you can read the label on those chips to the person you're going to buy from, they can do the matching for you.

• Be reluctant to buy used chips. They may be dead or injured from static electricity damage, even if they look okay on the outside.

• Be reluctant to buy used chips. They may be dead or injured from static electricity damage, even if they look okay on the outside.

Boards

Acculogic
Amkly Systems
Boca Research
Everex Systems
IBM
Micron Technology
Nevada Computer
Orchid Technology
STB Systems
Tenex Computer Express

Above Board Plus. Intel's AboveBoard, as shown in Figure 5-3, does support EMS 4.0 expanded memory, but it does not have any alternate mapping registers. And while the Above Board can hold as much as 14MB, with a piggyback board attached, it does not use SIMMs, but DIPs. It comes with a 5-year warranty and plenty of software, including configuration programs.

RAMpage Plus. AST's boards, shown in Figure 5-9 a and b, support 32 alternate mapping registers for EMS 4.0 expanded memory. They also support back-filling and other expanded memory options, and come with lots of software. Configuration and installation is through software, too.

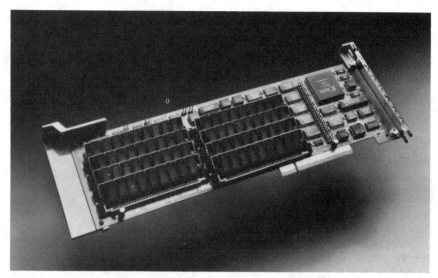

Figure 5-9a. AST's RAMpage Plus Board for the Micro Channel Bus (courtesy AST)

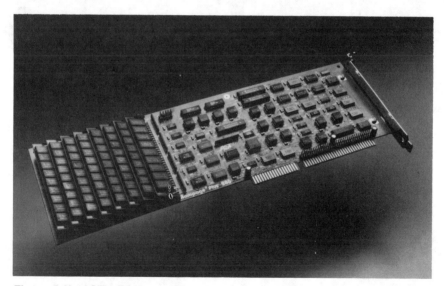

Figure 5-9b. AST's RAMpage Plus Board for the ISA Bus (courtesy AST)

Memoryzation. Newer Technology's board can hold up to 16MB as 82MB SIMMs. It works in IBM PS/2 Models 70, P70, and 80 with the MCA bus.

Figure 5-10. Newer Technology's Memoryzation for the Micro Channel Bus (courtesy Newer Technology)

Rapidmeg. STB System's board can hold 8MB tops, from 1MB SIMMs. It supports EMS 4.0, though part of that support is through software. It can handle some back-filling and has software configuration.

Elite 16 Plus HyperCache. This board from Profit Systems supports EMS 4.0 for expanded memory and is unique because it has its own SRAM cache for faster performance. The cache is either 16K or 32K bytes, which lets you use slower and cheaper DRAMs on the rest of the board. The result is 120ns DRAMs giving 80ns performance. The Elite board can hold as much as 16MB of memory in SIMMs, though that full amount would occupy one and a half slots. It also offers optional serial and parallel ports. It only has a single alternate mapping register set.

What To Ask for In Boards

• Is it extended or expanded?

• If expanded, does it support LIM EMS 4.0? (And does it offer multiple register sets, DMA, backfilling, and other niceties as mentioned in the expanded memory section later in this Step?)

• What sort of PC and slot does it plug into?

• Does it take up more than one slot?

• How much memory can it hold?

• Is there an option of a daughterboard that will piggyback on to it to hold even more memory?

• Is it restricted in speeds?

• Is installation simple, and automatic with software instead of switches for configuration?

• Can you buy it empty (and buy additional chips cheaper someplace else?)

• Does it have optional I/O ports?

• Does it use generic SIMMs? (These are the least expensive and easiest to install)

• Does it come with software (for installation, diagnostics, print spooling, disk caching, RAM disk creation, Expanded Memory Management, LIMulation, and memory analysis?)

• How long is the warranty good for?

Accelerators, BIOS Upgrades, and Motherboards

You may want to do more than plug in memory chips or boards. You may also want to change a PC's hardware memory management abilities, without having to look into an expanded memory board. You can do this by changing the BIOS chip or by putting a 386SX, 386, or 486 processor into your PC as an accelerator board or a new motherboard.

Throughout this book you'll see evidence that the 386SX, 386, and 486 processor chips not only run much faster than previous PC microprocessors, they offer far greater memory management features. For example, these processors can create expanded memory without an expanded memory board.

BIOS Upgrades

In some PCs and compatibles you have the option of buying a new BIOS on a ROM chip to replace the one you have. The newer BIOS may have better support for the latest in memory management. Instructions on the replacement come with the chip. Award Software is one company which sells BIOS upgrades.

386SX Processor Replacements

One way to get into the 386 generation is to use a 386SX mini-board to replace a 286 processor. Because the 386SX chip can function in most ways as a 286 chip, it can replace a 286 in an AT or compatible. However, it is not exactly the same shape. So several companies have made miniature circuit boards with 386SXs on them, that plug into the socket where the 286 was. To change one of these boards remove the 286, plug in the 386SX mini-board (this doesn't require an expansion slot). Because the 386SX has all the memory management powers of the 386 chip, this sort of upgrade increases the memory management of your AT, and can speed it up a bit— though not much because the rest of the system remains the same. Companies such as Cumulus and SOTA Technology offer these 386SX mini boards. SOTA Technology boards are shown in Figures 5-11a and b. 5-11a shows a 386 accelerator for PCs and XTs. 5-11b is for ATs and 286-based PS/2s.

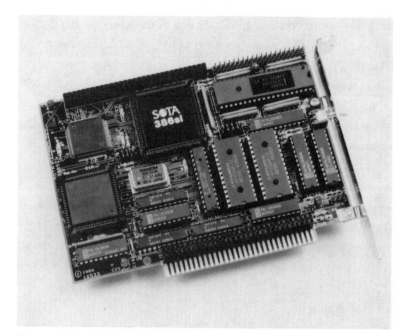

Figure 5-11a. SOTA 386si Accelerator for PC's and XT's (courtesy SOTA)

Figure 5-11b. SOTA Express/386 Accelerator for AT's and PS/2's (courtesy SOTA)

Accelerator Boards

This is a circuit board with its own faster processor. It plugs into one of the expansion slots in your PC, and then takes over processing from the original microprocessor chip. People with 8088-based systems generally buy 286 turbo boards, whereas people with 286-based ATs buy 386SX and 386-based turbo boards. Sometimes installation requires unplugging the original processor—these are re-placement processor boards. Other times the processor is left in to handle simple tasks such as controlling input and output of information to the disk drive and the display monitor. These are called coprocessor boards.

Coprocessor boards are the easier ones to install, as you just plug it into a slot. And because you retain your original processor, you can revert to using it if for some reason the new board is incompatible with one or more of your programs. But because the coprocessor board must work through the slot it is in and the bus to reach memory, it will be slower than a processor that is on the same board as the memory. For example, the standard AT bus runs at 8MHz—which would slow any 10, 12, 16MHz or faster processor. (Some coprocessors come with their own memory on board, thereby alleviating this problem). Another element of delay in coprocessor systems is that most buses (MCA and EISA excepted) don't understand that a processor in an expansion slot might "want to communicate" with boards in slots. Therefore, the coprocessor must first set signals on the main processor board before it can directly deal with any other expansion board in the computer. Coprocessor boards can be expensive too, because they are essentially complete computers on a board. Processor accelerator boards are a bit tougher to install than coprocessors because you not only plug them into a slot, but unplug your original processor and plug a special extension cable from the accelerator board into that now empty socket. This means direct control of the computer, direct communication with other slots (through the cable and the original processor socket), and direct communication with memory on the motherboard. Such a board with a RAM cache will run even faster.

Gems Computers, Arlington Computer Products, AOX, Quadram, Orchid, MicroWay, and others offer accelerator boards. Intel makes the Inboard 386/PC, to turn any PC into a 386 machine, or a product called Inboard 386/AT to make any 256 machine into a 386 machine. Intel says it will run about 85% of speed of new 386-

based systems. Inboard 386/PC comes with 2MB of memory and has slots for as much as 4MB more.

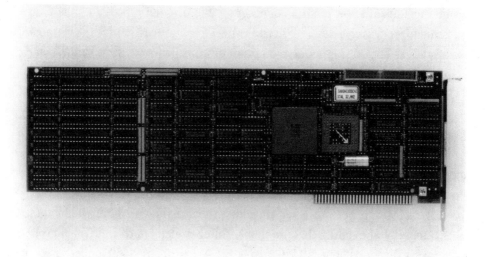

Figure 5-12. Intel's Inboard 386/PC (courtesy Intel)

Replacing the Motherboard

This means pulling the original main board out of your computer, and replacing it with a new circuit board with a faster processor and other parts. It lets you retain your power supply, disk drives, chassis, and other large elements of the PC, and lets you plug your expansion boards back in and continue to use them. This installation is a major undertaking, but it is not too complicated. At least you don't have to deal with individual chips. And moving to a new motherboard can give you not only a 386-generation processor but high-speed 32-bit memory to go with it. And if your system only had 8-bit slots, a new motherboard could get you 16-bit and 32-bit slots, for faster I/O performance too. Figure 5-13 shows a typical motherboard replacement.

Figure 5-13. Motherboard Replacement Example (courtesy Hauppage)

Motherboard replacements can be relatively inexpensive. You must find a motherboard replacement that fits your chassis (the box that surrounds your PC parts—they're not all the same size.) The PC and the XT, for example, have motherboards that are just about the same size, but the slots aren't spaced the same, so your cards from one may not fit into the other—and the new motherboard may not fit the holes in the back of the chassis.

If it is tough finding a motherboard that fits, you might want to buy a new chassis, and even a larger power supply, for that new board. But by that point you may be spending more than it would cost just to buy a new computer.

What To Ask About Motherboards.

• Make sure your intended new motherboard has been tested for network and OS/2 compatibility, even if you're not interested yet in using either. OS/2 is

185

touchier about hardware than DOS is.

• Ask which BIOS it uses. Phoenix, AMI, and Award are the best known and tested.

• Make sure it has enough expansion slots and ports for what you do.

How to Replace the Motherboard.

• Ground yourself to get rid of static electricity.

• Open the PC case.

• Make a map of the layout of cables inside the PC and mark them with tape (the same color or label for the plug and the right connector for each). Include the orientation of the cable where it meets the plug—there's a "pin 1" setting here, as with chips.

• Unplug the cables. Leave the cables connecting the disk drives to the disk controller boards if you can.

• You don't have to remove the disk drives or power supply in many systems.

• Remove the mounting screws or flared plastic holders (squeeze these together with pliers) that hold the motherboard down. Most PCs have two of these screws, some as many as nine. Install memory chips on the new motherboard, using any memory from the old motherboard if appropriate (right size, speed, and so on).

• Place the new motherboard in the case and attach it with whatever screws, standoffs, and other hardware necessary.

• Replace the add-in boards.

• Reconnect the cables.

• Close the case.

Sources of Motherboards. Hauppage is one of the best-known sources for replacement motherboards. Others are American Computer Systems and JDR Microdevices.

Special Accelerator Upgrades

A few systems put their original processors on an add-in board that you can slip out and replace. This can make it easy to upgrade in one way—putting the new board in will be easy. But it makes it less easy in another—the system will certainly be proprietary, and therefore more expensive than a generic motherboard would be. AST and Advanced Logic Research make some PCs along these lines.

Adding Power Backup for your Memory

The other item to plug in to your PC to improve its memory hardware is a backup power supply. When RAM loses its power, from a blackout or a tripped-over power cord; all the information stored in it vanishes. A UPS (Uninterruptible Power Supply) can avoid this sort of problem by, providing enough power to at least save information to disk, if not to just keep computing off stored battery power. Network server computers that cater to dozens of individual PC workstations should absolutely have a UPS. You can get UPS listings from most computer magazines or computer stores. Dakota Microsystems is one supplier of UPS systems.

CMOS Batteries

Another power supply your PC needs is the battery in AT and compatibles that keeps the information in CMOS RAM. This RAM holds the system configuration information, such as how your memory is set up. If the little CMOS RAM battery dies, the information expires, and you'll have to reconfigure your memory and disk.

The typical CMOS RAM battery should last about 10 years, but many don't make it for even a fraction of that. Rupp makes a replacement battery. Accumation makes a battery that plugs into your PC's power supply so that it always stays fully charged.

Configuring Memory

As explained in Step 1, there are several types of memory. Not all programs can use all types of memory; nor do all types of memory perform at the same speed. The type of a chip depends on the memory chip's address, both its original, physical address and any logical change of address it gets when remapped by a special software or hardware driver. In other words, the chips are always the same, but their position in your computer's hardware and software scheme can change, and that is what determines their type.

Conventional memory is generally considered to refer to the chips with addresses up to the 640K mark. This is the memory that DOS and all programs can use. High-DOS or reserved memory refers to the chips that can be at addresses from 640K to 1024K. That's 384K of memory addresses that are used for system ROM chips and video information, and sometimes for relocated TSR utilities and drivers.

Extended memory refers to the chips from the 1024K or 1M address to the 16M address. DOS cannot directly use chips at these addresses, though some other operating systems can. Extended memory can be converted to expanded memory, used for some utilities such as RAM disks, or reached through the use of a DOS extender.

HMA or High Memory Area memory is the 64K of chips just above the 1024K or 1MB address mark. Technically it is a part of extended memory, but some programs that can't reach the rest of extended memory can use the HMA memory.

Expanded Memory is as much as 32MB of chips outside the standard address space, that can be reached through the right expanded memory manager software and hardware.

The tools mentioned in Step 2 can tell you how much of each kind of memory you have. The results aren't set in concrete though. For example, you might have an expanded memory board—as explained below—that could reconfigure its chips to be expanded or extended, to your wishes.

Conventional Memory

Conventional memory is the most important type of PC memory—because DOS and every program uses it. It is also the type with the most profound limit: 640K, as shown in Figure 5-14. Although there are some tricks to add a bit to the 640K from high-DOS memory, they don't work with all programs or all of the time. In general, if you use a PC, you must concern yourself with the 640K limit.

As Figure 5-14 shows, you don't even get to use all of that 640K for your application programs. As much as 100K to 200K of it can be tied up with DOS information, TSR utilities, and device drivers.

DOS Interrupt Vectors, BIOS data, and DOS Data take up only about 700bytes (that's 700, not 700K). These are tables that keep track of where DOS can find things in memory and how the PC is configured.

IBMDOS.COM and IBMBIO.COM take up a few K more. (These are the names for PC-DOS. MS-DOS names are similar.) These are files DOS needs in memory to handle basic input and output functions.

Then come the BUFFERS, the tiny disk caching areas explained in Step 3 and Step 7. This may be as little as 0K or as much as 20K or more, depending on the number of BUFFERS you specify. See those steps for an explanation.

Next are any Device Drivers, such as the software that controls your mouse, your CD-ROM drive, and so on. These drivers stay in memory, adding abilities to DOS (which by itself could not understand your mouse or CD-ROM drive).

Then in memory you'll find the COMMAND.COM file of DOS. This file interprets the signals that come from your keyboard to the processor, and dictates what to put on the screen so you'll see the familiar C:\ prompt. COMMAND.COM has several parts. One is resident—it always stays in memory. The other is transient—it can be dumped from memory to make room for an application. When you quite that application, the transient part is copied back into memory from the disk drive. (If you use a RAM disk for this, as explained in Step 7, you can speed the copying process.)

Finally, some memory is occupied by TSR utilities. These are explained in Step 1. They stay in memory until you unload them.

What's left is ready for your applications. Certainly you'll want as much as you can get for these, so you should use the tips in Step 3 to minimize the amount DOS and your programs use, and the tips in Step 4 to push as many utilities and drivers out of the 640K as possible.

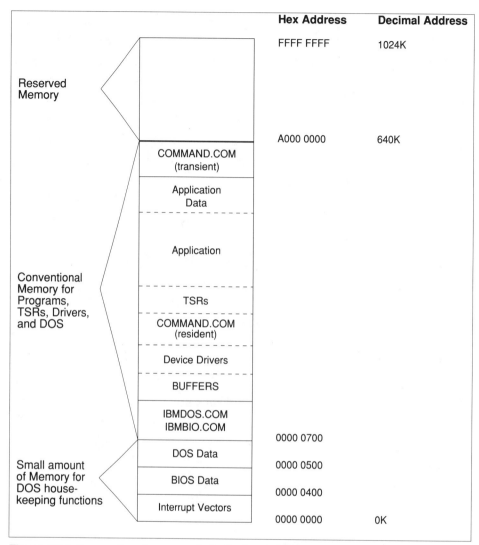

	Hex Address	Decimal Address
	FFFF FFFF	1024K
	A000 0000	640K
	0000 0700	
	0000 0500	
	0000 0400	
	0000 0000	0K

Reserved Memory

COMMAND.COM (transient)

Application Data

Application

Conventional Memory for Programs, TSRs, Drivers, and DOS

TSRs

COMMAND.COM (resident)

Device Drivers

BUFFERS

IBMDOS.COM IBMBIO.COM

DOS Data

Small amount of Memory for DOS housekeeping functions

BIOS Data

Interrupt Vectors

Figure 5-14. Conventional memory is limited to 640K under normal conditions.

But you should also make sure that your PC has a full 640K of memory chips to fill those conventional addresses. Every PC, whether for use in the most complex business or just to play games at home, deserves 640K of memory these days. Fill your 640K sockets first, check your inventory to make sure you have 640K, use additional memory to fill in any gap from 384K or 512K to 640K.

High-DOS Memory

The 384K of high-DOS memory can be reached by DOS, but can't be used for application programs under normal circumstances. It is reserved for special system functions, such as providing the addresses for the ROM memory chips that hold the Basic Input Output System programs (BIOS) and for holding the information that will be displayed on the video screen.

However, there are some utility programs that can borrow memory unused by the video, and add that to conventional memory—for some programs. This scheme could give those programs as much as 700K or even 800K of conventional memory, minus whatever is occupied by DOS and other utilities. High-DOS memory also has unused areas that can—with the help of the appropriate utility—be filled with TSR (memory-resident) utility programs, device driver programs, and network interface programs from conventional memory.

To use memory at the high-DOS addresses, as borrowed conventional memory or as a relocation area, you need both the appropriate utility software and chips at those high-DOS addresses. There are two ways to get RAM chips at those addresses.

One way is to buy a PC with, or fill your PC to, a full 1024K or 1MB of RAM memory. The first 640K will be the conventional memory. The remaining 384K will be available at the high-DOS addresses, with the help of the utility.

The second way is to have a PC with memory chips at addresses above 1024K, along with memory-management hardware and software (such as a 386 or 486 processor or a LIM 4.0 expanded memory board). This hardware and software can remap some of that memory to appear as if it is at the addresses from 640K to 1024K. The hardware to do this is mentioned earlier in this Step. The software is mentioned in Step 4 and in the following sections of this Step.

Conventional memory should be the first section of your memory to fill. Some programs demand expanded or extended memory, and that may put a priority on those, but in general high-DOS memory should be second because it is so vital to having the maximum conventional memory—through relocating TSRs and drivers to high-DOS.

Extended Memory

These are the chips at addresses from 1024K or 1MB to 16MB.

Extended memory cannot be added to 8088 and 8086-based PCs, such as the PC or XT or compatibles. The processor in those machines won't work with more than 1MB—so there's a hardware limit.

However, extended memory is easily added to 286-, 386-, and 486-based PCs, such as the AT and compatibles and PS/2s and compatibles. The processor in those machines will work with at least 16MB of memory (the 386 and 486 will work with much more), and IBM led the way in putting extended memory routines into its AT BIOS. There is no hardware limit, therefore, and all you must do is buy simple memory boards and plug them in. (You must also make sure that your conventional memory is full first: some PCs won't recognize extended memory unless they have a full complement of conventional installed.) Some PCs in this category even have enough sockets on the motherboard to hold 2MB or 4MB of memory—and anything beyond the first MB will be extended memory.

Unfortunately, DOS cannot directly use chips at these addresses, even if the processor and hardware can. Even so, extended memory can be quite useful, if managed by a:

- Different operating system than DOS

- DOS Extender

- RAM disk or Disk cache

- Task-switching, program swapping, or virtual memory program

- Expanded memory emulator

The standard for programs to follow in using extended memory is called XMS 2.0 (eXtended Memory Specification).

Different Operating Systems. Some operating systems treat 16MB of memory as conventional; providing much more room than DOS. Step 9 lists some examples. The disadvantage to this approach is that you lose some or all of your ability to run

DOS application programs.

DOS Extenders. DOS extenders are special programmer's tools that give a program the ability to use extended memory. On 386 computers they also give programmers access to 32-bit instructions that can speed applications. Some of the best known DOS extenders come from Phar Lap, Rational Systems Inc. and Eclipse Computer Solutions (formerly A.I.Architects). They are added to an application program while it is being written—so you don't have to know or do anything about it. The application then automatically can reach extended memory. DOS extenders do this by pushing the 286, 386, or 486 processor into protected mode where it can reach 16MB. Because the 286 chip can't easily switch from protected back to real mode—a flaw in the chip's design that's roundly criticized by computer makers— most DOS Extenders don't support the 286 chip. They stick instead to the 386, 386SX, and 486 chips, which smoothly and easily switch from real mode to protected mode and back again, and are also able to switch to the Virtual-86 or V86 mode.

However, to move to protected mode, the computer must leave DOS behind— it's a real mode operating system, after all. What the typical DOS extender does is to monitor PC activities, and move the processor alternately to real mode or DOS as necessary to carry out DOS functions, as shown in Figure 5-15.

Let me emphasize: *don't go out looking for a DOS Extender to help your PC get at more memory.* That's not how they work.

If you're a programmer you can look for a DOS Extender to use along with your programming language. You then build that Extender code into your new program so that your program can reach more memory.

But, as a user, you can only use a DOS Extender by looking for programs that have one built in. Look at the back of the program's box (if you're in the computer store) or read the reviews and descriptions in computer magazines. If the spreadsheet, CAD package, database, or other application you're curious about contains a DOS Extender, you'll know that application can use Extended memory. Check to see if it's a 286 DOS Extender (which naturally requires a 286-based PC) or a 386 DOS Extender (which will only run on a 386-, 386SX-, or 486-based PC).

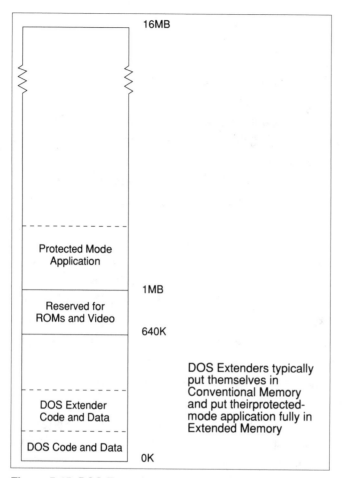

Figure 5-15. DOS Extender Diagram

Many famous programs now use DOS extenders, including Paradox 386, AutoCAD 386 and Release 11, 1-2-3 Release 3.1, and so on.

When you use a program with a DOS extender, you need to realize that:

It won't run on a PC, XT, or compatible—it needs a 286, 386, or 486 processor. (Those called "16-Bit DOS extenders" will run on 286, 386, and 486-based PCs. Those called "32-Bit DOS extenders," and sometimes just referred to as "DOS extenders" because they were the first kind available, run on 386 and 486-based PCs, not on 286s.)

DOS extenders may have trouble on a PC with shadow RAM turned on, because that RAM will interrupt the smooth set of extended memory addresses that the extender needs. Turn shadow RAM off in the PC's configuration screen to avoid such troubles.

It may conflict with other DOS extender programs or with programs that don't understand extended memory and the protected mode. To avoid these troubles, several companies have created specifications and standards for the use of DOS extenders and extended memory (particularly on 386- and 486-based PCs that might be using the V86 processor mode for multitasking). Microsoft and IBM, two of the largest influences in PC computing didn't sign on to the VCPI idea. Microsoft later came up with DPMI (DOS Protected Mode interface) which Phar Lap and most of the VCPI supporters then decided to support.

In the end, all you need to know about DOS extenders is this; if built into a program by a programmer, a DOS extender will enable that program to reach extended memory on a 286, 386, or 486-based PC. If all of your programs, those with DOS extenders and those without, follow either VCPI or DPMI they shouldn't conflict. (Or at least they are less likely to conflict. This is a fairly new part of software technology.) Otherwise it's best to stick to using one program at a time otherwise, the conflicting programs, vying for memory, might crash your PC.

RAM Disk or Disk Cache. Some disk cache and RAM disk programs—such as the VDISK utility that comes with recent versions of DOS—can immediately use extended memory.

Task-switching, Program Swapping, or Virtual Memory Programs. Some task-switching programs that swap utilities and applications in and out of conventional memory can use extended memory. When they do, they are essentially treating it as a disk, so the normal DOS rules don't apply—and the utilities and applications don't actually run in extended memory.

Expanded Memory Emulators. There are utility programs that can make extended memory behave like expanded memory. Particularly on 386 and 486-based PCs, the simplest and cheapest way to add to memory is to install it as extended, then have a utility convert some or all of it to expanded memory when needed.

Backfilling Conventional Memory. Some computers don't have a full 640K of conventional memory, and yet have some extended memory. There are utility programs, with the help of memory management hardware such as that built into a 386 or 486 chip or on an expanded memory board, that can back-fill this conventional memory to a full 640K by remapping the addresses of some of this extended memory.

Tips on Extended Memory. You should configure for extended memory:

• If you know your alternative operating system will use it.

• If your application asks for it (including Windows 3, which has a DOS extender built in).

• If you can use it as a RAM disk.

• If you have a 386 or 486, then get an expanded memory emulator (also known as a LIMulator) to convert part of it to expanded memory when necessary. Extended memory can be faster than expanded memory and doesn't require another driver program, as expanded does, which eats up part of your conventional memory.

HMA memory. These are the chips at the 64K of memory addresses just above the 1024K address. HMA is part of extended memory, and can be used as extended. But the HMA (High Memory Area) is different from the rest of extended memory because of a bug in the design of the 286 and 386 processors. These processors normally give programs the memory they need to work with in chunks of 64K—called a segment. It can place the beginning of any such segment at any address that's a multiple of 16 in the first 1024K of memory addresses. If that beginning point is less than 64K below the 1024K mark, the segment is supposed to wrap around to continue at the 0K address.

However, the bug or unintentional feature meant that by turning off a particular address signal, the processor could be told not to wrap around to 0K, instead it would just continue the segment beyond 1024K. If the segment starts at 1024K minus 16 bytes, the last possible starting point, it would continue to 1088K minus 16 bytes, adding almost 64K more to DOS memory.

Because this HMA area was not thought of when the high-DOS memory from 640K to 1024K was reserved for system functions, it is free to use. It is not contiguous with the lower 640K of DOS memory, so it cannot be used by all programs automatically, but it is available for holding TSRs, device drivers, network shells, and even parts of application programs. Unfortunately, it can only be used by one program at a time, whether that one program uses all 64K or just a few bytes.

All you need to use HMA is an HMA driver and memory chips at the HMA addresses—you don't need any special memory mapping hardware. The best known is Microsoft's HIMEM.SYS driver, which comes with Windows and a number of other programs. Quarterdecks' DESQview comes with its own QEXT.SYS driver to use the HMA memory.

HIMEM.SYS, for example, is a CONFIG.SYS device driver itself, that you install this way: Put a line in CONFIG.SYS that starts **device = himem.sys** and have the HIMEM.SYS file in a directory where DOS can find it (either in the root directory or with a PATH in some other directory). Then add the HIMEM.SYS parameters to that line as needed.

The parameters are: **/hmamin = n** which specifies the minimum amount of memory (in K) that a program can request from HMA. The default is 0, and the choice is anything from 0 to 63K. This is necessary because of the handicap that only one program can use HMA at a time. You wouldn't want a program that needed only a few bytes to grab the HMA, and thereby exclude another program from using 16K, 32K, or more of the HMA. That just wouldn't be very efficient. So by setting a minimum amount of HMA a program needs before getting it at all, you improve the efficiency of your memory use .

The parameter, **/numhandles = n** specifies the maximum number of extended memory block handles that may be allocated at any time. The default is 32, the choice is from 0 to 128.

The Windows version of HIMEM.SYS has two more switches, they are: **/shadow:on or off** which tells HIMEM.SYS to enable or disable RAM shadowing. Disabling it frees more RAM. (This doesn't work on all systems—particularly those that can't turn off shadowing through software.)

197

The parameter: /**machine** tells himem.sys the type of machine it is running on. The standard to follow for HMA use is the XMS (eXtended Memory Specification) which tells programs how to keep from bumping heads over extended memory in general and the HMA memory in particular. XMS 2.0 is the latest form. If you run a program that uses HMA or extended memory and that program is written to the XMS rules, any other program that wants to use extended memory and HMA must also support XMS.

Configure memory as HMA when you have a driver such as HIMEM.SYS or QEXT.SYS that can reach it and you have programs that will use it.

Expanded Memory

These are memory chips that don't have any standard addresses—not in the 640K, the next 384K, the next 15MB, or anywhere beyond that. Instead, chips configured as expanded memory are separate, outside the normal memory address range, and a computer trick puts them where DOS can find and use them. This trick is called "bank-switching" as explained in Step 1 and in the following sections.

EMS Specification. The standard for expanded memory today is called LIM EMS 4.0, for Lotus/Intel/Microsoft (three key companies in its invention) Expanded Memory Specification 4.0. The original specification was LIM EMS 3.0, followed quickly by 3.2, but the 3.2 version:

- Limited expanded memory to a maximum of 8MB

- Only permitted it to hold data—not programs

- Restricted the size and position of its page frame thereby limiting its speed and flexibility

After LIM EMS 3.2, a competing specification called EEMS (Enhanced Expanded Memory Specification) appeared, but its enhancements were noticed and copied in LIM EMS 4.0. You will still find some programs and memory boards that obey the LIM EMS 3.2 or EEMS rules instead of the LIM EMS 4.0 rules. You'll even find boards with 3.2 hardware and 4.0 utilities. These anachronisms will work with some programs, but they won't work as well as the more recent 4.0 stuff. If that's what you have, you should consider moving to 4.0. (The best way to do this is to get a 386 processor into your PC, by picking up a new 386 or 386SX PC or by adding a 386 accelerator to your PC. The 386 chip has LIM EMS 4.0 support built in.) Nowadays, the terms expanded memory and EMS generally refer just to LIM EMS 4.0.

How Expanded Memory Works. Expanded memory demands:

- Memory chips that are free to be configured

- Programs that are written to use expanded memory (either version 3.2 or 4.0)

- A software utility called an Expanded Memory Manager or EMM

- Hardware called a Memory Management Unit or MMU.

The MMU can come in four forms:

- An expanded memory board

- A special expanded memory chip (such as the ALL ChargeCard)

- A PS/2 with the Micro Channel Architecture bus (which has built-in MMU abilities)

- A chip set (such as the NEAT chips from Chips & Technologies) surrounding the processor, that have built-in EMS support

- A 386 or 486 processor (these have built-in MMU circuits)

The heart of the MMU is a set of registers for mapping. These hold physical or real addresses of chips and associated logical or temporary working addresses for memory chips.

It works this way. The EMM software sets aside a stretch of memory as the focal point for the expanded memory. This stretch is typically 64K of memory in the high-

DOS area. It is called a *page frame*. It is enough room for four 16K pages. The EMM also establishes contact with the expanded memory in your PC, which can range from only a few hundred K to as much as 32MB. Then the EMM waits for a program to "ask" for access to expanded memory. When that request comes, it will refer to a certain address on a certain page in expanded memory. The EMM will use the mapping registers of the MMU to give that certain page of the expanded memory the address of the page frame.

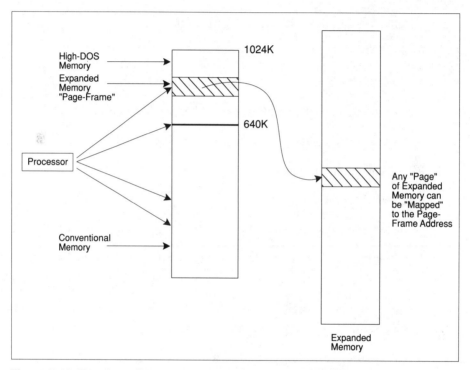

Figure 5-16. Mapping a Page of Expanded Memory to the Page Frame

Then the program will look for the information it needs on this page, or will store information to this page. If the next request involves some other page, the EMM will then assign the page frame addresses to that new page. The previous page that appeared in the page frame will be left undisturbed in expanded memory until needed again, its chips holding on to whatever information they acquired.

200

Try this analogy for understanding expanded memory. What if you wanted to send letters to homes in a town, but were prevented from using the street name. All you could do would be to put the house number on the envelope. Luckily you knew that every street in town used the same numbers on its homes. What you would need to be able to reach any of the homes on any of the streets would be an understanding with the mail delivery person. You would whisper to her what street you were aiming for, and off she would go, with an envelope that bore only a house number, but the knowledge of which street to take it to. You wouldn't be moving the people or the houses, just letting an intermediary carry the knowledge to map her delivery efforts to the proper street. The EMM software and the MMU hardware do just this for information that's being sent to, and retrieved from, expanded memory. They send it to a particular address in the page frame, but then depend on the EMM and MMU to keep track of which part of the expanded memory will appear in that page frame.

Page Frames. Notice that this scheme doesn't involve copying information from the expanded memory chips to chips at the high-DOS memory page frame address. It just involves temporarily changing the address of expanded memory chips so that they look like they're at the address of the page frame. This way, by switching addresses when necessary, DOS manages to work with a lot more memory, though with the disadvantage of having to work with it a bit indirectly. Expanded memory can hold as much as 32MB of information, but all of that information can only be manipulated through the 64K page frame by changing mapping register addresses.

Expanded memory boards that followed the original EMS spec, version 3.2, are called small-frame because they can only put the page frame in high-DOS memory—typically at D000 to E000.

There are two kinds of EMS 4.0 boards, with different page-frame abilities. The first can have a page frame larger than 64K and can put it anywhere in memory from 0K to 884K, but all of the parts of that page frame must be contiguous. The Intel AboveBoard Plus falls into this category. The most sophisticated EMS 4.0 board can have multiple page-frames of variable size, anywhere from 0K to 884K. (Both 3.2 and 4.0 reserve above 884K, DD00, for ROM.) The RAMpagePlus and concentration boards are of this type.

Back-filling. However, don't think that this address changing work means expanded memory is always slower than extended memory, which doesn't have to change addresses. For task-switching work where you want your PC to turn quickly from one large stretch of memory to another (see Step 6 for further explanation) expanded memory can be even faster than extended memory. Simply by changing the addresses in a few mapping registers, an eXpanded Memory Manager can have the same effect as copying 64K of new information into memory. Remember too that expanded memory can hold 32MB (if you have that many chips); extended can only hold 15MB maximum (again, if there are enough chips).

This advantage can be put to work by back-filling conventional memory addresses with expanded memory. That is, on some PCs and with some expanded memory boards and EMM utilities, you are given the choice of filling some of the memory addresses below the 640K line with expanded memory. Some PCs—such as 286-based PCs—only allow it from 256K to 640K, others—386-based PCs—can back-fill all of the conventional memory addresses, as shown in Figure 5-17. (Backfilling requires large-frame EMS memory.) In many cases this will mean disabling or turning off the chips that are already at those addresses. But once you do back-fill with expanded memory, you'll be able to switch tasks even more quickly. See the instructions of your particular expanded memory manager and expanded memory board to see if they allow this, and what the restrictions are. The DESQView environment (described in Step 6) makes good use of back-filled memory. Don't use back-filling unless you're interested in this sort of multitasking and task switching. For loading large files into a single program it's a waste of time.

Before EMS 4.0 the page frame could only hold 4 pages (that is, 64K holding four 16K pages). With EMS 4.0 the page frame can hold up to 8 pages when in memory above 640K, and any number when in memory below 640K. Some EMMs use all of the lower 640K as the page frame, putting the EMM itself into expanded memory. Version 4.0 supports pages of 16K and smaller. Some applications, however, may not work with the page frame below 640K.

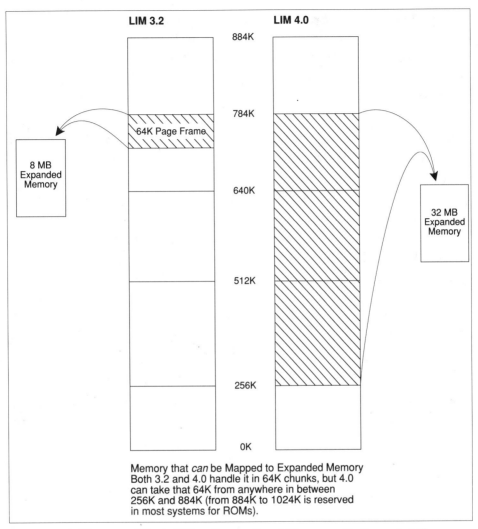

Figure 5-17. Diagram of Back-Filling Conventional Memory with Expanded Memory

Alternate Mapping Registers, Page-aliasing, and DMA Support. Expanded memory depends on mapping registers to keep track of such things as the address changes, and which page of memory holds what. The EMS 3.2 version requires at least one set; EEMS supported two sets. EMS 4.0 supports multiple sets, up to 32 sets. More registers means quicker task-switching, as shown in Figure 5-18.

Some EMS 4.0 boards have only the minimum number of registers; others have 32 or even more. One set per multitasked utility or application is about enough. Some programs even demand multiple register sets, just for themselves. If there aren't enough registers, however, the Expanded Memory Manager program can emulate them in software. However, software registers are slower than hardware registers. On an expanded memory board, 386 and 486 processors eliminate the need for registers because they have registers built in; they're created with memory mapping in mind. After a point, more registers of any kind are just superfluous, and don't add to performance.

Some EMS boards also have a feature called page aliasing. This permits a single section of expanded memory to be mapped to more than one DOS address, to let various modules of integrated programs share data simultaneously. Few integrated program do this, however, so the feature is only occasionally useful.

Full support of EMS 4.0 also provides for fast DMA (Direct Memory Access) transfers of information in memory without interrupting the main processor chip.

AST and Intel chips have page aliasing. Intel boards don't support the DMA. The Intel boards typically have 48 page registers, while AST boards have from 128 to 2048.

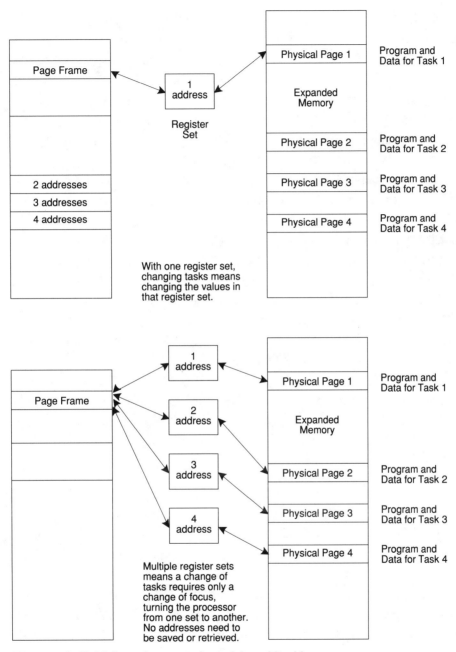

Figure 5-18. Multiple register sets for quick multitasking.

EMMs—Making Expanded Memory from Extended or Disk Memory. You don't have to get an expanded memory board to have expanded memory. You can also use an EMM (Expanded Memory Manager) program to turn some extended memory or hard disk memory into expanded memory. They emulate expanded memory in one of those other memory types—when a program wants some information from expanded memory, or wants to send information to it, the EMM redirects the request to extended memory or hard disk memory, following the rules of EMS. Another term for them is *LIMulators*.

Emulated Extended memory is slower than an EMS board on a 286 PC, faster on a 386 PC. Emulating in hard disk memory is always slower than an EMS board, as much as ten times slower. Some of these depend on the 386 and 486 processors, which have their own mapping registers. (The 386 microprocessor has special hardware that can map any 4K page of physical memory to any other 4K place.) Other EMMs create mapping registers in software, for the benefit of 8088 and 286-based systems that don't have hardware mapping registers.

There are two types of emulators. Some take advantage of the 386 chip's memory-mapping abilities. Some are more limited, copying 16K pages of memory from extended memory to conventional memory.

EMM386.SYS, XMAEM.SYS, and XMA2EMS.SYS—PC-DOS 4.01 comes with several drivers for turning extended memory into expanded memory in 386-based systems:

```
XMAEM.SYS
XMA2EMS.SYS
```

These are necessary because some DOS 4 command—including FASTOPEN and VDISK—can use expanded memory. You may get these drivers working in your PC by including them as **DEVICE=XMAEM.SYS**, and **DEVICE=XMA2EMS.SYS** in the CONFIG.SYS file.

XMAEM.SYS transforms extended memory on 386 systems into expanded memory. It emulates the PS/2 80286 Expanded Memory Adapter/A. It would look like this **DEVICE=XMAEM.SYS somenumber** where the word *somenumber* is actually a value for the number of 16K pages you want to create. The minimum is 64K pages, for one MB of expanded memory.

XMA2EMA.SYS is a LIM 4.0-compatible expanded memory manager for that memory transformed by XMAEM.SYS. Its line would look like this

```
DEVICE=XMA2EMS.SYS [FRAME=location] [P0=location] [P1=location] [P2=location]
[P3=location] [P254:location] [P255:location] [/X:pages]
```

where the square brackets indicate optional parameters tacked on to the one line. The **FRAME:location** parameter specifies the address of the default frame, somewhere between C000 and E000 in high memory.

The location parameters specify the addresses of the pages used by DOS. If they aren't specified, DOS commands cannot use expanded memory. The **/X:pages** parameter tells the amount of expanded memory to make, in 16K pages. The minimum is 4 pages. For more details on these drivers, see your DOS manual.

MS-DOS systems have the **EMM386.SYS** driver instead of XMAEM or XMA2EMS. It does the same work as the two: transforming extended memory on 386 systems into expanded memory, and then managing that memory.

These drivers don't offer all the features and options of other extended-to-expanded memory converters or "LIMulators", such as those mentioned in Steps 4 and 5 (QEMM and 386-to-the-Max are the best known). For example, they don't support 386 remapping for use of high memory.

EMS40.SYS—This is a public domain EMM you can find on bulletin boards such as PCMagNet. (See the Appendix on "Cheap and Free Software.") EMS40.SYS converts extended memory (but not hard disk memory), to expanded memory by emulating all 28 standard EMS functions, including the DMA functions in the alternate map register set. It is backwardly compatible with EMS 3.2 software—that is, it supports programs that want EMS 3.2 software. The control switches with EMS40.SYS only convert as much extended memory as you tell them to. (It comes in both assembly language and BASIC versions for programmers to inspect.) Once EMS40.SYS is installed, it can only be removed from memory by turning off your PC. In memory it takes up about 69K, which includes the 64K of the page frame.

EMS40.SYS is a device driver you put into your CONFIG.SYS file with a line like **device = d:\EMS40.SYS nnn** The path tells where the EMS40.SYS file is on your disk. *nnn* specifies the number of K of extended memory to convert to expanded. The default is 384K.

Tip: If EMS40.SYS seems to be incompatible with other software, you can try to avoid the problem by placing it as the first driver in the CONFIG.SYS file.

386Max—This memory manager from Qualitas can emulate expanded memory in extended, and can relocate TSRs and drivers to high-DOS memory. It requires a 386 PC, and lets you choose how much extended and conventional memory to keep as extended and how much to use as expanded.

QEMM-386—The QEMM-386 memory manager from Quarterdeck can relocate drivers and TSRs to high-DOS memory, and can emulate expanded memory from extended. In fact, it can transform all of memory, both conventional and extended, into EMS. QEMM lets you specify the number of register sets, the page frame details, and so on.

Memory Commander—This V Communications utility offers a number of memory management features, including relocation of TSRs and drivers, and expanded memory emulation. It can change the memory configuration "on the fly" without rebooting the computer, such as resetting the memory address for the page frame.

HI386—The HI386 memory manager from RYBS Electronics relocates drivers and TSRs to high-DOS memory, and can emulate expanded memory in extended.

Invisible RAM 386—This utility from Invisible Software emulates EMS 4.0 expanded memory in extended on 386 and 486 machines. Like QEMM-386 and 386Max it can also relocate drivers and TSRs into high-DOS memory (see Step 4 for details).

IOS-10/386—This is IO Data's device driver for 386-based systems, to convert extended memory into expanded. It also offers a RAM disk and a disk cache utility.

Other LIMulators that emulate with extended memory

CEMM   Compaq Computer's EMM supplied with Compaq PCs.
LIMSIM   Larson Computing's EMM.
VRAM   Biologic's EMM
V-EMM   Fort Software's EMM runs on 286-based PCs.

EMMs That Make EMS From Both Extended and Hard Disk Memory. Some EMMs can use extended or hard disk memory, whichever is in your PC or whichever you choose, to make expanded memory through emulation. These can also be thought of as virtual memory utilities because they are making more memory from disk, instead of from chips. They include:

Turbo EMS from Merrill & Bryan

Above DISC from Above Software

TC! Power EMS from Departmental Technologies Inc.

Tips on Expanded Memory. The more conventional memory you have free, the more access you'll have to expanded memory. That's generally true because you need some conventional memory to hold pointers to or parts of programs and data in expanded memory.

If you use hard disk memory as EMS, defragment the hard disk to make it as fast as possible.

Some programs that use expanded memory must have the page frame start at an address that's evenly divisible by 16K. (Paradox 2.0 was like this.) To meet the need, some EMMs have a switch to force such a page frame. Some spreadsheets only use EMS for certain types of data: text, formulas, fractions, and whole numbers larger than 32K.

Some programs, such as Javelin, use page-aliasing, and so aren't compatible with EMS emulators that don't provide page-aliasing. On a 286-based machine, emulated expanded memory is slower than expanded memory from an EMS board. On a 386, the emulated expanded memory can actually be faster, particularly if run from 32-bit memory.

- Expanded memory works on XTs; extended does not.

- More software is compatible with expanded that with extended.

- Expanded memory has strict rules for preventing program conflicts. Extended memory rules aren't so well set and broadly supported yet.

Virtual Memory: Adding Memory by Faking it

Virtual memory has been a vital part of minicomputers and mainframes for years. Now it is a possibility on personal computers. When you add virtual memory to a PC, you're not adding any chips or boards, nor are you freeing memory chips that were used for other purposes. What you're doing is forcing some disk memory to act as if it were chip memory. When virtual memory is working, a program or data file that needs more memory uses part of the hard disk—floppies are typically too slow and small—as if it were conventional, expanded, or extended memory. Any portion of the program or data file that is held in this virtual memory area of the disk can be moved into actual chip memory when it is needed, swapping places with some other part of the program or file that can move out to the disk. Remember, however, that this is not a magic bullet for avoiding the 640K conventional memory limit: that is still in place. Figure 5-19shows how virtual memory works.

Virtual memory is a wonderful invention because it uses something you have a lot of (disk memory) to fill in for something you rarely have enough of (chip memory). However, virtual memory is slower than real, physical memory. Not only are disks slower than chips, but something in your PC must keep track of what information is in physical memory and what is in virtual, what is waiting to swap in and what has been swapped out. If the operating system is doing this, it will work for all programs, but the swapping will be overhead that will subtract from the speed of your applications. (Programs still run fastest when they are entirely in real, physical memory.) If an individual application is providing its own virtual memory, that application will lose time from its other work when attending to swapping. Some PCs have hardware that supports virtual memory (the 386 and 486 chips have some circuitry for this) which eases that overhead burden, but even in those virtual memory is slower than the real thing.

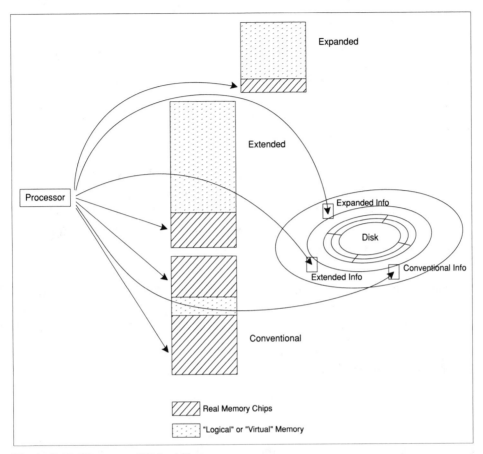

Figure 5-19. Diagram of Virtual Memory

The advantages of virtual memory are:

• Large space—hard disks can easily spare 5, 10, or more MB of space.

• Low cost—megabytes of disk space are always much cheaper than megabytes of RAM.

• Transparency—it's working and you don't even have to think about it, your PC just acts like it has more memory.

211

The disadvantages of virtual memory are:

• Uses disk space—a minor problem, but disk space is not unlimited.

• Incompatibility—it doesn't work with all programs.

• Speed—this is the big problem because virtual memory on disk is much, much slower than RAM memory.

The first flaw doesn't matter much in most systems. In a PC with 640K of RAM and a 30MB hard disk, for example, sacrificing 6MB of disk to virtual memory means a 20% disk cutback for about a 600% boost in RAM. Not a bad trade.

The second objection can be a problem. If you choose one of the general-purpose virtual memory programs, you'll find that some programs—perhaps some of your favorites—don't work with it.

The third objection is the most serious. Disks are much slower than chips, so even though a virtual memory system makes the software think there's more RAM, it can't fake the speed of RAM. You get more space, but not the same zip. And there's a limit to the efficiency of virtual memory when all of those megabytes of disk parading as RAM must shoehorn themselves in and out of that 640K of conventional RAM. This problem can be alleviated if the programs that make disk storage behave—except for speed—like expanded or extended RAM.

Types of Virtual Memory. There are several ways to get virtual memory on a PC: Overlays, Virtual Memory Utilities, Virtual Memory Environments, Virtual memory Operating Systems. Each has its own compatibility issues.

Overlays—Many PC programs have their own virtual memory built in as *overlays*. For years programmers have been using overlays as a trick to do more in a limited amount of memory. They let your memory feel larger than it is, at the expense of some extra copying from the disk. When a program was too big to fit into whatever memory a PC had, it was split into several pieces. A central, small piece might always stay in memory. But other parts would be copied in from the disk drive when they were needed, overlaying some other piece that was already in memory.

The piece that was covered up could then be copied in from disk again (where a permanent copy of it had stayed, untouched by the overlay process) when it was needed.

For example, a word processor might have its spelling checker in an overlay. Spelling checkers can be large because of the huge dictionaries they require. During most of the typical word processing work the spelling checker commands wouldn't be used, so why should the dictionaries and commands occupy precious memory? If they were kept separate in an overlay, they could be safe on disk until needed. Then, when the user decided to check some spelling, the dictionary and command instructions would be copied into RAM from the disk, obliterating some other program parts—perhaps those for changing the size and style of characters on screen—in the process. Then, when spell checking was done and the operator decided to again change some character sizes, the size and style overlay would be copied in from disk, knocking out the spelling checker (remember, the original is safe on disk).

Many large programs use overlays. You probably don't even know when yours is-there is no obvious sign. However, by looking to your program documentation or calling technical support to find out about overlays, you can use memory more efficiently. They are somewhat similar to virtual memory. Overlays can range from hundreds of K each down to the tiny 2K overlays of Borland's VROOM technology, used in Quattro. Overlays only work for the program they're in, not for your utilities and other programs. But they can let you get more functions and powers into your PC than your real memory chip space would allow. Try putting all the overlays from such a program onto a RAM disk, making that the swap space, and you'll see fast swapping.

Some DOS extenders that are built into programs to give them access to the 15MB of extended memory above 1MB also provide virtual memory to those programs. For instance, Phar Lap's 386|VMM virtual memory manager lets a program automatically use hard disk space. Only programmers need to think about this, however. Program users will only know that their manual says the program will use disk memory when necessary.

Virtual Memory Utilities. Some utilities provide a kind of virtual memory by swapping TSRs in and out of memory. These are called task-switchers or TSR managers, and are covered in a section of Step 6. Some of the most popular are: Extra, Software Carousel, PopDrop Plus, and Headroom.

Other utilities try to provide virtual memory for all the programs you run under DOS. They monitor what's in memory, and in a virtual memory area on disk, as well as swap programs and data in and out as needed. They can't be compatible with all programs, because DOS was not created as a virtual memory operating system, but they can provide virtual memory for many programs. And that may be the least expensive way possible to top your PC off with several MB of memory. Along with such a utility you may want a task-switching utility or environment that can handle the various programs you move in and out of the increased extended and expanded memory space.

Above DISC—Above DISC is a device driver program that makes expanded memory for PCs that don't have any or enough. It does this either by converting extended memory into expanded—as a LIMulator (see the section on LIMulators)—or by using virtual memory technology to make disk memory act like expanded memory. Above DISC can make up to 32MB of LIM 4.0 expanded memory. It uses 80K of memory itself. Figure 5-20 shows Above Disc's display.

In the meanwhile, it can also grab from 64K to 96K of unused video graphics memory above 640K to add to your conventional memory (see the section on borrowing memory in Step 4).

Above DISC comes with a special Lotus 1-2-3 add-in program called AboveMEM which converts up to 512K of extended memory into expanded memory just for 1-2-3 Release 2. AboveMEM uses only 11K of memory to run, far less than the 70 to 80K of many expanded memory managers.

And there's yet another utility with Above DISC, the AboveLAN memory manager for Novell NetWare that can put the NetWare 3 or 4 drivers into high memory or extended memory. NETBIOS and IPX remain in low memory. This saves up to 36K of conventional memory.

```
                              Above DISC

                              Ver. 3.1D
               Copyright (C) Above Software Inc. 1988, 1989, 1990
                  Expanded Memory Creator & Manager (EMS 4.0)

                         Written By: W. Glen Boyd
```

```
   1.    Install Above DISC on drive    [C]
   2.    Directory for Above DISC files [\RAMPACK                           ]
   3.    Specify number of 16K pages    [  21] =     336K of EMS
   4.    Expanded Memory Location       [ Extended Memory                   ]

   5.    SPECIAL OPTION (See Manual)    [ Specify Memory Segment            ]
   5a.   Memory segment to place page map [D000] Hex
   6.    Mode of processor operation    [   386   ]
   7.    Type of Bus in Computer        [ Standard Bus  ]

       Press ↑ and ↓ to move through specification items, Press SpaceBar or
       type in info which is requested.  Press F9 to exit/save configuration.
       Press ESCAPE to blank input fields.  Press F5 to reset to defaults.
```

Figure 5-20. Above Disc Display

Above DISC doesn't work with all programs Some problems crop up with Adobe Illustrator, Allways 1.0, Clipper (on some 386 machines), DisplayWrite 4 (on 386s), the PC Tools 5.0 cache, Publisher Paintbrush (on 386s), SuperCalc 5.0 rev B, Ventura Publisher 2.0 (on 386s), Codeview, Javelin, Lotus HAL, Oracle, and Windows/386.

Another way to buy Above DISC is to buy "The RamPack" from BLOC Publishing. This includes both PopDrop Plus and Above Disc.

Turbo EMS—Turbo EMS, from Merrill & Bryan, works much as Above DISC does, converting extended or disk memory into as much as 32MB of LIM 4.0 expanded memory. It automatically manages spillover of information between hardware expanded memory, extended memory acting as expanded, and disk memory acting as expanded. Its expanded memory supports Windows, Excel, DESQView, Ventura Publisher, and Lotus 1-2-3. Turbo EMS lets you create custom configurations of memory for your various applications, and you can switch between them without rebooting your PC. To do all this, it uses 74K of memory.

Turbo EMS can also relocate TSRs and device drivers into high memory, and it supports the VCPI and XMS standards. It installs automatically, automatically mapping TSRs and device drivers for the best fit in high-DOS memory. It detects VDISK and page frame memory areas, is compatible with HIMEM.SYS, and on 386 systems can even creates shadow RAM and back-fill conventional memory. Version 6.0 comes with the Microsoft VxD virtual device driver, so it is compatible with Windows 3. Finally, Turbo EMS can grab unused video graphics memory from high memory and add it to your conventional memory.

TC! Power—This utility from Departmental Technologies turns hard disk memory into expanded or extended memory. It can also convert some unused high-DOS memory between 640K and 1MB into extended or expanded. You can deactivate TC! Power by a DOS command, then activate it again later, and it works alongside RAM disks and caches.

Virtual Memory Environments. Some environment programs are built with virtual memory power, allowing any programs that run under them to swap out to memory on disk. Again, the compatibilities here won't be complete because programs must fully support the environment to use the virtual memory. The two best known are Windows and DESQView. See Step 6 for details on these.

Virtual Memory Operating Systems. DOS was not built with virtual memory at its core, but OS/2, Unix, and many other operating systems take virtual memory for granted, and provide it for all of their programs. The 286 and 386 chips even have special hardware to aid in virtual memory. The 286 supports up to 1GB of virtual memory, and the 386 up to 64 terabytes, (or 64 million megabytes). Other operating systems can take advantage of this support.

The disadvantage, naturally, is that moving to one of these other operating systems may prevent you from running your DOS programs that want more memory. See Step 9 for notes on alternative operating systems.

A Final Analogy: Memory as Your PC's Library

Think of yourself as your PC and your PC's memory as your library. This is the kind of library, though, where the you can both read books and write in the books.

Conventional memory would be the books lying on your desk: the most important and the immediately available. There's only so much room on the desk for books, and once the desk is covered, you wouldn't be able to open any more books. Part of the desk space, in fact, is taken up by a notebook or other such tools—the equivalent of the space DOS, TSRs, and device drivers occupy in conventional memory.

High-DOS memory would be the librarian's roll-top desk. Next to yours, the librarian would keep it locked. This desk would only be partially full. It would always be available to the librarian who needed the information from the books in it to keep the library open and running. However, with the help of a key (a memory management program), you could open this desk and use some of its space. You could rearrange the books in it so that there was some more space directly adjacent to your own desk—and so slide some of your books over to it—and you could slip some of your tools and books into unused niches in the desk. However, if you moved some of the librarian's books to where he or she could not find them, or replaced them with some of yours, the library might cease to function, and you could not work.

Extended memory would be a tall set of bookshelves that could hold 15 times as much information as your desk. If you were a PC or XT, this entire structure would be out of reach, except for use as a place to stack some books perhaps (as a RAM disk site). If you had a 286 or 386 PC your longer arms would reach the bookshelf and you would discover that it too was locked. With one special key—an HMA driver—you could reach and open one small shelf on it—64K—for immediate use. With another more general key—a DOS extender or alternative operating system—you could open the entire set of shelves for use. But you would have to read and write in the books at the bookshelves, not back at your desk.

Expanded memory would be another bookshelf unit, able to hold twice as many books as even extended memory. And you would be free to take books from this bookshelf back to your desk. However, the expanded memory bookshelf would be governed by some special rules. The librarian would only let you use it if you:

- Asked a library assistant to shelve or grab the book

- Took a single book from it at a time

- Put that book on your desk while in use

- Stuck to certain subjects while using the bookshelf

The library assistant would be the EMM and MMU. Without them the huge bookshelf of expanded memory would be useless.

The space you made on your desk for the single book in use would be the page frame. LIM 3.2 rules would tell you where to put this page frame. LIM 4.0 rules would let you put it just about anywhere on your desk—moving it to make it most convenient for whatever task you were engaged in.

The certain subjects rule would mean that only subjects relevant to this bookshelf (only programs supporting expanded memory) could get any use from it.

You could read or write in any book from the expanded memory bookshelf, but only one book at a time. Because of the restriction to a single book, this bookshelf would sometimes feel more restrictive than extended memory. Because you could take the book back to your desk, it would sometimes be more flexible than extended memory.

An expanded memory emulator, or LIMulator, could make all or part of an extended memory bookshelf follow the rules of an expanded memory bookshelf.

Virtual memory would be a huge bookshelf at some other library, from which you could request books, or to which you could send books. It could follow the rules of your desk, of extended, or of expanded memory, but would be much slower because of the time taken to move books to and from it.

And turning the power off to your PC would be a flash-fire in the library that within a fraction of a second would destroy your books. Only information stored in virtual memory would be spared.

Change Your Environment: TSR Managers, Task-switchers, and Multitasking Environments (Including DESQview and Windows)

Key Ideas:

- Task-switching and multitasking improve your computing efficiency. The PC's DOS operating system was not built as a task-switching or multitasking operating system. (Some of the alternative operating systems mentioned in Step 9 offer both.)

- To task-switch or multitask with DOS you need enough memory, the right memory-management software, and the right controlling software.

- DOS can task-switch by using

  Integrated programs alone (mentioned in Step 3).

  TSRs (memory-resident programs) with a TSR managing control program (described in this Step)

TSRs and standard applications with a task-switcher control program or environment .

- DOS can multitask by using: TSRs and standard applications with a 386 processor and the right controlling program or environment: such as Windows 3.0, DESQview 386, or GEOS (described in this Step).

Task-switching and multi-tasking environments and control programs sometimes simplify your memory management by centering it within a single program—adjust your task-switcher or environment's memory management and you're nearly all set.

Importance of Task-switching and Multitasking

Few of us work on a single project at a time, or use only a single tool even on a solitary project. That's true with or without computers. Unfortunately, for some time the majority of computers were only able to field a single program at a time. If that program didn't have every command or ability needed for the current task or project, we were faced with a frequent and time-draining need to:

- Close that program

- Locate and start another program that did have the necessary command

- Use the other program, then close it and return to the first program

This is called *context-switching* or *task-switching*. Figure 6-1 is a diagram of task switching. If it is cumbersome and slow, with your computer getting in your way, instead of making your work easier. If it is simple and quick, you can get more done with your computer, whether that means quickly changing from word processing to spreadsheet calculating (two separate projects), or just from formatting the text in a desktop publishing program to checking your electronic-mail for a last minute revision to that text (two tasks within a single project).

Sometimes separate computing projects or tasks require your full attention, they only progress when on the computer screen in front of you. But many times this isn't true, many times there are computer tasks that could proceed without your undivided attention. In terms of the task-switching examples given above, if you told the spreadsheet to make some complex calculation that would last one, two, or twenty minutes, your attention wouldn't be required again until that calculation was finished. If your electronic mail program was waiting for text corrections, there wouldn't be any need for your attention until that text was fully captured and ready to use.

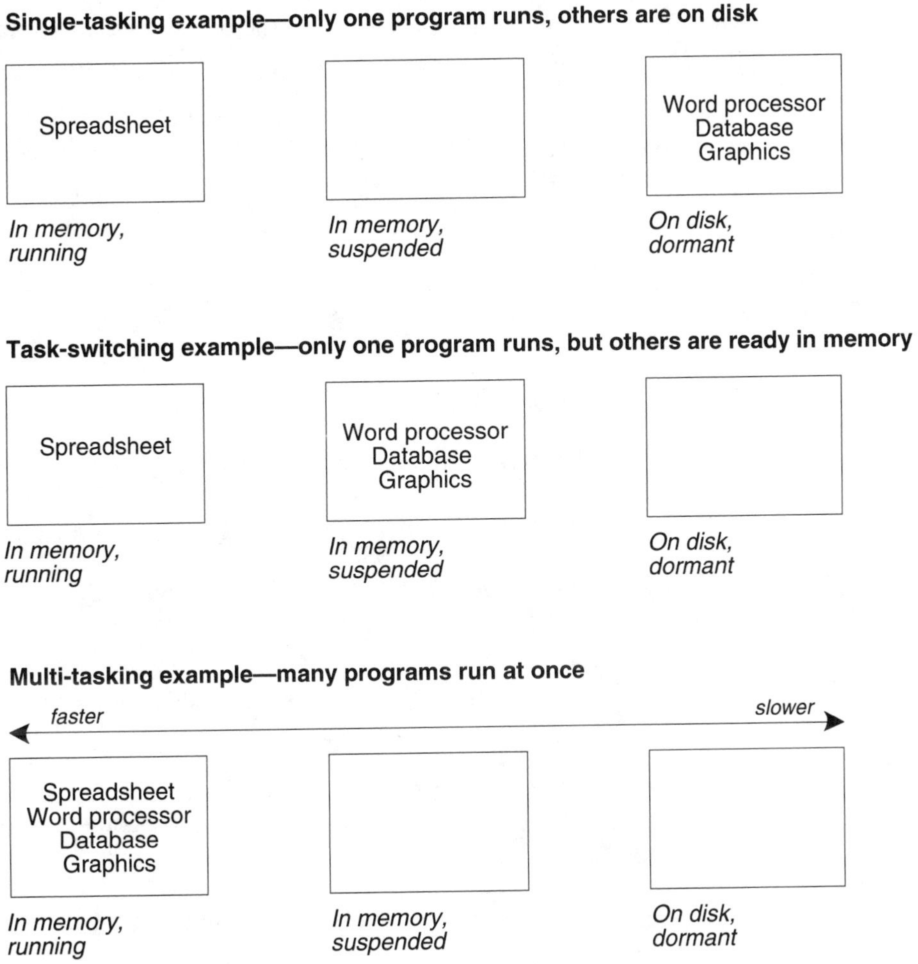

Single-tasking example—only one program runs, others are on disk

Spreadsheet		Word processor Database Graphics
In memory, running	*In memory, suspended*	*On disk, dormant*

Task-switching example—only one program runs, but others are ready in memory

Spreadsheet	Word processor Database Graphics	
In memory, running	*In memory, suspended*	*On disk, dormant*

Multi-tasking example—many programs run at once

faster ← → *slower*

Spreadsheet Word processor Database Graphics		
In memory, running	*In memory, suspended*	*On disk, dormant*

Figure 6-1. Diagram of Task-switching and Multitasking

In these cases, there would be a computer task (spreadsheet calculating or e-mail receiving) that needed some time to run, but didn't need your supervision. At the same time, other tasks (word processing or text formatting) would be awaiting your hands-on control. A computer that allowed both to occur at the same time, that could calculate the spreadsheet while you processed the words, that would capture the e-mail while you formatted other text, would be *multitasking*. It wouldn't just be switching you quickly from one task or program to another. It would be running more than one program at a time, some of them operating in the background and one of them operating in the foreground under your active control.

Multitasking isn't always necessary in a computer, but it is often useful, even for people who stick to a single program. A spreadsheet fanatic, for instance, might keep his or her spreadsheet on the computer screen eight hours a day, and not think in terms of task switching. But even that fanatic is likely to want to occasionally:

- Write a memo

- Send some e-mail

- Format a disk to save a new spreadsheet file

- Scan a disk for any defects or viruses

and so on. Even then, those are just the utilities that most computer users run. Handling them efficiently requires at the least good task-switching, but ideally, multitasking.

That same spreadsheet fanatic might want multitasking even within his or her spreadsheet, to calculate a difficult worksheet while editing another one or, to solve for a difficult set of values while creating a chart from some others.

In other words, task-switching and multitasking could be useful to just about every computer user, and I think they should be a fundamental component of computing.

- But not all computers are born to task-switch or multitask. They need:

- Enough processor power to handle more than one task

222

- Enough memory to hold more than one task

- The right hardware to manage that processor power and memory

- The right software to control that hardware

PCs certainly aren't born to task-switch or multitask. DOS, the PC operating system, was intended for single-tasking . It was created to load one program into memory at a time, and then to devote all of its energies and memory to that one program.

But you can make DOS task-switch, with enough memory and the right software. You can even make DOS multi-task, with enough memory, memory-management hardware, and the right software. That's what this Step is about.

Methods of Task-switching and Multitasking

There are several methods to task-switch and multitask, using different control programs. The more sophisticated forms offer smoother switching from one task to another, and even background processing for some programs, but they often demand more hardware (both processor power at the 386 level and more memory) and more expensive control software. This step lists some of the best-known control programs for task-switching and multitasking. It includes some tips for the best memory management in several of them, but is by no means a complete treatment of any of them because there just isn't enough space here.

Integrated Programs for Task-switching

The simplest form of task-switching on PCs comes from running an integrated program, a program that contains modules for more than one task. You choose from the program's menus to switch to another task, work on that for a while, then switch back to the initial task. Tasks switched away from are either turned off entirely or left suspended, not operating, but ready to come back to life. Integrated programs are nice because they put everything into a single package, with consistent commands and menus, that can run on any PC with enough memory. You don't need special memory management hardware or software to switch tasks. The disadvantage of integrated programs is that they confine you to the commands of the one program. Rarely is any one program good at all tasks, and most people have some preference in the word processor, spreadsheet, or even the minor utilities they want to run.

Shelling to DOS for Task-switching

The next simplest form of task-switching comes from programs that shell to DOS. These programs offer a DOS option in their menus that empties most of the program from memory and brings to the display the familiar DOS command screen. (A small part of the program is left in memory.) There you can type any DOS commands you want, or even run other programs (if there's enough memory for them). When you're done with DOS or the other program, you type **exit** and the rest of your original program is loaded back into memory, and the program continues off from where you left it. This shelling technique is somewhat cumbersome, and does not let you have several programs loaded into memory and ready to run, but it is quicker and easier than having to completely quit one program to run another. It appears in programs such as dBASE, Paradox, 1-2-3, WordPerfect, Word, and XyWrite. Some control programs take advantage of shelling to let you automatically move from one program to another, without stopping at DOS in between. This form of task-switching is not as difficult as moving from one program to another a single step at a time (quitting, loading, quitting, etc) but it is not as smooth as some of the more advanced forms mentioned later.

Dr. Switch. This task-switcher from Black & White International was once called Switch-It (there's another task-switcher by that name). It works on PCs, XTs, ATs, and PS/2s, but only works with programs that shell to DOS. You load it into memory, where it occupies 25K initially, and then set up partitions of memory—expanded, extended (including the HMA), or hard disk—to hold the applications you want to use. Each time you leave one of these applications Dr. Switch swaps it out of conventional memory and brings in the other desired program. While it does this it can unload any TSRs that are in memory, to make maximum room for the incoming application. Dr. Switch leaves only about 10K of itself in memory when applications are loaded. There is a cut-and-paste feature to move information between programs.

AutoSwap. This utility from the Lamba Group can task switch for programs that shell to DOS. It runs on PCs to 386 machines, and needs only 6K of RAM for itself. To use it you invoke any application's shell command to return to DOS, then type **as newprogram** ("newprogram" meaning the starting name of the new program). An image of the previous program will be saved to expanded memory, and the new program will load into memory and run. Each time you make such a swap, there will be another 6K chunk of memory occupied by an AutoSwap file in memory. To return to a previous program you need to work back through the chain of programs—you can't jump directly to it. There is no menu for making moves among programs.

TSR Managers and Task-switchers

Another form of task-switching comes from using TSRs, memory-resident programs. With the advent of DOS 2.0, programmers found a way to load programs into memory so that they would stay loaded, even after you had stopped using them, as explained in Step 1 and illustrated in Figure 6-2.

These "terminate and stay resident" or *TSR* programs then wait in memory for a signal to become active again, a signal from the keyboard (some special combination of keys you press) or from a timer in the computer, or from information coming in some port (such as information from a mode coming in the serial port). A TSR that is still in memory but not running is suspended, so this is not multitasking. But because you can load TSRs alongside each other, or alongside a standard application, they provide quick task-switching: press a key to jump to one program, press a key to jump back to another. TSR functions are commonly less extensive that you'd find in full-blown standard application programs because they, TSRs, must be relatively small to stay in memory.

The number of TSRs you can load at one time is limited by the amount of memory you have and by the various TSRs ability to get along with each other while in memory. (The memory limit can be eased by loading some of them into high-DOS memory, as described in Step 4.) TSRs can fight over which one gets which section of memory, and over their responses to interrupts, the various signals from the keyboard or communication ports. There are a number of control programs that manage TSRs, giving you more memory for them (swapping them out to expanded, extended, or disk memory). The swapping is most effective when going to expanded memory—even faster than to extended memory. If you can backfill your conventional memory with expanded memory to make it remappable too, your switching can be faster yet.

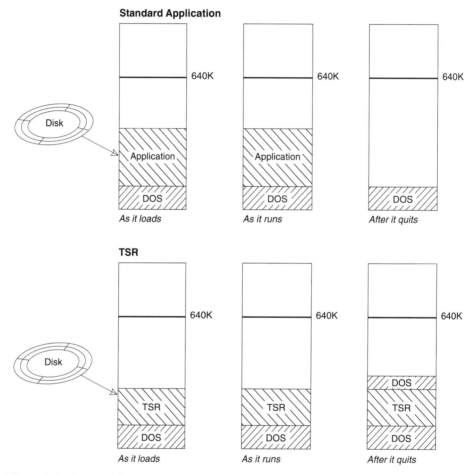

Figure 6-2. How a TSR Loads Into Memory

226

This sort of control of TSRs often gives another benefit: isolating the TSRs from one another, and so avoiding the memory and interrupt conflicts. This is done by putting each TSR, or set of TSRs, into separate memory partitions that are insulated from each other. Essentially this is a form of virtual memory and lets you act as if your PC has more than 640K of memory.

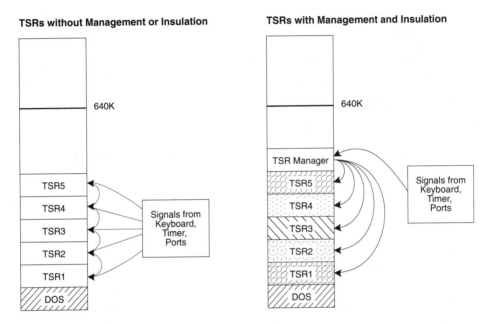

Figure 6-3. Diagram of Insulating TSRs from Conflicts

Some of the programs that manage multiple TSRs can also handle standard applications too, putting them into the memory partitions that are swapped in and out of activity and conventional memory. If you don't need background processing that comes with true multitasking, a task-switcher could be the ideal tool: it doesn't sap as much performance from your PC.

Tips on Using TSRs.

• Some TSRs can run in the background, offering a limited form of multitasking.

• Many TSRs come with the ability to load into LIM EMS 4.0 expanded memory—you should check if the latest version or upgrade of yours has added this feature.

• Some TSRs can remove themselves, some you can remove, and some can't be removed without turning off the PC. It is typically not possible to remove a TSR that's inbetween others, because that leaves a hole in memory which confuses and can crash your system.

• If your TSRs conflict, they may work if you merely change the order of loading.

• If some of your TSRs just don't get along at all, you can load them and unload them in compatible groups by creating appropriate batch files.

When TSRs are loaded one at a time, a copy of the DOS environment is loaded on top of each one. That can add up to lots of memory used for redundant information if you use many TSRs. To avoid the problem, use the smallest set of DOS environment variables possible (see Step 3) In your AUTOEXEC.BAT file for instance, load the TSRs before any PATH or SET commands.

Don't re-execute the AUTOEXEC.BAT file after you've booted the computer, or any other batch file that loads a TSR, because many TSRs don't check to see if they are already installed and so could install multiple times—eating up more memory than is necessary.

Most network drivers must be loaded before any TSR controller, because they must always be in memory and be active. However, many e-mail and communications programs can be swapped out of active memory because they are able to wait and "watch" for signals from a communications port to bring them back on-line.

Many print spoolers are TSRs and so can be swapped out of conventional memory—but nearly all will pause their operation when swapped out.

Things to Look for in Task-Switchers and TSR Managers.

- Number of programs that can be switched among—number of partitions.

- Menu of programs for easy identification and switching.

- Cut-and-paste utility for moving information between applications and TSRs.

- Ability to isolate TSRs from one another to prevent conflicts.

- Ability to load and unload TSRs in any order.

- Ability to load TSRs and device drivers into high-DOS memory.

- Whether it requires memory-management hardware to operate (such as LIM 4.0 boards or a 386 processor).

- Ability to jump directly from one TSR or application to another—not restricted to moving through the chain of applications and TSRs in the order in which they were loaded.

TSR Managers and Task-switchers.

Mark/Release—The simplest and least expensive way to control TSRs is to use the public domain *Mark* and *Release* programs. You can find these on PC MagNet (TSRC29.ZIP in Library 2 of the utilities forum), CompuServe (as MRKREL.ARC in Library 10 of the MSAPP Forum), through the Public (Software) Library, and on many other computer bulletin boards (see the Appendix on "Cheap and Free Software"). These programs are copyrighted, but free, from Turbo Power Software. You use them by putting the command **Mark** on the same command line for starting any TSR (including network shells, such as NetWare's) like this: **mark sidekick** for the SideKick TSR. Each copy of mark occupies about 1.5K. (A newer version called FMark uses only 150 bytes, putting the rest in a disk file. FMark also lets you name the various Marks in memory.) Then you can remove the TSRs, one at a time, in reverse order, with the **Release** command. You can load and unload TSRs in groups by simply placing marks after particular groups of TSRs. Release would unload all TSRs to the next Mark. Mark and Release can work on both conventional and expanded memory TSRs. Turbo Power also makes other TSR utilities, which let you view TSRs in memory (MAPMEM), as well as tracking how your TSRs act in memory (WATCH).

RAM Lord—This utility from Waterworks software can control up to 20 TSRs at a time. It allocates a piece of memory large enough for the most demanding TSR, and swaps TSRs in and out of that space as needed—sending them to expanded, extended, or disk memory It protects TSRs from interfering with one another, and is even compatible with OS/2. TSRs that are swapped out are not generally active, so RAM Lord does not claim to actually be a multitasking utility, though some TSRs are able to perform background operations.

Trading Places—This utility from Tate Publishing (part of Ashton-Tate, the company that makes the dBASE database manager) lets you have as many as 32 TSRs (or applications) on-line at once, swapping them in and out of memory. It uses only 11K of memory itself, and can store the TSRs that don't fit into conventional memory in expanded, extended, or disk memory.

Referee—Persoft's Referee manager controls TSRs, moving them in and out of memory. It lets you jump from one TSR to another, lets you isolate them so they won't interfere with each other, and lets you unload them (in order) even if they have no deinstall commands of their own, and lets you temporarily deactivate them if that is necessary.

Extra—This TSR manager from Delta Technology International can juggle as much as 700K or more of memory-resident programs. You tell Extra which TSRs to run, where they are on your disks, and which keys to use to bring them to life. Then you load Extra and it loads the TSRs into virtual memory on disk or into expanded or extended memory. If you tell it to load only one TSR at a time it looks for the largest TSR and reserves that much conventional memory, plus 35K more for itself. You can set it up to have more TSRs in conventional memory at a time, but that naturally requires more memory. The TSRs in virtual memory swap in as needed, responding to signals from the keyboard or from the Extra menu. Unlike PopDrop, Extra works while any application program that is running. You don't have to be at the DOS prompt to switch TSRs. You can also load TSRs before Extra, though these will then use their traditional amounts of memory.

Extra doesn't work with all TSRs, nor does it eliminate all conflicts between TSRs. Some programs that conflict with it include: PC Tools, Primetime Personal, Hot Line II, Graph-in-the-Box, 1-2-3 add-ins, some DOS shells, and SideKick Plus.

PopDrop Plus —PopDrop Plus, from BLOC Publishing, is really two programs: PopDrop and PopLoad.

PopDrop manages TSRs in conventional RAM. It can divide the 640K into as many as 16 layers (or groups) to separate and isolate the TSR in any given layer from the other layers. You can unload TSRs from the top layer down, even TSRs that normally unload only if you reboot your PC. PopDrop can also inactivate and reactivate layers at your command. It works with TSRs that use expanded memory and those that don't. You can view which TSRs are in each layer, as shown in Figure 6-4.

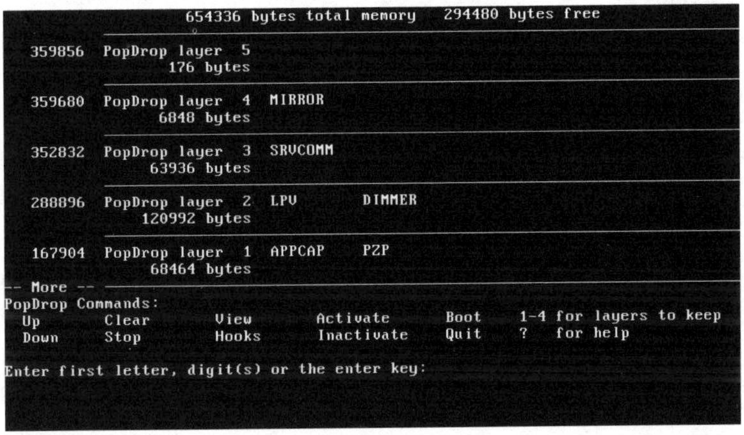

Figure 6-4. PopDrop's View of Memory (courtesy BLOC Publishing)

PopLoad takes up 23K of conventional memory to load up to 50 TSRs into expanded (LIM EMS 4.0) memory. You create a list or disk file of the TSRs to load that way and PopLoad does it automatically. When you want to use one of these

TSRs, you press the assigned hot key and that TSR is moved into high-DOS memory, where it can operate. Some TSRs don't work with this scheme, including SideKick Plus and Instant Recall. Nor can PopLoad work in PCs with active shadow Ram.

Task Switchers.

Back-and-Forth—This is one of the simplest task-switchers that works on all applications, not just those that shell to DOS. It is from Progressive Solutions, but is shareware—and is available on many bulletin boards on CompuServe (use the GO ZENITH then Section 13 commands). It offers a swap-definition screen where you define the amount of extended, expanded, or disk memory to be used for swapping. Back-and-Forth lets you set up a maximum of 50 partitions, and can run 20 of these at a time. Each partition has a size, name, program, and hot key that you dictate.

PC-Mix—PC-Mix from Proware can run and switch among up to three applications at once. You set up the configuration files for the groups of programs to run together, and the hot keys to use to move between them. This is one of the least expensive task switchers.

DOSamatic—A shareware task-switching utility available from such sources as PC-SIG, DOSamatic lets you load several programs and then transfer between them by pressing assigned combinations of keys. It offers menus and has commands for viewing, sorting, renaming, editing, printing, and otherwise handling files.

Omniview—A task-switcher from Sunny Hill Software, Omniview also comes in a multitasking version. It can move programs between conventional and expanded memory, and offers a display to show you which tasks are running and how much memory they are using. It offers menus to show you what you can switch to, but can also run in a smaller configuration that uses less memory but then you lose the ability to use the menus. Omniview does not have any cut-and-paste ability, and does not use extended memory. It does support the VCPI standard, and so can work with DOS extender programs.

Carousel—Carousel from SoftLogic Solutions is a task-switching utility for TSRs and applications. It does not offer multitasking. Carousel has been through several generations already, and used to be called Software Carousel. It both manages TSRs and swaps applications in and out of active, conventional memory to expanded, extended, or hard disk memory. It runs on PCs, ATs, and PS/2s. It is a fairly complicated switcher, with many screens of information for such details as setting the amount of memory for each of twelve possible partitions.

Carousel comes with a list of common applications and the memory they need for both program and data. If your applications aren't on this list, you'll have to experiment to find the same sort of information about them. Carousel can handle TSRs by loading them with any of the partitions—they will then be available only when that partition is active. You may also choose to load some TSRs before Carousel so that they are available to all applications—but this will eat into the available memory for all of the partitions.

There is a print spooler built into Carousel called "Print'n'Run." It can serve all of the dozen partitions. The latest version of Carousel can be joined by an option from SoftLogic called OLE—for Open Link Extender—that lets you execute network transactions in the background while using an application. OLE keeps the communications protocol active between your PC and a mainframe, minicomputer, or e-mail network that supports NETBIOS. Another utility program that comes with Carousel is called Magic Mirror. It provides a cut-and-paste ability to move information between programs and partitions.

Switch-It!—The Switch-It! utility from Better Software Technology is a task-switcher, and is similar to Carousel. It can manage up to 100 programs at a time, swapping them to expanded, extended, or hard disk memory. It comes with an automatic installation program to identify popular programs on your hard disk and then integrate these into the switching menus and options—as well as allowing you to set the memory partition sizes for them. It runs on any PC or PS/2 with at least 256K RAM. Switch-It! moves its own approximately 30K—in and out of expanded memory or hard disk, depending on how much memory the active application needs. It does have a cut-and-paste feature for moving information among programs. Switch-It! is compatible with Windows and GEM applications, and works in the OS/2 compatibility box. It can have some problems with graphics programs.

You can load TSRs in Switch-It, either into partitions with applications, or into their own partitions. To use extended memory with Switch-It! you need an EMM utility to convert it to expanded memory or a RAM disk program to make it behave as a disk drive. There's a configuration screen to show you what is in the various partitions and how much memory they occupy. If you have a 386-based PC with 386Max or QEMM, you can load Switch-It! into high-DOS memory, so that it doesn't use any conventional memory.

One tip when using Switch-It!: you should set up a more partitions than you need initially, so they are on hand if you want to load more applications. For instance, you might want to load two versions of a single program—such as 1-2-3—one in a small partition with room only for a small worksheet and another in a larger partition with room for a larger worksheet. That way you could sometimes use the smaller partition, which would operate faster, when you didn't need the larger worksheet space.

HeadRoom—Headroom from Helix Software combines task-switching, TSR management, and TSR relocation abilities (discussed in Step 4). There are related forms—Netroom and Connecting/Room—and optional Network Extensions that help you relocate or swap terminal emulation and networking drivers to high-DOS, extended, expanded, or hard disk memory. Headroom works on a PC, PS/2, or compatible with at least 256K RAM.

Headroom can swap any number of TSRs to extended memory or hard disk memory, leaving 51K of itself in conventional RAM. It handles standard applications the same way, essentially treating all programs as TSRs. You switch between the programs and TSRs with hot keys or by preset time alarms, and use the cut-and-paste feature to move information among them. TSRs in Headroom can pop up in the middle of programs they normally wouldn't work with. You determine the size of the memory partition for each program. You can save this configuration so that when you start Headroom again it will automatically find and load all the applications and TSRs.

Environments for Task-switching and Multitasking

The most advanced form of task-switching depends on an *environment control program*. These programs are more sophisticated forms of the partitioning mentioned above. They swap TSRs and applications in and out of conventional memory as necessary. They often provide the following navigational tools and special features: windows (putting each application program into its own section of the display screen, separate from the others), icons (tiny graphic images on the screen to represent files and commands), menus to move between and manipulate the windows and the programs in them, as well as utility programs, and cut-and-paste or linking features to move information from one partition to another. These environments sometimes contain their own memory management software to convert extended memory into expanded and to provide virtual memory to programs in the environment. Some environments can handle any DOS program. Some can only handle DOS programs that have been re-programmed to support the environment. Some handle both standard DOS programs and re-written programs, but offer more memory management and features for the re-written programs.

True multitasking is available in a few environment and control programs that use the ability of the 386 and 486 processors to create virtual-86 modes (see Step 1). These processor chips can carve memory into many slices, each independent of the others.

Windows. Windows is certainly the best known task-switching and multitasking environment for DOS. Microsoft, which makes DOS, also makes Windows, and has spent a great deal of time and money publicizing the software. Windows is not only a memory manager and environment, it is also a Graphical User Interface, (or GUI) attempting to present PC commands for all programs and for DOS as a set of menus and icons that can be learned quickly and easily and manipulated through the use of a mouse (a small input device that you hold and move about to move the cursor on screen) or the keyboard. It brings some of the Apple Macintosh's famed "ease of use" to the PC.

Windows evolved through several generations, from Versions 1.0 and 2.0 to separate versions for 286-based and 386-based PCs: Windows/286 and Windows/386. The latest version is Windows 3. If you have one of the previous versions the first move you should make is to upgrade to 3—it packs much better memory management as well as lots of other improvements.

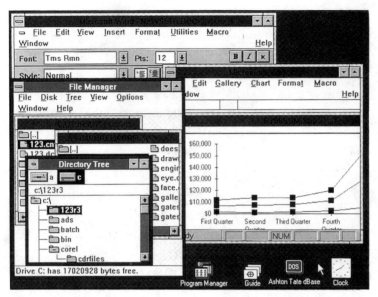

Figure 6-5. Windows Graphic User Interface on Screen (courtesy Microsoft)

Windows handles the memory management for programs that run under it. And it comes with its own disk cache program (SMARTDRV.SYS) and extended memory support (through the HIMEM.SYS driver). Windows 3 offers three operating modes, which have different capabilities and work on different PC hardware:

Real Mode, for PCs with an 8088 or 8086 processor and 640K of memory, or any other PC with less than 1MB of memory. Real mode is the same mode that older versions of Windows used. You can choose to start Windows in real mode by the command **win /r**.

Standard Mode, for PCs with at least a 286 processor and 1MB of memory (640K of conventional and 256K or more of extended or high-DOS memory). This mode multitasks Windows programs but not non-Windows programs. It runs 10 to 15% faster than 386E mode because it doesn't offer the full multitasking of 386E. You may choose to start in standard mode with the command **win /s**.

386 Enhanced Mode, for PCs with a 386 or 486 processor and at least 2MB of memory (640K of conventional, 384K of high-DOS, and 1024K of extended memory). Three or four MB of RAM is better. This mode offers real multitasking because it uses the Virtual 86 mode of the 386 chip. This mode also offers virtual memory, swapping programs to disk as needed.

No matter which Windows mode you use, you'll find utilities on hand, with names like: Write, Paintbrush, Terminal, Notepad, Recorder, Cardfile, Calendar, Calculator, and Clock. Windows has its own File Manager program to handle classic DOS tasks such as copying, deleting, and renaming files, and formatting disks.

Some programs are written specifically to run under Windows. These operate in any Windows mode, and offer menus for operation. But Windows can also run programs that haven't been rewritten to its dictates, programs that are just standard DOS applications. These don't stick to their own windows—unless you run in the 386 Enhanced mode—they occupy the entire screen. To run a program that is not built specifically for Windows, you need to create a PIF (Program Information File) for that program. This is also true for TSRs you want to run in Windows. For further information refer to Windows manual.

Installing Windows is an automatic process, but you need to answer a number of questions as you install. Also, once Windows is in place, you can adjust quite a few of its parameters, including many that dictate how much memory is used for various modes and processes. The Control Panel lets you customize the appearance of windows on screen, and lets you change printer installation, port assignments.

For the 386 E mode's multitasking you dictate how much of the computer's processing time is devoted to the Windows and non-Windows applications that run.

Windows comes with its own print spooler called the Print Manager (see Step 7 for a description of spooling) that can use memory to let your printing run in the background.

Tips for Windows—

• Check the Windows manual for information on memory settings and mode choices. Configure all memory for 386E mode as extended. Windows will appropriate expanded memory to programs that need it, creating it from extended memory.

237

• Use standard mode if you don't need to multitask non-Windows applications. Standard mode can run a single program 10 to 15% faster than the 386E mode can.

• Use real mode if you have Windows program versions created for previous Windows—such as Windows/286 or Windows/386.

• Several switches let you dictate expanded memory use in real mode. These switches don't affect standard or 386E modes. They are:

/e tells Windows how much conventional memory must be available to use large-frame EMS memory.

/l moves the EMS page frame up by 1K increments from the default position, when using large-frame EMS.

/n prevents Windows from using any expanded memory. It normally uses any expanded memory it finds.

• If you load TSRs into memory before starting Windows, they will be available to all Windows programs, but will also rob memory from the conventional memory available for each and every Windows application. A better way to use them is to load them as independent applications within Windows, and switch to them by changing Windows. This way they won't always be occupying part of the memory reserve.

• Use a compatible memory manager such as QEMM 5.1 or 386Max 5.1 to free as much conventional memory as possible before starting Windows.

• If you use 386E mode, make a permanent swap file on the hard disk for better performance. The Windows manual explains how to do this.

• Use the SMARTDRV disk cache that comes with Windows. This disk cache loads memory temporarily back to Windows when Windows needs it. Then reduce BUFFERS to 10 at most.

- If you have more than 1MB free for disk caching, use it instead as a RAM disk for the Windows temporary data files. Windows comes with the RAMDRIVE.SYS RAM disk program (which also ships with DOS 3.1 and later). To use this, put the line **device = c:\windows\ramdrive.sys 1024/e** into CONFIG.SYS.

- To make a 1MB RAM disk in extended memory. It will be assigned the drive letter *d* on most systems. You also need to change the temporary file paths by putting these lines in the AUTOEXEC.BAT file:

mkdir d:\temp
set temp = d:\temp

- If you run the RAM disk in external memory, the ramdrive.sys line must come after the himem.sys line in CONFIG.SYS.

- To conserve memory, get rid of device drivers and TSRs you don't need, such as any mouse driver: Windows comes with its own mouse driver.

- Standard mode has more memory if you check the No Screen Exchange and Prevent Program Switch options in the PIF Editor dialog box. But this prevents you from switching away from a program while that program is running.

- You can run some programs with built-in DOS extenders under Windows, but look for those that support the DPMI standard (see Step 5 for an explanation).

- To see how much memory is free, in Windows use the Resource Thermometer. In the Program Manager go to the Help option and click on "About Program Manager". The box there shows the free memory and Free System Resources. Free memory is the sum of unused extended and virtual memory.

- Some non-Windows applications use extended memory in a way that's incompatible with Window's HIMEM.SYS driver. If this is a problem, disable the HIMEM.SYS driver in CONFIG.SYS (remark it or precede it with a colon as explained in Step 3) and then restart your PC and run Windows in real mode.

In general Windows is better than DESQview if you:

• Use graphics-based programs, not text-based programs

• Want to run a Windows application

• Have a powerful PC with lots of memory and a fast 386 processor

• Need dynamic or "hot" links of information between windows or programs (it's called DDE for Dynamic Data Exchange).

DESQview. Quarterdeck's DESQview is not as well known as Windows, but is still quite popular with PC users. It has offered task-switching and multitasking for some time, even on 286-based systems (with expanded memory). DESQview task-switches faster if it has backfilled conventional memory. DESQview does not demand as much hardware power as Windows, partly because it is a text-based environment, where Windows is a graphics-based environment. Still, DESQview can manage your memory and provide separate windows for applications. It can run graphics programs, but they occupy the entire screen instead of just a single window. DESQview swaps the inactive programs out to disk, or to memory if there's enough. It comes ready to handle 100 popular programs, and can handle others once you've entered some information about the particulars of these programs. DESQview offers a scripting language to let you create complex custom procedures and setups.

DESQview 386 comes with the QEMM-386 memory manager program (see Step 4 for a description). QEMM's ability to relocate TSRs and device drivers to high-DOS memory will give you more of the 640K of conventional memory for each application you do run under DESQview. DESQview is also able to use the HMA (or High Memory Area), and was the first program to take advantage of HMA. Programs with DOS extenders built in, which use the rest of extended memory, run without trouble under DESQview too, alongside non-DOS extender programs. In fact, DESQview 2.3 with QEMM 5.1 can run Windows 3, in its real or standard mode, within a DESQview window. That's useful if you like DESQview but sometimes need to run applications created for Windows.

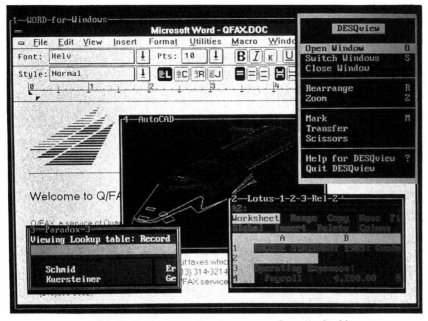

Figure 6-6. Typical DESQview Display (courtesy Quarterdeck)

Tips for DESQview—A 1K script buffer is set aside for each program you add to the DESQview environment. If you won't be using scripts with a program, don't waste that K of memory. Select **Open Window**, then **Change a Program**, choose the program, then press F1 for the **Advanced Options**, then Tab the cursor to the **Script Buffer** field and change the default from 1000 bytes to 0 bytes.

Use QEMM to get maximum memory with DESQview 386.

DESQview runs faster if its swap files are on a RAM disk. However, don't use a RAM disk if you have expanded memory or a 386-based system, because DESQview can use the expanded and extended memory more efficiently itself. To use a RAM disk, set up the RAM disk. Run the DESQview setup program on your hard disk, then choose Logical Drives, and set the Swap: type to the letter of your RAM disk.

If EGA and VGA displays are slowed by multitasking, use the QEMM DESQview 386 memory manager to move the ROM instructions to high-DOS memory. Put the line **ROM=C000-C3FF** in the CONFIG.SYS file.

DESQview switches between tasks best with lots of expanded memory, even backfilled memory occupying all of the conventional memory addresses.

DESQview requires a PC or compatible with at least 512K RAM (though 640K is better), DOS 2.0 or later, a hard drive, and LIM 4.0 expanded memory.

In general, DESQview is a better bet than Windows if you:

- Mainly use text-based applications, not graphics-based stuff

- Want maximum conventional memory for applications

- Don't have a 386-based PC with lots of RAM (necessary for Windows) but do have expanded memory don't need dynamic or hot links between windows, but can get by with cut-and-paste transfer of information.

GEOS. GeoWorks GEOS (Graphic Environment Operating System) is a GUI (Graphical User Interface) much like Windows. The two big differences are that Windows is much better known and that GEOS demands much less hardware to run. Hundreds of programs have been rewritten to completely support Windows. Few have so far been rewritten to support the much newer GEOS. But Windows needs at least a 386 processor a couple of megabytes of memory to run well. GEOS runs on PCs and XTs as long as they have a hard disk. It needs only 100K of memory for itself. When you run a GEOS program, though, all 70 bytes of GEOS are removed from memory, leaving the maximum amount of room for the application.

Even so, GEOS is not only a task-switcher but a multitasking and multithreading (multitasking within a single program, for different parts of the program) environment. That is even beyond the multitasking that Windows offers. Like Windows or DESQview GEOS adds to DOS; it doesn't replace it.

GeoWorks also makes Ensemble, a set of applications that run under GEOS. This includes GeoWrite, GeoManager (a simple database), GeoDraw, and GeoDex (an address manager), a NotePad, a Calendar, and a Calculator. GEOS can offer scalable outline fonts for these programs—something you get under Windows only with an added utility program. Figure 6-7 shows Ensemble.

When you install GEOS you have a choice of running it under Appliance, First Time, or Professional Level, determining the amount of multitasking, the options and the number of variables you can and may deal with.

242

Figure 6-7. Ensemble with the GEOS Environment (courtesy GEOS Software)

GEOS needs a PC with 512K of RAM, a CGA or Hercules graphics adapter, a mouse, DOS 2 or later, and three free megabytes of memory on a hard disk to run. It can use extended or expanded memory and runs in the processor's real mode.

GEM. GEM is a Windows-style environment and Graphical User Interface from Digital Research, the company that makes DR-DOS, the DOS alternative mentioned in Step 9. It does not provide multitasking or any route past the 640K barrier. However, it can run in a DESQview window, and use DESQview's memory management.

Like Windows, GEM demands that programs be rewritten to its style and rules. Not many programmers are taking this route because of the popularity of Windows. Even Ventura Publisher, the best-known GEM-based program, is now appearing in a Windows version.

Omniview. The 386 version of the Omniview, the context-switcher from Sunny Hill Software, provides real multitasking for DOS application programs. It needs LIM 4.0 or some other memory mapping hardware to do this. Omniview 386 allocates memory to the applications as they need it, and works with expanded memory, though not with extended. The 386 version comes with an EMM utility that can convert extended memory to expanded. Omniview can also relocate its routines to high-DOS memory, but it cannot move TSRs or DOS BUFFERS.

Deskmate. This environment from Tandy (the Radio Shack company) is a text-based set of menus and icons that demands less memory and processor power than Windows. It does not offer the task-switching or multitasking of Windows or DESQview, and does not provide any memory management capabilities. It is chiefly designed to create a standard set of menus for applications and a DOS shell to make DOS applications easier to use for beginners.

VMOS/3. VMOS/3, from Microdyne Corporation, needs a 386-based PC to run because it uses the 386's V86 mode to offer multitasking and virtual memory. Because it so thoroughly isolates applications from one another, you can even reboot one application without interrupting the others. This isolation is a drag on performance, though, slowing any program down. VMOS/3 has its own user interface, too. It lets you control details such as DMA channels, interrupts and ports. It provides a status screen to show how it is working, including a bar graph to show how much time each session is getting. And it does all of this without changing your CONFIG.SYS and AUTOEXEC.BAT files.

VM/386. This is a text-based environment from IGC. It requires a 386- or 486-based PC, and on such a machine can use the V86 mode to multitask DOS programs, including Windows. However, it can only show one program on-screen at a time. VM/386 isolates programs from one another, so rebooting one with the Ctrl-Alt-Del keys won't affect the others. It does not offer virtual memory. It also lets you plug terminals into a 386 PC's serial ports to have a multi-user system.

Each program running under VM/386 needs enough memory for DOS, for the program, and 40K more of its own buffers. In other words, you'd need 3 to 4MB to run several programs at once. VM/386 doesn't support the VCPI standard, so it won't run many DOS Extender programs. It does support the newer DPMI standard, and offers many customizing commands for experts to use in creating their own multitasking system.

Do More With Memory

After you've found, added, and configured memory, and set it up with applications, TSRs, drivers, environments, memory managers, and whatnot, you may find that you have a bit of memory left over. You can use that extra memory to make your computing faster and your printing easier with disk caches (pronounced "cashes"), RAM disks, and spoolers. In fact, these three memory tools are so powerful that you should make sure you have memory left over to set them up in your PC.

Key Ideas

- Spoolers intercept any print task you send to the printer, save it in a memory buffer, and dole it out in the background at the slow speed that a printer can accept. This cuts the time you have to wait to get back to work after giving a print command.

- Disk caches and RAM disks can speed up nearly every PC operation, but are especially potent for those programs that frequently use the disk drives—such as database management and accounting, and word processing large documents. Disk caches use a small amount of memory to speed the apparent operation of a disk drive. RAM disks use larger amounts of RAM and act as if they are a very fast disk drive. Each has advantages and disadvantages.

Printer Spoolers

No matter what application program you run, memory is part of the hardware team involved in the calculations, computations, and manipulations that lead to a finished page that's ready to print. Once the result is ready for printing, your computer could just send it directly to the printer without any further use of memory.

This is rarely the case, because it is not efficient. Memory can hold the information to print before that information squirts out through a serial or parallel cable to the printer. Memory in the printer can hold the information to print before the graphics or text are actually put on the page. (These same rules hold for most other output peripherals, such as plotters and film-recorders. You can follow all of the advice in this chapter when using those devices too—just make sure whatever spooling utility you choose supports the device you want to use.) For each role, you can make printing better and easier by using the memory more efficiently or by adding memory. (Ah, haven't we heard that before.) This Step covers the memory in the computer; Step 8 covers the memory in the printer.

Printers are Slower than Chips

You see, even the fastest printers are slower than the slowest processor or memory chips. (printers and disk drives are the slowest parts of PCs because they're mechanical instead of electronic. Electricity works at the nearly the speed of light, while mechanical operations are a million times slower. The computer would send the first character (for text printing) or dot (for graphics printing) and the printer would go through its process to put that on a page. While the printer huffed and puffed at its work, the computer would wait, and wait, and wait, and wait, and wait ten thousand times more. Finally it would get to send the second character or dot, and then wait ten thousand times again.

The PC is always kept waiting while feeding a slow, steady stream of data to the printer. Complicated or long documents can take hours to print, even on today's fast laser printers. That means your PC could be held hostage to a much slower printer for hours at a time. (Even the couple of minutes for printing a quick memo can be annoying.) Why tolerate such a waste of time?

Intercepting the Flow

You don't have to wait on a slow printer. Spooling or buffering can eliminate this wait. It doesn't take all the power of the computer to feed a character or dot at a time to a printer. So just as disk caching uses a small controlling program and some memory to speed slow disk operations, spooling and buffering use a small controlling program and some memory to speed up slow printer operations. Instead of sending the print information to memory in dribs and drabs, at the sedated printer speed, why not send it all to memory as fast as the program can put it out? Then feed it from the memory spool or buffer to the printer's mechanisms at the printer's comfortable speed. Figure 7-1 shows this information flow.

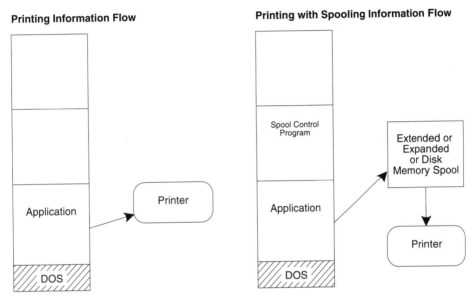

Figure 7-1. Diagram of Information Flow in Spooling or Buffering a Print Job

Background Operations: Avoiding Tie-up

After the spool or buffer captures the print results and starts feeding them to the printer, the computer's processor and memory can get back to work on other things. The printing can continue in the background, and you can get back to work in your spreadsheet, word processor, in seconds instead of minutes, or minutes instead of hours. The pages won't necessarily appear any sooner from the printer, though in some cases they may if the spooler program has special routines to efficiently shuttle information to the printer, but your computer will be ready for other work much sooner. For example, if you're using 1-2-3 to create a large report, and have a spooler running in the background, you could give the command to print the report, and quickly turn to working on another spreadsheet or to some other program, perhaps a word processor. The report would zip from 1-2-3 to memory, and would eventually come rolling out of the printer. Most spoolers and buffers can work in the background, operating even while other programs are running. This primitive form of multitasking is possible even on computers that aren't officially capable of multitasking.

Four Locations for the Buffer

There are basically four places the buffering memory can be:

- In the computer (using part of its conventional, expanded, or extended memory or even its hard disk)—called spooling in this book.

- In the computer, on a special plug-in controller card for the printer (where it doesn't use the computer's own memory)

- In a box between the computer and the printer, called a standalone buffer or printer-sharing buffer in this book.

- In the printer.

Watch out for the terms here. The terms spooler and buffer are often confused, and are sometimes used interchangeably. Some people think a spooler is in the computer's memory, a buffer in the printer's, and the box in between is a standalone buffer. Whatever—they're all buffering the flow of information, and any buffering for print work is called spooling.

Each location has its own advantages and disadvantages.

- Spooling in the computer—uses up some of your computer's memory, but offers great flexibility in handling different printers (even at the same time) and in a large number of print management options and commands. It also lets you use the memory for other work when not printing.

- Used on a special plug-in controller card in the computer, it can offer a very high-speed transmission cable to the printer, and leave your computer's memory undisturbed. However, with a special processor and memory devoted only to printing, this can be an expensive solution. It is typically used only for very high resolution prints from controller boards that push laser printers to their limits. (Step 8 covers this sort of dedicated printer memory.)

• In a box between computer and printer—this makes it easy for several PCs to share a single printer. It doesn't use any of your computer's memory, but can also be an expensive solution—with the memory only useful for printing.

• In the printer—doesn't use any of your computer's memory, but means the memory can only work on printing, and that the memory moves with the printer. If you move your computer or buy a new printer, the buffer in the old printer is no longer yours to use. However, it also means that any other PC that uses the printer gets the advantage of the extra memory. (Step 8 covers memory within the printer.)

Spooling is one of the easiest and cheapest things you can do with extra memory. In fact, it was one of the few things people could do with extended memory for a long time (along with disk caching). Spooling isn't necessary for every computer user, but if you have been waiting on printing jobs it could be just the ticket for you.

Spoolers

The only catch in this dreamy tale of spooling is that you need a special spooling program. This utility will be the organizer that sets aside part of memory, accepts print information from your application, stuff it into the set-aside memory, and then passes the information on, at a slower speed, to the printer. Think of a host who must set up accommodations and welcome a thousand guests within minutes, and then usher them out the door, in exactly the order they arrived, at the rate of one an hour.

Most multitasking operating system—that can do several things at once—spool automatically. You keep computing with one program while a separate printer management program conscientiously doles out the information to the printer. That's one reason to use multitasking software—or to move to a multitasking operating system—such as OS/2 or UNIX. But there's even a simple spooler in DOS for ASCII text file printing: the DOS PRINT command. This doesn't help for most applications, but is easy to use and free for any printing you call on from the DOS prompt. There are a variety of shareware and commercial spooling utilities for DOS. Local area network servers almost always have a spooling utility—a single, central catchpoint for printing files from many computers. Sharing an expensive printer is a key reason to have a network.

Features to Look For

Not all spoolers have the same features. Here are some things to look for:

• Able to work in conventional, expanded, extended, or disk memory. The more places the spooler works, the more chance you'll get to use it no matter what kind of PC you have and what you're doing with memory. Most spoolers will put at least some of their program into conventional memory—even if only a few K. But it's important that you be able to push the actual buffer—especially if it's large—into extended, expanded, or even disk memory.

• Low overhead. The spooler uses memory in two ways: for its own program code (also known here as the "overhead") and for the buffer that holds your printer information. The program code is almost always a memory-resident program that will eat up from 5 to 100K of your own, precious, conventional memory. Try to keep the overhead to a minimum, around 5K to 20K. The buffer itself can generally be any size you set it to, from just a few K for printing small text files to a megabyte or more for printing, long, complicated graphics documents. Figure 7-1 shows how spoolers have a small program in RAM and a large buffer in RAM or on disk.

• Dynamic use of memory. This is an advanced feature that's wonderful to have. Instead of setting aside some large piece of memory turf and protecting it jealously for spooling, a dynamic spooler will start with only the memory it needs and then reach for more as it needs it. In fact, it will shrink it's demands again once there is less to keep in memory—releasing memory for other programs and uses.

• Broad (or at least relevant-to-your-equipment) compatibility. Most commercial spoolers now support all kinds of printers, including laser, dot-matrix, inkjet, and even plotters. Older spoolers and inexpensive spoolers may have more limited capabilities, supporting only dot-matrix printers, for example. This compatibility can also include the ability to spool for more than one printer at a time—something you might like if you have a laser hooked up for polished prints, an inkjet for drafts, and a plotter for drawings.

• Ability to handle multiple printers. If you have one printer for drafts, another for finals, and yet another for color prints, this suggestion is obviously important. It can also come in handy if you only occasionally use a different printer, but might want to spool results for that printer off to a separate file.

• Low price. See the discussion that follows on "Where to Find Spoolers."

• Speed. A few spoolers can actually speed printing by sending information in a more efficient manner to the printer. PrintCache is famous for this.

• Has queue management commands. (Not everyone needs these.) Some people just need to send a file off for printing and forget it, while returning to their work. But if you're printing lots of documents, or working on a network spooler where many people are printing documents at once, it could be very useful to set priorities for different printing files, to change the order of files waiting in the queue, and to even flag certain printing files for off-hours printing. Some of the commercial spoolers have these commands.

• Has print management commands. These include making multiple copies of a print, scaling or rotating the print, and so on. Most programs can do these things, but having the spooler do them relieves the program of some work.

• Interruption protection. Some spoolers do a better job than others of recovering from a power outage or other interruption. Some spoolers just close down entirely; others ask if you want to restart a print job that wasn't complete.

Terms of Confusion

Here are some spooling terms you should know when shopping. There's confusion on using these, with even the experts muddying the waters.

- Spooling—using memory in your computer to temporarily hold print information.

- Spooler—the program that sets aside and manages spooling memory.

- Buffering—using memory in your printer or in some intermediate box between computer and printer to hold print information.

- Buffer—any chunk of memory set aside for holding information temporarily. Often used to refer to the area of the computer's memory set aside for spooling.

- Queue—the list of names of the files waiting in the spooling memory for their chance to be printed. Sometimes used to mean the files themselves, not just the file names.

- Printer cache—synonym for spooler, buffer, queue, or other related term.

- Printer Buffer—sometimes means the buffer in the printer.

- Print Buffer—sometimes means the spooler in the computer.

Where to Find Spoolers

Spoolers are all around you. You probably already own one, though it may not have all of the features you want. Here are some places to look for spoolers:

- Your application program. For example, if you're using WordPerfect, you already have a built-in spooler with that program. It may not have all the features you want, but it's free. Unfortunately, it will probably only work for that particular program. Other programs in this category include Framework, DisplayWrite, MultiMate, and Windows-compatible applications (it's built into Windows 3).

• Your operating system or environment. Windows, for example, has its own spooler (though it only works for Windows programs). DOS has only the very-limited PRINT.COM spooler built-in, but most other operating systems offer more.

• Your utility package. Many utility packages, such as PC Tools Deluxe, have a print spooler as one of their many utility programs.

• Your add-in memory board or accelerator. Most add-in boards come with a disk of utility programs, and a spooler is a typical denizen of such a disk. Intel's Above Board Plus, for example, comes with a spooler. You can decide during the board's SOFTSET installation program process to set up the print buffer. There's a pop-up menu of spooling controls for assigning the buffer to a particular printer, for canceling or resuming printing, for printing whatever is on the screen display, and for emptying the buffer of print information.

• Your user-group or favorite computer bulletin board. Spoolers are a staple in the diet of user groups and bulletin boards. They're often public domain stuff (they're free, see the Appendix on "Cheap and Free Software").

• A Shareware distributor. Shareware spoolers are generally inexpensive, and you can try them before paying the full price. (See the Appendix on "Cheap and Free Software" for more information on this.)

• Commercial software. There are several excellent spoolers for sale. Check retail stores or mail-order catalogs. Note that the prices at mail order can be half what they are in the store. Commercial spoolers generally have more commands for print and queue management, more flexible use of memory, and more up-to-date compatibility with various printers and plotters.

Spoolers Gallery

Here's a directory of some popular spoolers. My favorites are:

• Any spooler that comes free with an add-in memory board. (These typically do the job just fine, and are free with the board.)

• The Windows 3 or Carousel spoolers if you use either of those environments.

• PrintCache 2.2—if you want small, fast, and the unique ability to print full-page graphics on a LaserJet with only 512K RAM, but don't care about queue or print management commands.

• PrintRite 1.3 for its long list of print and queue management options.

• Super PC-Kwik Spooler—because it's such a great deal when it's part of the Power-Pak bundle of utilities, including a disk cache.

Spoolers in Environments and DOS.

PRINT.COM in DOS—The PRINT command in DOS is actually a memory-resident spooler for ASCII file printing. It comes free with every copy of DOS, gives you some print management commands, and can run in the background. That's the good news. Near the end of this chapter you'll find a detailed explanation of PRINT.COM's commands and options. Unfortunately, the bad news is that PRINT.COM isn't much of a spooler for most of us because it only handles ASCII files—any standard spreadsheet, word processor, database report, or desktop publishing page is way beyond PRINT.COM's abilities.

Carousel's Print Spooler—As Step 6 explains, Carousel is a task-switching program that lets you load several programs into memory at once. (It was previously called Software Carousel.) It comes with its own print spooler utility that can run in the background, called Print'n'Run. Any of the programs in one of Carousel's 12 partitions can direct printing to this spooler, which will use all available RAM—extended, expanded, and hard disk. Print'n'Run doesn't use any conventional RAM.

Windows Print Manager Spooler—Windows 3.0 has a print spooler built in, called the Print Manager. It only works with Windows applications though. The memory this spooler uses depends on the mode Windows 3 runs in, and can include conventional, expanded, extended, and disk. Whenever you print from a Windows program, the results head straight to the Print Manager, which stacks them into a queue for printing. It will hold them there waiting for a printer to be connected and ready to print. The Manager has commands for changing the order of the print queue, for removing files from the queue, for pausing, resuming, or canceling printing, and for setting the priority of printing. Figure 7-2 shows the print manager's display. Any files left unprinted in the queue when you exit Windows are not printed—the queue is simply discarded. Windows can also show you the printing progress of any files that are sent to a network spooler, distinct from the print manager's local spooler. The Windows users guide explains the spooler in some detail.

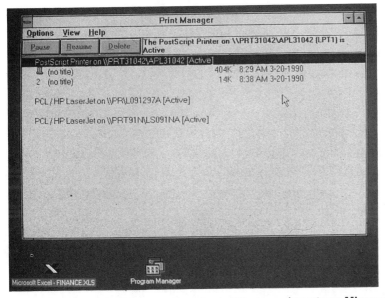

Figure 7-2. The Print Manager Spooler in Windows (courtesy Microsoft)

Public Domain and Shareware Spoolers.

PC Spool—This spooler is available free on PC Magazine's PC MagNet, as explained in the Appendix on "Cheap and Free Software." It can spool for several programs at once, and is easy to set up and use.

Disk Spool II 2.0—Disk Spool II 2.0 is a shareware spooler from Budget Software. It spools print files to disk and can hold files there indefinitely—protecting you from lost printing if the computer loses power. It builds a separate file for each document. Spooling to disk this way also adds the unique ability to print even when no printer is attached to your computer. The information to print is stored on the disk, and can then be printed either when a printer is hooked up or when the disk file is transported to another system that does have an attached printer. Disk Spool II offers a pop-up menu to control spooler activities, to print through more than one port at a time, and to fine-tune the printing-spooler system for the best speed. The registration fee is $34. A $44 update is faster and adds context-sensitive help. Available through PC-SIG.

FPRINT.COM.—You can find enhanced versions of PRINT.COM in some shareware and public domain collections. For example, the Printer Utilities 4 disk from PC-SIG comprises more than three dozen printer utilities, including FPRINT.COM (an enhanced DOS print spooler) and SP.EXE (a print spooler).

Commercial Spoolers.

PrintCache 2.2—PrintCache from LaserTools replaces the Torq (for dot-matrix printers) and LaserTorq (for laser printers) spoolers. It can use any type of memory—including conventional, expanded, extended, and disk—and lets you vary the buffer size to fit your particular needs. The program itself is quite small; it normally needs about 9K, but can be trimmed down to a mere 5K if you don't need the pop-up status screen. This small control program doesn't offer as many queue management options as some spoolers, because of a design decision that few people actually use these commands, and nearly all want a program that takes up minimum memory. For instance, it can't set the priority for printing a particular document, limiting itself to the basic commands for ejecting a page, suspending printing, or clearing the buffer.

PrintCache is quite fast. It can send serial output at up to 115,000 baud—that's about the same as bits per second—the highest speed most serial ports allow. (HP

LaserJets take data at up to 19,200 baud). It handles parallel ports with a special algorithm, to push them to their highest speed possible.

PrintCache supports most types of printers—including dot-matrix, daisy-wheel, inkjet, HP LaserJet, PostScript laser, and plotters. It can spool print information for several printers at once. PrintCache has optimized drivers for dot-matrix and inkjet-printers and even spools for plotters. It also supports printer-sharing devices and has optimized printer port drivers for PS/2 computers.

A unique feature in PrintCache is its ability to squeeze the white space out of graphics documents to let you print many full-page, 300 dpi (dots per inch) graphic images on an HP LaserJet IIP, Plus, II, and IID printer or compatible with only 512K of RAM (in the printer). Unfortunately, this feature doesn't always work. Without PrintCache you need at least 1MB in your LaserJet to print any full page of high-resolution graphics. This can be an inexpensive alternative to memory upgrades for your printer. Figure 7-3 illustrates this operation.

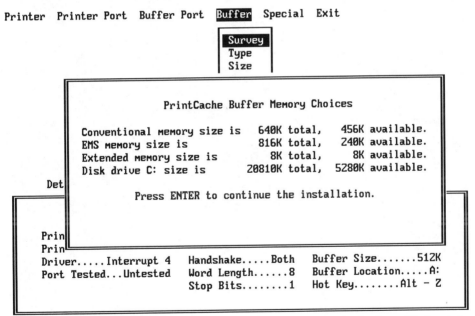

Figure 7-3. PrintCache can squeeze graphic images to fit 512K laser printers.
         (courtesy LaserTools)

PrintRite 1.3—PrintRite 1.3 from Bloc Publishing supports most printers and also supports networks. It is not as small as PrintCache 2.2, using 50K of RAM for the control program, but can keep the spool file size relatively small by compressing print jobs. It comes with pull-down menus for a long list of sophisticated queue and print management, such as changing the printing order, specifying multiple copies, aligning forms, and even printing sideways on any laser printer. It can even group types of printing together—handling all the spreadsheets, then the text, then the graphics—for the most efficient process. The status display tells you the files waiting to be printed, the source application for each file, and the file's time and date of entry to the queue, status, and total pages. It also lets you view files without printing.

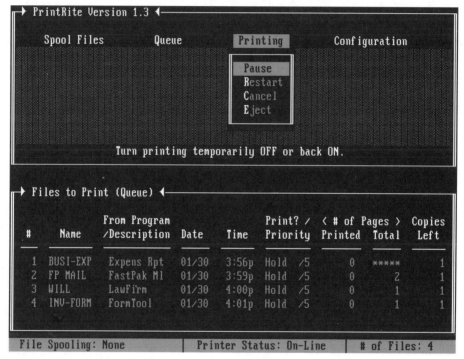

Figure 7-4. PrintRite's Control Display (courtesy BLOC Publishing)

PrintRite spools each file separately, not as a single spooling file, and can queue up to 225 entries and control five printers at once. PrintRite spools to disk, and so protects your printing information. This also makes it a fine spooler for a laptop without an attached printer, where sending a file to the spooler feels just like printing, and that spooled file can later be printed at a computer that is hooked up to a printer.

Super PC-Kwik Spooler—This spooler works in extended, expanded, or disk memory. It has a pop-up control window and can compress print data. Perhaps its most outstanding feature—besides the low price as part of this utility bundle—is its ability to dynamically share memory with the disk cache that accompanies it in the PC-Kwik Power Pak utility bundle. The Power Pak has lots of utility programs, including a RAM disk, a screen and a keyboard accelerator, a disk cache, and the print spooler.

PrintQ 4.0—Print Q from Software Directions works with dot-matrix, daisy-wheel, inkjet, and both HP and PostScript laser printers. It comes in both single-user and 4-user network versions, and can use hard disk instead of RAM for the buffer. Print Q needs 55K RAM and isn't particularly fast. But it packs lots of print and queue management functions in its pop-up control program, including: hold or archive for later printing, print multiple copies, manage multiple queues, restart printing from a particular page, set printing priorities, and view files before printing.

Printer Genius—NOR Software's Printer Genius spooler uses 47K RAM and can control up to three printers at a time. Its TSR printer and queue management program has some features you won't find on most other spoolers, such as an editor for labels and notes, and font-selection commands.

Spool-Q—Insight Development's Spool-Q is an inexpensive spooler that can forward files directly to a printer or to a disk file. Each print job is a separate file on the disk.

PrinTools—This spooler from Insight Development is a set of utility programs for HP LaserJet and compatible printers. It can initialize printers, directly capture output to a disk file for later printing and processing, capture a screen image as text or graphics, and use the plotter abilities built into LaserJets.

Specialized Spoolers.

P.D.Queue—Funk Software's P.D.Queue spooler is only for Lotus 1-2-3 Release 2.x and Symphony Release 1.1 or later. It is an add-in that becomes part of the 1-2-3 or Symphony command structure, adding 36K to their RAM use (and also taking up hard disk space for the actual spooled files). Funk also makes the popular formatting add-ins Sideways and Allways. It can handle any 1-2-3 output on most any printer, including 1-2-3 files enhanced with Allways, Sideways, Impress, or other utilities. P.D.Queue can hold up to 99 print jobs in the queue at once, and lets you rearrange the queue or pause printing. Because it uses hardware interrupts, it doesn't steal much processor time from 1-2-3 or Symphony: it won't slow them down while printing in the background.

SuperPrint—SuperPrint, from Zenographics, is a replacement for the built-in spooler of Windows 2.1 or 3.0. It is a utility that runs under Windows. There are two parts to SuperPrint. First is a font handling part that lets you mix and match Adobe Type 1, Bitstream Fontware, Nimbus Q, HP LaserJet bit-map, and Agfa Compugraphic Intellifonts on a page, giving PostScript quality prints on non-PostScript printers. It manages this in as little as 1K of memory, where competing programs—such as FaceLift and ATM—sometimes need hundreds of K. However, it does not create screen fonts "on the fly." SuperPrint comes in versions for HP, CalComp, Tektronix, and Mitsubishi Electronics America printers, and for Presentation Technologies film recorders. The package includes 22 scalable typefaces.

The second part of SuperPrint is the SuperQue spooler, which can be much faster than the spoolers that come with Windows 2.1 or 3.0.

Using the DOS PRINT.COM Spooler

The DOS PRINT command is actually a memory-resident spooler program called PRINT.COM for ASCII file printing. It comes free with every copy of DOS, gives you some print management commands, and can run in the background. Here's how to use it.

PRINT.COM basics. PRINT is one of DOS's external commands. (The DOS 4.0 shell has this print command in its FILE menu.) That is, it isn't automatically available at all times as internal commands are. You must have it available on disk before using it. The command PRINT.COM lets you send information from a disk file to all sorts of devices, but the typical destination is a printer attached to your PC's parallel port. Hook the printer up, and type **PRINT filename** then press Return to print the file titled "filename". If it is an ASCII file and your printer can easily handle

ASCII text, you'll soon see the file appear on the printed pages. Some printers, however, need special control codes that PRINT.COM won't produce, and their output may be worthless.

Choosing Serial or Parallel Output. You can use PRINT to send to a serial ported printer too, with the following DOS command, **MODE LPT1:=COM1**

MODE.COM is another DOS external command. LPT1 is the first parallel port in your PC. COM1 is the first serial port. This MODE command tells the PC to redirect information that's headed to the parallel port, and to send it instead to the serial port. Part of the MODE command is a memory-resident or TSR program—it loads into memory and stays there until you reboot your computer. This part is quite small, however.

Using Switches for PRINT.COM Options. PRINT.COM has a number of operation options that you control with switches. You use these as you would the options of any DOS command, by typing a slash after the PRINT command and then typing the switch letter (uppercase or lowercase, it doesn't matter). The only time you can use these switches is when you first run or load PRINT.COM into memory. After that, the only way to change the switch settings is to restart your PC (either by turning off the power or by pressing Ctrl-Alt-Del) and then running and loading PRINT.COM again with the new switch settings. Because PRINT.COM is often inserted into the AUTOEXEC.BAT file so that it will automatically be active whenever you run your computer (AUTOEXEC.BAT runs every time you turn on your PC), you may have to edit AUTOEXEC.BAT to change the PRINT.COM options.

Managing the PRINT.COM Queue. PRINT's buffer is kept on disk and can be large enough to hold several files in line. (Remember, the *print buffer* is the memory area that holds the files. The *print queue* is the list of filenames waiting to print. The *spooler* is the program that set aside the buffer and maintains the queue. They aren't the same thing, but they are closely related: the queue lists what's in the buffer which is created and managed by the spooler.) The files in the queue will print one after the other, in the order they were sent to the queue. And because part of PRINT is a TSR program—staying in memory to control the buffer—those files will print in the background to some extent: allowing you to use other DOS commands while the PRINT queue is still queuing up the jobs to be printed.

To send more than one file to the PRINT queue, you can use a sequence of PRINT commands, such as **PRINT filename1** and **PRINT filename2** or you can just put more than one filename in a command such as: **PRINT filename1 filename2**. The filename1 file will print before the filename2 file.

You can even use DOS wildcard symbols with PRINT, such as **PRINT *.txt** to print all of the text files, sending them into a long PRINT queue. Even if you're using other DOS commands in between, each new PRINT command will send another file to the queue, to be lined up behind all those that haven't printed yet. To see the full PRINT queue type **PRINT**. A list will show, as in Figure 7-5, with the name of the file being printed and the names of all others in the queue.

```
C>print *.bat *.txt *.sys
PRINT queue is full

  C:\DOS\README.TXT is currently being printed
  C:\DOS\TRIAL.TXT is in queue
  C:\DOS\CONFIG.SYS is in queue
  C:\DOS\AUTOEXEC.BAT is in queue
  C:\DOS\GOMOUSE.BAT is in queue
  C:\DOS\README.TXT is in queue
  C:\DOS\TRIAL.TXT is in queue
  C:\DOS\ANSI.SYS is in queue
  C:\DOS\CONFIG.SYS is in queue
  C:\DOS\COUNTRY.SYS is in queue

C>
C>
C>
C>
C>
C>
C>
C>
C>
C>
```

Figure 7-5. The DOS PRINT Queue List

To cut a file from the queue, type **PRINT filename /c** The "c" stands for "cancel". The command **PRINT filename1 /c filename2 filename3** cuts several files from the queue. You may use wildcards here too. The /t terminates printing. It stops the current print and empties the queue, like this **PRINT filename /t.**

PRINT.COM's Buffer Size. The default PRINT buffer size is only 512 bytes. That will only hold about a quarter of a page of text. Because that buffer is small, it fills and emptys quickly, so PRINT must frequently grab more print information from the disk drive. A larger buffer cuts down on disk work and time and can let you build longer PRINT queues. You can change the buffer size, but as mentioned above, you can only make option changes like this the first time you use PRINT, until you restart your computer and DOS, that is. Use the **PRINT /B:bytes** command with any value from 512 to 16,000 for the bytes. Do this in increments of 512 bytes. Here are some rules of thumb for the PRINT.COM buffer size when printing only a few files at a time.

- If you're printing 4K bytes or less, use a 2048 byte buffer

- If you're printing 4K to 8K bytes, use a 4096 byte buffer

- If you're printing more than 8K bytes, use an 8192-byte buffer More files at a time demand more buffer space, so increase those amounts if you're planning to queue more than 5 or 10 files at a time.

PRINT.COM's Queue Size. If you're planning to queue more than 10 filenames at a time, you'll also need to enlarge the print queue (the length of the list of files that can sit in the buffer). The default holds only 10 names (I say "only," though that's more than I've ever printed at once with PRINT.COM). If you don't enlarge the queue, you'll get the error message **PRINT queue is full** from DOS. To enlarge the PRINT queue, use the /Q switch, like this: **PRINT /Q:number** with "number" being any value up to 32. If it is too late to use Q, you'll see an error message such as: **Invalid switch-/Q:32**

PRINT may have already been run, and loaded into memory. Check the AUTOEXEC.BAT file for a PRINT command. You can use the switch next time you start the computer—you might have to extract any PRINT command from AUTOEXEC.BAT, or add the /q option to that command.

Controlling PRINT.COM's Speed and Timing. As mentioned above, PRINT can run in the background. That is, you can use other DOS commands and even applications programs while the PRINT buffer feeds its queue of files to the printer. PRINT handles this multitasking by giving some processor time to your other work and some to PRINT. You can determine how much time goes to each.

DOS has a timer that ticks. On a PC the typical tick is about 55 milliseconds long. That means there are about 20 ticks in a second. DOS's default setting is to give itself 8 ticks and then to give PRINT 2 ticks. Then it's 8 more ticks for DOS work (or your application) and 2 more again for PRINT. You can increase the number of ticks for DOS—running your application faster and your printing slower—or you can increase the ticks for PRINT—slowing your application and speeding the print. You can also set the number of ticks that PRINT waits after getting a busy signal from a printer, the time it waits before trying to send printable information again to that printer.

/s   is the switch for DOS ticks. (The default is 8.)

/m   is the switch for PRINT ticks. (The default is 2.)

/u   is the switch for waiting ticks after PRINT gets a busy signal. (The default is 1.)

To balance DOS and printing, for instance, you might use **PRINT /s:20 /m:4 / u:2**

If the printer buffer is larger than 2K, start with a larger /m value to give PRINT time to fill the large buffer. Then you should probably increase /s to keep the proportions between DOS and PRINT the same. Experiment with the settings, but don't spend too much time on it—there is no perfect balance for all computing work.

Printer-sharing Buffers

Memory that can hold printer information doesn't have to be in your computer. It can be in the printer itself, or in some intermediate device. Most of these in-between boxes aren't satisfied to just offer a wad of memory. Typically they add a set of parallel and serial ports, some electronic logic to back them up, and even some software to control the whole thing. Then the box can not only buffer printing, but can accept and translate slower serial information into faster parallel, and can accept input from several PCs and send output to several printers. It can let PCs share printers, without the higher cost and complication of a local area network or LAN—the chief other way to share information between computer devices.

These boxes differ in the number and type of ports they have, in the amount of memory they start with, in the maximum amount of memory they can hold, and in the control packed into their hardware and software. Some have LED panels and switches to avoid the possibilities of conflict from TSR control programs. Some can daisy-chain to connect more printers to more PCs. Some even let PCs share files. A standard buffer is 256K, though some inexpensive buffers have as little as 64K. The maximum memory is typically 1MB to 4MB. You'll need to examine your own applications to see how much memory you need. Multiple graphics printing jobs would strain a 1MB box, for example. Figure 7-6 shows a typical standalone buffer.

Figure 7-6. A Stand-Alone Print Buffer Box (courtesy Buffalo Products)

Printer-sharing buffers aren't as flexible as the spoolers in individual PCs, or as powerful as local area networks (which can have their own spoolers), so I don't cover them in much detail in this book. Just make sure you pay attention to the following considerations.

- Additional memory for the box doesn't cost too much.

- The box's TSR Control programs that run on your PC don't eat up too much of your PC's memory.

Here's a list of some printer-sharing buffers:

- Print Director PD6SP from Digital Products comes with TSR control programs that run on your PC, and a buffer box with 4 serial and 2 parallel ports. It can hold from 256K to 1MB of RAM.

- Buffalo SL 1000 from Buffalo Products has a TSR control program that needs only 9K of conventional RAM because the rest of it can run in expanded memory. The box comes with four parallel and six serial ports or eight parallel and two serial ports. It can automatically route printing to a free printer. It's initial complement of 1MB of RAM can be increased to 4MB.

- The SimpLAN Serverjet from ASP Computer Products plugs into the I/O slot of an HP LaserJet. You can then stretch up to 2000 ft of phone cable to as many as 10 different computers who can share the LaserJet, simultaneously printing at 115,200 baud using the 256K or 1MB buffer.

- The Share Spool ESI-2094A from Extended Systems lets up to four PCs simultaneously reach a LaserJet printer. It comes with a 1MB buffer and DMA-assisted input channels for speed. The ESI-2020A has a 64K dynamically-allocated buffer to let two PCs share a LaserJet IIP.

- The Microfazer printer buffer from Quadram can have as little as 64K RAM or as much as 512K. Its controls let the PC user stop printing, clear the buffer, make multiple copies, pause, or restart printing.

• Local Union from LaserTools can link four or eight PCs to a printer. The boxes can be daisy-chained and come with the PrintCache spooler program.

Tips for Using Spoolers and Buffers

Spoolers are very important when sharing a printer with someone else because without one you might find yourself waiting, not only for your own printing to finish, but for all the printing tasks sent to the printer to finish before you can use your computer again.

Spoolers are very easy to use and will save time whenever you print. Print jobs won't appear any sooner in most cases, but your computer will have more time to work on other jobs while it is printing.

• Put the spooler in extended or expanded memory if you can.

• Check to see if any of your programs have a built-in spooler that you can use immediately.

• If you use Windows-compatible application programs under Windows 3.0, you have the built-in print manager spooler.

• If you use a network, look for a central spooler program built-in to the networking software. (Step 8 discusses network spooling in more detail.)

• Spoolers in your PC and standalone buffers are not especially useful when your printer has a large built-in buffer. Spoolers and buffers are also useful for redirecting output—sending it to different output devices.

• Use the hard disk spooling option if your spooler has it, because then any files saved in the queue will be protected from power outage or other interruption and you'll use less precious RAM. Only the spooler control TSR program will occupy any RAM.

• Don't use more than one spooler or buffer at a time as they can conflict. If there's a spooler in your environment or program, disable it before setting up another spooler.

• Use parallel connections to your printer whenever possible—they're faster than serial.

• If you're spooling to a printer through a serial port, remember to set up the serial port for the highest rate of information transfer, using the DOS MODE command.

• Use a buffer that's large enough or you won't see much speed improvement. Estimate 4K for each text page and 256K for each graphics page. For simple word processor files 50K will certainly be enough. The smallest files could even get by with 5 to 10K. But desktop publishing and graphics work could use 1 to 2MB. You'll need to experiment to find your own best solution. The easiest thing to do could be to get a dynamic buffer, such as that with Multisoft's PC-Kwik spooler, that can share memory with a disk cache, each using what it needs as circumstances change.

• The built-in spoolers of programs such as WordPerfect often take up more extra memory than the program would take without them.

• The 4MB of memory that OS/2 Presentation Manager programs such as Excel and PageMaker need to get started is sometimes free after startup for tasks such as spooling. Spooling is one of the easy things you can do with extended memory, including that 384K of extended memory that would have been in the high memory addresses on the typical AT clone with 1MB of RAM installed.

• EMS 3.2 memory is also prime territory for a spooling buffer. Although it can't be used for programs, it can be used for data such as this, with the spooling program itself in conventional RAM.

• If your network has a spooler on the server or printer, you may not need a spooler on your local PC or workstation.

Disk Caches and RAM Disks

Disk drives are a lot slower than RAM memory chips. If you time how long it takes the typical RAM memory chip to return some stored information, and compare that to how long it takes the typical hard disk drive, this is what you'll see:

RAM memory chips: 100ns
Hard disk drive: 28,000,000ns

That means RAM memory chips are nearly a million times faster than disks. It shouldn't be surprising. After all, RAM memory chips work with electricity that's moving at nearly the speed of light while hard disk drives are working with motors and levers which are moving at mechanical speeds.

Why do we bother with mechanical disk drives at all then? Why not just use RAM memory chips for all of our program and data storage? Three reasons:

- Expense
- Size
- Volatility

As for expense, take a look at a cost comparison, in typical 1991 prices for a megabyte of memory (as a SIMM strip for the chips and a 100MB hard disk for the disk). Here's what you'll see:

RAM memory chips (per megabyte): $80
Hard disk drive (per megabyte): $5

So RAM memory chips are between ten and twenty times as expensive as disks. That's one reason they're not the only storage in a computer.

As for size, disk drives take up considerably less room and power than do RAM memory chips. As one indicator, consider what fits in a typical PC add-in slot,

RAM memory chips (max in typical slot):   8MB
Hard disk drive (max in typical slot):   80MB

RAM memory chips take up ten times as much room.

What's volatility? Simple, a *volatile memory* only keeps its information as long as it has power. When you turn off the computer's power (or it is shut off accidentally by a blackout, lightning strike, child tripping over the plug, etc.):

RAM memory chips: data is lost
Hard disk drives: data is retained

A computer wouldn't be too practical if it forgot all of your files and programs every time you turned it off. So RAM memory chips don't make it as the only storage in a computer (There are ways around this volatility, such as attaching a backup battery to the RAM memory chips to ensure power, or using special memory chips that aren't volatile. Either scheme costs more than standard RAM memory chips, making the cost comparison with a hard disk even worse.)

Floppy disk drives, incidentally, aren't part of my comparison here because they are no longer used in most PCs as a main storage medium. Instead they have become an information transfer medium. They are much slower than hard disk drives, hold much less information, but are non-volatile just like hard disks. ROM chips aren't used in the comparison because they can't accept new information. They may be non-volatile like disks, but you cannot write to them so they cannot store your programs and files as RAM can.

Trade-Offs

As you can see from the comparison above, each type of memory has its own advantages.

RAM memory chips: Fast, expensive, large, volatile
Hard disk drives: Slow, cheap, compact, non-volatile

Computer designers know these facts, and so try to balance the computer with some of each. RAM memory chips are used for processor and video memory, which must be fast and can be relatively small. Hard disk drives are used for longer-term memory, which must be large and non-volatile.

But the decisions the computer designers make are not written in stone. You can buy more memory and hard disk, and what's more, you can trade one against the other. You can improve your computer's performance by using software that makes part of one memory type act like another. You can:

- Use disk memory as chip memory—that's called virtual memory (Step 5)

- Use chip memory as disk memory—that's called disk cache or RAM disk (refer to this Step for more information).

RAM caches and RAM disks can speed up your computing work. The two schemes are not the same, though. They have different pleasures and perils. Nearly all computer owners can benefit from at least one of them. Many can use both at once.

How Caching Works

Caching increases the apparent horsepower of your computer. Caching uses a smaller amount of a faster memory to hold the most frequently-used information from a larger amount of slower memory. (A bit of a tongue and brain twister, I know. But once you see how it works, it's almost obvious.)

Caching depends on one fact of computing: most programs stick to a using a small section of memory for many steps in a row, then jump to another small section and use it for many steps in a row. Few programs leap about throughout memory, grabbing and storing information in wildly different places with each successive operation.

For example, in a computer with 1MB of RAM, a program may execute a hundred instructions in a row reading and writing from one 16K slice of RAM just above the 512K address. Then for the next hundred instructions it might jump to using a 32K slice of memory near the 256K address. All of this reading and writing would run at the 100ns or so speed of those RAM memory chips.

Picture this, then. The computer designer puts a 32K chunk of fast memory chips—rated at 20ns or so—in next to the regular RAM. And she hooks them up so that they don't just add 32K on top of the 1MB. Instead, they don't have any permanent memory address. What they do have is a special controller chip that monitors the addresses your programs are reading from and writing to, and copies the most recently used memory information to that 32K chunk or cache. Then the controller tells the program to look to the cache for its reading and writing.

For that first hundred operations, the program will work with memory that runs at 20ns—much faster than the regular memory chips. It will find the same information in the cache that it would have found in the regular RAM at the 512K address, but it will find it faster. Then when it needs to use the memory addresses near the 256K address, the cache controller will say "hold on a moment," will dump the information that's in the cache, and then will quickly copy what's in those addresses at 256K into the 32K cache. Then the controller says "go ahead, use the cache" to the program. And again the program will be working with 20ns of memory. The result is that a machine with 1MB of 100ns chips looks like a machine with 1MB of 20ns chips, just a little bit slower because of the time to copy the information from regular RAM to the cache. And this computer is a lot cheaper than one that actually contained 1MB of 20ns chips. Nearly all the speed without much of the expense. That's RAM caching from fast RAM to slow RAM.

Disk caching is similar to RAM caching (and the names are sometimes confused). It uses a chunk of the computer's regular RAM as a cache for disk information. A controlling program (itself running in memory, or contained in special hardware) sets 32K, 128K, or some amount of RAM aside as a disk cache. Then the controller monitors the reading from and writing to disk, and copies the most frequently or recently used disk information to the RAM cache. (In fact, the control method is called MRU for Most Recently Used. The more a piece of information is used, the more weight it gets when time comes to decide what stays in the cache and what goes.) Finally, the controller tells programs, and even DOS itself, to look first to the cache for information. In that way, some of the speed of the RAM chips can "rub off" on the disk drive, making it function must faster than its mechanics would ever allow. Whenever the needed information is in the cache, the disk doesn't even get used.

Many of todays fastest computers have both a RAM cache and a disk cache. The RAM cache makes RAM work faster; the disk cache makes the disk drive work faster.

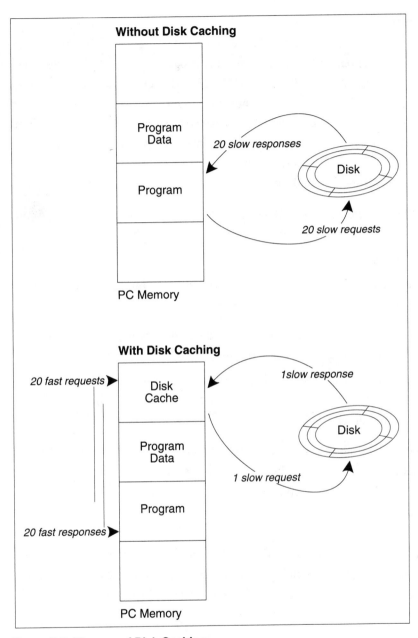

Figure 7-7. Diagram of Disk Caching

Cache Efficiency

All caches, both RAM caches and disk caches, measure their efficiency as a *hit rate*. That rate is the percent of of the times the program asks for information and finds it in the cache. A low hit rate would mean slower operation, because the program would often have to wait while new information was copied into the cache. Hit rates of 90% to 95% are excellent. They're also what most cache makers claim, although such claims must be viewed somewhat skeptically because the hit rate will depend mightily on the testing procedures.

The hit rate will be affected by:

• The kind of program used (some programs stick to a small piece of memory, while others tend to jump around more). Database and accounting programs improve the most.

• The operation tested (some operations within a single program stick to a small memory area more than other operations do).

• The size of the cache (a larger cache can hold more information, and so be more likely to have what's wanted). Once the cache is large enough for your application and use, making it larger won't increase the hit rate much. It's difficult to know how large that is, but this Step includes some tips and programs that will help you guess.

• The caching algorithm (the smarter the controller is at keeping the right information in the cache, the higher the hit rate). Rating the algorithms is like rating computer's speed—you need to read reviews and try the controllers for yourself.

Keep in mind that a cache can actually slow performance when it misses because of the time needed to copy new information to the cache. You may want a cache that you can turn on and off for different applications that would have different hit rates.

Caching Writing Schemes

All disk caches copy information from the disk to the RAM for quick read operations. But not all disk caches behave the same when it comes to writing information. This is tricky because if the program wants to achieve the best speed, it would write to the cache, and not to the disk. But then the information in the cache would differ from that on the disk—and they are supposed to be the same! At some point any changes to the cache must be copied back to the disk, to keep the disk information up-to-date. The cache controller decides when that writing to disk happens.

Some caches just write-through immediately, to avoid the danger of confused information. What if your PC lost power before the write finished? Your program would have saved something, but the saved data would evaporate when the RAM lost power. The disk would only have the older version. Write-through slows a cache down a bit, but is safest.

Some caches offer delayed write, writing information to the cache, then waiting for a moment when the program isn't busy to copy those changes to the disk. This is a bit riskier, but is faster than write-through caching.

Some caches let you choose when to use write-through and when to use delayed-write caching.

Disk Cache Choices

Nearly everyone can use a disk cache. That's not to say all programs tolerate a disk cache in your system. Some don't get along with this or that cache controller. Some PCs don't have enough memory left over for the cache—remember you need enough room to run the cache controller program plus enough RAM for the cached information itself. The more you and your programs use your disk drive, the more speed you'll gain from using a disk cache. What you need is a little free RAM and a controller program.

For most people a disk cache will improve performance more than a RAM disk will.

A 256K cache is good, a 1MB cache better, a 2MB cache fantastic. What you devote to caching should depend on what your computer does.

Don't use a disk cache when running a program's installation routine that includes copy-protection. The two can collide and cause trouble.

There are free controllers (one comes with every PC), shareware and commercial controllers, and even controllers built into disk drives. Some are easier to set up than others; some boost your computing speed more because of better caching algorithms. Here's a list of some of the most popular.

DOS Buffers. DOS comes with a built-in caching option called the *BUFFERS* statement. BUFFERS sets aside a number of areas in memory to cache the most recently used information from disk.

You call upon BUFFERS by including a statement in your CONFIG.SYS file, such as: **BUFFERS=20** (that's for DOS 3.3 and before), or **BUFFERS=25,4/x** (that's for DOS 4.0 and later)

Without a BUFFERS statement, your PC defaults to a certain few buffers (mentioned as follows), each about 523 bytes of memory. But you can specify some other number of buffers in your CONFIG.SYS file. The best number of BUFFERS depends on the application you're using, and how you want to balance increased speed against decreased RAM. (More buffers means more disk speed, up to some point of diminishing returns. But more buffers also means less memory left for other uses.)

Versions of DOS before 3.0 could improve disk performance about 10% by the right BUFFERS setting. But with the wrong settings, these DOS versions could actually hurt disk performance, spending more time reading through the buffers than would have been spent just grabbing the information directly from disk.

DOS 4.0 improved the efficiency of BUFFERS. It lets your PC read more than one sector from the disk at a time, using what's called "lookahead". (Meaning an intelligent guess about what information might be needed next.) When the program needs information from a certain disk sector, that sector and as many as seven following sectors are read all at once. DOS 4.0 also gave BUFFERS the right to use expanded (EMS) memory. That frees more of the conventional 640K of RAM. You should be careful with this feature, however. Because of a bug in PC-DOS, too many programs running at once and using expanded memory can sometimes corrupt the buffers. That is, they can change and ruin the information in the buffers. This isn't as much a problem with MS-DOS, though there are reportedly a few programs that use expanded memory pages—such as Paradox, DesqView, and SideKick Plus—that can hurt the buffers.

Setting Up the Buffers—To change the number of buffers, change the value at the end of the **BUFFERS=** statement in the CONFIG.SYS file (use a text editor or word processor that can output pure text ASCII files). Then restart ("reboot") your computer.

If you have DOS 4.0, you can set lookahead for anything from 1 to 7 sectors. It reads like this **BUFFERS=20,2** for 20 buffers and a lookahead of 2 sectors. Each lookahead sector eats up an additional 512 bytes.

DOS 4.0 has a switch to tell the buffers to "live in" expanded memory. It looks like this **BUFFERS=20 /x.**

If you use another cache, cut the buffers down to 4 or 5 or you could hurt performance.

The Optimum Number of Buffers—In DOS 3.2 and earlier you could have from 1 to 99 buffers. In DOS 3.3 you can have from 2 to 255. In 4.0 you may have from 1 to 99, unless you choose the /x switch to put buffers into expanded memory. Then you may use from 1 to 10,000 buffers.

The default buffer settings, the number of buffers DOS sets up if you don't specify a number yourself, depends on your PC. Here are the defaults:

If your PC has a floppy larger than 360K:	3
If your PC has more than 128K RAM:	5
If your PC has more than 256K RAM:	10
If your PC has more than 512K RAM:	15
If your PC doesn't fit any of these categories:	2

A typical number to use is 15 or 20. If you have 512K or more RAM and DOS 3.3 or later, you don't need more than about 15. If you use spreadsheets or word processors, you can use DOS 4's lookahead capability, and you'll need only 2 to 4 buffers. Accounting or database programs with DOS 4.0 can best use 2 or none. If you use 2 buffers and notice a slower disk pace, change to 0 buffers. In general, the trial-and-error method to find the optimum number is to start with 15 or 20, then increase 5 at a time until you get the best performance. There are also some utility programs, mentioned below, that will automatically analyze what setting you should use. Remember, you lose about .5K (532 bytes) for each buffer you set up. The more memory you have, the more buffers you can afford. But too many buffers can actually hurt performance because it gives the program too many little caches to search through before turning to the disk. With 60 or so buffers your PC would be searching through 30K of memory for each disk access.

Here are some tips about buffer settings:

For a PC with a floppy drive try: 8
For an XT with a hard disk try: 16
For an AT or PS/2 with a floppy drive try: 16
For an AT or PS/2 with a hard disk try: 32

You'll usually need more than the DOS defaults for best results. BUFFERS=25,4 is typical for good performance on an average system. Check your program manuals to see if any programs demand a certain minimum buffers setting.

If you can, use a good disk cache instead of buffers—you'll get a better overall performance. Buffers aren't really intended as a full-purpose cache, but as a tiny cache for the directory and FAT information on your disk that gets used time and again. If you do use a cache, cut down on your buffers.

BUFFER Utilities—Some commercial programs can estimate how many buffers you should use by looking at the number of files on your disks and the fragmentation level (disorganization) of the disk. (I advise that you de-fragment your disk with a utility package such as PC Tools to avoid fragmentation trouble.)

Other programs, such as the public domain program THRASHER, take the empirical approach. You specify a range of BUFFERS numbers to test—such as 20 to 50—and THRASHER tries them, exercising your disk, and automatically changing the CONFIG.SYS file for each trial. Eventually it writes an ASCII report file for you telling what worked best.

FASTOPEN. This is a DOS cache-style command that I don't recommend you use, unless you're a DOS expert willing to risk some incompatibilities. FASTOPEN speeds your access to files on disk by storing information about their disk location in RAM. But many programs bypass DOS when looking to disk, and so will bypass FASTOPEN. Such actions could change the file locations on the disk without FASTOPEN's knowledge, and so confuse both FASTOPEN and your computing. You could even lose data. Programs such as DesqView, Javelin, Paradox, and SideKick Plus have shown such troubles. (This is also a potential problem with any cache or buffering program. But it doesn't happen with most, they've been ironed out to avoid such troubles.)

In DOS 4.0 FASTOPEN added the ability to use expanded memory. (IBM's FASTOPEN, however, still cannot.) Placing the /x switch after the FASTOPEN command tells it to use expanded memory for its data. Look to a DOS manual for more details on FASTOPEN.

IBMCACHE.SYS. This is the caching program IBM tosses in with DOS versions 4.0 and later. It is definitely better than just using BUFFERS. It works with extended memory, but not with expanded. Version 2 of IBMCACHE can cache floppies. It installs as a device driver, rather than as a TSR program. This is the CONFIG.SYS statement to install it:

```
DEVICE=IBMCACHE.SYS number /e
```

The number is the size of the cache. The /e switch pushes the cache into extended memory. IBMCACHE has look-ahead, making it a fairly intelligent disk cache.

DCACHE. DCACHE.COM is a public domain utility you can get from *PC Magazine*'s PC Magnet bulletin board. It is a TSR program (loads into memory and remains there) that can supposedly cut your disk access time by as much as 50%. If you want to see the details of disk caching control, you can get the assembly language or BASIC listing for DCACHE from a back issue of *PC Magazine*.

You install DCACHE by including it in your AUTOEXEC.BAT file. This is the form: **DCACHE /off or on /u /mx /e /hx.**The backslashes here contain optional switches.

The /off or /on switch is how you turn the cache on or off. You would normally start by turning it on. Then you could turn it off if you were concerned that it was hurting the performance of a program. Then you could turn it back on when you wanted a cache. Note, however, that turning the cache off would not return the memory for other uses. For that you need the /u switch.

The /u switch can remove the DCACHE from memory, but this only works if DCACHE was the last TSR installed. If the BIOS disk interrupt 13H has been changed since DCACHE was installed, something some TSRs do, DCACHE will tell you with an error message that it cannot be removed.

The /m switch tells how large a cache to make. DCACHE defaults to a 64K cache. If you add the /m switch and some value, you change that. The choices are 16, 32, 64, 128, 256, 512, 1024, 2048, 4096, and 8192K bytes. For example, /m128 would create a 128KB cache. (The DCACHE controlling program takes up about 1200 bytes.)

The /e switch lets you put the DCACHE in expanded memory. For caches larger than 256K, expanded memory use is required.

The /h switch lets you dictate which hard disk to cache in a system with more than one hard disk drive. The primary hard disk is the default. Use /h0 and you're just confirming the default. But if you use /h1 you'll cache for the secondary disk. DCACHE treats a partitioned disk drive as a single disk drive, by the way. It acts on physical disks, not logical disks.

Finally, if you use **DECACHE ?** you'll see a list of help information about DCACHE, without even installing the program. If you try this and DCACHE is already installed, you'll only see information about turning the cache on, off, or removing it from memory. DECACHE only works on hard disks, not floppies.

SMARTDRIVE. This cache comes with MS-DOS 4.x versions and with Windows. It has decent performance but cannot be removed from memory without rebooting your computer (a failing that IBM's IBMCACHE also has). It also has few tuning features for optimizing performance. SMARTDRIVE can automatically free memory when Windows needs more.

Compaq's CACHE.EXE. Compaq computers come with the CACHE.EXE disk cache utility that includes such features as buffered writes and a performance report. It can create a cache as large as 2MB, using at least 16K of conventional RAM. The cache can sit in expanded or extended memory. You can disable this cache entirely, disable only its write buffer, or adjust the track buffer, but you can't remove the cache from memory.

To use it you put a line like this in the CONFIG.SYS file:

```
device = cache.exe 512 /ext
```

The number tells the system how much memory to use for the cache, from 128K to 2048K (2MB). The default is 256K. The /ext part of the command tells the cache to get into extended memory. You may also choose either /exp for expanded memory or /bas for conventional memory.

EMC 1.10. EMC is a free cache controller, a public domain program you can find in user groups and on bulletin board systems such as CompuServe. It works only in expanded memory and only with some (though the most common) disk drive types (MFM and RLL drives). It is easy to use, but relatively slow. It works with DOS 3.3 and earlier versions.

EMC lets you specify the maximum and minimum number of expanded memory pages to use for caching. It can be enlarged, reduced, or disabled after you start it. EMC caches a maximum of 8MB of memory, and needs at least 4K to run.

Super PC-Kwik. This commercial caching program from Multisoft seems to capture more awards than any of the others. It is fast, easy to install and use, and compatible with most other software. It comes by itself or with other utilities as part of the PC-Kwik Power Pak (which includes a RAM disk, a print spooler, a keyboard accelerator, and a screen accelerator). Super PC-Kwik can cache in conventional, expanded, or extended memory. It can share this memory with other programs, such as the print spooler that comes with the Power Pak; a unique feature. The other utilities borrow memory from the cache and give it back when done. Through this dynamic sharing of memory above 640K, the PC-Kwik software uses the same RAM to buffer and speed whatever the slowest current operation is.

The cache can be turned on or off, has many tuning options for customizing its operation, and offers statistics to tell how much it is helping your computing. Super PC-Kwik uses 10K for the controlling routines, and needs DOS 2.0 or later to run. The cache can be as large as 16MB. It works with most hard disk drives, is compatible with DesqView and Windows, and with NetWare drivers. It's tuning options include track buffering (read-ahead), redundancy check, write buffers, caching user-specified drives, cache disabling, write-buffer disabling, cache removal from memory, adjustable track buffer size, and cache location at a specific memory location.

Vcache. This program from Golden Bow Systems is one of the most powerful commercial caches. It is fast when operating, but isn't very simple to install. Vcache lets you adjust the drive and memory type, the size of the cache, the lookahead buffer size, and the delay time for buffered writes. It uses as little as 9K for the controlling program, works with any form of memory, and can cache up to 15MB of information. Larger caches need more controller space—approximately 10K can control a 300K cache, 20K can control a 1MB cache. Vcache works under DOS versions from 2.0 to 4.0. It is compatible with most major application programs but can be removed from memory if there is trouble. It is not compatible with DesqView/386 and Windows/386.

FLASH V Disk Accelerator. This cache from Software Masters works in conventional, expanded, extended, or a combination of those types of memory. It has a menu to make installation easy and, unlike many other caches, can cache for floppy disk drives. FLASH has lots of tuning options, such as saving the current cache configuration so you can keep different configurations for different applications. It lets you force certain files to stay in the cache. FLASH can buffer writes. It will tell you if you remove a disk before that disk is updated (necessary for floppy caching with cached writes). FLASH won't let you reboot using Ctrl-Alt-Del before writing to disk is complete. It uses 20K of memory minimum for its control, and eats up more memory in relation to the size of the cache you've created. Figure 7-8 shows the installation menu for FLASH.

PC Tools Deluxe. The popular PC Tools utilities package from Central Point Software comes with a disk cache, among other utilities. It actually uses a simplified version of Super PC-Kwik's disk cache program, calling it PC-Cache. You can choose the amount and kind of RAM you want to use for this cache, set the number of sectors to read into the track buffer, exclude drives from the cache, and remove the cache from memory at will. You cannot disable this cache nor does it offer a write buffer. This frugal cache uses 12K for an extended memory cache or 5K for an expanded memory cache, no matter how large the expanded memory cache.

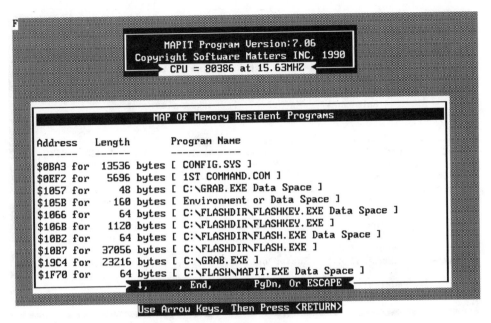

F

```
        MAPIT Program Version:7.06
     Copyright Software Matters INC, 1990
          CPU = 80386 at 15.63MHZ

              MAP Of Memory Resident Programs

Address     Length        Program Name
-------     ------        ------------
$0BA3 for   13536 bytes [ CONFIG.SYS ]
$0EF2 for    5696 bytes [ 1ST COMMAND.COM ]
$1057 for      48 bytes [ C:\GRAB.EXE Data Space ]
$105B for     160 bytes [ Environment or Data Space ]
$1066 for      64 bytes [ C:\FLASHDIR\FLASHKEY.EXE Data Space ]
$106B for    1120 bytes [ C:\FLASHDIR\FLASHKEY.EXE ]
$10B2 for      64 bytes [ C:\FLASHDIR\FLASH.EXE Data Space ]
$10B7 for   37056 bytes [ C:\FLASHDIR\FLASH.EXE ]
$19C4 for   23216 bytes [ C:\GRAB.EXE ]
$1F70 for      64 bytes [ C:\FLASH\MAPIT.EXE Data Space ]
             ↓,       , End,       PgDn, Or ESCAPE

         Use Arrow Keys, Then Press <RETURN>
```

Figure 7-8. The FLASH Disk Cache Installation Menu

The Mace Utilities. This utilities package from Fifth Generation Systems includes many useful tools, such as virus testing, automatic saving, disk defragmenting, and file recovery. It also packs a caching program.

Control Room. This utility and system analysis package from Ashton-Tate, described in Step 2, has its own disk cache with some unique features. The cache is fault-tolerant, meaning that it is immune to programs that sometimes cause troubles with other caches. It is careful to protect you from any data loss such incompatibilities could cause. The Control Room cache can run in conventional, expanded, or extended memory. Figure 7-9 shows the disk cache within Control Room.

The Norton Utilities. As of version 5.0, available from Symantec, the famous Norton Utilities includes a cache. If you use QEMM or 386-to-the-Max, you can load most of the cache into high memory.

Lightning. This cache from the Personal Computer Support Group company comes in two versions: an inexpensive copy-protected version and a more expensive un-copy-protected version. It is easy to use, but does not support extended memory caching.

```
┌─────────────────────────────────────────────────────────────────────┐
│ Help   Keyboard  [Disk]  General  Memory  Config  Expert  Summary  Tasks  Quit │
├─────────────────────────────────────────────────────────────────────┤
│                                                                       │
│            Press ↵ to adjust hard disk settings.                      │
│                                                                       │
│            ── Safe park ──         ── Basic data ──                   │
│            Safe park:  Yes<No>     Formatted size:   21 MB            │
│            Park delay:<3>10 30     Average access:   20 MS           │
│                                                                       │
│   ──────────────────── Jet-Cache settings ─────────────────          │
│   Cache:<On>Off          Number of physical reads:   1,937 - 91%     │
│   Location:<Main>EMS XMS  Number of cached reads:       203 -  9%     │
│   Cache size: 64   KB     ··········· Cache status ···········        │
│   Track read ahead:<On>Off  Active in main RAM, no faults detected    │
│   Fault analysis: Low<High>  with 0 minutes, 0 seconds saved today.   │
│                                                                       │
│   ── Access time ──      ── Interleave ──       ── Miscellaneous ──   │
│   Track-to-track:    4 MS  Track optimum:   1:1  Controller type:  Advn│
│   Average access:   20 MS  Current:         1:1  CMOS drive type:    2 │
│   Maximum access:   33 MS  Sector optimum:  1:1  Disk cache type:  C/R │
│                                                                       │
│        ── Physical layout ──    Transfer    Amount      Speed         │
│        Bytes per sector:   512  ────────  ────────   ────────         │
└─────────────────────────────────────────────────────────────────────┘
```

Figure 7-9 The Disk Cache in Control Room

PolyBoost. This collection of several utilities from Polytron Corp includes a keyboard accelerator, an on-line editor, a screen accelerator, and disk de-fragmenter, and a cache.

Power Cache Plus. This cache from Intelligent Devices Corp. uses as little as 5K of conventional memory for the control. It is compatible with Windows 3.0. This cache from Intelligent Devices can speed the operation of any DOS-compatible mass storage device. It works with conventional, expanded, extended, expanded *and* extended, or even high memory and can cache up to 23MB of information. It automatically configures itself, keeps a running log of its operation, has built-in help and status screens, and includes some disk performance testing utilities.

Fast!. This cache from Future Computer Systems works with hard or floppy disks and caches in conventional, expanded, or extended memory. It is compatible with Windows 3, AutoCAD 386, DesqView, dBase IV, and many other programs. Fast! uses only 8K of RAM.

Cache86. This cache from The Aldridge Co. has different programs for working in conventional, expanded, and extended memory. There's also a version optimized for 386-based PCs with their different instruction set and 32-bit bus. Along with Cache86 you get the program C86STATS that shows a log of the requests for cache information and the hit rate, so you can monitor the efficiency of your caching.

```
Tree86 - 352K
C:\CACHE86>c86

Cache 86 (tm) utility program version 3.51g:

        Cache86 version number          3.51f
        Caching is enabled
        Cache is in extended memory
        Cache size                      512 Kb
        Total read requests            1291
        Percentage of reads from cache   85 %
        Convetional memory footprint   6912 bytes

Tree86 - 352K
C:\CACHE86>
```

Figure 7-10. Report From Cache86 Utility Testing Disk Cache Efficiency (courtesy The Aldridge Co.)

PC-Kwick. This is an old shareware caching program you can find in many software libraries, such as PC-SIG, and bulletin boards. It automatically uses memory above 360K in conventional memory that is not used by DOS or other TSR programs. It works with any DOS from version 2.0 to 3.3, and requires a system with at least 384K RAM.

SpeedCache. Version 1.4.1 of SpeedCache comes bundled with hard disks from Storage Dimensions, along with the SpeedStor formatting and partitioning utility. You may also buy SpeedCache separately. It is a reasonable cache when bundled with a system, but has few tuning options and a rather tough installation.

Caching Controllers

The Cache Control program doesn't have to be loaded into and run from your PC's memory. You can also get controllers that are built into disk drives. These caching controller disk drives are also equipped with RAM to hold the cached information. Because these controllers are built into hardware, they can work faster and more efficiently than PC memory cache controller programs. They also don't occupy any of your precious PC memory, either with the controller program or with the cache. However, the memory isn't available for other uses when not caching, and can only cache for the one disk drive, not for any others your PC might call upon. A 2MB disk cache can outperform many caching controllers, and leave memory more flexible.

Caching controller disk drives are growing more popular all the time. Hard disks without caching controllers can't be much faster than 12 milliseconds average access time. That's not as fast as some sophisticated users would like, and is definitely a bottleneck in many network systems where a central disk drive must be on call to dozens or even hundreds of computer users. Even moving from one interface—such as the SCSI interface—to a faster one—such as the ESDI interface—doesn't improve speed enough.

A disk caching controller can cache frequently used programs and data. And it can also hold FAT (File Allocation Table—that tells you where files are on a disk) and disk directory information. That adds yet more speed to your disk work.

Here are some sources for caching controller disk drives.

Perceptive Solutions Inc. This firm makes the Hyperstore/1600 Dual-Mode Caching Controller. Because this emulates the popular WD 1003 controller, it is compatible with most drives (including MFM, RLL, ESDI, and SCSI technology drives). It plugs into the standard AT bus.

UltraStor Corporation. UltraStor's caching disk controllers are aimed at both single and multiple user systems. They can co-reside with another hard drive or floppy disk controller, and can support up to three floppy drives as well as a hard disk, and support drives of more than 528MB without extra software (some controllers need special utility programs to do this).

Other sources include:

Distributed Processing Technology offers caching controllers that supposedly make drives 3 to 5 times faster. DPT also makes solid-state disk drives.

Quantum Corporation offers a cache controller for its drives that incorporates lookahead with a 64K buffer to improve disk access by about 35%. These controllers have built-in self-testing for fine-tuning the cache parameters to the operating system as well as any applications you use.

Zenith Data Systems is building caching controllers into its latest PCs, to give sub-millisecond access.

Compaq is also building caching controllers into its latest systems, such as the SystemPro with a 512K cache for network server operation.

Plus Development's Hardcard II 40 has a 64KB on-board cache, one of the largest available on a hard disk card.

Data Technology Corporation's caching controller boasts .5ms access times.

RAM Disks

If your disk drives aren't fast enough, even with caching, why not try a RAM disk? That is, set aside a larger piece of RAM than you would with a cache, and make it act just like a disk drive. You assign it a drive letter (such as D:), and copy files to and from it just as if it were another hard or floppy disk in your system. It will have its own directory and subdirectories, and will respond to DOS commands just as other disk drives do.

The advantages?

• RAM disks are much faster than mechanical disks.

• RAM disks are easily set up in extended memory, which is sometimes left wasted otherwise.

The disadvantages?

• RAM disks can use up a lot of your memory.

• RAM disks are almost always smaller than mechanical disks—perhaps 128 to 512K instead of 512K to 40MB or more.

• RAM disks are *volatile*, in other words they lose information when you turn the power off. You must remember to copy RAM disk files back to a mechanical disk before turning off your system.

• You can't just set up a RAM disk without a control program.

• You need to know the appropriate files to put on the RAM disk (it'll be too small to just copy all your files to the disk).

Still, despite the disadvantages, RAM disks can add fantastic zip to many programs. The speed is definitely worth it, if you find the right control program and you have the memory to spare.

When to Use a RAM Disk. RAM disks are especially useful with applications that frequently read and write disk information. Monitor such programs by watching the disk drive light on your PC—if it turns on a lot, your disk is active. But even for applications that use the disk a lot, only some of that application's files need to be on the RAM disk. An application may consist of a dozen or more different program, library, and font files, and only one, two, or a half-dozen of these might be the subject of frequent disk activity. Programs with many overlay files are particularly ripe for a RAM disk. (Large programs are sometimes broken into smaller pieces called overlays to fit into memory.) The WordStar word processor, for example, gets a lot of speed from a RAM disk because it has many overlays on disk. The Lotus 1-2-3 spreadsheet, in contrast, doesn't change much when run from a RAM disk because it keeps its program and data files in RAM. Check your program manuals or call for technical support to find out if a RAM disk would help, and which files to put on it.

You may think of putting your working data files—word processor document, spreadsheet worksheet, or whatever—on the RAM disk. Although you could speed your computing considerably, you do need to be careful as a RAM disk can lose all of your files if your PC loses power for any reason. It would be one thing to lose a program file which you could easily reinstall once the power was back up, but obviously, if you lose data files you lose all of the time you've spent working on them.

Many programs also create temporary or backup files as they work. These too you might want to direct to the RAM disk, though you need to be careful of the power loss vulnerabilities.

There are also some DOS files you might copy to a RAM disk for better performance, such as COMMAND.COM. This fundamental DOS program is frequently dumped from memory when you load an application program, and then loaded again when you're done with the application. Putting it on the RAM disk can speed your application loading and unloading.

Whatever impermanent files you put on your RAM disk, copy them frequently to your floppy or hard disk to save them. Or buy a UPS (Uninterruptible Power Supply) that will guarantee power to your PC even if there's a blackout or someone trips over your PC's plug.

Some copy protected programs won't run from a RAM disk because they expect to find certain codes and signals on the original disk. Step 3 mentions the many individual programs and files that are most appropriate for RAM disk treatment.

How Large a RAM Disk to Use. You can guess at the optimum RAM disk size by adding up the size of the flies you want to keep on that disk. However, you need to allow an ample safety margin for any temporary working files your programs make create—remember that you don't know in advance precisely how large these will be. Also remember that some RAM disk programs ask you to set a maximum limit on the number of files that can fit on the disk—on the directory entries for the RAM disk. Give yourself some breathing room there too. If guessing and experimentation isn't enough, you can turn to utility programs that monitor your disk use and suggest a RAM disk size.

There are also utilities that let you expand and shrink the size of your RAM disk dynamically, without having to reboot your computer in between changes. However, even these utilities often require that you copy your files to the RAM disk again after the change—they wipe out everything on the RAM disk.

You may have more than one RAM disk, just as you have more than one floppy or hard disk drive in a system. Each will use its own memory and have its own drive letter.

RECORDER. Recorder is a free utility from *PC Magazine*'s PC MagNet bulletin board. It measures your disk input and output use, keeping track of how many times each of your files is accessed. That lets you select the best files to put in a RAM disk. (You can get similar information from some disk optimization programs that tell you which files to keep closest to the FAT.)

To use Recorder, download the program from PC MagNet, then issue this command **RECORDER n /r** with the n and r as optional parameters. The *n* specifies the maximum number of files the recorder can hold in the table. The default is 200, but you can keep tabs on as many as 2000 files. Each one in the table uses 20 bytes of RAM. The */r* resets the table if it is filled. A reset table loses all entries and starts recording again from scratch. For example, **RECORDER 100 /r** would start recording from scratch, keeping a table on 100 files.

Once recorder is running, just compute as you normally would. After a while, view the RECORDER table by typing **RECORDER** again at the DOS prompt. Choose the most popular files for your RAM disk.

Tips for Using RAM Disks. To save yourself the chore of copying appropriate files to the RAM disk each time you start your system, and to automate backing those files up to more permanent disks, you should cobble together a batch file or AUTOEXEC.BAT routine.

As explained in Step 1, an AUTOEXEC.BAT batch file runs automatically when you first turn on your computer. If you're always copying the same files to your RAM disk, then you should put the commands to do so here. But if you sometimes use differing RAM disk setups for different applications, you could put your file copying commands into a series of batch files, one for each setup.

Some people forget to put path statements into the CONFIG.SYS file to make sure that the RAM disk is the first place checked for the important files. If you copy a file to the RAM disk, but leave a copy on your hard disk, and your computer looks first to the hard disk for that file, the RAM disk won't do you any good. Make sure the RAM disk path is listed first, like this: **PATH = D:\;C:\DOS;C:\UTIL**.

If you make a batch file for your application, then that batch file can automatically resume working when you quit the application, and copy your data files from RAM disk to hard disk or floppy. For example, this SPREAD batch file would do the backup trick for worksheet files of Lotus 1-2-3:

```
C:
CD C:\LOTUS
COPY *.WKS D:\LOTUS
D:
CD D:\LOTUS
123
COPY *.WKS C:\LOTUS
C:
```

This batch copies all the Lotus .WKS worksheet files to the RAM disk (assumed here to have the drive letter D:), then switches to the RAM disk, runs Lotus 1-2-3 and lets you work. When you're done with Lotus and choose to Quit, the batch file takes up again automatically, copying your changed worksheet files back to the C: drive.

Most every RAM disk user should consider putting the DOS COMMAND.COM program on the RAM disk. This program is frequently loaded and unloaded, especially when using large programs such as WordPerfect, and you can save time by having a RAM disk copy. (It helps most on floppy-based PCs, where loading command.com can take quite a few seconds each time.) Use an AUTOEXEC.BAT file that tells DOS where to find the new copy of command.com, like this:

```
COPY COMMAND.COM C:
SET COMSPEC=C:\
COMMAND.COM
```

In fact, you can speed autoexec itself by splitting it into two pieces, and running the second from a RAM disk. Assuming you've put a device driver such as VDISK into your CONFIG.SYS file to set up a RAM disk, then put these lines at the beginning of the AUTOEXEC.BAT file:

```
IF EXIST D:AUTOEXEC.BAT
GOTO CONTINUE
COPY AUTOEXEC.BAT D:
D:AUTOEXEC
:CONTINUE
```

RAM Disk Choices. There are lots of shareware and public domain RAM disk programs around, and most expanded memory boards come with a RAM disk utility. But you probably don't need either source because most PCs get a free RAM disk program as part of DOS. These RAM disk programs set up and format the RAM disk, assign it a drive letter, and install it as a device in your system, ready for use. All you need do then is copy files to and from this drive, and then execute programs from it as you would from any other disk drive. By the way, few RAM disks use conventional memory for the actual disk, because it is so precious. Most use extended or expanded. Windows, for example, comes with a RAM disk that uses expanded memory.

VDISK and RAMDISK—Many PCs with the DOS operating system come with a free RAM disk program called VDISK or RAMDISK. Since PC-DOS 3.0 IBM PC's have had VDISK, compatible PCs have had a similar program called RAMDISK or SUPERDRV since MS-DOS 3.2. They all operate in pretty much the same way, as explained here. (VDISK is IBM's name, it stands for Virtual Disk. RAMDISK is what most other computer makers call their VDISK replacement.) VDISK is easy to use, though not particularly flexible. It works in conventional memory or extended memory. In fact, for some time it was the only practical use for extended memory on the early AT and AT-compatible systems. Yet many people don't know about it, and few use it. Look for the VDISK or RAMDISK driver as a file in with your DOS files. It will be called something like VDISK.SYS or RAMDISK.SYS. (Check your DOS documents for information about it.)

Here's a quick rundown on using VDISK. (RAMDISK programs will run in pretty much the same way, though you can check your DOS manual for details and differences.) Although widely used, many people think VDISK is primitive.

In your CONFIG.SYS file put this line: **DEVICE=VDISK.SYS**.That will set up the RAM disk, once you tag on the parameters—total size, sector size, and entries—and switches—to using expanded or extended memory.

The total size is measured in KB, from 1 to all available memory. The default is 64 (for 64K). Most people want more than 64K. If you specify a size that is too large to fit into the available memory, VDISK uses the largest size that will fit. (PC MagNet offers a utility called XPANDISK that lets you change the size of VDISK RAM disks without rebooting—though it does erase everything that's already on the RAM disk.)

Sector size specifies how large the sectors of the disk are: 128, 256, 512, or 1024 bytes. Large sectors on real disks provide faster performance, but that isn't true on a RAM disk. Use 128 most of the time for the most efficient use of memory—using larger sectors can waste memory because of partially-filled sectors.

Entries specifies the number of directory entries there may be for the disk. The default is 64, but you can set entries to any number from 2 to 512. To determine how best to set this, think of the number of files you'll be putting on the RAM disk, and then leave room for any temporary files your applications may create. Use at least 64, although 128 is probably best for most uses, even with small applications. If you run out of directory space, your RAM disk is functionally full, even if there's memory left in it.

If you want VDISK to use extended memory in your computer, use the /E switch. After the E you can specify the number of sectors VDISK can transfer at a time, from 1 to 8. The default is 8.

If you want VDISK to use LIM expanded memory, use the /X switch. After the X switch you can specify the number of sectors VDISK can transfer at a time, from 1 to 8, with 8 as the default. (Before DOS 4.0, VDISK worked only in conventional or extended memory. RAMDRIVE offered expanded operation with DOS 3.2.)

If you specify /x you can't also specify /e.

The entire CONFIG.SYS statement for VDISK will look like this example: **DEVICE=VDISK.SYS 128 128 128 /E:4** which would set up a RAM disk of 128K in extended memory with 128 bytes per sector, 128 directory entries maximum, and capable of transferring 4 sectors at a time. When you restart your computer and DOS runs into this statement in the CONFIG.SYS files, it will show you a message like this:

```
IBM DOS Version 4.00, VDISK virtual disk D:
Buffer size adjusted
Sector size adjusted
Directory entries adjusted
buffer size:        128KB
Sector size:        128
Directory entries:  128
```

It will have assigned the letter D: to the VDISK. (If the VDISK.SYS file is in a DOS subdirectory, you must use a full path in the DEVICE statement so that DOS can find the file.)

With VDISK and RAMDISK you should put their device driver line first in the CONFIG.SYS file, loading ANSI.SYS, expanded memory drivers (that convert extended memory to expanded), and other such devices later. If you don't have extended memory, put the expanded memory driver first, to activate the expanded memory board, then put the extended memory simulator, then any RAM disk program (such as VDISK or RAMDISK mentioned below) that wants to use extended memory. VDISK wants to be the first driver to have a claim on any extended memory. Assigning extended memory drivers before the VDISK can result in a loss of data, or create an addressing conflict later.

You could call on the VDISK driver more than once, setting up multiple RAM disks. Just use another line in CONFIG.SYS and specify the parameters and switches as you need them. DOS will assign a different driver letter to the other RAM disk or disks, giving them sequential letters. (The first RAM disk will typically be D: because your hard disk is C:. The next RAM disk will be E, and so on.)

NJRAMDSK—This shareware RAM disk's name is an acronym for Nifty James' Famous expanded Memory RAM Disk Drive. It is fast and uses only a small amount of DOS memory: 720 bytes or less. There's a special version that runs faster on 286 and 386 machines. The NJRAMDISK makes a click to tell you when it is operating, sort of a virtual disk light, which you can turn off if you wish. You can find it on bulletin boards, or from Mike Blaszczak (see the Addresses appendix).

Compression and RAM Disks. You can get more information on to your floppy disks and hard disks by using a compression utility. (There are also some compression chips you can plug into PCs.) By squeezing redundant information out of programs and files, a compression utility can put more files in less disk space. The utility then decompresses the file to a usable shape when you run the program or open the file. (Most are constantly available because they run as TSR programs.) You must wait a few seconds for compression or decompression, but in exchange you get twice as much apparent disk space. General-purpose compressors can get 40 to 60% more space for you. Specialized compressors, that know about the specific kind of file they're tackling, can sometimes get you as much as 80% more usable space.

Some utilities work on only certain file types (such as spreadsheet files or fonts). Some work on all files. Some can work just on certain sectors within a single file or program. Many of these compression utilities don't work with RAM disks, but a few do. Here's one:

Squish Plus—This compression utility from Sundog Software works on all files including program files (those ending with the .EXE and .COM extensions to their names). It works on hard disk, floppies, silicon disks, RAM disk, and tape cartridges. It is not a TSR program but a device driver. Compression is automatic when files are stored on the "virtual drive" that Squish creates. When you store a file, Squish compresses it, then automatically decompresses it when you retrieve it. Most disk utility programs are compatible with Squish Plus.

Silicon Disks. Most times when you hear about a RAM disk you're hearing about a piece of the PC's memory that's been set aside to act like a fast disk drive. But there are also dedicated RAM disks, sometimes called *silicon disks* or solid-state disks, collections of RAM chips dedicated solely to acting like a disk drive. The chips in these RAM disks are separate from your PC's conventional, expanded, and extended memory.

This kind of independent RAM disk is sometimes called a solid-state disk. It is expensive, far more expensive than an equivalent disk drive. But they are much faster. Some are even designed, either with special chips or with battery back-up power, to be non-volatile. That is, they'll hold on to your information after you turn the power off, just as a mechanical disk drive would. (RAM disks in your PC's regular memory lose their data when power is turned off.) These independent RAM disks are often on circuit boards you plug into your computer's slots. Their large capacity (compared to RAM itself) and their non-volatility makes them popular in tough working environments such as laboratories. However, unlike mechanical disks where it is sometimes possible to recover files after you mistakenly delete them, deleted files on independent RAM disks are gone completely.

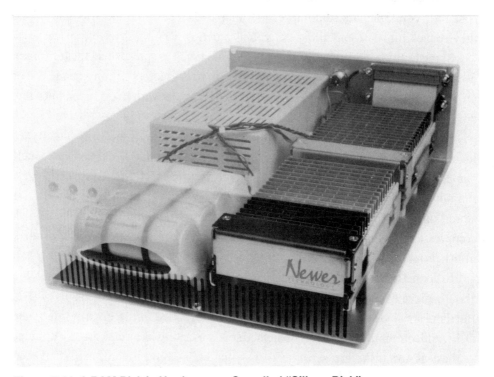

**Figure 7-11. A RAM Disk in Hardware—a So-called "Silicon Disk"
(courtesy Newer Technology)**

Their key advantage in memory management is that they don't use any of your conventional, expanded, or extended memory. Their disadvantage is that you pay a lot for a collection of RAM chips which can then only be used as a disk drive, not as conventional, expanded, or extended memory.

Here are some independent RAM disks:

Dartcard—Newer Technology's Dartcard can hold tens, hundreds, or even more MB of memory. It fits into full or half-height disk drive bays on the PC chassis. You can upgrade a Dartcard in 4, 16, or 64 MB increments, and can daisy-chain the cards together to get more storage space. Dartcard's can work through standard AT, SCSI, and ESDI interfaces. They have an option of continuous power for non-volatility. They also have an option to be BIOS-compatible for booting: you could start your PC from the Dartcard, speeding startup considerably. They have EDC (Error Detection and Correction) logic built-in to protect against lost or corrupted memory bits. And the Dartcard has the unique feature that up to 8MB of its RAM can be used as expanded LIM EMS 3.2 memory.

Flashdisk—Digipro's Flashdisk can have 2, 4, or 8MB of memory. It offers an access time of 240ns and a data transfer rate of 2048KB/second. The Flashdisk is non-volatile, but does not require batteries. It is resistant to power problems too, able to withstand surges. The Flashdisk is also mechanically tough, resistant to vibrations, dust, humidity, and extreme temperatures. it can be removed from your PC and then returned later without losing or corrupting any data.

Solid State Disk Drive—Vermont Research's solid state disk drives connect to a PC through a SCSI port. They have 5 ms access times and can hold from 8MB to 320MB of information. The transfer speed checks in at 2.8MB/second for asynchronous work and 5MB/second for synchronous. The drives are available in full and half-height modules to fit in standard PC disk drive bays.

Manage Your Peripheral Memory

Your PC doesn't have a monopoly on memory or memory management. Many computer peripherals—such as printers, network servers, display subsystems, and even modems—come with their own RAM and ROM memory. The ROM stores instructions that help the peripheral do its job. The RAM holds working information, either as a buffer to hold data that is being moved or as a scratch-pad area for calculations and manipulations of the information.

This section discusses the uses and abuses of memory in the most memory-sensitive peripherals and devices: the printer, the video display, the network, and the PC-Host connection.

Printers

Key Ideas

- Add memory to your printer's built-in buffer if you print documents with many fonts or lots of graphics.

- Use a spooler for printing.

Print Buffers

Printers depend on memory. They use it to hold:

- Text to print

- Graphics to print

- Forms to print

- Font shapes for text printing

- Instructions for text or graphics formatting

This memory can be in the PC that's driving the printer, but many printers also have their own memory for these tasks. This section is about that memory in the printer, how to add to it, and how to determine when you have enough.

Dot-Matrix Printer Memory

Laser printers are faster, quieter, and produce higher-quality prints than older dot-matrix impact printers. (Impact refers to the print head with tiny wires or hammers that put ink on a page.) In 1990 laser printer prices dropped low enough that impact printers became obsolete for most computer printing. But dot-matrix systems are still important in a few niches, such as for printing on forms where the print must push through several copies or layers of paper. Only an impact printer can do that.

Dot-matrix impact printers often have small buffers of 4K to 64K built right into the printer. These buffers may hold such things as printing instructions, fonts, or forms, but are often only used to hold text for immediate printing. This smooths the printing flow. The buffers are essentially tiny spoolers (see Step 7 for a complete definition of spooling) that ensure a constant flow of print information to the print head.

PCs create the information that a printer will print. PCs can send this information much faster than a dot-matrix printer can get it on the page. If there were no buffer, the printer would stop each time the PC was interrupted by any other task. Also, without a buffer, the PC would have to carefully help the printer through the entire printing process, feeding it information at the slow pace it could accept.

However, with a buffer, the PC and the printer can both make more efficient use of their time. The PC can send information at high speed to the printer's buffer. If the PC is temporarily diverted from sending print information to the printer, a full buffer will prevent any interruption in the printing process. And once the PC has sent an entire document to the buffer, it can get back to other work, and not have to baby-sit the printer through the slow printing process.

If the buffer is holding fonts or forms, it is saving the PC the trouble of sending the same character shapes or page basics for each page that is printed. Instead the PC can just send the information that is different for each page.

The buffers in dot-matrix printers can be small because these printers typically handle simple text, without many fonts and with little graphics. Simple text only eats up about 2K to 4K per page of printing.

Even so, most dot-matrix printers with buffers have optional add-in memory to increase the buffer's size. The Panasonic KX-P1654, for example, has an optional 32K RAM chip that can add to the built-in buffer or 42K for a total buffer of 74K.

Unfortunately, you typically pay a lot more for this memory than you do for memory in your PC. If you can use some of the PC's memory to buffer your dot-matrix printing, you'll save money. You'll also have memory that can be used for other things when it isn't busy buffering a print. (See Step 7 for details on dynamic spoolers that can flex this way.)

Bottom Line for Dot-matrix Impact Printers.

• Add memory to the built-in buffer if you print multiple copies of forms or use fonts that will be stored in that buffer (check the printer descriptions or ask a salesperson).

• Don't add memory to the built-in buffer if it won't help you with forms or fonts. Instead use a print spooler in the PC's memory.

Laser Printers

Memory is more important to laser printers than it is to dot-matrix impact printers. Dot matrix printers typically print a line at a time of simple text, so even small buffers of 16K or so can be sufficient. They can be enough to let the computer quickly return to other work.

Memory Holds the Page. Lasers are page printers; they hold the entire page in memory before printing it. It works this way; the PC sends the description of a page of text, or graphics, or both to the laser printer. A processor—essentially another computer—built into the laser printer translates those instructions into the pattern of dots that will cover the laser printed page, dots that will form the text or graphics for that page. The laser printer keeps that dot pattern in memory before using a laser to put the dots onto the electrically charged surface that will roll against the paper.

Because a typical laser printer works at 300 dpi (dots per inch), a square inch of a laser printed page has as many as 90,000 dots. A typical 8.5 x 11" page can have as many as 8,415,000 dots. A single bit of memory can be on or off, and so can represent a position that has a dot or one that doesn't. The eight bits of a byte can hold 8 dots, therefore, an 8.5 x 11" page "eats up" approximately 1MB of memory.

The page won't occupy the entire MB if it isn't full of graphics, however. A half-page of graphics takes up only 512K. The blank half can be signified in just a few more bytes saying, basically, "don't print anything here." The individual dot positions don't need to be explicitly specified as "blank" by the PC.

Or, if graphics are printed at lower resolution, they won't take up as much memory. A full page of 150 dpi graphics, for example, needs only one fourth the memory of a page of 300 dpi graphics. Images that are dark, and scanned photographs take up the most memory.

There are exceptions to this rule too, where a 512K printer can use some of your computer's memory to print a full page of graphics. The LaserJet Series II, for instance, has this capability. Also, a page that has text will take up much less memory than a page of graphics, since text characters can be specified as a few bytes saying "this character, at this position, in this style and size" rather than specifying each individual dot of the character.

Memory Holds Fonts and Forms. Memory isn't only used to hold the final page image before the laser heats up. It also holds:

- Fonts—keeping the dot patterns for various sizes and styles of text characters. These are called *downloadable fonts*.

- Forms—keeping the dot pattern for a master page design that will be used over and over.

Laser printing a page with a variety of fonts, especially of large characters, can easily fill 512K to 1MB just with the fonts. You can install about 15 to 20 12-point fonts in 512K RAM, but a single 30-point character can "eat up" as much as 143K. Headlines and other large-character text bits need lots of RAM.

However fonts aren't only available as downloaded patterns in RAM. Individual fonts don't change from one day to the next, so they can be easily kept in ROM chips too. Most laser printers have at least some fonts in built-in ROMs, and have slots to plug in extra ROM cartridges with yet more fonts. These ROM fonts can save you from using RAM in the printer for downloaded fonts. A few printers even have their own hard disks to hold fonts, though moving fonts from that disk to the printer's RAM isn't as quick as having the fonts in RAM or ROM. There are some utility programs—such as those mentioned later in this chapter—that help you manage downloaded fonts, to use as little memory as possible.

More built-in fonts, or fonts plugged in as ROM cartridges, means less need for downloaded fonts in RAM. Having ROM fonts also saves downloading time, though downloaded fonts can be more flexible. For memory's sake, buy your printer with an eye to the maximum amount of built-in and cartridge fonts.

Printer memory of 512K is typical, although rarely enough. As explained previously, some printers can put a whole page into 1MB of RAM; others have less efficient formatting systems and need as much as 2.5MB of RAM for that work. All need RAM for holding fonts and forms. Most laser printers, though, start with only 512K. A few have 1MB as standard equipment. That's a holdover from the days when memory was much more expensive than it is now.

The HP LaserJet is the most popular laser printer family. It has evolved through several generations, from the LaserJet and LaserJet Plus to the LaserJet II and III. Many competing laser printers are made to be "LaserJet compatible" so they can use the same fonts and talk to PCs the same way a LaserJet would. The original LaserJets had only 59K built in. That was soon beefed up to 512K, which became the standard for LaserJets and LaserJet compatibles. The competing IBM LaserPrinter, for example, follows this 512K tradition. Even the latest LaserJet, the III, only doubles that amount to 1MB of built-in memory.

The result of this memory shortage is that the garden-variety laser printer:

• Cannot print an entire page of 300 dpi graphics. (There are a few compression products, including the PrintCache spooler described in Step 7, that can sometimes elude this restriction.)

• Is very slow to print pages with many fonts, especially fonts that aren't in the printer's ROMs. (Downloading new fonts to the limited RAM takes time. If one font must replace another, and then is needed again for the next page, the PC and printer will spend lots of time swapping fonts and not as much actually sending and printing the document.)

You can tell if your printer doesn't have enough memory, if:

• Printing takes too long (though there can be other reasons for this too).

• Printing fails—the printer doesn't eject a page after working on it. You might have to eject it manually. If what comes out is a partially printed page—too little memory could well be the cause.

LaserJet III Example. The LaserJet III builds pages in its memory in strip buffer sections. It can print some full pages of text and graphics with only the standard 1MB of memory. But if the page has many fonts, or rotated type, or overlays a number of graphic and text elements, the LaserJet III may not be able to process each section fast enough to keep up with the printer engine (the mechanics that actually put the ink on paper). In that case, you'll see an error message such as the following, **Error 21 message (print overrun).**

If this occurs, you need to install more memory or simplify the page. Another way to avoid this effect, though you need 2MB of memory to do it, is to turn on the Page Protect feature from the printer's front panel menu. The LaserJet III will then process the entire page and store it in memory before printing. The solution to the memory shortage is simple—add more memory to your laser printer.

Adding Memory to Your Laser Printer. Most printers have slots or sockets for added memory. The IBM LaserPrinter, for example, can have 1, 2, or 3.5 more MB of memory added to it. The LaserJet Series II can be filled to 4.5MB (4 MB plus the original 512K). The LaserJet III has two memory slots that can increase its original 1MB up to a 5MB total. Some printers have even more room, offering expansion to as much as 12MB.

Installing extra memory in your printer is even easier than putting it into your computer. The printer manufacturers assume nearly everyone will be adding memory. There are slide-in boards and other simple means to put more memory in your printer.

Add-in memory boards sometimes offer other features, such as dynamic allocation between fonts or page images and spooling. Spooling memory can allow several PCs to share a single printer more easily.

Now for the Bad News:

Printer memory often costs more than PC memory. Printer memory boards aren't standard. That is, the board for one company's printer is unlikely to work on any other brand of printer. In fact, even the different printers from a single company—including industry leader HP—can demand differing memory add-on boards. (Printer hardware standards aren't as solid as those for the PC. Applications and downloadable fonts have been standardized on the HP style. Although there is some standardization on HP ROM font cartridges, which will fit many other printers besides HP's.)

Testing Your Printer's Memory

The first step in adding memory to your printer is learning how much is already there. Almost every printer has a diagnostic or test routine that will give you this information. Many even print it on a status sheet when you first turn on the printer.

For example, to test how much memory is in a LaserJet, turn the printer on and wait for it to warm up. Then press the ON-LINE button so that the indicator light disappears. Next press and hold the PRINT FONTS/TEST button for 5 seconds. On the LED panel you'll see the following message: **05 Self Test**.

The printer will then test itself and print a test page. That page shows the number of pages that have been printed, the ROM date, the user settings for printing, and the total installed memory (in KB). For example, 1024 means 1MB. Now that you have the results, turn the printer off or press the ON-LINE button to get back to normal printing modes.

Every printer has a different memory add-on procedure. Some have sockets waiting for memory chips. Others require that you buy a special printer memory add-on board.

If all you need is chips, look to Step 3 on buying chips and plugging them in. Check your printer documentation to see what speed and type of chips you'll need.

If you need a memory board for your printer, you can buy it from your local computer dealer or possibly from one of the sources below. The cheapest way to buy the board from your printer manufacturer is stripped. That is, buy the board without any chips. This is sometimes referred to as 0K. Then order chips from one of the sources mentioned below, or your own local reseller and install them yourself. (Most printers will work with 1MB chips running at 120ns speed or faster.)

It might be worth your while, though, to see if one of the sources below has a board with chips that will suit your printer. You'll pay a little more than buying the chips yourself, but less than buying a board with chips from the printer manufacturer in most cases. You won't have to plug the chips in and worry about bent leads and bad connections, and the board with chips will have been tested.

Check your computer's documentation for the place to slide the memory board into the printer system, and for any switches or front-panel menus you'll have to change to let your printer know it has been given more RAM. Figure 8-1 shows a typical laser printer add-on memory board.

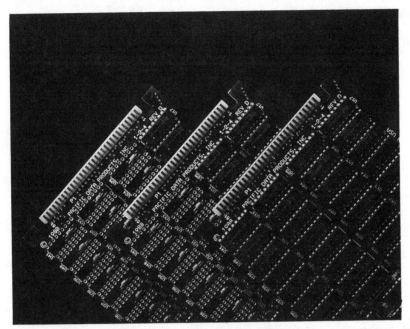

Figure 8-1. Laser Printer Add-on Memory Board (courtesy Pacific Data Systems)

Printer Memory Sources

There are a variety of companies that will sell you additional printer memory. Some of the best known are:

Pacific Data Products
Micron Technology
Computer Peripherals

Remember that memory in a printer on a network can be used by all of the PCs on that network, so it can be more cost-effective to add lots of memory to a shared printer than to add some memory to a number of independent printers.

307

Ways to Conserve Printer Memory

There are ways to stretch your printer's memory farther.

• Print with lower-resolution graphics. Cutting the resolution in half cuts the memory use by 75%.

• Use a spooler in your PC. That way the printer doesn't have to use any of its memory to spool.

• Print with fewer fonts. This cuts the downloading time and memory space.

• Print with fonts that are built into the printer or are on a plugged-in cartridge. (Buy cartridges of the fonts you use most often.)

• Avoid large fonts. These can eat up an enormous amount of RAM.

• Use a utility program that manages font downloading.

BackLoader 2 from Roxxolid, for instance, loads into the PCs memory as a TSR program and waits for your application to send a command to the printer to use a "soft" (downloadable) font. It then interrupts and downloads that font so that the font reaches the printer before the command does. Applications will "think" the fonts are resident in the printer, that they are built into the printer or are in cartridges. You won't, in turn, need batch files or macros to download the fonts, saving you both the time and trouble of creating those. BackLoader tracks the fonts use, and saves the printer from downloading the same fonts over and over. When BackLoader sees that the printer has almost filled the printer's memory, it tells the printer to reclaim the memory space from the least recently used font (just as caches do), to make room for a more needed font. BackLoader takes only 21K of PC memory, or when there is expanded memory to use, takes only 10K of conventional memory. It works on LaserJet, DeskJet, and compatible printers with at least 1MB of RAM.

BackLoader can work in conjunction with Isogon's FontSpace, which can quickly decompress font files on your hard disk when they're called for, and then compress them when they're not, to save hard disk space. This can squeeze 10MB of font files into 500K or so, using only 3K of conventional memory and 45K of expanded memory to do its work. The compression slows font movement by about 10%.

Printvision, a TSR utility from BLOC Publishing, lets you see a full-page preview on your PC's screen of what your HP-compatible laser printer will print. This saves you from printing something you don't really want. This could save lots of memory if you're sharing a printer with other PCs, whose jobs might have to wait for your job that turns out to be incompletely or mistakenly formatted or set up.

Other Add-ins for Laser Printers

Laser Printers are fertile ground for other add-ins besides memory. You can buy:

- Font cartridges (mentioned above).

- Plotter-compatibility cartridges—so your printer will act like a standard plotter for drawing drafting pages. The LaserJet III has this plotting ability built-in.

- PostScript cartridges.

PostScript is a printer language that helps PCs and printers work together to make smoother text characters and better-looking graphics. PostScript can produce an unlimited range of font sizes without the font-making programs and utilities of HP LaserJet printers.

Some laser printers have PostScript built-in. (This is the competing standard to the HP LaserJet mentioned above.) But many HP-LaserJet compatible printers can have PostScript added on either by working with a PostScript-emulation program running in your PC (and using PC memory) or a PostScript cartridge plugged into the printer. Expect to need at least 2MB to 2.5MB of printer RAM for using a PostScript-compatible cartridge.

Some Sources of PostScript-compatible printer programs and cartridges include;

- Custom Applications for Freedom of Press (PC program)

- Personal Computer Products for ImageScript (cartridge)

Special Controllers

You can also put special printer controller cards into your PC. Some use PostScript; many do not. These cards typically offer to push your printer to higher resolution prints. And most communicate with the printer through a very high-speed video cable instead of through the slower parallel or serial cables used by most printer connections. These controller cards often come with their own megabytes of memory, though sometimes they also need to borrow some of the PC's memory. The Tall Tree Systems JLaser Plus AT 2 board has 2MB of memory that can be used as expanded PC memory when not in use for printing. The Intel Visual Edge boards need megabytes of expanded or extended memory from the PC to work well. Figure 8-2 shows an example of such a controller card.

Companies that make these controller include: Intel, Lasermaster Corp., Advanced Vision Research, Tall Tree Systems, QMS Laser Connection, Destiny Technology Corp., Conographic Corp. Memory in one of these boards can't be shared by other PCs, the way memory in the printer itself can.

Bottom Line for Laser-printer Memory

Have enough memory in your laser printer to:

- Hold the pages you'll print.

- Print any high-resolution graphics on those pages.

- Hold the downloadable fonts for your fancy text printing.

- Hold any forms or macros for repetitive printing jobs.

Figure 8-2. JLaser Plus AT 2 Board (courtesy Tall Tree Systems)

For a laser printer, you should use a print spooler in your PC and you should add memory to the printer's built-in buffer to match your style of work. Some estimates for a single printer are:

One PC	printing simple text	512K
One PC	printing long or fancy text	1MB to 2MB
One PC	printing text and graphics	2MB to 4MB
Several PCs sharing the printer	printing simple text	1MB
Several PCs sharing the printer	printing long or fancy text	2MB
Several PCs sharing the printer	printing text and graphics	4MB or more

Video

Key Ideas

• Have enough memory on your video card to provide the colors and resolution you need.

• Capture any unused video memory for relocated TSRs and device drivers or to add to conventional memory.

• Copy the video ROM instructions to RAM for a faster display.

• Use 16-bit video for a faster display, and don't disable it by an installation conflict with an 8-bit peripheral.

How Video Memory Works

The central processor and memory of the computer run the application programs. It's these programs that create displays and images to be shown on the screen.

But it's the video adapter circuits that turn the results from those applications and utilities into signals the screen understands. Many different adapters are used on PCs. Some come on cards that plug into a PC slot; others are part of the PC's main circuit board. All use memory for two purposes. Memory holds instructions that tell how to translate PC signals into screen signals. And memory holds the display information those instructions work on. This is called the frame buffer or video buffer memory.

Most programs use the standard video instructions. But because they can be quite slow at times some programs bypass them and use their own instructions to write information directly to the video buffer memory.

The standard video instructions don't change often, and so are often kept in ROM chips at one address in memory. The display information changes constantly, and so are kept in RAM at a different address. To get the fastest display, with the most colors and the highest resolution, you need instruction memory that's fast and video buffer memory that's both fast and large enough.

Video Goals: High-resolution, Many Colors, Fast Display

Resolution, Color, and Speed are the three important factors in your PC's display. And if you use desktop publishing, presentation, or CAD software, these factors are more than just important—they're vital. All three are affected by memory.

Resolution is the number of dots on the screen. More dots means smoother graphics and sharper text. Color refers to the number of different colors that can appear on the screen at once. Some displays are only monochrome, offering essentially the two colors: black and white. Others offer up to 16, 256, thousands, or even millions of colors at a time. There are also gray-scale monitors that offer many different shades of gray instead of different colors.

Most color adapters also limit the palette that these simultaneously displayed colors can be chosen from. For example, an adapter might be able to display 16 colors at a time from a palette of 256 colors. If the adapter was only showing 8 colors on the screen and wanted to add another, but that other color wasn't among the 256 in the palette, it could not be shown.

Speed is a measure of the time it takes to put an image on the screen. Some video systems are so fast you don't even realize it takes time—the image is just there. Some can be quite slow. Some complex drafting images, for instance, might take anywhere from 10 seconds to a minute or more to be drawn on screen. Then when the image changes, you might have to wait that much time again for the modified image to appear.

More memory, of the right kind, can give you higher-resolution display images, more colors, and faster-changing images.

Text Mode and Graphics Mode

There is a division in adapters between graphics modes and text modes. Adapters running in a text mode see the screen as a grid of rows and columns, with each intersection consisting of a cell that's able to hold a single character, punctuation mark, or tiny graphic shape. Each cell can be made up of anywhere from 49 to 126 or more pixels or dots. The computer and its programs need only to specify which character will be in each cell. The adapter circuits will then look up that character's pattern of pixels for the cell in a special ROM chip. The final result is a series of pixels

313

sent to the display to form letters, numerals, punctuation, or tiny graphic shapes. (These shapes can be placed adjacent to shapes in other cells to build larger graphics.) Text mode doesn't use much memory because it only sees the screen as a set of approximately 2000 (80 columns by 25 rows) cells. Each cell requires only a single byte to record and store its character. (More bytes would be necessary for color information about that character, however.) A typical text screen could be held in 4K of memory, even granting plenty of room for color and special-effects (blinking, underlining, and so on) information.

Adapters running in a graphics mode see the screen as a field of pixels, so many across and so many down. Graphic images and text can be built from the individual pixels. Text made this way is called bit-mapped text, because it is built entirely from the individual bits and pixels, instead of from pre-formed character shapes inserted into cells. Both graphic and text constructions are stored in memory before being sent to the display. More pixels in the field means higher resolution. The latest resolutions are 640 x 480 to 1024 x 768. Because each pixel needs at least a single bit of memory (for monochrome), or as much as three bytes of memory (for millions of colors), graphics modes use much more memory than do text modes. For example, a 640 x 480 monochrome needs nearly 40K. An 800 x 600 display of 256 colors—an excellent display for running such environments as Windows—needs 512K. That's not 512K of memory in your PC; that's 512K of memory just for the graphics, above and beyond any other memory in your computer. Often the number of colors trades off against the resolution. The highest resolution mode won't offer as many colors as a lower resolution mode—because there isn't enough memory to show both the top resolution and the top color possibilities at the same time.

Video Adapter Standards

The highest-resolution, most-colorful, and highest-speed video adapters are often expensive products from companies that specialize in graphics hardware. These adapters are nearly always plug-in circuit cards, with a processor chip of their own and several MB of memory on the card. If there's a processor on the video adapter, the computer's main processor can avoid some work. Instead of saying "drawing this dot here and this dot here" the main processor can just tell the graphics co-processor to "draw a line from here to here." Then the graphics coprocessor figures out which dots go where, and puts those into the video memory.

Most PCs depend on standard video adapters, however. These follow IBM designs, just as PC-compatible computers follow IBM's overall computer design.

Some standards are set outside of IBM. The Hercules company was able to leapfrog IBM at one point, setting a monochrome video adapter standard that many other companies followed. Also, a number of companies later surged past IBM's VGA standard to create a SuperVGA standard. And Texas Instruments has led a group of graphics companies making TIGA (Texas Instruments Graphics Architecture) into a new standard, that can push resolution into the thousands of pixels horizontally and vertically, and color into the millions.

Each new generation of video adapter typically supports the previous generations, while adding its own new modes for more resolution and color. The 8514/A and TIGA don't follow this, but can run alongside a VGA adapter that will provide all of the previous video modes.

Here's a list of the important video adapter standards, their typical resolution and color modes, the amount of memory they use, and the addresses of that memory. The list is in chronological and performance order, from the oldest and least powerful to the latest and most powerful video adapters.

MDA (Monochrome Display Adapter)	80 x 25 text in monochrome	4K
CGA (Color Graphics Adapter)	640 x 200 in monochrome or 160 x 200 with 16 colors	16K
HGA (Hercules Graphics Adapter)	720 x 348 in monochrome	64K
EGA (Enhanced Graphics Adapter)	640 x 350 graphics with 16 colors from palette of 64	64K to 256K

VGA (Video Graphics Adapter)	640 x 480 with 16 colors from a palette of 256K or 320 x 200 with 256 colors from a palette of 256K	256K
MCGA (Memory Controller Gate Array) (a subset of the VGA mentioned above)	320 x 200 with 256 colors from 256K palette	
SuperVGA	640 x 480 with 256 colors from palette of 256K, or 800 x 600 with 16 colors from palette of 256K, or 1024 x 768 with 4 colors	256K to 1MB
8514/A	1024 x 768 with 16 colors	512K to 1MB
XGA (Extended Graphics Adapter)	1280 x 1024 with 256 colors.	1MB
TIGA (Texas Instruments Graphics Architecture)	1024 x 768 to 4096 x 4096 with millions of colors.	1MB on up

Other Video Adapters. An example of another, very-high-powered video adapter is the Horizon 860 from True Vision Inc. It is built around the Intel 33MHz i860 graphics coprocessor. This board can have up to 46MB of its own RAM. (But it costs more than many powerful PCs do.)

How Much? Adding Video Memory

Memory is a relatively cheap part of an entire computer system, but it can be a large fraction of the cost of a video adapter board. Even when memory costs $50 a MB, adding that MB to a video adapter board that only costs $200 is a major decision.

That's why most of the latest video adapters don't automatically come with the maximum amount of useful memory. Instead they keep their prices lower by letting you add more memory if you need or want it.

The first memory question to ask about your video is "Do I have enough memory for the colors and resolution I want to display?" Each adapter points this question in a different direction. For adapters that do give you a choice, adding memory and moving a few switches will let you display more colors at once, or work at higher resolutions.

MDA, HGA, and CGA boards don't give you the choice of adding RAM. They set aside what they need above the 640K address, and that's that.

EGA boards come with at least 64K of memory, but can often be beefed up to 256K with additional memory. Do this if you must stick with EGA but want more colors, but my advice is not to bother, as EGA is obsolete. VGA can do everything it does and a whole lot more and do it faster. So you're better off moving to a Super-VGA board, though you may also need to buy a new monitor.

VGA uses analog monitors, in place of the digital monitors the CGA and EGA use. VGA and Super-VGA boards often come with 256K of memory and sockets to plug in enough more memory to make a full MB. Each board is different. Figure 8-3 shows an example Super VGA board. This board starts with 256K, and with that much memory can handle standard VGA modes. With a full 1MB it can produce 1024 x 768 with 256 colors. The MB also lets it emulate the 8514/A graphics. EGA and VGA boards manage to handle more than 64K of memory by switching it in and out in banks of 64K at a time to the video frame-buffer memory addresses.

To add memory to the board you buy the DRAM chips and plug them in. Pay attention to the speed and type of chips the documentation says you'll need. DRAMs with an 80ns speed should fit most any board, but some can get by with slower DRAMs, at say 120ns or so. Some boards demand the more expensive VRAM chips, as explained later in this chapter. For details on and pictures of chip insertion, see Step 3. You'll also need to move a jumper or switch on some boards to let them know you've added memory. Other boards can sense the change automatically.

Figure 8-3. Example Super-VGA Board With Empty Sockets for Add-in Video Memory (courtesy Everex)

TIGA, 8514/A, and other advanced boards typically start with at least 512K of memory and offer more colors or resolution if you add more memory. Some can even perform faster with more memory, using special software that puts more of the work onto the boards processor, relieving the computer's main processor. Some boards accept more memory chips; others connect to daughterboards with more memory. The IBM 8514/A board, for example, can be attached to a 512K expansion option daughter card that will increase its color capability to 256 simultaneous colors.

Grabbing Video Memory for Applications

Many PCs chug along without using all of memory reserved for the video frame buffer. You can have your PC grab that unused memory, and hand it over to applications, TSRs, and device drivers that need it. This is one of the cheapest and easiest ways to get more memory in your PC.

In particular, you can often add that unused memory to the conventional memory in your PC. This is the only legal way to actually get more than 640K of conventional memory, the most immediately available memory to most applications.

For example, if you choose to run in MDA text mode but have a CGA adapter, you can grab 12K of the CGA's 16K and add it to your conventional memory. If you run an EGA or VGA adapter in a less memory-hungry mode, you can grab even more, getting 64K or more to add to conventional memory. In fact, you could total as much as 736K or even 800K of conventional memory for loading your device drivers, TSR programs, and applications. Such unused memory can also be grabbed and used as high memory for relocating drivers and TSRs, without adding it to conventional memory.

Using this memory for anything but video work, however, limits your flexibility some. You cannot quickly and automatically switch into the graphics modes that would employ this memory if it is already busy as conventional or relocation memory. See Step 5 for a thorough explanation of relocation and high memory use.

Video Speed

Faster video displays—putting the information on the screen as soon as possible—is good for just about any PC. It is critical for graphics applications such as animation, desktop publishing, drafting, and presentations. Speed or video performance becomes more important the higher the resolution and the more color on screen. Every color Super-VGA screen can, after all, mean moving about one fourth MB of information.

There are several memory factors to video speed: 8-bit vs. 16-bit, VRAM vs DRAM, and ROM BIOS operation vs. BIOS shadowing

Video Adapter Speed—8-bit versus 16-bit. Some video adapters plug into 8-bit slots and move video information 8 bits at a time. Some more recent, more expensive VGA video adapters are 16-bit, requiring 16-bit slots and moving 16 bits of video information at a time. The 16-bit adapters are faster than the 8-bit adapters, approximately twice as fast.

Adapter Conflicts—8-bit and 16-bit. Plug-in adapters of either 8- or 16-bit speed can conflict with each other in several ways. The most obvious is if they're trying to occupy the same address. To solve that problem you just reset the address of one of the two—see the documents to tell you how.

But there's another, more insidious conflict that many PC owners don't know about. This conflict sets 8-bit cards against neighboring 16-bit cards, and strips the 16-bit cards of their higher speeds.

This other conflict stems from a simple PC fact: the PC sets aside blocks of high memory for either 8-bit or 16-bit I/O operation. If a block is set for 8-bit operation, any 16-bit card in it will only work on 8 bits at a time. The second punch in this combination, though, is that even if a block is set to 16-bit operation, if there are both 16-bit and 8-bit cards inside that block, the PC cannot let them run at those different speeds. Instead, it slows the 16-bit card down to the 8-bit speed, making it run as an 8-bit card. That will spoil the anticipated performance of any 16-bit video adapter.

There are also potential conflicts between 16-bit adapters and VCPI-compatible memory managers. To avoid these conflicts you might need to reconfigure a 16-bit VGA card to 8-bit operation and exclude a region, such as the banks A through D of memory from use by any 16-bit applications. This problem is a bugbear for 286-based PCs; it is only an annoyance to 386s because they can remap memory in small pieces to avoid the problem of neighboring 8-bit and 16-bit operations.

VRAM Versus DRAM. When you buy a video adapter card, you can choose to get one with VRAM memory chips instead of the more common DRAM. VRAM chips, as shown in Figure 8-4, are specially made with two ports on the chip. These VRAMs can be read from (by the video display system) and written to (by the processor and program) at the same time. Standard DRAMs are slower. They must take this one step at a time, giving information to the display system, then turning to accept information from the processor and program.

However, VRAMs are more expensive than DRAMs, sold at a 50% premium, both for the original amount on the video board and for any extra amounts you want to add. Although some VRAM board manufacturers claim significant speed improvements from using VRAMs, my own experience and research suggests that the improvement is only slight, and certainly less than the difference between using 8-bit and 16-bit video adapters.

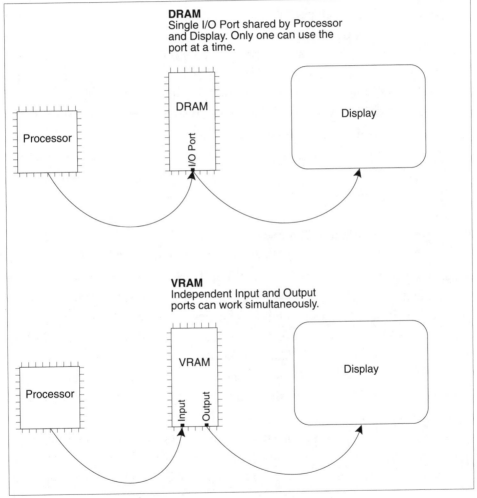

Figure 8-4. VRAM chips are faster for video than DRAMs because they can be read from and written to at the same time.

Some Sources of VRAM Video Boards—

Western Digital
Video Seven
Headland Technology
Everex

There are also other chip solutions that increase video adapter speed. Western Digital uses FIFO buffer chips (First In First Out) that work like VRAM, moving information in one side and out the other. But the FIFO scheme isn't as expensive as VRAM because it just adds a couple of the special FIFO chips to a board that relies primarily on DRAMs. ATI Technologies uses page-mode RAM chips and a 16-bit bus. Everex sells a VRAM board that automatically senses the CPU type and selects the fastest execution mode for the system it's in.

In general, you shouldn't pay too much of a premium for special architecture video adapters unless you can be shown that they will significantly improve the video performance of your particular system and application.

Copying BIOS to RAM and Shadow RAM

A PC's BIOS (Basic Input Output System) is a set of small programs that help run the basic parts of the computer system. The BIOS includes graphics instructions that can perform simple drawing operations on the video display. Some computer programs avoid the BIOS instructions for graphics. Instead of asking DOS to ask the BIOS to draw a line on the screen or fill an area, they just do it themselves, by directly writing information to the video frame buffer. They bypass BIOS because they want faster video, and the BIOS can be one of the slowest links in the video chain. But you can speed the BIOS for the benefit of all those programs that do use it by using shadow RAM.

The ROM BIOS in most video adapters is an 8-bit or 16-bit chip, offering its instructions in 8-bits or 16-bits at a time to programs that call for them. Often it is put into a slow EPROM chip. However, you can copy that BIOS full of instructions from whatever ROM it is in to faster RAM chips. There are then two copies of the BIOS in your PC. If you direct all requests for BIOS instructions to the RAM copy, your video can run faster than it ever could from an 8-bit or 16-bit ROM.

Some PC programs can copy the ROM BIOS to conventional RAM. This can speed video—the amount of improvement depends on the system—but it uses up some of that precious conventional RAM.

Other PCs copy the ROM BIOS to high memory RAM. This is called BIOS shadowing, using shadow RAM—RAM that's at the same address that the ROM would normally be. Figure 8-5 shows these two ROM BIOS copying schemes.

In a PC with an 8-bit ROM, copying to 8-bit RAM doesn't increase the speed much. In an 8MHz AT, a 16-bit video ROM copied to 16-bit RAM still doesn't improve the speed much. But in a 386 or 486 PC with 32-bit RAM, copying to RAM can make a big difference. The faster the processor in the PC—such as in very fast ATs running 12 or 16MHz—running from RAM has more impact.

Many 386- and 486-based systems, and some 286 systems such as those with the Chips & Technologies Chip Set, offer shadowing as part of the setup options. It is also built into some video adapters as an option. Using the shadowing feature of a 386 or 486 system is often better than using the video card's option, because the 386 can use extended memory while BIOS drivers use 12K or so of conventional memory below 640K.

Remember that BIOS shadowing doesn't help with programs such as Lotus 1-2-3 and Windows that write directly to video frame memory, speeds scrolling and cursor movement, but doesn't change redraw time.

You should also know that shadow RAM can conflict with some software, such as programs that use extended or expanded memory (Lotus 1-2-3 is an example) and some networks—that expect to put their routines in the RAM taken by the shadow copy of the BIOS. If you have such troubles, you should stop using either shadow RAM or the conflicting driver. You can check CONFIG.SYS and pull drivers out of it one at a time until you find the unhappy culprit, turn off shadow RAM in the PC's Setup window, or stop using the utility that produces shadow RAM. If the conflict has frozen your PC, turning off the power should free your system again.

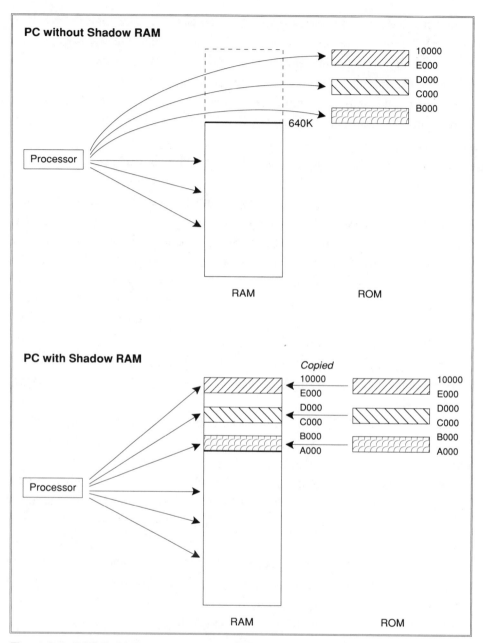

Figure 8-5. ROM BIOS Copied to Shadow RAM

Here are a few programs that provide RAM BIOS operation for PCs that don't have it as a built-in setup option:

Invisible RAM. Invisible Software's Invisible RAM program helps you use shadow RAM in 386 and 486 systems and in ATs and compatibles with the Chips & Technologies NEAT chipset. (About 80% of AT compatibles use that chip set.) This lets you load the ROM BIOS into high memory above 640K, and extend DOS conventional memory above 640K. It also lets you load as much as 224K of TSRs and device drivers, including AUTOEXEC.BAT and CONFIG.SYS drivers, into high memory. Invisible Software claims that some programs that have trouble in shadow RAM systems—such as Lotus 1-2-3—can run when Invisible RAM is handling the shadowing. When used with Invisible Software's NET-30/EMS Network Operating System, Invisible RAM can also load the network drivers into expanded memory or shadow RAM.

MOVROM. This shareware program works on some PC and XT-generation machines, particularly those from IBM. It copies the ROM to RAM and runs it from there.

Networks

Local area networks connect PCs so they can easily share data files and programs. LANs make some special demands on memory, however. This section explains those demands and what you can do about them. The most crucial—the need for LAN Driver space—will be explained last.

Key Ideas

- Each PC needs to run some sort of network driver program that takes up part of RAM. If you can load this driver into high, expanded, or extended memory, you'll have more conventional memory for running applications.

- Each LAN has at least one disk server PC, dedicating part or all of its powers to managing a large hard disk for the use of all the connected PCs on the LAN. This server is more efficient if it has lots of RAM for disk caching.

• Each LAN typically has at least one print server PC, dedicating part or all of its powers to managing a central printer for the use of all the connected PCs on the LAN. This server is more efficient if it has lots of RAM for spooling and has a network spooling program.

LAN Adapter Address

The LAN Adapter board you use to physically connect a PC to a network plugs into one of the PC's slots. Just as video adapters and disk drive controllers do, this board occupies an I/O address in high memory above 640K. Most any PC will have an address available, but address conflicts are quite possible. That is, the address the LAN adapter board first wants may be taken by some other board—in which case you'll need to change the address assignment for one of the two boards. Or the address the LAN adapter takes may be in memory that a high-memory relocation program is using. In that case, you'll need to reset the relocation configuration files. You'll need to let QEMM, 386-Max, or whatever other remapping and relocating tool you use "know" that there's a new board in the system.

LAN Disk Server Memory for Caching

Most networks of any size have a disk server and a print server. These may be the same machine. A server can be a powerful PC completely dedicated to serving the other PCs on the network, or a server can be just one of the jobs of one of the PCs on the net.

A disk server holds central files and programs that PCs on the network can request and share. A print server accepts printing jobs from all the PCs on the network, organizes them into a queue, and then prints them on a central printer.

Both disk servers and print servers depend on memory, lots of memory. First there's the memory they use for running programs. All servers must run their own programs, either applications if the server is doubling as a workstation PC, or network monitoring and analysis applications if the server is dedicated to network tasks.

Then there's the memory used for disk caching. Hard disk speed is critical to networks because servers are constantly storing and retrieving data from a large hard disk. A hard disk can be made much faster by using chip memory (which runs at electronic speed) to hold the most frequently used information from the disk (which, running at mechanical speed, is thousands of times slower).

The cache for a network server can be much larger than the cache used by a solitary PC. Where a single PC might need no more than 128K of cache, a network cache should be in the range of 1MB of cache for every 100MB of disk. With network disks often reaching or exceeding 300MB, that means 2 to 4MB of cache for best performance, depending on the number of users and the applications. (Database management and accounting, for instance, gets more help from a cache than do graphics programs.)

There are several ways to implement a network cache.

Some network operating systems, such as NetWare, LAN Manager, IBM's PC LAN, and LANtastic, have efficient RAM-caching schemes built in. Another option is to turn to one of the cache programs that's listed in Step 7, if it supports network operation.

Yet another way is to use a disk drive controller with a built-in cache. The memory in this cache won't be available to other PC or network uses, only to caching for that particular disk drive. But this is the smoothest way to get better disk speed, and is increasingly popular.

Whichever way you choose, don't delay writes in the cache program. It is quite difficult to recover from a power outage when the information on disk is obsolete and must be recreated from a score of different programs and workstations.

LAN Print Server Memory for Spooling

Just as a single PC can use memory to spool printing jobs for most efficient printing, a network server can spool all of the printing jobs from many PCs for most efficient printing. A LAN spool such as this needs more memory than a single PC spool does, and needs a spooler program intended for network operation.

Most network operating systems come with a spooler utility. For example, Novell's Advanced NetWare 286 and SFT NetWare 2.15 installations have long included printer-server features. But such built-in spoolers are not your only choice, or the most powerful choice, for network spooling. For example, it was only recently that the new print server utility with NetWare allowed PCs on the net to share printers that were attached to particular PCs, instead of directly connected to the net. Also, the NetWare spooler commands such as CAPTURE and ENDCAP had to be sent at the DOS prompt; they weren't available from a pop-up menu as most spoolers are. And NetWare's spooler does not offer sophisticated queue control.

Independent network spoolers have many capabilities, such as sending configuration commands to the printer, signalling the end of a print job, and managing print jobs in the queue. They track the progress of print jobs, and let you assign priority levels to them. Some let you send messages to other workstations, and some can reach remote hard disks on the network. Here are a few of the most popular LAN spoolers. In them you should look for small memory use—the spooler could add yet another burden to all those network software modules mentioned in the next section. The memory use ranges from approximately 4K to 190K.

LANSpool. LANSpool from LANSystems, Inc., is a print spooler for Advanced NetWare 286. It lets you attach multiple shared printers to a single PC—they don't have to be attached to the NetWare server as some levels of the NetWare spooler demand. LANSpool works with existing NetWare utilities including Pconsole, Printcon, and Printdef. It runs as a Novell VAP in non-dedicated mode using the least memory on the print server. It needs only 2K to 6K or so in your PC.

PrintQ LAN. PrintQ LAN from LANsmart/NV serves NetWare 2.1 or later or any NetBIOS network. It uses 70K of RAM in a system with extended memory or 140K in systems without. It cannot use expanded memory. PrintQ LAN supports 4 printers per print server, has password security for queue control, and offers 9 priority levels for printing. It also provides commands for naming queues, a chat mode for messages, starting or stopping a print, resending a job, reprinting a single page, banner control, and forms control. It can find all jobs that use a certain form and do them in a batch. PrintQ LAN doesn't use NetWare's Printcon database for printer sharing, so you can log out of NetWare on the print server but still receive print jobs from other PCs on the network. If there's enough memory in the server, PrintQ LAN can set up a RAM disk and send spooled print jobs to it for faster processing.

Q Assist and Printer Assist. These TSR programs from Fresh Technologies can manage NetWare's spooled print jobs. They work with NetWare ELS I version 2.0a and NetWare 2.0a. They can assign priorities to print jobs. Together they use only 19K to 24K.

Windows Workstation. Windows Workstation from Automated Design Systems provides NetWare spooling for Windows users. Most spoolers are made as pop-up TSR programs, but Windows doesn't work well with such TSRs. Within Windows Workstation is a print-management utility for NetWare that can route print jobs to local or server-based printers and can manage print queues from inside Windows.

LAN Software Space

The Network operating system software adds network abilities to your main operating system (which is typically DOS). The Network OS takes up RAM space in each and every workstation on the network. Most networks load several programs into RAM: a driver to connect to the network adapter card, a shell to provide network commands for the PC user, and other utilities to manage printing and communications. Technically speaking you will have a transport-layer module for the card and a redirector module for the network, and may also have a menu shell, email, and various communication modules. Some of these must remain in RAM the entire time your PC is on and connected to the network. Most network OSs also take up even more RAM on any servers in the network.

Unfortunately, the network OS RAM bite can be large and painful. Some "eat" as much as 100K or more from conventional memory, leaving you little space to run applications or to load other drivers you might need—such as mouse drivers, operating system utilities, and TSRs. Novell, the most popular network operating system, needs 50K to 70K.

This is the focus of networks and memory: how to cut down on the network driver's hunger for memory. There are two answers:

- Relocate network drivers to high, extended, or expanded memory

- Use a network with smaller drivers

Relocate Network Drivers High. If your network OS shell or driver is taking up more RAM than is comfortable, you can use many of the memory management programs mentioned in Step 5 to load the shell or driver into high or extended memory. Figure 8-6 shows a memory map of such a relocation. Novell's popular NetWare operating system (NOS) has drivers large enough to frustrate many PC owners—they are prime targets for relocation.

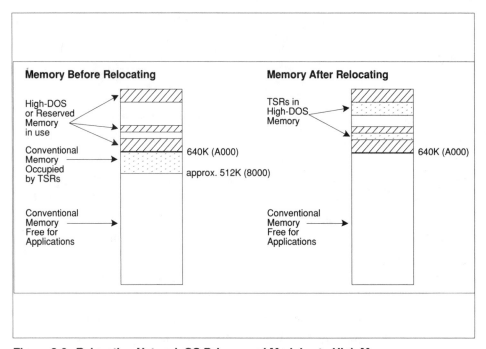

Figure 8-6. Relocating Network OS Drivers and Modules to High Memory

Even with relocation, you still need memory for the driver, but at least you're not using precious conventional memory that is so necessary for running application programs. By relocating the driver into high memory, you can often save 20K to 100K or more of conventional memory for other uses. See Step 5 for more details—especially in the "Relocating" sections. Here are a few products and tips relevant specifically to network driver relocation. Remember that not all memory managers mentioned in Step 5 can relocate all network modules, and that some of the utilities mentioned here can relocate not only network software but also other drivers and TSRs.

HiNet—Fresh Technology Group's HiNet program loads Novell NetWare workstation shell software into expanded memory, freeing 35 to 42K of conventional memory. It can be installed or deinstalled as you want and is compatible with such memory management programs as QEMM and Microsoft's HIMEM as well as with several popular RAM disks.

LANSpace—LANSystems' LANSpace program loads the NetWare shell into extended memory on systems with at least 64K free extended memory. This can free up to 56K more of conventional memory. LANSpace can also unload the NetBIOS software for applications that don't need it, saving more memory.

The RAMPack—BLOC Publishings team of PopDrop Plus and Above DISC includes the latest version of Above DISC, which can load Novell NetWare drivers into extended memory. See Step 5 for details on Above DISC, which can also turn unused extended memory into LIM 4.0 expanded memory.

NetRoom—Helix Software's NetRoom is from the same people who make the HeadRoom memory manager mentioned in Step 5. NetRoom can relocate Novell's hardware drivers and software modules—including IPX, NetBIOS, and NET3/NET4—into high, extended, or expanded memory. It can also relocate the drivers for IBM's PC LAN program, 3Com's LANs, Banyan's VINES LAN, and others. It runs on any PC from the original 8088 design to today's 486 compatibles. NetRoom also comes with a utility called DISCOVER that can quickly report on the hardware and software configuration of your PC.

Para-Mail—There are also differences in the memory that various network applications need. Some of the popular email packages, for example, need 75K or more. That's too much for them to run alongside large applications, so many people with these programs must quit their applications, send and receive mail, then restart their applications. But there are alternatives such as Para-Mail from Paradox

Development, that don't use as much memory. Para-Mail needs only 15K, and comes with a text editor, folders, priority levels, phone messages, and conversation tracking.

NetWare Relocation Tips. The NetWare Operating System has been a troublesome character for memory managers. Until recently, for instance, the NOS shell occupied 56K of memory. It could not be loaded into expanded or extended memory and could not be removed from memory without rebooting the PC, even if you logged off from the network. However, the latest NOS has customizing commands and switches that can be tuned to cut back on NetWare's use of RAM. In fact, there were two shell files—IPX and NET3 or NET4 (depending on the DOS version you use)—and a third file, NETBIOS, that added another 26K for point-to-point communication on the net. (This is explained in more detail in Step 3.) Most PC applications, such as WordPerfect, 1-2-3, and typical e-mail programs, need only two-way communication with the server, and so don't need NetBIOS. IPX eats up 17K. It tells the network the address and interrupt channel of the network interface card and which transfer protocol to use.

The latest NetWare lets you use EMSNET3 or EMSNET4 and XMSNET3 or XMSNET4 to put part of the NetWare shell into expanded (EMS) or extended (XMS) memory. Only the IPX module, occupying 16K of memory, and a 6K or 7K piece of EMSNET or XMSNET (respectively) will remain when you log off the network. However, your PC must be highly compatible with IBM's PCs to use these new modules. Reportedly even some PS/2s aren't compatible enough. These new files also won't work properly unless the network supervisor installs the new versions of some other NetWare utilities on the system server.

If you want to run Windows 3 on a NetWare network, you must have DOS Client Version 3.01 installed. This lets you deinstall NET3 or NET4 and NetBIOS when you log off the network. Windows users must also remember to load the NetWare modules, then load Windows, then log on to the net. Don't log on to the net and then try to load Windows.

Banyan Vines Relocation Tips. Vines 4.0 lets you move 37K of the network software to high memory, leaving only 83K in conventional memory. This is possible with QEMM, HIMEM.SYS, and other memory managers that support the XMS memory standard.

Using a Network with Smaller Drivers

Novell isn't the only network operating system in town. There are others which take up less memory in both workstations and servers. Here are a few of the best known:

LANtastic. The LANtastic network from Artisoft is generally touted as the smallest network operating system around. This thrifty network takes up less than 40K per server and 10K per node. Even these minor amounts can be cut back by using QEMM or some other memory manager to load parts of the OS modules into expanded or extended memory. A workstation doing that can devote as little as 1.5K of conventional memory to LANtastic.

It also rates well for easy installation, good speed, and low cost. LANtastic has full DOS 3.1 file and record-locking support and fully implements NetBIOS for all network communications. This is a true peer-to-peer network that can share hard disks, floppy disks, and printers among all of the nodes. LANtastic has its own print spooler and e-mail, and even has a unique ability to capture, store, and send voice messages (it comes with a telephone handset for the job).

The server software may be hard to fit into high memory because although it needs only 23 to 27K in memory, it needs more than that during loading. Also, any 286-based PC with an EMS board can have trouble with that board which may try to use the same memory as the LANtastic adapter card. There can be conflicts with video memory too. Some users report that Lantastic has some compatibility problems with DESQview and VM-386. If relocation troubles are too sticky, you can buy a daughterboard from Artisoft that has its own memory. Plug this board into the LANtastic adapter card, and the network software can load into the daughterboard's memory.

Invisible Network. Invisible Software's Invisible Network is a memory-thrifty network operating system. Net/30 isn't as easy to install as LANtastic, and doesn't have as many features, but it can use as little as 3K per workstation and 13K per server if there is expanded memory for software relocation. Without expanded memory it uses 60K per workstation and 80K per server. The Invisible Network has file sharing, print spooling, file/record locking, e-mail, a menu system, security, network management, and diagnostics. (Invisible Software also makes memory boards and memory managers, such as the Invisible memory software that can grab unused video memory for use as conventional memory.)

PowerLan. Performance Technology's PowerLan doesn't have a particularly small appetite for memory—using 87K per server and 42K per workstation—but it does let you load those drivers into high memory. PowerLan runs on inexpensive, standard Arcnet cards instead of the proprietary network adapter cards that most nets use.

Gateways and Terminal Emulators

Many PCs hook up to more than a local area network; they are also communicating with mainframe computers and distant networks through PC-HOST connections (and terminal emulation software) and gateways. But for each extra protocol that a PC needs to send and receive information with other computers, there's probably another module to fit into conventional memory. The squeeze can be particularly acute when the PC user wants to download data from a mainframe, for instance, and then chart that data using a graphics program or spreadsheet. Of the 640K of conventional memory, DOS uses 60K or so, a Windows 3 kernel needs about 45K more, the network needs some for itself, the PC-HOST connection some more, and any extra protocols, such as IPX, TCP/IP, ISO TP-4, and IBM's APPC yet more. What's left for the graphics program that may want 512K to 640K? Perhaps as little as 200K to 400K.

There are some long-term solutions, such as the new standard that IBM, DEC, 3Com and others are working on, to let multiple protocols run through a single network adapter card. There are also graphics programs that don't need as much memory—the latest versions of many graphics programs reflect the cries of mainframe communicators and take up less memory. (Ashton-Tate's Applause, for example, once needed 640K. Now it wants only 512K. Lotus Freelance shrank 20% to ease the memory squeeze.)

Again, however, you can look for terminal emulation, protocol, and gateway programs that are smaller or that can be relocated to high, expanded, or extended memory. Here are some examples:

3270/Elite. This SNA gateway, 3270 DFT-mode terminal emulator from Network Software Associates is the smallest I can find: it takes only 60K of conventional memory. 3270/Elite runs with practically any coaxial adapters, network, or Token-Ring attachment. It offers full SAA/CUA screens.

NSA also makes APPC for DOS. Use this with Windows 3.0 and you won't need to move to OS/2's Extended Edition Communication manager or to multiprotocol network adapters and memory cards. From Windows, this program can swap between protocols locally into extended memory.

Connecting/Room. Helix Software's Connecting/Room relocates terminal emulation software to extended or expanded memory, or to disk when those memory types aren't available.

Defect From DOS: a New OS if You Must

Key Ideas:

• If the DOS memory limits are too tight for you, even with improved memory management, or you are attracted by multitasking, multi-user systems, switch to another operating system such as DR DOS, OS/2, Unix, or even the Apple Macintosh.

• Even if you're happy with DOS combined with a memory-management environment such as Windows, you should consider a DOS-compatible operating system such as DR DOS 5.0 or the imminent DOS 5.0 from Microsoft. These can give you more memory for use inside each program running in Windows.

Sometimes Extending DOS is Not Enough

The DOS operating system is the villain in memory management these days. There are a few older PCs and XTs whose hardware limits your memory might, whose processor chip cannot easily work with more than a megabyte of memory. But it is DOS that restricts memory use for every PC owner. DOS imposes the hated 640K limit on memory. DOS can reach beyond 1MB only through convoluted or indirect schemes such as expanded memory and extended memory. Don't get me wrong—these schemes can help your computing enormously. But how much nicer it would be for you and your computer if your operating system just let each and every program have as much memory as it wanted, without you having to worry about how it was done.

This book has been a tour of DOS extension, enhancement, and avoidance techniques. But there's a more straightforward way to beat the 640K DOS limit: leave DOS altogether. If the memory problems of DOS hurt enough, you might just want to give up on it and try another operating system.

PCs can run other operating systems than DOS. And many of these other operating systems don't have the DOS 640K limit. They have limits of their own, but these limits are typically much looser than those in DOS. This Step explains the ins and outs of those other operating systems.

Pros and Cons of Other Operating Systems

DOS can be forced to use more memory than 640K, and to use it better, but DOS is not the only operating system around. There are other software foundations for your PC that can offer such advantages as:

- Better memory management

- Multitasking

- Multi-user support

- Better networking support

If more than one of these advantages grabs your attention, you should at least consider switching operating systems. Keep in mind though that there are several disadvantages to leaving DOS:

- Expense

- Retraining

- Application incompatibility

The Expense disadvantage will hit you in several ways. You'll have to pay for:

- Hardware—such as additional memory chips or disks to run the new OS.

- Software—for the new OS itself and any additional utilities it might need, as well as for any new versions of application programs you'll need.

The retraining disadvantage is really another expense factor. You'll spend time and money switching to a new OS. There will be an installation process, new commands to grasp, new support procedures to learn, and exceptions to study.

What exceptions? compatibility exceptions—the third and key disadvantage: you can't count on using your present software. Nor can you count on all of your hardware peripherals working.

This is the most painful fact about leaving DOS: you cannot automatically run DOS programs under another operating system. Word Perfect, Lotus 1-2-3, Word, dBASE, even little utility programs you use without thinking much about them: these are all created with DOS in mind. You lose the right to use some or all of them if you defect from DOS.

Because DOS is so popular and important, some of the alternative operating systems can run many or even most DOS programs. But you can't be sure that every program will run, or that every feature will work properly in each program. And some of the alternative systems can't run any DOS programs at all. These alternative systems can run programs of their own, but none support the number and variety of programs that DOS can.

The hardware compatibility problem can crop up with plug-in boards such as network adapter cards, or with special peripherals such as CD-ROMs that don't have software driver connections to the new operating system. You may need to buy new interfaces, new peripherals, or at the very least re-install those peripherals.

Hardware Demands of New Operating Systems

Some alternative operating systems work on any PC. A fair number, however, get their improved memory management by exploiting the 386 chip, and so work only on 386 and 486-based PCs. (The 486 can do everything the 386 does.) The Virtual-86 mode and huge memory address space of the 386 and 486 suit them well to multitasking and the use of massive memory. The operating systems that do require the 386 and 486 don't carry the burden of supporting simpler PCs, a burden that restricts what DOS can do.

Some alternative operating systems also demand more RAM memory and more disk memory than DOS requires. The expense of that extra hardware is sometimes a key reason in remaining with DOS.

Types of Operating Systems

There are three kinds of alternative operating systems for your PC.

DOS-Compatible—Systems in this first group look and feel a lot like DOS, but have more features and commands and improved memory management. These are the best at running DOS software, and include: Other versions of DOS, DR DOS, Concurrent DOS, and PC-MOS.

OS/2, Unix, and Similar OS—Systems in this second group are fundamentally different from DOS, and far more powerful. These can run some or most DOS programs through special emulation. This group includes OS/2, Theos, QNX, Unix, and Xenix.

Finally there are operating systems that won't run at all on PCs, that are built for different computers. If you're frustrated enough with the PC you may want to leap out of its way entirely. Even these systems have some emulation abilities to run PC software. Unix Workstations and the Apple Macintosh are the leading examples in this group.

DOS-compatible Alternatives

Other Versions of DOS

Your first choice for another OS is... another version of DOS. After all, as explained in Step 3, DOS has changed through the years, and you don't have to stick to the latest version. Some versions eat up less memory than others, and some offer more functions and commands for inspecting memory. The practical DOS choices are (and will be): DOS 3, DOS 4, and DOS 5.

DOS 3. DOS version 3 is an all-time favorite. Many programs only demand version 2.0 or later, but most PC owners can upgrade from 2.0 to 3.1, 3.2, or 3.3 without losing any compatibility. If you do upgrade, you'll have more powerful directory and disk abilities and a stable version of DOS that IBM and Microsoft are still supporting. What you won't have is some of the bug problems of DOS 4.0. Version 3.3 is still a live product, even though it hasn't been the latest DOS for several years. It outsells version 4.01, which has a bad reputation because of some early bugs. DOS 4 is also famous for using more RAM than DOS 3 does, so switching back to 3 from 4 can sometimes save you a few K.

DOS 4. DOS 4, actually DOS 4.01, is the most recent version of DOS as I finish this book. It does use a bit more memory than DOS 3, but it comes with some memory management tools you won't find in 3, such as a MEM command to see what programs are in memory. DOS 4 also has a shell that makes it easier to use for many beginning computer users.

DOS 5. Finally, you might live with DOS as best you can waiting for version 5.0, which is scheduled to appear in mid 1991. DOS 5.0 will add some sophisticated memory management abilities to DOS, such as the ability to relocate some of its own code from conventional memory to high-DOS or reserved memory. DOS 5 should also be smaller than previous versions of DOS. Microsoft intends it as a replacement for both DOS 3.3 and for DOS 4.01. (It will clearly cut into the market for utilities such as QEMM and 386Max that provided relocation abilities.) Finally, this new DOS won't be available only when each computer manufacturer gets around to adapting it, but instead will be sold at retail stores for less than $100.

5.0's new memory features may include:

• Loading DOS into high memory, a relocation option that could open all but about 15K of your 640K for applications. (This will be done with the EMM386.SYS program that lets TSRs and device drivers sit in high memory.)

• Task switching—swapping active application programs to and from disk. Running from ROM on portables, saving more of the 640K for applications.

Other advantages of 5.0 will include:

• Direct support from Microsoft—instead of support only through your PC's manufacturing company or your dealer.

• A Shell that looks something like the shell of DOS 4.0 and that interface of Windows 3.

• New commands such as undelete and unformat.

• A full-screen text editor to replace the EDLIN line editor.

• On-line help for all DOS commands.

341

- The Quick Basic Interpreter for programming.

- A command-line buffer to recall and edit any commands you have typed.

- A File Search utility program.

- Installation over previous DOS versions, with the ability to return to the previous version when necessary.

Advantages of Sticking to DOS. When you stop and consider a DOS with extenders and memory management environments such as Windows 3.0, DOS has to some extent passed newer operating systems such as OS/2. You'll certainly gain the following advantages by sticking with DOS:

Compatibility—All of your existing applications, utilities, and device drivers should still work (or more than would with alternative operating systems, at least) This won't be entirely true with a new DOS such as version 5.0, but should be more dependable than switching to an OS from any other company.

Low-cost—You won't have to buy new hardware or software, nor will you face much retraining expense. At worst you'll pay a small upgrade price.

Disadvantages of Sticking to DOS.

- No virtual memory built in.

- DOS won't be able to use the advanced features of the 386 and 486 chips, such as virtual memory support.

- Limited networking and communications ability.

- Even the new DOS 5 doesn't' promise to change the bedrock fact that DOS wasn't created to neatly network machines or handle multi-user task.

- The 640K limit is still there, hampering your operations.

Bottom Line. Use DOS 3.3 for maximum free memory now, but if you like DOS, switch to DOS 5.0 as soon as it is available and you're sure it is compatible with your programs.

For more details on DOS versions, look to Step 3.

DR DOS

DR DOS isn't DOS. It's a very similar operating system from the company that set the OS standard before Microsoft. In fact, DR DOS 5.0 looks a lot like Microsoft's scheduled new DOS 5.0, but has been on the market for a while before DOS 5.0. DR DOS lets you run all of your DOS programs, but has better memory management than DOS.

Digital Research Inc. (DRI) made CP/M, the most common operating system before the IBM PC made DOS the best seller. (In fact, some people think DOS copied CP/M's commands and file handling.) In 1984 Digital Research came up with Concurrent DOS, a DOS competitor that could run DOS programs, and like DESQview had some multitasking ability. Later DRI came up with GEM, a graphic environment that ran on top of DOS. But GEM lost the market popularity battle to Windows.

Now Digital Research is offering DR DOS 5.0, pronounced "dee are DOS" not "Doctor DOS." This is not an addition to DOS, (as Windows and DESQview are) it is a full-blown operating system on its own. But it is an operating system that can run all DOS programs. (You may find some that don't run, or don't run in all of their modes, but the list will be quite short.) You run it just as you would DOS, typing the same commands and using your programs the same way.

But DR DOS adds some things to DOS:

• More file and disk handling commands.

• A full-screen, WordStar-style text editor for viewing and changing files such as CONFIG.SYS and AUTOEXEC.BAT. DOS has only the feeble EDLIN.

• A history buffer for the command line, so you can automatically call up and repeat complex commands.

• Help information for all commands. Just type /h after any command to see what the command does and how to use it.

• A password protection option for files and directories.

• Larger hard disk partitions, more than the DOS maximum of 32MB.

• Power control options (BatteryMax). Designed originally for laptop computers with batteries, DR DOS can automatically check for activity, and if nothing is happening, puts the system into a standby state to save power and extend battery life.

• A graphic shell (ViewMax) like that in DOS 4 for beginners and experts who prefer to use a mouse to copy and move files and start programs.

• A file transfer utility (FileLink) utility that can send or receive files over a serial link to a second computer.

• A Disk Cache utility that can use expanded or extended memory.

• A Setup program that is interactive and can automatically create, or change, or put options into the CONFIG.SYS and AUTOEXEC.BAT files.

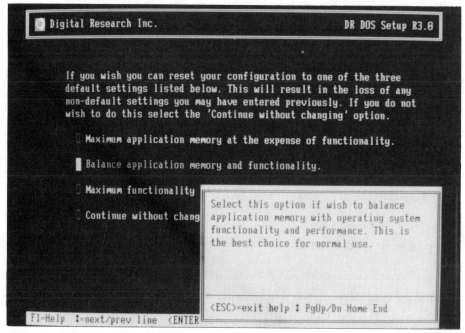

Figure 9-1. DR DOS Options in CONFIG.SYS and AUTOEXEC.BAT
(courtesy Digital Research)

DR DOS Advantages. Beyond these additional utilities and commands, DR DOS has some distinct advantages as an alternative operating system. It is:

• Compatible, running DOS applications, TSRs, network and device drivers. (It even runs Windows 3 and DESQview.)

• Easily installed over DOS, seeking and replacing DOS on your hard disk. It doesn't bother files that aren't involved, and it preserves the hard disk partitions, which few new operating systems do.

• Thrifty with your 640K of memory because it can load most of itself (and TSRs and device drivers) into memory above 640K (on systems with 386 or 486 processors or 286 processors with the Chips & Technologies support chip set). This is like having QEMM or 386-Max built in. EMS 4 emulation sup on 386 and 486. Users report as much as 639K free for application use.

• Compatible with the VCPI and DPMI (DOS Protected Mode Interface) standards for using DOS extenders with extended memory. That means DR DOS can run Lotus 1-2-3 Release 3, AutoCAD and other such DOS extender programs.

• Inexpensive. It costs just $199 for DR DOS and its utilities—nothing more for additional hardware or software.

• Popular, with reportedly as many as several million users.

• Well supported, with unlimited, toll-free, charge-free, customer support direct from Digital Research. DOS doesn't have any direct support yet from Microsoft or IBM.

DR DOS Disadvantages. DR DOS isn't all good news, though. It still has the disadvantages of the:

- Same 640K limit as DOS.

- Single-tasking foundation—there's no multitasking built in.

- Compatibility questions. Even new versions of DOS have some trouble running all of the old DOS software. DR DOS has a share of these problems too. QEMM-386 5.0 has trouble with DR DOS, so does DESQview. And when DR-DOS writes files onto floppies formatted with DOS, not all DOS machines can read those files.

Bottom Line. DR DOS is a superset of DOS 3.3 and 4.0, with a bunch of useful utilities and built-in memory management to free more of your 640K. It competes directly with DOS 5.0, but it doesn't eliminate the 640K barrier.

Concurrent DOS and DOS XM

Digital Research, which makes DR DOS described above, also makes several other operating systems for PCs. These are dedicated to multitasking and multiuser work. With one of these operating systems, a single PC can keep several attached terminals busy. Because terminals are cheaper than PCs, and provide better security for a central database or accounting file, these OS choices are popular in dedicated systems for accounting and medical offices. Multiuser systems are cheaper to set up than Local Area Networks too, though they don't have all the power and features of networks.

DOS XM is aimed at 8086 and 80286-based PCs. Concurrent DOS 386 and Concurrent DOS 386/MGE (Multiuser Graphics Edition) can multitask several DOS programs at a time on a 386 PC. These are fully compatible with the commands and files of DOS.

All of these Digital Research operating systems support EMS LIM 4.0 expanded memory and up to 4GB of extended memory on standard memory add-in boards. There are some holes in this support, however. For example, DOS XM doesn't support a full 32MB of expanded memory as well as some other features of EMS 4.0.

Extra memory is essential when you have a single, central PC running applications for three or four terminals. Concurrent DOS, for example, can multitask up to 4 operations at a time on the main PC while running two more on each satellite terminal, for a total of up to 255 different tasks at a time. The real limit on all these multitasking, multiuser work would be memory.

Advantages of Concurrent DOS Include:

• Runs most DOS programs

• Inexpensive multiple user system for sharing programs and databases

• Supports expanded and extended memory

Disadvantages of Concurrent DOS.

• Still has 640K limit for applications.

• Graphics programs only run on the central system, unless using the more expensive MGE (Multiuser Graphics Edition) version.

• XM can't run programs such as Lotus, dBASE, and WordStar, that don't carefully follow video display conventions.

Bottom Line. Turn to concurrent DOS or one of the other multiuser operating systems only if there's a special application program for your market—such as medicine, retail, or accounting—that runs under that OS. Don't use them hoping for a memory fix—you'll need even more memory in the central system to support all the attached terminals.

PC MOS

PC-MOS from The Software Link is sold as a modular operating system. (MOS stands for Modular OS.) It looks like DOS when on a the PC screen, but it is a multiuser, multitasking operating system for up to 25 users. It is easily installed, and doesn't require you to reformat your hard disk or change your file system (the directories and subdirectories on your disks.) It even uses normal DOS AUTOEXEC.BAT and CONFIG.SYS startup files.

PC-MOS can work on a simple PC or XT. On a 386 system (as PC-MOS|386) or a 286 with memory remapping ability (perhaps through an All ChargeCard), PC-MOS has some powerful memory management abilities. It can relocate part of its kernel to extended memory above 1MB to make more room in the lower 640K. In some cases it can even get more than 640K into a partition (an area of memory for one of the multitasking programs) by grabbing unused video memory and by remapping stuff from the lower 640K into high memory. That is, it has relocation abilities built in, that DOS gets only through special utilities and memory managers. PC-MOS will test various memory ranges to determine whether or not they are available. Unfortunately it can make a mistake in this testing and optimizing, missing some potentially useful memory or grabbing addresses that are needed by some vital function. For example, it could take a piece of high memory for relocation work from addresses that are actually necessary for the interface of some plug-in board if that board didn't signal its need during startup. That would crash the system when the board did decide to sign on and use those addresses. However, you can avoid these kinds of problems by entering FREEMEM statements in the CONFIG.SYS file. In other words, you can and sometimes have to fine-tune the memory management, just as you would on a DOS system with QEMM or 386-MAX or other DOS memory relocation utilities.

PC-MOS also uses the 64K of high memory, the wraparound memory that most 386 systems can address above 1MB. It has its own EMS emulator to convert extended memory into expanded memory, and has a disk caching program.

Advantages of PC-MOS.

- Compatible with most PC programs.

- Has built-in remapping and relocation software to put drivers, TSRs, and even itself into high memory.

- Has EMS Emulator and disk cache utility.

- Easy installation, without reformatting hard disk.

- Multitasking and multiuser—and attached terminals can be running DOS.

Disadvantages of PC-MOS.

- It is not compatible with all PC programs.

- It still lives in a world of the 640K memory limit, with the exceptions noted.

Bottom Line. PC-MOS buys you multitasking and multiuser operation as well as built-in utilities for memory management that you'd have to buy separately for DOS. It doesn't eliminate the 640K barrier however, and doesn't have all the extra utilities in DR DOS 5.0 or rumored to be in DOS 5.0.

OS/2, Unix, and Similar Operating Systems

An OS doesn't have to be compatible with DOS to work on your PC. It can just replace DOS entirely, using your PC hardware but ignoring that DOS software you've been taking for granted as a necessity. To compete with DOS, most of these other OSs have more power, in everything from memory management to networking. They can typically run some DOS programs through a compatibility or emulation option. But they aren't as compatible with DOS programs and peripheral drivers as DOS itself or any of the DOS-compatible OS options mentioned above. Certainly the leader in this category is OS/2, though it is in a tough battle with Unix, to set the next business-world standard for OS on PCs.

OS/2

OS/2 can use 16MB of memory. What is extended memory for DOS is just conventional memory for the OS/2 operating system, as you can see in the OS/2 memory map of Figure 9-2. Also, OS/2 is built to take multitasking, multi-user, and networking operation for granted, while DOS is not.

OS/2 Versions and Confusion. Because of those advanced abilities, and because it has both IBM and Microsoft behind it, OS/2 has been touted by many experts and most of the PC magazines as the natural successor to DOS. Although there are some proponents of Unix for this position, and you'll find a few people who swear by DR DOS or PC-MOS, OS/2 has been the leading alternative for those who were cramped by DOS memory limits and lack of multitasking.

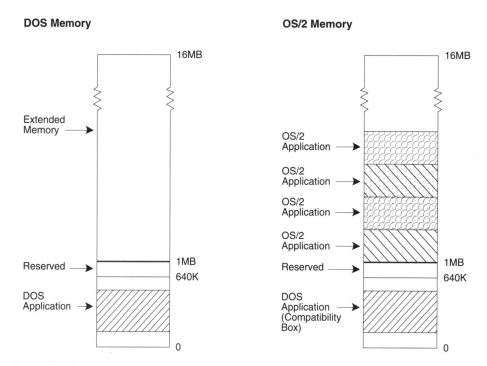

Figure 9-2. OS/2 Memory Map

In fact, IBM and Microsoft developed OS/2 together, and expected DOS to give way to OS/2 in the late 1980s. (At one point it was even known as DOS 5, the next logical step in the evolution of DOS.) That didn't happen for several reasons. For one thing, although OS/2 can work with more memory than DOS can, it also needs more to get started. You can't run any version of OS/2 in less than 2MB of RAM, and realistically you need 4MB or more to use any of its sophisticated powers. OS/2 running on a database server asks for as much as 8MB and more. And just as OS/2 was coming out in 1987 and 1988 the price of RAM chips temporarily soared, making OS/2 economically impractical. Then, as memory prices fell and OS/2 was getting ready for another big surge in 1989 and 1990, Microsoft's Windows took off, stealing the headlines from OS/2. Instead of the new, untested OS/2 operating system that couldn't run all DOS programs and needed lots more RAM and disk, DOS users could take the smaller step of adding Windows 3.0. This new Windows offered better use of memory, multitasking, and other such OS/2 benefits but didn't need as much memory as OS/2 and wasn't as expensive.

The incomplete and changing nature of OS/2 also slowed its acceptance. The DOS-compatibility box in OS/2 1.0 wasn't very compatible with DOS. But IBM and Microsoft assured people that this would improve in Versions 1.1 and 1.2. Unfortunately, those versions took some time to appear. Then there was the difference between standard OS/2 from Microsoft and Extended Edition OS/2 that you could only get from IBM. On top of that was the difference between OS/2 and OS/2 with its Presentation Manager graphic interface. The Presentation Manager is to OS/2 what Windows is to DOS. It was a big part of the early excitement about OS/2, but didn't appear for nearly two years after OS/2 was announced.

In the meanwhile IBM and Microsoft have shifted their OS/2 plans several times. The original OS/2 plan was for a new operating system that could use the protected mode of the 286, 386, and 486 chips to reach 16MB of memory and to handle multitasking. The 16-bit 286 chip was chosen as the base processor because the more advanced and more powerful 32-bit 386 was thought to be too far in the future. Because of the delays in OS/2 development, disagreements between IBM and Microsoft, and the quick popularity of the 386 chip in the market, there are now plans for IBM to make a newer OS/2, called OS/2 2.0, while Microsoft makes an even more advanced OS/2 3.0. These advanced versions of OS/2 will handle 32-bits at a time and will have a faster paged memory addressing scheme like that of Unix, leaving behind the small 64K segments that are the basis of memory addressing in both DOS and 16-bit OS/2. Both would need yet more memory, though. Typical systems would have perhaps 8 MB of RAM, and would be able to handle as much as 64TB (terabytes). When they will be available and just what their capacities will be, though, is still an open question.

Finally, to add to the confusion, at times IBM has been rumored to be planning a smaller version of OS/2. This is dubbed by some PM Lite. It would run on PCs with less memory—needing only 3MB instead of 4MB or more—and so would compete more directly with Windows 3.

OS/2 Applications. A few DOS applications have been rewritten to work under OS/2, but there is no single new "killer" application for OS/2 yet that is convincing people to leave DOS behind. Through 1990, the most popular uses for OS/2 were for proprietary, specialized programs within large corporations, and as the central software for a database server running in a network. Those are important tasks, but they aren't the bulk of the market, and they aren't enough to cut seriously into the DOS world.

The similarity between Presentation Manager and Windows may mean that companies creating Windows programs now will have a relatively easy time moving those programs to OS/2 and Presentation Manager later.

DOS Compatibility in OS/2. OS/2 1.2 has a DOS compatibility environment or DOS box feature for running DOS programs. It sets aside 640K of memory and lets a DOS program run within that familiar, comfortable, cramped limit. Figure 9-3 shows this running inside the Presentation Manager. It cannot just let DOS programs run in more memory as they aren't built for it. In Version 1.2 this box often had as little as 500K left for an application after loading operating system routines and the like. Many DOS programs won't even load with that little memory. There is no provision in 1.2 for expanded memory for the DOS programs. ·

OS/2 2.0 will have more in the range of 624K free in the Box, up to as much as 721K. What's more, Version 2.0 will be able to run as many as sixteen DOS boxes simultaneously, multitasking DOS programs. It will also provide expanded memory and offer cutting and pasting of information between DOS programs and between DOS and OS/2 programs. OS/2 2.0 will even be able to run Windows 3.0, though it won't handle the protected mode or other DOS extenders, either of which would interfere with its own extender technology.

Tips for Memory Management in OS/2. OS/2 1.2 may be able to reach 16MB, and OS/2 2.0 thousands of times that much memory, but both still need smart memory management to make the fastest and most efficient use of the memory in your computer. Here are some tips to that end (though you'll find many more in a book devoted entirely to OS/2).

• More memory means faster processing, so try to have as many MB as possible.

• Use Dynamic linking in OS/2 programs to conserve RAM. It allows applications to share one physical copy of some software routines.

• Keep lots of hard disk free for the virtual memory swapping. Certainly have at least 5MB free.

• Don't worry about TSRs eating up memory; OS/2 doesn't have TSRs. All programs can run side-by-side in a multitasking system, so any program can behave like a TSR does in DOS, ready to pop up at any time.

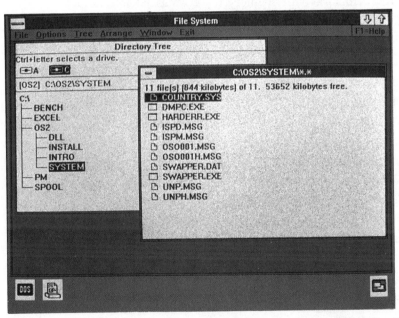

Figure 9-3. DOS Compatibility Box of OS/2 Running in the Presentation Manager (courtesy Microsoft)

CONFIG.SYS is a big deal in OS/2. It affects dozens of operating system defaults and settings, as shown in the example in Figure 9-4. Use the CONFIG.SYS file to set a whole range of memory values.

Disk—If you have only 2MB and are running OS/2 and the PM, performance will be hurt by all the time spent swapping information to your hard disk. You'll get much better disk performance if you increase the disk cache size to at least **diskcache=128** or if you have 4MB or more RAM, use **diskcache=256** or better yet, **diskcache=512**

DOS Box—If you don't run DOS programs in the compatibility box, change **protectonly=no** to **protectonly=yes** so that no memory will be reserved for real-mode programs.

Then place **REM** and a space in front of **DEVICE=c:/ega.sys**

This will free as much as 600K memory. if you want to enable the DOS Box later, remove the REM and change protectonly back to no.

Incidentally, some IBM-designed device drivers when scanning DEVICE= line can't recognize optional switches specified in lowercase.

Or, if you're going to use the compatibility box only for programs that need less than 640K, change rmsize to 256 to 640.

Threads—Threads are OS/2's name for active operations. Multitasking always requires multiple threads, but even a single program can use more than one thread (such as a word processing program that was checking spelling and re-paginating at the same time). However, OS/2 sets aside 2K for each possible thread, so you don't want to configure to have a huge number of possible threads (you probably won't ever use that many anyway). The maximum possible is 255, the minimum 32, the default 128. To conserve memory, change **threads=128** to **threads=64**. Sometimes, however, 64 may not be enough for the programs you'll run. Then you'll have to increase the value again in CONFIG.SYS.

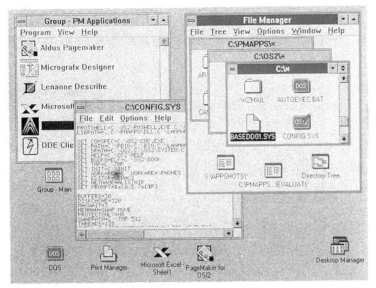

Figure 9-4. Example CONFIG.SYS File for OS/2 (courtesy Microsoft)

Advantages of OS/2.

• Built-in memory management—Version 1.2 can use 16MB of memory; Version 2.0 can use many times that amount. It has memory management built in to track where software is in memory and to make sure that different programs don't interfere with each others use of memory.

• Built-in virtual memory—It has built-in virtual memory, called storage overcommitment, to swap programs and program segments to and from the disk. Because of this any program should run on any OS/2 system. There won't be "minimum memory" statements on program packages, however, there will be "recommended memory" statements.

• Multitasking—It is multitasking and multi-threaded. That is, even within a single program it can multitask different routines and functions of that program.

• It uses a flat memory space that will work faster and more easily than the convoluted memory space of DOS.

• There's a DOS compatibility box to run many DOS programs. Version 2.0 should be able to run Windows.

• Communication between applications and networking are built-in features.

• There's a graphic interface called the Presentation Manager for OS/2.

• Some popular programs are available in OS/2 versions, including AutoCAD, 1-2-3, WordPerfect, and more.

• It is modular, and so should be able to adapt to future changes more easily than DOS could.

• It can be set up in a "dual-boot" option with DOS on a single hard disk, so the PC user can decide when turning the PC on which OS to use.

• It has the "HPFS" (High Performance File System) that is more efficient than the file system and directories in DOS.

Disadvantages of OS/2.

• Few applications. There aren't many programs written to take advantage of OS/2's features. In fact, there aren't that many rewritten just to be compatible with OS/2.

• Expensive applications—OS/2 programs typically cost more than DOS programs.

• RAM hunger—OS/2 needs at least 3 or 4MB, several more for PM, more yet for multitasking.

• It is not a multi-user system, though you can now find special versions of OS/2 made for multi-user work (from companies such as Citrix).

• The DOS compatibility box in OS/2 Version 1.2 only offers 500K or so for DOS programs, and doesn't have expanded memory at all.

• No support for DOS extenders such as VCPI. So many recent DOS applications will not run in DOS windows.

• OS/2 2.0 offers limited support for DOS device drivers.

• OS/2 1.2 doesn't use special features of 386, even as much as Windows 3.0 does.

• Little printer support so far.

• Complicated installation process.

Bottom Line. Move to OS/2 only if your applications call for it and you can afford the tough installation and extra hardware costs. Don't move if you plan to use the DOS compatibility box a lot.

Unix and Xenix

Unix is older than any of the other operating systems discussed in this chapter. It first appeared 20 years ago at Bell Labs as an OS for minicomputers. For a long time it was very expensive, unless you were in a university, where it was nearly free. So generations of programmers, scientists, and engineers grew up on Unix and that orientation has remained strong. Even in the 1980s Unix was wildly popular with scientists and engineers using *workstations*, those high-powered computers that were more than personal computers but less than minicomputers. However, many versions of Unix also appeared that worked on personal computers. Unix only sells 1% as many systems as DOS does, however. Because it is such a smaller market, Unix software is typically more expensive than DOS software—the same development costs can't be spread over as many copies.

Unix is a multitasking and multiuser operating system with sophisticated memory management abilities such as built-in virtual memory. What DOS thinks of as extended memory is just conventional memory to Unix—it can use many megabytes of RAM.

It is a powerful operating system and many programs are available for it, but the majority of these are programming and technical tools. Until the last few years Unix has been a difficult OS for beginners to use because it was honed for experts—able to do a lot but demanding an in-depth knowledge of cryptic commands and computer structures. It is an ideal environment for programming in the C language.

Although some proponents claim that Unix promotes portability of programs, it hasn't quite worked out that way. There are many different versions of Unix that cannot share software. To name a few, there are System V (AT&T or The Santa Cruz Operation), OSF, BSD, Mach (NeXT), AIX (IBM), VP/ix, and Xenix. Xenix is the most popular of these on PCs—it probably represents 90% of the PC Unix market. (Microsoft promotes it—the same Microsoft that offers OS/2 and DOS.) Many of these can swap programs if you're willing to recompile the program for each different Unix, and then pick out a few bugs. That's called source-level compatibility, and is less than most PC owners want. Binary compatibility is the goal for many Unix software developers, where no recompilation would be necessary. Another name for this is shrinkwrap compatibility, where you would be able to walk into a software store and buy an application for Unix, without worrying about which particular computer or Unix version it was for. A new approach called the Architecture Neutral Distribution Format would make it possible, but this isn't a standard yet.

To make Unix easier to use there are now several graphic interfaces that give it the look of Windows, the OS/2 PM, or the Apple Macintosh. These include Motif, OpenLook, X Windows, and NextStep. Again, there isn't a standard yet. (A new program called DESQview/X will soon be available that will let DOS PCs use X Windows.)

Unix can run DOS programs, using a DOS emulator (a special program) such as DOS-Merge, VP/ix (Interactive Systems), and Merge 386 (Locus Computing). The PC-Elevator software added to a high-resolution graphics card from Applied Reasoning Corporation lets you run Windows 3.0 and its applications under X Windows. PC Elevator X comes with a VCPI DOS extender for applications that use 386 protected mode and virtual memory. But don't turn to Unix if its very important for you to run DOS programs. These emulators aren't fully compatible with all the twists and turns of PC DOS software and hardware. Figure 9-5 shows an example of a DOS program running in a Unix window under such an emulator.

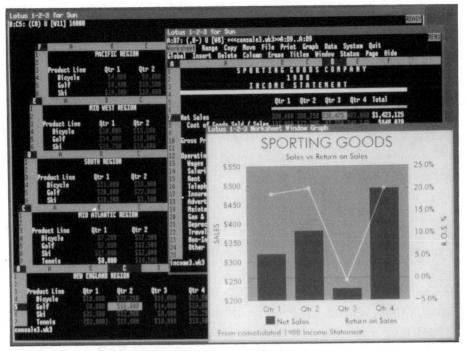

Figure 9-5. DOS Emulation in Unix (courtesy Sun Computer)

Advantages of Unix.

- Relatively bug-free because of long history

- Can use almost any amount of memory

- Built-in virtual memory

- Powerful interface for programming

- Excellent networking abilities

- Multitasking and multiuser

- Can run some DOS programs through emulation

- Can run both Xenix and DOS from a single 386 PC, even sharing files on the disk

359

• Some popular DOS applications are available in Unix versions, including Word Perfect, AutoCAD, and Oracle

Disadvantages of Unix.

• Complex installation, configuration, and maintenance which often requires a specialist, known as a Unix guru.

• Sizable hardware demands. Typical Unix configurations need at least a 60MB hard disk drive and 4MB of RAM.

• DOS emulation not completely PC compatible. That is, most popular applications will run under emulators, but not all will. (For example, DOS extenders won't work.)

Bottom Line. Unix will eliminate DOS memory management problems such as the 640K limit, but you may have trouble running your DOS applications under Unix and Unix is difficult to install, run, and maintain. In other words, only move to Unix if you know about it and still like it.

QNX

QNX from Quantum Software has been around for 10 years. It's a Unix-like OS for PCs that runs identically on 8088, 286, 386, or 486-based PCs. QNX has many of the same benefits as Unix, such as multitasking, advanced file system organization, multiuser support, networking, and powerful software development tools. Even its command structure is like that of Unix. But QNX's "microkernel architecture" takes as little as 135K, compared to the megabytes that Unix needs. It's a modular system where most of the work is handled by special managers that run with the application. In fact, the main kernel can use only 10K, leaving lots of room for applications even in a PC that has only 512K or 640K of memory. QNX runs in both real and protected modes. Networking is built into the base of QNX. There are 100,000 QNX sites installed, and hundreds of application programs that run under QNX—many of them for accounting. QNX can run DOS as a task, and so can run some DOS application programs.

Bottom Line. QNX gives many of Unix' benefits—such as multiuser and multitasking operation—without eating up all the memory that Unix demands. However, it is not as well known as Unix, so there are fewer applications available for it. It can run some DOS programs by emulating DOS, but this is no guarantee. Get QNX if you like Unix but don't want to feed it all the memory and disk it wants, and if you know your important programs will run under QNX.

Theos

Where QNX is built in the Unix style, Theos follows IBM's old CMS operating system. CMS was made for mainframes when interactive terminals, were first appearing. The company claims 80,000 sites that use Theos and over 1000 third-party application programs that run under Theos. Theos 86 is a multiuser OS for PCs and XTs.

Theos 286-V is a multiuser, multitasking OS for AT-class 286 and 386 systems. It uses the protected mode for 286 to reach up to 16MB of memory and so support up to 32 users and as many as 256 different tasks. A user can switch among twelve active programs on the main console by simply hitting hot keys. Theos 286-V supports VGA, EGA, CGA, MDA, and HGA graphics.

Theos 386 release 3.1 is the latest Theos version. It has its own disk cache and supports as much memory as the 386 chip can address—up to 4GB. It is a multi-user system that can handle as many as 128 users at a time. Theos has e-mail, a fast file system, advanced command interpreters, and a scripting language built-in.

THEO+DOS is powerful software add-on for Theos 386 that can run standard DOS programs under Theos. Using the Virtual 86 mode of the 386 chip it can run DOS programs at the same time as Theos 386 programs, using standard PC-DOS or MS-DOS internal, external, and batch commands. Legal DOS file operations, for instance, are converted automatically to equivalent Theos operations, reading and writing in the Theos file system. There's a Theo+DOS feature called Memory Plus that can transfer TSRs in a Virtual 86 DOS partition into high memory. Memory Plus can also grab unused video memory, and so provide you with more of the 640K for DOS applications. Theo+DOS also has an EMS emulator for up to 8 MB of expanded memory. Using device drivers such as network cards need may give you some trouble under Theo+DOS.

To run Theos 386 and Theo+DOS you'll need at least a 386 or 486-based system with 2MB or more of RAM. 4MB is recommended, and would give room for six Theos users (there are hundreds of Theos applications available) and two Theo+DOS sessions.

Bottom Line. Theos is a multi-user and multitasking operating system that can access lots more memory than DOS. It lets you replace PCs with less expensive serial terminals, and can run many DOS programs under Theo+DOS option. But Theos is not as popular as DOS, DR DOS, OS/2, or Unix, and so there are far fewer applications available for it. Switch to it only if you want a multi-user system and know that the programs most important to you will run under Theos.

Operating Systems on Other Computers

The IBM PC and all of the PC-compatible systems aren't the only type of microcomputers, naturally. There are also popular systems from manufacturers such as Commodore and Atari (both popular in Europe), and Fujitsu (popular in Japan).

In the US the two most popular challengers to the PC's lead are the Apple Macintosh family and Unix workstations.

Unix Workstations

Sun Microsystems, Hewlett-Packard, NeXT, and even IBM make many different high-powered computers that run the Unix operating system. These systems commonly cost from $10,000 to $100,000. Until two years ago they were largely used by scientists and engineers. As they've dropped in price, they've started to be practical choices for some graphic designers, publishers, and other professionals. Each company tends to run a slightly different version of Unix, so there aren't many programs for any individual system, especially once you eliminate all of the specialized scientific and engineering programs. But as was mentioned with PC Unix above, these Unix stations have excellent memory management abilities including built-in RAM from 4 to 8 or even 32 MB, multitasking and multi-user foundations, and virtual memory. Unix workstations can also be very fast, and very smoothly networked with other workstations and personal computers.

Figure 9-6. A Typical Unix Workstation (courtesy of Sun Microsystems)

Bottom Line. Consider a Unix workstation if networking and high-speed computing are very important to you, if the software you want runs on the system, if you can afford the higher expense than with PCs, and if you can live with the more difficult installation and maintenance.

Apple Macintosh

The Apple Macintosh costs about the same as PCs from IBM or Compaq, runs similar software, and is popular enough to have a wide variety of inexpensive software. But the Mac has an entirely different operating system—famous for its graphic display and standard menus between programs that are driven by a mouse. This Mac OS can directly address 16MB of RAM. There's no 640K limit here.

And the Mac OS MultiFinder program makes it simple to load multiple programs into memory at the same time, and switch between them with a click of the mouse's button. The Mac OS also has *desk accessories*, small programs that can pop up at any time, and play the same role as the PC's TSRs.

The new System 7 release of the Mac OS, scheduled for 1991, will add virtual memory to the Macintosh, pushing it even farther beyond DOS. With its simple, linear address area, the Mac doesn't have to worry about expanded memory, extended memory, high memory, and the other details of PC memory management. It just lets you assign a certain amount of memory to each program, without concerns about any limit below 16MB or as much memory as you actually have plugged in. Figure 9-7 shows an Apple Macintosh. Figure 9-8 shows the Mac screen with two programs running at the same time, and a utility showing how much memory each is using.

Figure 9-7. An Apple Macintosh IIsi (courtesy of AppleComputer—photo Will Mosgrove)

Bottom Line. Switch to the Apple Macintosh if you can afford the higher hardware prices in exchange for a more easily learned and installed system. Make sure the kind of software you want can be found on the Mac, which can run a wide range of programs, but not as wide a range as the PC.

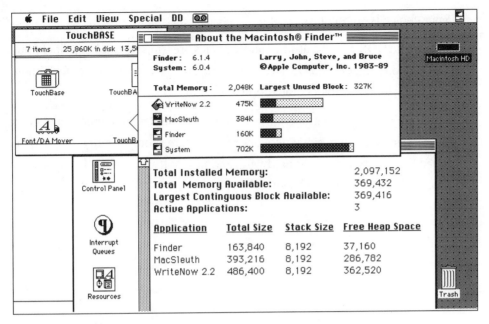

Figure 9-8. MultiFinder on the Apple Macintosh

Conclusion

DOS is clearly too confining for some people. Not only does it have severe memory limits, but it also isn't well suited to networking operations, intense graphics work, or multi-user environments. OS/2 and Unix are technically superior to DOS for all these things, but are more expensive, need more memory and disk hardware to get started, and are more difficult to use. They also are supported by as large a library of software, though they can run some DOS programs through emulator options.

There are other alternative operating systems, from new versions of DOS, through DOS-compatible offerings such as DR DOS, to competitors to Unix, and even different computer systems such as the Macintosh. Nearly all can boast more memory than DOS can, and some are smaller and less expensive than OS/2 or Unix. But moving to any one of them means giving up some DOS compatibility—you can't count on running all of your DOS programs and using all of your DOS hardware.

Your choice is simply this:

•   Extend DOS with the utilities and schemes presented in this book (including new versions of DOS and DR DOS mentioned in this chapter) to get some more memory with only small compatibility risks, or

•   Switch to a different operating system to get lots more memory and other benefits (multitasking, better networking) with large compatibility risks and the expenses of retraining, new hardware, and new software. OS/2, Unix, and the Mac are the best supported alternatives.

The Quick Solution Guide: My Advice

If you've read through this whole book, you may feel as I do at this point: that's a lot of pages and ideas—where do I start? This step summarizes memory management, and gives you my advice on priorities for several categories of computer use. Naturally these rules of thumb are generalized—they can't take into account every detail of your particular computer status and needs.

Computing Style: Compute, Data, or Switch-intensive

Some computer tasks are dominated by lots of calculations on small amounts of data. These are sometimes called compute-intensive or processor-intensive. Engineering programs, complex graphics, and some spreadsheets are good examples. Surprisingly, desktop publishing can be too, because of all the processing time it takes to calculate the shapes and positions of complex graphics and fancy fonts. The time it takes to perform such tasks depends mainly on the processor's speed and the speed of the chip memory. Compute-intensive tasks can sometimes be sped by having all of the program and the file in memory. (A math coprocessor is also a good idea.) They aren't helped much by disk caching and RAM disks.

Other computer tasks are dominated by simple calculations or comparisons on large amounts of data. These are sometimes called data-intensive or disk-intensive. Database management and large spreadsheets are examples. The time it takes to perform these tasks depends mainly on the disk memory's speed, and (because of buffering and caching) on the amount of chip memory. Data intensive or disk intensive programs can be sped considerably by a RAM disk or disk cache. Sometimes they're helped by having the full database or document in memory.

Some peoples computing work is dominated by switching tasks, moving from some word processing to checking electronic mail to updating a spreadsheet calculation to looking up some information in a database and back to the word processor. For these people, lots of fast memory is vital. They need: an integrated application with all their functions and the memory to run it; or lots of TSR utilities that can handle their work, and a TSR switching manager that can swap them in and out of memory; or 4 or 5MB of memory and a fast 386 processor running DesqView or Windows and all the applications they want on line at once.

To know how to manage your memory best, you need to think about whether your computing style is compute-intensive, disk-intensive, switching-intensive, or some mixture of those.

The Simple PC: the PC or XT

Description: The home PC, dedicated to home finance, basic word processing, education, and games. It's probably an older PC, mostly likely a PC, XT, or compatible based on the 8088 or 8086 processor. It may have only 256K, 384K, or 512K of memory with two floppy-disk drives or a small (10MB) hard disk and CGA graphics.

Advice: If this PC is running the software you want it to, don't spend much time or money on memory management.

However, if you want to add some power inexpensively, to run a new program or some new utilities, or to make it run faster:

• Read to understand what memory management offers to help you know if and when you should move up to a more powerful system (Step 1).

• Check for tips that will help you configure your application and DOS to use less memory (Step 3).

• Add conventional memory to reach 640K (see Step 5).

• If you do have a hard disk, use a virtual-expanded memory program to let you work with larger files when using programs that employ expanded memory (Step 5).

- If you switch tasks much, you should consider getting an EMS 4.0 expanded memory board (Step 5) and using a task-switching utility (Step 6).

- Optimize your Buffers setting to optimize your disk performance (Step 7).

- Add a hard disk, if you don't have one.

- Use GEOS if you want an environment with a graphic user interface (Step 6).

The Business PC: the AT or 386SX

Description: The business PC is used for more complex word processing, spreadsheet calculations, database management, simple chart drawing, and electronic mail shuffling. It's at least an AT-compatible or PS/2 with an 80286 processor and may have a 386 processor. It has at least 512K or 640K of RAM, and may have as much as 2MB. The disk drive is a hard disk of 20 to 40MB and the graphics are EGA or VGA.

Advice: Remember that the application that's used most dictates the best memory management scheme.

- If yours is a 286-based system, buy a new system or an accelerator to move up to 386SX or 386 class. This chip offers far superior memory management possibilities, and a solid future for your computing needs (Step 5).

- Determine just how much memory you do have (Step 2).

- Fill conventional memory to 640K if it isn't there already (Step 5).

- Configure your applications and DOS to use memory for the minimum size or optimum performance for your tasks (Step 3) or use DOS 5 or DR DOS (from Step 9).

- Use high memory relocation to push any memory-resident utilities or drivers out of conventional memory (Step 4).

- Add 2MB of extended memory, or use the extended memory you've already got (Step 5).

- Set up a disk cache for best disk performance (Step 7).

- Set up a RAM disk in extended memory (Step 7).

- Use an expanded-memory simulator to convert extended memory to expanded (Step 5).

- Consider using DesqView if you want a windowing environment and some multitasking (Step 6).

- If you print long documents, or many documents, use a print spooler in extended memory (Step 7).

- If you use a laser printer, make sure it has enough memory (Step 8).

The Power PC: the 386 or 486

Description: The power PC is used for business work that processes large files or includes graphics. This means such tasks as word processing with desktop publishing, spreadsheet calculation on large files resulting in fancy printed reports with charts, database management on very large databases, or color design and drawing work. This system is a 386-based AT compatible or PS/2, though in some cases it may even have a 486 processor. It has a full 640K of conventional memory and probably at least 2MB of extended memory. A 40 to 80MB hard disk, VGA or better graphics (such as XGA or TIGA), a connection to a network, and a laser printer round out the hardware. It may be running Windows or DesqView.

Advice:

- Analyze just what you've got (Step 2).

- Get a 386 memory manager program (Step 5) and use it to relocate TSRs and drivers to high memory (Step 4). If you use Windows, make sure you get a memory manager version that's compatible with it.

- Set up a RAM disk or a disk cache (Step 7). (Some programs do better with a RAM disk but these days most people get the most from a large disk cache and no RAM disk.)

- Assure yourself of enough printer memory (Step 8).

- Assure yourself of enough video adapter memory for the color and resolution you need (Step 8).

- If you want to multitask, or to run Windows, add more memory—first fill any high-speed 32-bit memory slot in the system, then add extended memory in 32-bit slots (Step 5).

- Fill any expanded memory demands of programs by using an expanded memory simulator to transform part of extended memory to expanded (Step 5).

- Read about other operating systems to know if and when to change away from DOS to OS/2, Unix, Macintosh, or some other operating system (Step 9).

The Portable PC: a Laptop or Notebook computer

Description: The portable PC is a lightweight system that can be carried on trips. It is used for word processing, electronic mail handling, and spreadsheet calculations. They fall into two categories: the older PC-compatible laptops and the newer AT-compatible laptops and notebooks.

The older PC-compatible laptops have 512K of memory or so, DOS in a ROM chip, and a single floppy disk drive. The newer AT-compatible laptops and notebooks (so-called because that's the size they are) have a 286 or 386 processor, 640K of RAM (and sometimes 1MB of extended memory), and a 20MB hard disk.

Advice for older, PC-compatible laptops:

- Configure your DOS and software to use the least memory (Step 3) or move to a small application or an integrated application.

- Use high memory relocation to open up more of conventional memory (Step 4).

Advice for newer, AT-compatible laptops and notebooks:

- Generally follow the advice given for business PCs above.

- If there are no slots for easy memory expansion, add what memory you can and then use a virtual-memory program to let your hard disk behave as extended or expanded memory (Steps 5 and 6).

Final Words

Memory management is not a destination, it's an attitude and a process. Even after you've worked your way through the 9 previous steps in this book, you should always keep on your toes to use your PC's memory efficiently (and to know when to get more). Not only will your expectations rise as you see the speed and ease that better memory management yields, but programs and files will continue to get bigger and ask for yet more memory. That well-managed megabyte today will certainly be obsolete in a few years, dwarfed by machines with 16MB handling 10MB desktop publishing files and 50 MB video files through virtual memory.

A couple of tips:

Buy a 386, not a 286.

Buy a system that accepts SIMMs, not one that accepts DIPs.

Outfit your PC with 4MB of memory: 1MB for DOS, 1 to 2 for a disk cache, and 1 to 2 for other uses.

Don't make your system configuration too complex or obscure or you'll have trouble running new programs. Keep a boot floppy (one with DOS on it) in case your system crashes.

Remember that saving 5K can make a different when that 640K limit is staring in your face.

PS: If you disagree with any of my recommendations, please let me know—I'll listen to your advice for any future versions of this book.

And, thanks for reading.

APPENDIX A

Getting Cheap and Free Software

Some of the programs that analyze, test, count, manage, and use your memory are in the public domain. That is to say, they are free and anyone may copy them and use them. Some are distributed free to customers of a specific software or hardware company, to entice people to buy or use other programs from that company. Some come with memory boards or printers. Some are simply created and then distributed by generous programmers.

Some memory management programs are called *shareware*. Although sometimes mistakenly understood to mean free, shareware actually refers to a program that you may copy and try, but that you should pay a registration fee for if you intend to keep and use. Registration is the legal and ethical requirement, but it also often gains you better documentation for the program and free technical support. (Some shareware programs also pay a bonus to the source of registered programs. For instance, if you give a copy to a friend and convince that friend to register, the software company then sends you a check.)

Shareware programs are often copied and given to friends as if they were public domain programs. You can tell the difference by watching for a copyright statement at the beginning of the program, just after you start it running. A shareware program will have some kind of "Please register your software by sending x amount of money to the following address" statement.

How do you find public domain and shareware programs for memory management?

1. Contact or join any users group to find such software. Look for listings of local groups in regional computing publications in your area. There are also

373

user groups with national and international memberships, such as the Boston Computer Society.

2. Contact a company that specializes in gathering shareware and freeware and selling it as a collection of programs on a disk for $5 or $10 a disk. Two of the most famous of these are:

Public (Software) Library
Houston, TX
(713) 665-7017
(800) 242-4775

PC-SIG, Inc.
Sunnyvale, CA
(408) 730-9291

3. Read *Public Domain Software & Shareware*, by Rusel DeMaria and George R. Fontaine, (M&T Books, 1988). It lists hundreds of inexpensive programs, for memory management and other work.

4. Another good source for shareware and public domain software (sometimes called "freeware") are bulletin-board systems and on-line services. These are computers especially set up to receive calls from other computers through modems. On-line services, such as BIX, CompuServe, and Prodigy, are commercial ventures running on huge computers, with hundreds of thousands of callers. The bulletin-board computer is often a single PC and may be dedicated to some non-computer interest (writers, hunters, dog-owners) or maybe to a particular niche of computing. Most on-line services and bulletin boards have a section devoted to software, that you can retrieve using your modem. Dial the system with your modem (there are plenty of books on using bulletin boards—or have a friend show you how) and then look for a listing of available programs. Then follow the instructions for downloading the program. It may be in compressed or archived form (often

with the label ARC attached). To use such a squeezed program (which can be downloaded faster because it is smaller, making for smaller phone bills), you'll need to first download a decompression or de-archiving utility program. The bulletin board listing should direct you to one of these too.

One particularly fine bulletin board for PC owners interested in memory management is PCMagNet, run by *PC Magazine* through CompuServe. (Though you don't have to be a CompuServe member to get PC MagNet.) PC MagNet costs $12.50 an hour for 1200 or 2400 bps service, and $6 an hour for 300 bps. MasterCard, Visa, and American Express numbers can sign you up on the phone. The programs are copyrighted—so although most are free for your own use, you may not sell them to anyone else, and they are not for commercial use.

To reach PC MagNet, you need to have a computer and modem. You may call (800) 346-3247 (or 800-635-6225 in Canada) and ask for a PC MagNet modem phone number. Or you may call CompuServe's voice customer service number for finding other dial-in numbers. That's (800) 848-8990 in most of the US, or (614) 457-8650 in Ohio and outside the US.

Here are a few PC MagNet modem phone numbers:

Phone Numbers

Boston	(617) 542-1796
New York	(212) 422-8820
Chicago	(312) 693-0330
SF	(415) 956-4191

Protocols

You'll need to set your communications software to use these protocols: 300 or 1200 bps, 7 even 1, full duplex.

Procedure

Once you're on PC MagNet you can use 2400 bps after signing on by typing **Go Phones** and then follow these instructions:

After dialing, use the following commands:

type Ctrl-C after the connection is made

type CIS after HOST NAME appears

type 177000,5000 after USER ID appears

type PC*MAGNET after PASSWORD appears

type Z10D8912 after Enter Agreement Number appears

type Go Utilities to reach the utility programs area,

or choose PC Magazine Utilities from the menu

choose Direct Utility Download

type the name of the utility you want

answer Y to the question Do you wish to Download?

select a downloading protocol (and set the same protocol in your own communications program) and downloading will begin.

You may need the PCARC and PCXARC or PKZIP and PKUNZIP utility programs to decompress programs in the ARC format. These are all shareware programs. (The ZIP programs are newer.)

Product List— Alphabetical

	@Base	Personics
	@Liberty 2.01	SoftLogic Solutions
	1-2-3 and 1-2-3/G	Lotus Development
	3-for-3	Iris Associates
	3270/Elite	Network Software Associates
	386MAX (386-to-the-MAX)	Qualitas
	386MAX Professional	Qualitas
	386SX Card	Cumulus
	386|DOS-Extender	Phar Lap Software
	386|VMM	Phar Lap Software
A	AboveBoard Plus	Intel
	Above DISC	Above Software
	AboveLAN	Above Software
	AboveMEM	Above Software
	Agenda	Lotus Development
	ALL ChargeCard	ALL Computers
	AMIDIAG	American Megatrends
	Ami Professional	Samna
	Applause	Ashton-Tate
	ASQ	Qualitas
	Atlas Board	Atlas Technology
	AutoCAD	Autodesk
	AutoSketch	Autodesk

B	BackLoader 2	Roxxolid
	Baler	Baler Software
	BASICA	Microsoft
	BetterWorking Eight-in-One	Spinnaker Software
	Beyond 640K	Intex Solutions
	BlueMax	Qualitas
	Bootcon	Modular Software Systems
	BOOT.SYS	Hans Salvisberg
	Buffalo SL 1000	Buffalo Products
C	Cache86	The Aldridge Co.
	Carousel	SoftLogic Solutions
	CEMM	Compaq Computer
	ChargeCard	All Computers
	Check 1-2-3	Lotus Development
	CheckIt	TouchStone Software
	Clipper	Nantucket Corporation
	CompuServe	CompuServe
	Concentration	Newer Technology
	Concurrent DOS/386	Digital Research
	CONFIG.CTL	PC Magazine
	Concurrent DOS	Digital Research
	Connecting Room	Helix Software
	Control Room	Ashton-Tate
	CP/M	Digital Research
	Ctrl-Alt	Biologic
D	Dac Easy Accounting	Dac Easy Software
	Dartcard	Newer Technology
	dBASE	Ashton-Tate
	DCACHE	PC Magazine
	Designer	Micrografx
	DeskJet	Hewlett-Packard

	DESQview	Quarterdeck Office Systems
	DESQview/386 with QEMM	Quarterdeck Office Systems
	Discover	Helix
	Disk Spool II	Budget Software
	DisplayWrite	IBM
	DOS XM	Digital Research
	DoubleDOS	SoftLogic Solutions
	DPMI	Microsoft
	Draw Applause	Ashton-Tate
	DR Chips	Alpha Group
	DR DOS	Digital Research
	Dr. Switch	Black & White International Inc.
E	EDLIN	Microsoft
	Elite 16 Plus HyperCache	Profit Systems
	EMS40.SYS	PC Magazine
	Excel	Microsoft
	Extra	Delta Technology
F	Fast!	Future Computer Systems
	Flashdisk	Digipro
	Flash V Disk Accelerator	Software Matters
	Fontware	Bitstream
	FoxPro	Fox Software
	Framework	Ashton-Tate
	Freedom of Press	Custom Applications
	Freelance	Lotus Development
G	GeoWorks Ensemble	GeoWorks
	Graph-in-the-Box	New England Software
	GW BASIC	Microsoft?
H	Hardcard	Plus Development
	Harvard Graphics	Software Publishing Corporation

	hDC First Apps	hDC Computing
	Headroom	Helix Software
	HiCard AT	Rybs Electronics Inc.
	HiNet	Fresh Technology Group
	HiRez	Lightning Zoom
	Horizon 860	True Vision
	Hyperstore	Perceptive Solutions
I	i860	Intel
	ImageScript	Personal Computer Products
	Inboard	Intel PCEO
	InfoSpotter	Merrill & Bryan
	Intellifonts	Agfa Compugraphic
	Interleaf Publisher	IBM
	Invisible EMS	Invisible Software
	Invisible Network	Invisible Software
	Invisible RAM	Invisible Software
	IOS-10/386	IO-Data
J	JLaser Plus	Tall Tree Systems
K	King Jaguar	Sheng Labs
	KX-P1654	Panasonic
L	LANSpace	LANSystems
	LANSpool	LANSystems
	LANtastic	Artisoft
	LaserJet	Hewlett-Packard
	Letter Perfect	WordPerfect Corporation
	Lightning	Personal Computer Support Group
	Limsim	Larson Computing
	Local Union	LaserTools
	LotusWorks	Lotus Development
	Lucid 3D	PCSG

M	Macintosh	Apple Computer
	Magellan	Lotus Development
	Managing Your Money	MECA Software
	Manifest	Quarterdeck Office Systems
	Maximizer	Softnet Communications
	Memory Commander	V Communications
	Merge 386	Locus Computing
	Microfazer	Quadram
	Move'Em	Qualitas
	MS-DOS	Microsoft
	MultiMate	Ashton-Tate
N	NEAT Chipset	Chips & Technologies
	NET-30/EMS	Invisible Software
	NetRoom	Helix Software
	NetWare	Novell
	NJRAMDSK	Mike Blaszczak
O	Omniview	Sunny Hill Software
	Oracle	Oracle
	OS/2	IBM or Microsoft
P	PageMaker	Aldus
	Paradox	Borland
	Para-Mail	Paradox Development
	PC MagNet	PC Magazine, Ziff-Davis
	PC Tools Deluxe	Central Point software
	PC-DOS	IBM
	PC-Kwik Power Pak	Multisoft
	PC-MIX	ProWare
	PC-MOS	The Software Link
	PC Tools Deluxe	Central Point Software
	PC Write and PC Write Lite	Buttonsoft

P.D. Queue	Funk Software
Periscope	The Periscope Company
Personal Measure	Spirit of Performance Inc.
PFS: First Choice	Software Publishing
PFS: First Publisher	Software Publishing
PFS: Professional Write	Software Publishing
PFS: Professional File	Software Publishing
PolyBoost	Polytron Corp.
PopDrop	Bloc Publishing
PostScript	Adobe
PowerCache Plus	Intelligent Devices
PowerLan	Performance Technology
Power Meter	The Database Group
Power-Pak	Multisoft
PrintCache	LaserTools
Print Director PD6SP	Digital Products
Printer Assist	Fresh Technologies
Printer Genius	NOR Software
PrinTools	Insight Development
PrintQ	Software Directions
PrintQ LAN	LANsmart/NV
PrintRite	BLOC Publishing
Printvision	BLOC Publishing
ProComm Plus	DataStorm Technologies

Q

Q&A	Symantec
Q Assist	Fresh Technologies
QEMM	Quarterdeck Office Systems
QNX	Quantum Software
QRAM	Quarterdeck Office Systems
Quattro Pro	Borland
Quick BASIC	Microsoft
Quicken	Intuit

R	R:Base	MicroRim
	RAMPage Plus	AST
	RapidMeg	STB Systems
	Recorder	PC Magazine
	Read RAM	Corvus Systems Inc.
	Reflex	Borland
S	Service Diagnostics: The Kit	SuperSoft
	Share Spool ESI-2094A	Extended Systems
	SideKick and SideKick Plus	Borland International
	SimpLAN Serverjet	ASP Computer Products
	SmartDrive	Microsoft
	Software Carousel	(see Carousel)
	SOTA Pop	SOTA Technology Inc.
	SpeedCache	Storage Dimensions
	Spool-Q	Insight Development
	Squish Plus	Sundog Software
	STB Rapidmeg	STB Systems Inc.
	Super PC-Kwik	Multisoft
	SuperPrint	Zenographics
	Switch-It!	Better Software Technology
	Symphony	Lotus Development
	System Sleuth	Dariana Technology
T	TC! Power	Nordra Technologies Inc.
	The Mace Utilities	Fifth Generation Systems
	The Norton Commander	Peter Norton Computing/Symantec
	The Norton Utilities	Peter Norton Computing/Symantec
	The RAMPack	BLOC Publishing
	Theos	Theos Software
	Turbo Assembler	Borland
	Turbo Debugger	Borland
	Turbo EMS	Merrill & Bryan Enterprises

	Turbo Pascal	Borland
	Type 1	Adobe
V	V-EMM	Fort's Software
	Vcache	Golden Bow Systems
	VCPI specification	Phar Lap Software
	Ventura Publisher	Xerox
	Vines	Banyan
	Visual Edge	Intel
	Vopt	Golden Bow Systems
	VMOS/3	Microdyne Corporation
	VP/ix	Interactive Systems
	VRAM	Biologic
W	Windows	Microsoft
	Windows Workstation	Automated Design Systems
	WinSleuth	Dariana Technology
	Word	Microsoft
	Word	for Windows Microsoft
	Word Perfect	Word Perfect Corporation
	WordStar	WordStar Corporation
	Works	Microsoft
X	X-Bandit	Teletek
	Xenix	Microsoft and The Santa Cruz Operation
	XMA2EMS.SYS	Microsoft
	XYWrite	XyQuest

APPENDIX C

Company Addresses

Above Software Inc.
3 Hutton Centre, Suite 950
Santa Ana, CA 92707
(800) 344-0116
(714) 545-1181 in Canada

Acculogic Inc.
18023 Skypark Circle, Unit E
Irvine, CA 92714
(800) 234-7811

Accumation, Inc.
8817 Southwest 129 Terr.
Miami, FL 33176
(305) 238-1034

Advanced Vision Research
2201 Qume Drive
San Jose, CA 95131
(408) 434-1115

ALL Computers Inc.
1220 Yonge St, 2nd Floor
Toronto, Ontario
Canada M4T 1W1
(416) 960-0111
(800) 627-4825

Alpha Group Operation
3953 Glenn Meadow Dr.
Norcross, GA 30092
(404) 448-2828

American Computer Systems
780 Montague, Ste. 305
San Jose, CA 95131
(408) 432-6277

AMI (Single Source Technology)
1346 Oakbrook Drive, Suite 120
Norcross, Georgia 30093
(800) U BUY AMI
(404) 263-8181

Amkly Systems
60 Technology Drive
Irvine, CA 92714
(714) 727 0788

AOX
486 Totten Pond Rd.
Waltham, MA 02154
(800) 232-1269

Applied Reasoning Corporation
86A Sherman Street
Cambridge, MA 02140
(617) 492-0700

Arlington Computer Products, Inc.
1970 Carboy St.
Mt. Prospect, IL 60056
(800) 548-5105

Artisoft, Inc.
575 East River Road
Tucson, AZ 85704
(602) 293-6363

Ashton-Tate
20101 Hamilton Ave.
Torrance, CA 90502-1319
(213) 329-8000

ASP Computer Products, Inc.
1026 W. Maude Ave., Suite 305
Sunnyvale, CA 94086
(408) 746-2965
(800) 445-6190

AST Research Inc.
2121 Alton Ave.
Irvine, CA 92714
(714) 863-1333
(714) 727-4141

ATI Technolgoes, Inc.
3761 Victoria Park Avenue
Scarborough, Ontario
Canada M1W 3S2
(416) 756-0718

Atlas Technology
3900 Montclair Road
Birmingham, AL 35213
(800) 326-9555

Autodesk
2320 Marinship Way
Sausalito, CA 94965
(415) 332-2344

Automated Design Systems, Inc.
375 Northridge Rd., #270
Atlanta, GA 30350
(800) 366-2552
(404) 394-2552

Award Software
130 Knowles Dr.
Los Gatos, CA 95030
(408) 370-7979

Baler Software Corp
1400 Hicks Rd.
Rolling Meadows, IL 60008
(800) 327-6108

Banyan Systems Inc.
120 Flanders Road
Westboro, MA 01581
(508) 898-1000

Better Software Technology Inc.
55 New York Ave.
Framingham, MA 01701
(508) 879-0744
(800) 848-0286

Biologic
7950 Blue Gray Circle, Suite 1622
Manassas, VA 22110
(703) 368-2949

Black & White International Inc.
P.O. Box 1040
Planetarium Station
New York, NY 10024
(212) 787-6633

Bloc Publishing Corporation
800 S.W. 37th Avenue, Suite 765
Coral Gables, FL 33134
(305) 445-0903
(800) 888-2562

Boca Research Inc.
6401 Congress Ave.
Boca Raton, FL 33487
(407) 997-6227

Borland International
POB 660001
Scotts Valley, CA 95066
(408) 438-8400
(800) 331-0877

Buffalo Products Inc.
2805 19th St., S.E.
Salem, OR 97302
(503) 585-3414
(800) 345-2356

Burr-Brown Corp.
1141 West Grant Rd., MS 131
Tucson, AZ 85705
(602) 746-1111

Capital Equipment Corp.
99 S. Bedford
Burlington, MA 01803
(800) 234-4232
(617) 273-1818

Central Point Software
15220 N.W. Greenbrier Parkway, #200
Beaverton, OR 97006
(503) 690-8090
(800) 888-8199

Chips & Technologies
521 Cottonwood Dr.
Milpitas, CA 95035
(408) 434-0600

CMS Enhancements
2722 Michaelson Dr.
Tustin, CA 92715
(714) 259-9555

CompuAdd
12303 Technology Blvd.
Austin, TX 78727
(800) 627-1967

Computer Peripherals Inc.
667 Rancho Conejo Blvd.
Newbury Park, CA 91320
(805) 499-5751
(800) 854-7600

Corvus Systems Inc.
160 Great Oaks Blvd.
San Jose, CA 95119
(800) 426-7887

Cove Software Group
P.O. Box 1072
Columbia, MD 21044
(301) 992-9371

Cumulus
23500 Mercantile Road
Cleveland, OH 44122
(216) 464-2211

Custom Applications, Inc.
900 Technology Park Drive, Building 8
Billerica, MA 01821-9923

D-Link Systems Inc.
5 Musick
Irvine, CA 92718
(714) 455-1688

Dac Easy, Inc.
17950 Preston Rd., Suite 800
Dallas, TX 75252
(800) 877-8088

Dakota Microsystems, Inc.
301 E. Evelyn Ave., Bldg A
Mountain View, CA 94041
(800) 999-6288
(415) 967-2302

Dariana Technology Group Inc.
7439 La Palma Ave., S-278
Buena Park, CA 90620-2698
(714) 994-7400

Data Technology
Division of Qume Corporation
500 Yosemite Drive Milpitas, CA 95035
(408) 262-7700

DataStorm Technologies, Inc.
PO Box 1471
Columbia, MO 65205
(314) 474-8461

Definicon International Corp.
11 Business Center Cir.
Newbury Park, CA 91320
(805) 499 0652

Delta Technology Intrnational
1621 Westgate Road
Eau Claire, WI 54703
(715) 832-7575
(800) 242-6368

Departmental Technologies, Inc.
PO Box 645
Andover, NJ 07821
(201) 786-6878

Destiny Technology Corporation
300 Montague Expressway, Suite 150
Milpitas, CA 95035
(408) 262-9400

DiagSoft Inc.
5615 Scotts Valley Dr., #140
Scotts Valley, CA 95066
(408) 438-8247

Digipro
3315 South Memorial Parkway, Suite 2
Huntsville, AL 35801
(800) 662-6802

Digital Products Inc.
108 Water St.
Watertown, MA 02172
(617) 924-1680
(800) 243-2333

Digital Research Inc.
Box DRI 70 Garden Ct.
Monterey, CA 93940
(408) 649-3896
(800) 443-4200

Distributed Processing Technology
132 Candade Dr.
POB 1864
Maitland, FL 32751
(407) 830-5522

Everex Systems Inc.
48431 Milmone Dr.
Fremont, CA 94538
(415) 498-1111

Extended Systems
6062 Morris Hill Lane
Boise, Idaho 83704
(208) 322-7163

Fifth Generation Systems
10049 N. Reiger Rd.
Baton Rouge, LA 70809
(800) 873-4384
(504) 291-7221

Fort's Software
P.O. Box 396
Manhatten, KS 66502
(913) 537-2897

Fox Software, Inc.
134 W. South Boundary
Perrysburg, OH 43551
(419) 874-0162

Fresh Technology Group
1478 N. Tech Blvd., Suite 101
Gilbert, AZ 85234
(602) 497-4242

Funk Software
222 Third St.
Cambridge, MA 02142
(617) 497-6339

Gems Computers
2115 Old Oakland Rd.
San Jose, CA 95131
(408) 456-9300

GeoWorks
2150 Shattuck Ave.
Berkeley, CA 94704
(415) 644-0883

Golden Bow Systems
2665 Ariane Dr., #207
San Diego, CA 92117
(800) 284-3269
(619) 483-0901

Hans Salvisberg
Foreschmattstr. 40
CH-3018
Bern, Switzerland
(800) 242 4775
(713) 524 6394
or on CompuServe 73237,3556
or Internet salvis@ahorn.iam.unibe.ch

Hauppage Computer Works, Inc.
91 Cabot Ct.
Hauppage, NY 11788
(800) 443 6284

hDC Computer Corporation
6742 185th Avenue NE
Redmond, WA 98052
(800) 321-4606

Helix Software Co.
8365 Daniels St.
Briarwood, NY 11435
(718) 262-8787
(800) 451-0551

Hewlett-Packard Co.
19310 Pruneridge Ave.
Cupertino, CA 95014
(800) 752-0900
in Canada (800) 387-3867

IBM
Entry Systems Division
1000 N.W. 51st Street
Boca Raton, FL 33432
1-800-426-3333

IBM Corp.
Old Orchard Road
Armonk, NY 10605
(800) IBM-2468

IGC
1740 Technology Dr., #300
San Jose, CA 95110
(408) 441-0366

Insight Development Corporation
2200 Powell Street, Suite 500
Emeryville, CA 94608
(800) 825-4115

Intel PCEO
5200 N.E. Elam Young Parkway
Hillsboro, OR 97124
(503) 681-8080
(800) 538-3373

Intelligent Devices Corporation
112 Harvard Ave, Suite 295
Claremont, CA 91711
(714) 920-9551

Interactive Systems
2401 Colorado Ave.
Santa Monica, CA 90404
(213) 453-8649
(800) 346-7111

Intex Solutions, Inc.
161 Highland Ave.
Needham, MA 02194
(617) 449-6222

Invisible Software
1165 Chess Dr., Suite D
Foster City, CA 94404
(415) 570-5967

IO Data Equipment
1-5-41 Honmachi, EkiNishi
Kanazawa 920, Japan
81-0762-21-4812

Iris Associates
239 Littleton Rd., Suite 8D
Westford, MA 01886
(800) 225-5800
in MA (508) 692-2800

Isogon Corporation
330 Seventh Ave.
New York, NY 10001
(212) 967-2424
(800) 662-6036

JDR Microdevices
2233 Branham Lane
San Jose, CA 95125
(800) 538-5000

LANSystems Inc.
300 Park Ave. S
New York, NY 10010
(800) 458-5267

Larson Computing
1556 Halford Ave. #142
Santa Clara, CA 95051
(408) 737-0627

LaserMaster Corporation
7156 Shady Oak Road
Eden Prairie, MN 55344
(612) 944-9330

LaserTools Corporation
5900 Hollis St., Suite G
Emeryville, CA 94608
(800) 346-1353
(415) 420-8777

Leo Electronics, Inc.
P.O. Box 11307
Torrance, CA 90510
(800) 421-9565
(213) 212-6133

Lerman Associates
12 Endmoor Road
Westford, MA 01886
(800) 233 4671
(508) 692-7600

Locus Computing
9800 La Cienega Blvd.
Inglewood, CA 90301
(213) 670-6500

Lotus Development Corporation
55 Cambridge Parkway
Cambridge, MA 02142
(617) 577-8500

Merrill & Bryan Enterprises Inc.
9770 Carroll Center Rd., Suite C
San Diego, CA 92126
(619) 689-8611

Microdyne Corp.
P.O. Box 7213
491 Oak Rd.
Ocala, FL 32672
(904) 687-4633

Micron Technology, Inc.
2805 E. Columbia Rd.
Boise, ID 83706
(208) 368-3800

Microsoft Corporation
One Microsoft Way
Redmond, WA 98052-6399
(206) 882-8080
(800) 323-3577

Microway, Inc.
POB 79
Kingston, MA 02364
(508) 746-7341

Mike Blaszczak
112 Verlinden Dr.
Monroeville, PA 15146-2041

Modular Software Systems
115 W. California Blvd., #113
Pasadena, CA 91105
(818) 794-7602

Multisoft Corporation
15100 S.W. Koll Pkwy., Ste. L
Beaverton, OR 97006
(800) 888-5945
(503) 644-5644

NEC Electronics
401 Ellis St.
Mountain View, CA 94039
(415) 960-6000

NEC Technologies Inc.
159 Swanson Rd.
Boxborough, MA 01719
(800) 632-4636

Network Software Associates
39 Argonaut
Laguna Hills, CA 92656
(714) 768-4013

Newer Technology
1117 South Rock Road, Suite 4
Wichita, KS 67207
(800) 678-3726
(316) 685-4904

Nevada Computer Corp.
684 Wells Rd.
Boulder City, NV 89005
(800) 654-7762

NOR Software
POB 1747
Murray Hill Station
New York, NY 10156
(212) 213-9118

Nordra Technologies Inc.
POB 645
Andover, NJ 07821
(201) 786-6878

Novell Corporation
122 E. 1700 South
Provo, UT 84601
(800) 526-5463

Opus Systems
20863 Stevens Creek Blvd., Bldg. 400
Cupertino, CA 95014
(408) 446-2110

Orchid Technology
45365 Northport Loop W
Fremont, CA 94538
(415) 683-0348

Pacific Data Products
9125 Rehco Rd.
San Diego, CA 92121
(619) 552-0880

Paradox Development Corporation
7544 Trade St.
San Diego, CA 92121
(619) 586-0878

PC Magazine Labs
One Park Ave., 4th Floor
New York, NY 10016
(212) 503-5570

PC-SIG, Inc.
1030D East Duane Avenue
Sunnyvale, CA 94086
(408) 730-9291

Peerlogic Inc.
555 DeHaro St.
San Francisco, CA 94107
(800) 873-7927
(415) 626-4545

Perceptive Solutions Inc.
2700 Flora St.
Dallas, TX 75201
(800) 486-3278
(214) 954-1774

Performance Technology Inc.
800 Lincoln Center
7800 IH-10 West
San Antonio, TX 78230
(512) 349-2000

Persoft, Inc.
465 Science Dr.
Madison, WI 53711
(608) 273-6000

Personal Computer Support Group
4540 Beltway Drive
Dallas, TX 75244
(214) 351-0564

Perx
1730 S. Amphleett Blvd., #222
San Mateo, CA 94402
(800) 722-7379
(415) 573-0834

Peter Norton Computing
100 Wilshire Blvd., 9th Floor
Santa Monica, CA 90401
(213) 319-2000

Phar Lap Software, Inc.
60 Aberdeen Ave.
Cambridge, MA 02138
(617) 661-1510

Polytron Corporation
1700 Northwest 167th Pl.
Beaverton, OR 97006
(503) 645-1150

Profit Systems, Inc.
30150 Telegraph Rd.
Birmingham, MI 48010

Programmer's Connection
(800) 336-1166

Programmer's Shop
(800) 421-8006

Progressive Solutions Inc.
131 Washington St.
Lodi, NJ 07644
(800) 833-4400
(201) 473-2000

Proware
POB 551314
Dallas, TX 75355
(214) 349-3790
(800) 842-3787

QMS Inc.
POB 81250
Mobile, AL 36689
(205) 633-4300

Quadram
One Quad Way
Norcross, GA 30093
(404) 564-5522

Qualitas
7101 Wisconsin Ave., Suite 1386
Bethesda, MD 20814
(301) 907-6700
(800) 733-1377

Quantum Corporation
1804 McCarthy Blvd.
Milpitas, CA 95035
(408) 432-1100

Quantum Software Systems, Ltd.
175 Terrence Matthews Crescent
Kanata, Ontario
Canada K2M 1W8
(613) 591-0931

Quarterdeck Office Systems
150 Pico Blvd.
Santa Monica, CA 90405
(213) 392-9851

Roxxolid Corporation
3345 Vincent Rd.
Pleasant Hill, CA 95423
(415) 256-0105

Rupp Corp.
835 Madison Ave.
New York, NY 10021
212 517 7775

RYBS Electronics Inc.
2590 Central Ave.
Boulder, CO 80301
(303) 444-6073

Semiconductor Express International
63-3 North Branford Road
Branford, CT 06405
(203) 481-5562
(800) 875-5562

Sheng Labs, Inc.
4470 SW Hall St., Suite 282
Beaverton, OR 97005
(800) 548-1270

SoftLogic Solutions Inc.
One Perimeter Road
Manchester, NH 03103
(603) 627-9900
(800) 272-9900

Softnet Communications Inc.
15 Hillcrest Drive
Great Neck, NY 11021
(800) 627-7060

Software Directions Inc.
1572 Sussex Turnpike
Randolph, NJ 07869
(800) 346-7638

Software Matters Inc.
6352 North Guilford Ave.
Indianapolis, IN 46220
(317) 253-8088

SOTA Technology
551 Weddell Dr.
Sunnyvale, CA 94089
(800) 933-7682
(408) 745-1111

Spinnaker Software Corporation
One Kendall Sq.
Cambridge, MA 02139
(800) 826-0706
(617) 494 1200

Spirit of Performance
73 Westcott Rd.
Harvard, MA 01451
(508) 456-3889

STB Systems Inc.
1651 N. Glenville, Suite 210
Richardson, TX 75081
(214) 234-8750

Sundog Software Corporation
264 Court St.
Brooklyn, NY 11231
(718) 855-9141

Sunny Hill Software
POB 55278
Seattle, WA 98155
(800) 367-0651

SuperSoft Inc.
POB 611328
San Jose, CA 95161
(408) 745-0234

Symantec Corporation
10201 Torre Ave.
Cupertino, CA 95014
(408) 253-4092

Tall Tree Systems
POB 50690
Palo Alto, CA 94303
(415) 493-1980

Teletek Enterprises Inc.
4600 Pell Dr.
Sacramento, CA 95838
(916) 920-4600

The Aldridge Co.
2500 CityWest Blvd.
Houston, TX 77042
(713) 953-1940

The Lambda Group, Inc.
555 DeHaro St.
San Francisco, CA 94107
(415) 626-4545

The Periscope Co.
1197 Peachtree St.
Atlanta, GA 30361
(800) 722-7006
(404) 875-8080

The Software Link
3577 Parkway Lane
Norcross, GA 30092
(404) 448-5465
(800) 451-5465

THEOS Software Corporation
1777 Botelho Drive, Suite 360
Walnut Creek, CA 94596-5022
(415) 935-1118

TouchStone Software Corporation
2130 Main Street, Suite 250
Huntington Beach, CA 92648
(800) 531-0450
(213) 598-7746

Turbo Power
P.O. Box 66747
Scotts Valley, CA 95066
(408) 438-8608

V Communications Inc.
4320 Stevens Creek Blvd., Suite 275-
PCS
San Jose, CA 95129
(408) 296-4224
(800) 662-8266

Vermont Research Corporation
Precision Park
North Springfield, VT 05150
(802) 886-2256

Waterworks Software, Inc.
913 Electric Avenue
Seal Beach, CA 90740
(213) 594-4768

Western Digital Corporation
800 E. Middlefield
Mt. View, CA 94043
(415) 960-3360

WordPerfect Corporation
1555 N. Technology Way
Orem, UT 84057
(801) 225-5000

XyQuest Inc.
44 Manning Rd.
Billerica, MA 01821
(508) 671 0888

Zenographics
4 Executive Circle, Suite 200
Irvine, CA 92714
(714) 851-6352

Glossary

8086

Microprocessor chip used in some PC compatibles. Can address 1MB of memory. Slightly faster than the 8088 (see Step 1 for details).

8088

Microprocessor chip used in original PC and XT. Also used in many PC compatibles. Can address 1MB of memory. The slowest chip in the family (see Step 1 for details).

80286

Microprocessor chip used in original IBM AT, and in many compatibles. Can address 16MB of memory, though limited to 1MB when using DOS operating system. Faster than the 8088 and 8086 (see Step 1 for details).

80386

Microprocessor chip used in fast AT-compatibles and in some PS/2 systems. Can address 4GB of memory, though limited to 1MB when running DOS. A 386 chip includes circuits for handling expanded (EMS) memory and other memory management circuits for easy remapping of memory. (This chip is sometimes called the 80386DX.) Faster than the 80286, 8086, and 8088 (see Step 1 for details).

80386SL

Low-power version of the 80386SX chip, tailored for use in portable computers.

80386SX

Inexpensive version of the 80386 microprocessor chip.

80486

Microprocessor chip in most recent (1990 and 1991) AT and PS/2 compatibles. Combines 80386 chip and a math coprocessor, so has all memory addressing abilities of 80386, but is faster, particularly so on complicated calculations. The fastest chip in the family (see Step 1 for details).

accelerators

New processor chips or boards with processor chips plugged into a PC or compatible to give it more processing speed.

address

A location in memory. Memory is organized by assigning *addresses* to all the locations where information can be stored. It's the same idea as assigning numbers to houses on a street, to organize and identify them. Memory addresses start at 0 and increase, the end point depending on how much memory is in the computer. Addresses can be in decimal numbers (12, 63555), in binary (00101, 11111), or in hexadecimal (FF00, A0). The term address can also be a verb, meaning "the computer reaches out and finds" a certain location in memory.

address space

The amount of memory a computer can address. A larger address space means the computer can handle larger programs and files.

alternate register set

Expanded memory depends on a set of registers or memory locations that keep track of what memory is being swapped where (See listing for *expanded memory* for more details). Having an alternate register set on an EMS board means being able to handle more complex swapping situations, which means faster and smoother processing, especially for computers trying to run more than one program at a time.

application

A computer program that handles a specific working task, such as word processing, spreadsheet calculations, or database management. Distinct from computer programs that handle basic system functions (such as an operating system), or communications with peripherals (such as drivers).

ASCII

An acronym for "American Standard Code for Information Interchange." You don't need to know that. What it means for memory management (and most other PC uses) is "plain text." That is, some files of information on disk have lots of special codes that indicate such things as fonts and graphics. ASCII files only have the basic text characters, symbols, and numerals.

AUTOEXEC.BAT

A file of information on your disk that DOS automatically looks to for its initial instructions. Many memory management techniques require that you put instructions into the AUTOEXEC.BAT file. This is a "plain text," or ASCII file, that you can change with any word processor that can save its files in ASCII form.

backfill

Expanded memory can sometimes be used to replace or "backfill" conventional memory. Doing so gives faster task switching. (See *expanded memory* for more details.)

background

When a program is said to run "in the background," that means it can keep doing some processing, even though it is not the "top" or active program on the screen. Few programs running under the DOS operating system can actually multitask or run entirely in the background, but some can at least perform calculations or monitor a phone-line connection. The more programs that can run in the background, the more you can get done in the same amount of computer time.

bank-switching

One way to let a computer address more memory than it's natural address space permits is to "bank-switch". For example, a stretch of 16K of memory addresses is singled out as a swapping area. Then the information that is stored in other 16K chunks of memory is moved into and out of that location. If information is needed from one particular chunk, that chunk is given those addresses. If a program then needs information from another chunk, the first chunk is moved out and the second chunk is moved into the swapping location. Special registers or program instructions are used to keep track of which chunk is needed at which time, and to redirect requests to the swapping area so that they actually target the needed information. Expanded memory functions as a bank-switching scheme like this.

batch file

DOS will try to run as a program any file with a .BAT extension on its name. You can create your own batch file by typing a sequence of DOS commands into a word processor, then saving them as an ASCII file with a .BAT file extension name. The most famous batch file is AUTOEXEC.BAT (See that listing for more details).

binary

Computers deal with all information as strings of 0s and 1s. Since this means only two possible fundamental values, it is known as base two or binary information. The computer can build up complex numbers and values by stringing lots of these 1s and 0s together.

BIOS

The most fundamental software in the PC, even more elementary than the DOS operating system, is the stuff that tells the PC processor how to start, where to find the disk, where the display screen is, and so on. This is the BIOS or Basic Input/Output System subroutines and startup code, and is typically kept in a ROM chip.

bit

A single piece of information in a computer is a binary digit, or "bit" for short. (See *binary*)

boot

Computer language meaning "start the computer." Cold boots occur when you turn on the power. Warm boots occur when you tell the processor to start from scratch, while keeping the power on. (Most PCs do this when you hold down the Ctrl, Alt, and Del keys simultaneously.)

boot sector

Information on disks is organized into sectors. The sector that contains the first information to be read when you boot the computer is called the boot sector. This contains the first parts of the operating system, which tell how to load the rest of the operating system into memory where it can operate.

bus

A bus is a team of electrical lines carrying information in a computer. Most processor chips have a data bus that carries any data signals, and an address bus that carries any address values the processor sends to locate information in memory. Bus is also used to mean the combination of data, address, and other signals that are brought together at slots where you can plug in extra circuit boards. For a PC to accept and use such a board, that board must be compatible with the type of bus the PC uses. See EISA, ISA, and MCA, the major bus types.

byte

Eight bits of information taken as a single packet is called a byte. This is the smallest practical unit of information in most computers. (See *bit*)

CGA

Color Graphics Adapter, the first color video adapter hardware IBM produced for the PC. Many compatible computer makers then made CGA-compatible adapters for their PC-compatibles. CGA is a low-resolution display that's no longer popular.

clone

A computer that is entirely compatible with an IBM design is sometimes called a clone. This word also connotes an inexpensive compatible, from a relatively unknown company.

command

DOS, application programs, and utilities have commands, or functions they can perform when you issue the command to do so. Various methods of issuing these commands exist—each program has its own. Other times you type the name or acronym of the command and then press Enter or Return. Sometimes you select the command from a menu. Programs that run under environments such as Windows have their commands organized in similar ways, and use similar methods of issuing commands. This makes new programs easier to learn.

command path

(See *path*.)

compatibility box

The OS/2 operating system tries to appeal to DOS users by having a compatibility box within which DOS programs will run. It's not a physical box; it's a software way of organizing memory so that DOS users don't have to abandon their application programs. Reports from users indicate that the DOS compatibility box is not entirely compatible with all DOS programs, and offers them limited memory for those programs.

compatible

When one computer or program works in the same way as another, it is called "compatible." There are many different kinds of compatibilities. A computer that can run the same programs as another computer is *compatible* with that computer. A program that can use the same operating system, files, commands, or drivers as another program is also considered to be compatible with that program.

compression

To reduce the amount of disk space that a file occupies, a compression program can squeeze redundant information out of the file. Some memory management programs "compress" the ROM BIOS in a different way, by leaving out unnecessary or rarely used parts of it— such as the BASIC language—when copying it to higher-performance Shadow RAM.

compute-intensive

A program that depends on lots of calculations is called compute-intensive. The opposite is a program that's disk intensive, depending on lots of data movement to and from the disk drives. Which type a program is, affects the best ways to improve its performance using memory. A compute-intensive program will get less from a RAM disk than a disk intensive program will.

COMSPEC

A DOS setting that affects how memory is used. (See Step 3 for details.)

concurrent

When two programs run at once, the computer is said to be "multitasking," or running them concurrently.

CONFIG.SYS

This file, along with the AUTOEXEC.BAT file is the one that DOS always looks for on your disk when you start your computer. It contains instructions on the system configuration—such as how much memory to set aside for buffers and where the driver is for the mouse. You can create or change your PC's CONFIG.SYS file with any word processor that can save a file as plain ASCII text.

configuration

Computers and programs have a configuration or setting. This refers to such things as which options are turned on and how commands will behave. How a configuration is set will affect how the computer or program uses memory.

conventional memory

Memory is given different names, depending on how it is organized for the computer to use. The most basic memory is called conventional. This is the most important memory for most programs, and the memory that is most often exhausted because of so-called "RAM-cram": trying to get too much data into a limited space. It is the memory from address 0 to address 640K. (See Step 1 for further explanation.)

CPU

Central Processing Unit, a generic name for the microprocessor that is the heart of most computers. The type of CPU used is a central factor in determining how much memory a computer can use, and how it uses it.

data

Data is information, the stuff programs work on, and store.

database

A database is an organized collection of information. A program that handles that database is called a database manager, though that name is sometimes shortened to just database.

DDE

Dynamic Data Exchange is a feature of the Windows environment, and of the OS/2 operating system. DDE lets two programs or files automatically exchange information. This is typically used to keep information up to date when it appears in several places. For example, if a chart that has been pasted into a word processor document is based on a spreadsheet file, and the values in that spreadsheet change, a DDE link would automatically copy the changes to the chart.

debug

Programmers must eliminate any mistakes or bugs from programs by debugging them.

DesqView

DesqView is an environment that helps organize and manage the memory in a PC, and allows the PC to run more than one program at a time. (See Step 6 for details.)

device driver

Most peripherals—such as modems, printers, and special video adapter boards—need a small program called a device driver to "tell them" how to communicate with other software in the computer.

DIP

Dual In-line Package. This is the traditional way of packaging memory chips, putting single chips into small plastic or ceramic packages with two parallel rows of legs.

disk cache

A small piece of memory can be set aside as a disk cache to hold frequently accessed information from a disk drive. This increases the apparent speed of the disk drive.

disk-intensive

A program that depends on reading and writing a lot of information is called disk-intensive. This is the opposite of compute-intensive. Disk-intensive programs can be given a big performance boost by using a disk cache.

document

The information that you're working on in a word processor, spreadsheet, or other program is called your *document*.

DOS box

(See *compatibility box*.)

DOS

Disk Operating System, from Microsoft and IBM. (See *operating system*.) This is the basic software that runs on almost all PCs. Most of this book is about managing memory under the DOS operating system.

DOS extender

A special piece of software that lets DOS reach beyond its normal limit of 1MB of memory address space is called a DOS extender. Extenders don't let just any program reach the extra memory. DOS extenders are typically built into individual programs by the programmer—the user doesn't even know they are there. The VCPI and DPMI specifications help avoid conflicts between programs that use DOS extenders and other programs. (See Steps 1 and 6 for details.)

DPMI

DOS Protected Mode Interface, a specification for programs that want to use DOS Protected mode and Extended memory. Programs that support DPMI, such as Windows 3.0, won't conflict with each other. Similar to, but more advanced, than the older VCPI standard for DOS and Extended memory.

DRAM

Dynamic Random Access Memory, the most common type of memory chip. (See Step 1 for more details.)

driver

(See *device driver*.)

EDC

Memory can be accompanied by Error Detection and Correction circuits, that will prevent any mistaken bits from creeping into the information. (Damaged chips or cosmic rays—as science fictional as that sounds—can change the bits in memory chips.) Few PCs have EDC, but many do have so-called "parity chips," a ninth bit added to each set of eight bits, that detects errors.

EEMS

Enhanced Expanded Memory Specification, the improved expanded memory scheme introduced by AST and several other companies to outperform the Lotus Intel Microsoft EMS Version 3.2 specification. The EEMS innovations became part of the LIM EMS 4.0 standard.

EEPROM

Electrically Erasable Programmable Read Only Memory. A chip like an EPROM, but erased with electricity instead of ultraviolet light, and so easier to use. EEPROMs can be reprogrammed—stored with new data and programs—without being removed from the PC.

EGA

Enhanced Graphics Adapter, the video adapter that IBM introduced after CGA. EGA has higher resolution and more color than CGA, and was the standard for several years, and was copied by many compatible makers.

EISA

The Extended Industry Standard Architecture bus. This is a fast, new bus that accepts both ISA bus boards and newer 32-bit boards. It comes from an association of compatible-making computer companies, and competes in the market with the MCA bus.

electronic disk

Another name for a RAM disk.

EMM

Expanded Memory Manager refers to software designed to handle expanded memory.

EMS

Expanded Memory Specification, the specification for LIM (Lotus Intel Microsoft) expanded memory. (See *expanded memory*.)

environment

1) The DOS settings that describe how memory is set up 2) A piece of software that adds to DOS, to manage memory, present menus, and display windows for programs. Windows and DesqView are two of the best known environments.

EPROM

Erasable Programmable Read Only Memory, a type of ROM memory chip commonly used to hold the BIOS. ROMs cannot be erased for reprogramming; EPROMs can, by exposure to special ultraviolet light, which requires removal of the board from the PC.

ESD

When you install or inspect memory chips, you can damage them through static electricity. Even small charges on your body, built up without your knowledge, can cause ElectroStatic Discharge, which can weaken or ruin chips.

expanded memory

A type of memory that through bank-switching lets a PC reach more than its normal 1MB of memory. Version 3.2 of the LIM EMS standard for expanded memory restricts the expanded memory to holding data, and so is obsolete. It has been replaced by Version 4.0 which allows programs and memory to be stored in up to 32MB of memory outside of the standard 1MB. (See Steps 1 and 6 for details.)

expansion slot

Many PCs have slots which you can plug new circuit boards into, to add more memory or a peripheral to the computer.

extended memory

Memory above the 1MB address that normally limits DOS programs is called extended memory. This is not bank-switched memory, like expanded memory. It cannot be used by normal DOS appliations. It appears only on systems that use the 80286, 80386, or 80486 chips, not on systems with the 8088 or 8086 microprocessors. Most PCs can use extended memory for RAM disks. Programs with DOS extenders built-in can use 15MB of extended memory. Expanded memory simulation programs, or LIMulators, can make extended memory behave like expanded memory, making it useful to many more programs. Some operating systems, such as OS/2, can use extended memory as their own conventional memory.

file

A file is the smallest element of information that's assigned a name on a disk. Programs, documents, and operating system information are stored in files. When you see a directory of what's on your disk, you're seeing a list of the files on the disk.

flash EEPROM

A new kind of memory chip that may replace hard disks in portable computers. Flash EEPROM can be erased faster that traditional EEPROMs can.

format

1) Any disk must be formatted before information can be stored on it. Formatting puts down signposts of information on the disk so that the disk drive can later "know" where information was put, like putting street signs on streets. 2) The arrangement of information in a file is called the file format. For example, the TIFF (Tagged Image File Format) format for graphics files specifies how the initial bits of the file describe the file's size and details, and the later bits are the actual graphic image. A graphics program trying to load a TIFF file, but understanding only some other format, wouldn't know how to interpret the bits in the file, and so couldn't open or use it.

FRAM

Ferroelectric Random Access memory, a new kind of memory chip that is nonvolatile—that doesn't need power to keep the information that is stored on it safe. If FRAMs become cheap enough, they could replace today's DRAMs, and lead to computers that you could turn off, and then turn on again and still see your programs and files open just as they were when you turned the system off. Today when you turn a PC off and on again you must reload all your programs and files.

gigabyte

A large amount of memory, about a billion bytes, but more exactly 1024 megabytes.

Graphical User Interface

Software that displays windows, menus, and icons on the PC screen to make identifying and manipulating files and information easier. Graphical User Interfaces demand a lot of memory. The Apple Macintosh had the first popular Graphical User Interface. Windows is a PC Graphical User Interface.

graphics

Curves, lines, and images on the computer screen instead of just text (alphanumeric symbols). Graphics demands more memory than text.

GUI

Acronym for Graphical User Interface

hard disk

A type of disk drive that's much faster and can hold much more information than floppy disks. Most hard disks are not removable, the disk remains in the computer permanently.

Hercules

A graphics adapter type, one of the few video graphics adapters not created by IBM that has become a standard and has been copied by compatible computer manufacturers.

hexadecimal

Base-sixteen counting, using the numerals 0,1,2,3, 4,5,6,7,8,9,A,B,C,D,E,F. Hexadecimal is very convenient for computer scientists counting memory addresses, and so appears in many memory management programs. (See Step 1 for more details.)

high memory

1) The 384K of memory above 640K and below 1024K (1MB). (See Step 1 for details.) This memory cannot be used by most programs and data files, but can be used for video, BIOS, and other uses, and can be borrowed for use of TSRs, device drivers, and other small programs (See Step 5). High memory is also used in expanded memory schemes. 2) The 64K of memory just above 1024K, which can be used by some PCs because of a trick in the microprocessor, which is only supposed to be able to reach 1024K. Sometimes spelled "hi memory."

icon

A small image used to represent files or commands in a graphical user interface.

ISA

The Industry Standard Architecture bus. This is the bus that IBM introduced with the IBM AT, and that was widely copied in AT compatibles. It isn't as fast as the EISA or MCA buses.

K

1024 bits of memory equals 1K. 1024 is used to count many things in computers. The value is 1024 rather than 1000 because 1024 is a multiple of 2 and memory is organized in powers of 2. (See Step 1 for details.)

KB

Acronym for kilobyte.

kilobyte

1024 bytes is 1KB. Don't confuse this with 1Kb, which means 1KiloBit, or 1/8 of 1KB (there are 8 bits to a byte).

LAN

An acronym for "Local Area Network"—electrical hardware and appropriate software to link a group of PCs together so they can share files, electronic mail, peripherals, and even programs.

laser printer

A printer that uses a laser (or sometimes an LED array) to quickly print high-resolution pages of text and graphics. Laser printers use more memory than older dot-matrix and daisy-wheel printers.

LIM EMS

An acronym which stands for Lotus Intel Microsoft Expanded Memory Specification. (See *expanded memory*.)

MB

Acronym for megabyte.

MCA

The Micro-Channel Architecture bus. IBM introduced this bus with the PS/2 systems. It is a fast, 32-bit bus that competes with the EISA.

MDA

Monochrome Display Adapter, the original monochrome video adapter standard used by IBM for its PC, and copied by many compatible computer makers. MDA is low resolution, and is no longer used much.

megabyte

1024K of memory, the maximum amount a standard PC can address.

memory

Storage area in a computer for information. Disk drives store information too, but most references to memory, including the title of this book, refer to the semiconductor circuit chips in a computer that are the quick memory used for computing.

memory-resident

Traditional application programs stay in memory only until you're done using them. When you quit the program, it is dumped from memory. Memory-resident programs stay in memory, though they aren't active, while you use other programs. Some are drivers that the computer user doesn't pay attention to. Some are utilities that can be brought back to activity by pressing a specified combination of keys. Also called TSRs.

menu

A list of commands you can choose in a program.

microprocessor

As the engine is to the car (or even more accurately, as the driver is to the car), the microprocessor is to the computer. The microprocessor is the main chip that handles the calculations and comparisons that are vital to any program.

millisecond

A millisecond equals 1/1000 of a second. Disk drive speeds are measured in milliseconds.

modem

A peripheral device that connects a computer to a telephone line so that it can communicate information to other computers with modems.

monitor

Another name for the display screen of a computer.

motherboard

The main circuit board in a PC. It typically contains the microprocessor and memory. Some people increase the speed of their PCs by
swapping motherboards, by taking out the original motherboard
and replacing it with a new motherboard with a faster microprocessor
and faster memory chips.

mouse

A small, hand-held pointer device commonly used with graphical
user interfaces.

MS-DOS

Microsoft's version of DOS.

multi-tasking

Running more than one program at a time, or capable of doing so.
Multitasking systems demand more memory than single-tasking
systems. DOS is not a multitasking OS, though with an environment
such as Windows 3 or DesqView, it can perform some multitasking.

multi-threading

Running more than one part of a single program at a time. Essentially this is multitasking within programs. DOS is not a multi-
threading OS; OS/2 is.

multi-user

A multi-user system involving a single computer which runs programs for more than one person at a time. This requires both a multi-user OS (which DOS is not), and a set of terminals (keyboards and displays) connected to the single computer so that several users at once can send commands and observe displays.

nanosecond

1/1000000000 of a second or, one billionth of a second. Memory chip speeds are measured in nanoseconds.

network

Short for "Local Area Network" or LAN.

NVRAM

Nonvolatile RAM. Refers to memory chips that won't lose their information when power is turned off. This can be done by adding battery back-up power to SRAM chips, or by using new RAM technologies. Many PCs use NVRAM for small sections of memory that hold configuration, clock, and calendar information.

operating system

The fundamental software that animates a computer. The operating system takes requests from applications and utilities, and shuffles information from and for them to and from disk drives. The OS also handles tasks such as sending the appropriate signals to the display screen, monitoring the keyboard to see which keys are pressed, and so on.

OS

Acronym for Operating System.

OS/2

Operating System/2, the successor to OS offered by Microsoft and IBM for those who are no longer satisfied with DOS. See Step 9 for details.

page frame

A 16K block of memory addresses used by expanded memory for bank-switching.

PATH

A DOS command for telling the operating system where to find files.

PC

The original IBM desktop computer model. Also a generic name for desktop computers, or for desktop computers that are compatible with IBM's PC and DOS standards.

PC-AT

The IBM PC successor based on the 80286 microprocessor.

PC-DOS

IBM's version of DOS.

PC/XT

The IBM PC successor that added a hard disk to the original PC structure.

peripheral

A piece of hardware not vital to computer operation, that is connected to the computer. Printers, modems, even special disk drives can be considered peripherals.

pixel

Short for "picture element," the smallest dot of light on a computer display screen. Putting more pixels on the screen gives higher resolution, and therefore better images. However, more pixels requires more memory.

protected mode

A microprocessor mode available on the 80286, 80386, and 80486 chips that can reach 16MB of memory. DOS cannot run in protected mode without the help of special software such as DOS extenders. OS/2 is a protected-mode operating system.

PS/2

The new family of computers that IBM introduced in 1987, to succeed the PC family (PC, XT, AT).

public domain

Free software that is available to anyone.

RAM

Acronym for Random Access Memory. The most common type of memory chip.

RAM disk

A section of memory set aside to behave like a very fast disk drive. (See Step 7 for details.)

real mode

The operating mode of the 8088 and 8086 microprocessors, able to address 1MB of memory. The DOS operating system is designed to work in real mode. (See *protected mode*.)

register

A memory location for holding specific information during processing. The microprocessor has its own registers that aren't part of conventional, high, expanded, or extended memory. EMS boards also have registers.

remapping

Logically changing the addresses assigned to areas of memory, to rearrange what is in conventional, high, expanded, and extended memory. (See *address*.)

ROM

Acronym for Read Only Memory. A type of memory chip that holds information, but can't be written to, but can store new information. ROMs are typically used to hold permanent program routines, such as the BIOS and diagnostics in a PC.

shareware

Software that you can freely copy and try, but that you should pay a registration fee for if you want to keep.

shell

A user interface put on top of an operating system. Typically simpler than an environment. DOS 4.0 comes with a shell.

SIMM

Acronym for Single In-line Memory Module. This is a way of packaging memory chips, placing them in sets on small circuit boards and calling the results modules. A typical module has 9 1Mbit or 4Mbit chips, one chip for parity and 8 to make 1MB or 4MB total. SIMMs take up less space than the older DIP packaging method. (See Step 4 for more details.)

software

Lists of instructions that computer hardware follows. (See Step 1 for comments on the different kinds of software.)

spooler

A spooler intercepts information that is sent to the printer, stores it in memory or on disk, and then forwards it to the printer at the chosen time. A spooler can allow an application program to return to activity sooner—by relieving it of the job of monitoring the print process.

SRAM

Static Random-Access Memory. This type of RAM chip can be faster than DRAMs, but is more expensive and takes up more space. SRAMs are commonly used only in caches.

surface-mount

A way of packaging chips, including memory chips. Takes up less space than DIP packaging.

Terabyte

1024 GB, or 1024 x 1024 MB, or 1024 x 1024 x 1024 bytes. 1,048, 576 MB. No PC uses this much memory, so there's no great reason for having this word in the glossary, except that some 386 and 486 chip documents refer to "x" number of terabytes worth of virtual memory.

TSR

Acronym for Terminate-and-Stay-Resident. Shorthand way of saying memory-resident program.

Unix

An operating system that can reach more than DOS's 1MB of memory, and that also offers multitasking. (See Step 9 for details.)

V86

Short for Virtual 86 mode.

VCPI

Phar Lap Software and Quarterdeck's Virtual-86 Control Program Interface. This specification is for DOS extenders. (See Steps 1 and 6 for details.)

VGA

Video Graphics Adapter, the IBM video adapter standard that succeeded EGA. With greater resolution and color possibilities than EGA, VGA has become the business computing standard, and is widely copied on PC compatibles. VGA uses more memory than EGA. (See Step 8 for details.)

virtual disk

Another name for RAM-disk.

Virtual-86

The Virtual 86 mode of the 80386 and 80486 processor chips. These chips can run any number of V86 modes, each mode pretends it is an 8086 chip with only 1MB of memory. Each V86 operation is protected in the 80386 or 80486 memory from any other operation. This allows the 386 or 486 to multitask DOS programs.

volatile

Memory that loses what is stored in it when power is turned off is called volatile. DRAM and SRAM chips are volatile. Some forms of RAM chips, such as SRAMs backed up by batteries, are non-volatile. Disk drives are also nonvolatile.

window

A space on the computer display screen that's reserved for a particular task. By placing tasks or programs in their own windows, and letting those windows overlap on the screen, the computer tries to replicate the familiar image of multiple sheets of paper arranged on a desktop.

Windows

The memory management and graphical user interface environment from Microsoft. (See Step 6 for details.)

XGA

The IBM video graphics adapter standard that may succeed VGA, with more resolution and graphics, and higher memory demands. (See Step 8 for details.)

XMS

eXtended Memory Specification. The standard for using extended memory in PCs. (See Steps 1 and 6 for details.)

Bibliography

If you want to know more about memory, you should read magazine articles and books, ask plenty of questions at your local computer store, and talk to other PC owners at user groups, conventions, and through on-line bulletin board systems. Here are some magazines, books, and on-line services that I use.

Magazines

BYTE

InfoWorld

PC/Computing

PC Magazine

PC Week

PC World

Books

Extending DOS, by Ray Duncan, Charles Petzold, M. Steven Baker, Andrew Schulman, Stephen R. Davis, Ross P. Nelson, Robert Moote. (Addison-Wesley, 1990). This is a good book if you're a programmer. It presents details on handling EMS and XMS memory in your programs, how to use VCPI and DPMI, and the roles of Windows and DesqView. There are many program examples. It's not for novices or those who just want to use more memory—only for those who want to write programs that make the most of expanded and extended memory.

On-line Services

These are services which you can sign on to with a modem to read news, exchange mail and messages, ask for technical support from various hardware and software company representatives, and to download free and inexpensive programs.

BIX

CompuServe

PC MagNet

Index